Foundations of Business Leadership: I & II

2011-2012 Edition

University of Georgia

∴ CENGAGE
Learning™

Australia • Brazil • Japan • Korea • Mexico • Singapore • Spain • United Kingdom • United States

CENGAGE
Learning™

Foundations of Business Leadership: I & II, 2011-2012 Edition

MGMT 3, 3rd Edition
Chuck Williams

© 2011 Cengage Learning. All rights reserved.

ORGB 2, 2nd Edition
Debra L. Nelson | James Campbell Quick

© 2011 Cengage Learning. All rights reserved.

Understanding Business Strategy: Concepts and Cases, 2nd Edition
R. Duane Ireland | Robert E. Hoskisson | Michael A. Hitt

© 2009 Cengage Learning. All rights reserved.

The Leadership Experience, 5th Edition
Richard L. Daft

© 2011 Cengage Learning. All rights reserved.

Executive Editors:
Maureen Staudt
Michael Stranz

Senior Project Development Manager:
Linda deStefano

Marketing Specialist:
Courtney Sheldon

Senior Production/Manufacturing Manager:
Donna M. Brown

PreMedia Manager:
Joel Brennecke

Sr. Rights Acquisition Account Manager:
Todd Osborne

Cover Image:
Getty Images*

*Unless otherwise noted, all cover images used by Custom Solutions, a part of Cengage Learning, have been supplied courtesy of Getty Images with the exception of the Earthview cover image, which has been supplied by the National Aeronautics and Space Administration (NASA).

For product information and technology assistance, contact us at
Cengage Learning Customer & Sales Support, 1-800-354-9706

For permission to use material from this text or product,
submit all requests online at **cengage.com/permissions**
Further permissions questions can be emailed to
permissionrequest@cengage.com

This book contains select works from existing Cengage Learning resources and was produced by Cengage Learning Custom Solutions for collegiate use. As such, those adopting and/or contributing to this work are responsible for editorial content accuracy, continuity and completeness.

Compilation © 2011 Cengage Learning

ISBN-13: 978-1-133-66517-5

ISBN-10: 1-133-66517-9

Cengage Learning
5191 Natorp Boulevard
Mason, Ohio 45040
USA
Cengage Learning is a leading provider of customized learning solutions with office locations around the globe, including Singapore, the United Kingdom, Australia, Mexico, Brazil, and Japan. Locate your local office at:
international.cengage.com/region.

Cengage Learning products are represented in Canada by Nelson Education, Ltd.
For your lifelong learning solutions, visit **www.cengage.com/custom.**
Visit our corporate website at **www.cengage.com.**

Printed in the United States of America

CONTENTS

MGMT 3010-3020 – Foundations of Business Leadership I

CHAPTERS

CASES

Case: "Thomas Green"

Case: "Where Have You Been?"

Case: "Into the Fray"

Case: "Charlotte Beers at Ogilvy & Mather Worldwide (A)"

CONTENTS

MGMT 4010-4020 – Foundations of Business Leadership II

CHAPTERS

CASES

Challenges for Managers

After reading this chapter, you should be able to do the following:

1 Describe the factors that affect organizations competing in the global economy.

2 Explain how cultural differences form the basis of work-related attitudes.

3 Describe the challenges and positive influences diversity brings to today's business environment.

4 Discuss the role of ethics, character, and personal integrity in the organization.

5 Explain five issues that pose ethical dilemmas for managers.

Key challenges managers face today stem from the fact that business is increasingly global in scope.[1] Globalization is driven by the spread of economic logics centered on freeing, opening, deregulating, and privatizing economies to attract investment as well as technological innovations that are revolutionizing communication.[2] The challenges it creates for managers can be viewed as both opportunities and threats.

What major challenges must managers overcome in order to remain competitive? Chief executive officers of U.S. corporations have cited four crucial issues: (1) globalizing the firm's operations to compete in the global village; (2) leading a diverse workforce; (3) encouraging positive ethics, character, and personal integrity; and (4) advancing and implementing technological innovation in the workplace.[3]

LEARNING OUTCOME **1**

Competing in the Global Economy

Only a few years ago, business conducted across national borders was referred to as "international" activity. The word *international* implies that the individual's or the organization's nationality is held strongly in consciousness.[4] *Globalization*, by contrast, suggests that the world is free from national boundaries and is borderless.[5] U.S. workers now compete with workers in other countries. Organizations from other countries such as the auto manufacturers Honda, Toyota, Nissan, and Daimler Benz are establishing subsidiaries in the United States.

Similarly, what were once called multinational organizations (organizations that did business in several countries) are now referred to as transnational organizations. In **transnational organizations**, the global viewpoint supersedes national issues.[6] Transnational organizations operate across long distances and employ a multicultural mix of workers. 3M, Dow Chemical, Coca-Cola, and other transnational organizations operate worldwide with diverse populations of employees.

Social and Political Changes

Social and political upheavals have led organizations to change the way they conduct business and

6 Describe the effects of technological advances on today's workforce.

©Mike Kemp/Rubberball/Getty Images

transnational organization
An organization in which the global viewpoint supersedes national issues.

Start thinking about yourself as a global manager. Do the "What about You?" activity on the Chapter 2 Review Card.

encouraged their members to think globally. In the Soviet Union, for example, *perestroika* led to liberation and created opportunities for U.S. businesses, as witnessed by the long waiting lines at Moscow's first McDonald's restaurant.

Business ventures in China have become increasingly attractive to U.S. companies. One challenge U.S. managers have tackled is understanding the Chinese way of doing business. Chinese managers' business practices were shaped by the Communist Party, socialism, feudalistic values, and *guanxi* (building networks for social exchange). Once *guanxi* is established, individuals can ask favors of each other with the expectation that the favor will be returned. For example, many Chinese use *guanxi*, or personal connections, to conduct business or obtain jobs.

The concept of *guanxi* is not unique to China. There are similar concepts in many other countries, including Russia and Haiti. It is a broad term that can mean anything from strongly loyal relationships to ceremonial gift-giving, sometimes seen as bribery. *Guanxi* is more common in societies with underdeveloped legal support for private businesses.[7]

Americans can learn to build their own *guanxi*; understand the Chinese chain of command; and negotiate slow, general agreements in order to interact effectively with Chinese managers. Using the foreign government as a local franchisee may be effective in China. For example, KFC's operation in China is a joint venture between KFC (60 percent) and two Chinese government bodies (40 percent).[8]

The opening of trade barriers is a third issue that affects organizations competing in a global economy. In 1993, the European Union integrated fifteen nations into a single market by removing trade barriers. At that time, the member nations of the European Union were Austria, Belgium, Denmark, Finland, France, Germany, Greece, Ireland, Italy, Luxembourg, the Netherlands, Portugal, Spain, Sweden, and the United Kingdom. By 2007, Bulgaria, Cyprus, the Czech Republic, Estonia, Hungary, Latvia, Lithuania, Malta, Poland, Slovakia, and Slovenia had also joined. Europe's integration provides many opportunities for U.S. organizations to engage 494 million potential customers. Companies such as Ford

guanxi

The Chinese practice of building networks for social exchange.

Motor Company and IBM, which entered the market early with wholly owned subsidiaries, were able to capitalize on their much-anticipated head start.[9] Competition within the European Union will intensify, however, as will competition from Japan and the former Soviet nations.

The United States, Canada, and Mexico dramatically reduced trade barriers with the North American Free Trade Agreement (NAFTA), which took effect in 1994. Organizations found promising new markets for their products, and many companies located plants in Mexico to take advantage of low labor costs. Prior to NAFTA, Mexico placed heavy tariffs on U.S. exports. The agreement immediately eliminated many of these tariffs and provided that the remaining tariffs be phased out over time.

Given these changes, managers must think globally and adopt a long-term view. Entering global markets requires long-term strategies.

[McDonald's Learns to Appreciate Cultural Diversities]

Since the 1908 introduction of the Model T by the Ford Motor Company, standardization has been synonymous with the American way of business. American corporations often attempt to maintain standard operations in the global market, ignoring cultural complexities in favor of proven strategies. Large sectors of the global population resent and resist Americanization, suggesting that it threatens cultural diversity by imposing corporate imperialism. There was a time when fast-food restaurant chain McDonald's was vilified for pushing American values onto the world, but recently, the corporation has amended its practices to be more culturally sensitive. While they were once bound to rigid guidelines, McDonald's operations around the world are now free to produce and promote their own buns, bags, and business practices. The approach has been a huge success for the company, most of whose business now comes from global markets.

Amid disinterest in the Big Mac sandwich, the hugely successful Big Tasty was developed in Germany and launched in Sweden. France, one of the company's best-performing and busiest markets, offers the Croque McDo, which consists of sliced ham and Swiss cheese on toast. Because many Indians do not eat beef, they have the option of the Maharaja Mac: two chicken patties topped with smoke-flavored mayonnaise. The Netherlands offers the McKroket, a deep-fried patty of beef; South Korea recently unveiled the Bulgogi Burger, a pork patty marinated in soy-based sauce; and Taiwan offers the Rice Burger, which consists of shredded beef sandwiched between two rice patties. The global success of McDonald's is being achieved through accommodation, not through domination.

SOURCE: P. Gumbel, "Big Mac's Local Flavor," *Fortune*, Vol. 157, Issue 9, 00158259.

Cultural Differences

One key for any company competing in the global marketplace is to understand diverse cultures. Whether managing culturally diverse individuals within a single location or managing individuals at remote locations around the globe, organizations must appreciate the differences among cultures. Edgar Schein suggests that to understand an organization's culture, or more broadly any culture, one should dig below the surface of visible artifacts and uncover the basic underlying assumptions at the core of the culture.[10]

Microcultural differences (i.e., differences within cultures) are key to our understanding of the global work environment.[11] The gap between generations is an important microcultural difference. Toyota, for example, is learning to speak to the 60-million-strong "millennial" Generation Y.[12]

When considering differences among cultures, symbols are extremely important, as they can generate misunderstanding or inhibit communication if not understood. The thumbs up sign, for example, means approval in the United States, while it is an obscene gesture in Australia. Many European countries don't use manila file folders and therefore do not recognize the icons used in Windows applications.[13]

Do cultural differences translate into differences in work-related attitudes? The pioneering Dutch researcher Geert Hofstede investigated this question. He and his colleagues surveyed 160,000 managers and employees of IBM working in sixty different countries. The researchers were able to study individuals from the same company in the same jobs but living in different countries. Hofstede's studies showed that national culture explains more differences in work-related attitudes than do age, gender, profession, or position within the organization. He found five dimensions of cultural differences that formed the basis for work-related attitudes.[14] These dimensions are shown in Figure 2.1.

Management careers have taken on a global dimension. Working in transnational organizations may give managers the opportunity to work in other countries.

> ## Whether managing culturally diverse individuals within a single location or managing individuals at remote locations around the globe, organizations must appreciate the differences among cultures.

Expatriate managers, those who work in a country other than their home country, benefit greatly from knowledge of cultural differences.

International executives are executives whose jobs have international scope, whether they have an expatriate assignment or deal with international issues. What kind of competencies should an individual develop in order to prepare for an international career? There are several attributes, all of them based upon core competencies and the ability to learn from experience. Some of the key competencies are integrity, insightfulness, risk taking, courage to take a stand, and ability to bring out the best in people. Learning-oriented attributes of international executives include cultural adventurousness, flexibility, openness to criticism, desire to seek learning opportunities, and sensitivity to cultural differences.[15] Further, strong human capital generally has a positive effect on internationalization.[16]

Because workplace customs vary widely, understanding cultural differences becomes especially important for companies that are considering opening foreign offices. Carefully researching this information in advance helps companies manage foreign operations. Consulate offices and companies operating within the foreign country provide excellent information about national customs and legal requirements.

Table 2.1 presents a business guide to cultural differences in three countries: Japan, Mexico, and Saudi Arabia.

Another reality affecting global business practices is the cost of layoffs in other countries. As the economy has become more global, downsizing has presented challenges worldwide. For example, dismissing a forty-five-year-old middle manager with twenty years of service and a $50,000 annual

FIGURE 2.1 Hofstede's Dimensions of Cultural Differences

Individualism	Collectivism
High power distance	Low power distance
High uncertainty avoidance	Low uncertainty avoidance
Masculinity	Femininity
Long-term orientation	Short-term orientation

SOURCE: Reprinted with permission of Academy of Management, P.O. Box 3020, Briarcliff Manor, NY 10510-8020. *Cultural Constraints in Management Theories.* G. Hofstede, *Academy of Management Executive 7* (1993). Reproduced by permission of the publisher via Copyright Clearance Center, Inc.

expatriate manager
A manager who works in a country other than his or her home country.

TABLE 2.1 Business Guide to Cultural Differences

COUNTRY	APPOINTMENTS	DRESS	GIFTS	NEGOTIATIONS
Japan	Punctuality is a necessity. It is considered rude to be late.	Conservative for men and women in large to medium companies, though pastel shirts are common. May be expected to remove shoes in temples and homes, as well as in some ryokan (inn) style restaurants. In that case, slip-on shoes should be worn.	Important part of Japanese business protocol. Gifts are typically exchanged among colleagues on July 15 and January 1 to commemorate midyear and the year's end, respectively.	Business cards (*meishi*) are an important part of doing business and key for establishing credentials. One side of your card should be in English and the other in Japanese. It is an asset to include information such as membership in professional associations.
Mexico	Punctuality is not always as much of a priority. Nonetheless, Mexicans are accustomed to North Americans arriving on time, and most Mexicans in business, if not government, will try to return the favor.	Dark, conservative suits and ties are the norm for most men. Standard office attire for women includes dresses, skirted suits, or skirts and blouses. Femininity is strongly encouraged in women's dress.	Not usually a requirement in business dealings though presenting a small gift will generally be appreciated as a gesture of goodwill. If giving a gift, be aware that inquiring about what the receiver would like to receive may offend.	Mexicans avoid directly saying "no." A "no" is often disguised in responses such as "maybe" or "We'll see." You should also use this indirect approach in your dealings. Otherwise, your Mexican counterparts may perceive you as being rude and pushy.
Saudi Arabia	Customary to make appointments for times of day rather than precise hours. The importance Saudis attach to courtesy and hospitality can cause delays that prevent keeping to a strict schedule.	Only absolute requirement of dress code is modesty. For men, this means covering everything from navel to knee. In public, women are required to cover everything except the face, hands, and feet by wearing an *abaya* (standard black cloak) and headscarf.	Should only be given to the most intimate of friends. For a Saudi to receive a present from a lesser acquaintance is so embarrassing that it is considered offensive.	Business cards are common but not essential. If used, the common practice is to have both English and Arabic printed, one on each side so that neither language is perceived as less important by being on the reverse of the same card.

SOURCE: Adapted from information obtained from business culture guides accessed online at http://www.executiveplanet.com.

salary varied in cost from a low of $13,000 in Ireland to a high of $130,000 in Italy.[17] Laying off this manager in the United States would have cost approximately $19,000. The wide variability in costs stems from the various legal protections that certain countries give workers. In Italy, laid-off employees must receive a "notice period" payment (one year's pay if they have nine years or more of service) plus a severance payment (based on pay and years of service). U.S. companies operating overseas often adopt the European tradition of training and retraining workers to avoid overstaffing and potential layoffs. Appreciating the customs and rules for doing business in another country is essential to global success.

Hofstede found the United States to be the most individualistic country of any studied. It ranked among the countries with weak power distance, and its level of uncertainty avoidance indicated a tolerance of uncertainty. The United States also ranked as a masculine culture with a short-term orientation. These values have shaped U.S. management theory, so Hofstede's work casts doubt on the universal applicability of U.S. management theories. Because these dimensions vary widely, management practices should be adjusted to account for cultural differences. Managers in transnational organizations must learn as much as they can about other cultures in order to lead their culturally diverse organizations effectively.

LEARNING OUTCOME 2

Cultural Differences and Work-Related Attitudes

Hofstede's work has implications for work-related attitudes. We'll now take a closer look at how his five dimensions of cultural differences are manifest in a variety of countries.

Individualism versus Collectivism

In cultures where individualism predominates, the social framework is loose. Employees put loyalty to themselves and their families first, while loyalty to their company and work group comes second. Cultures characterized by collectivism are tightly knit social frameworks in which individual members depend strongly on extended families or clans. Group decisions are valued and accepted.

North American and European cultures are individualistic in orientation. Managers in Great Britain and the Netherlands, for example, emphasize and encourage individual achievement. In collectivist cultures, such as Israeli *kibbutzim* and Japan, people view group loyalty and unity as paramount. Collectivistic managers seek to fit harmoniously within the group. They also encourage these behaviors among their employees. The world's regions are patterned with varying degrees of cultural difference.

Power Distance

Power distance relates to the acceptance of unequal distribution of power. In countries with a high **power distance**, bosses are afforded more power, titles are used,

formality is the rule, and authority is seldom bypassed. Managers and employees see one another as fundamentally different kinds of people. India, Venezuela, and Mexico all demonstrate high power distance.

In societies with low power distance, people believe in minimizing inequality. People at various power levels are less threatened by and more willing to trust one another. Managers and employees judge each other equally. Managers are given power only if they have expertise. Employees frequently bypass the boss in order to get work done in countries with a low power distance, such as Denmark and Australia.

Uncertainty Avoidance

Cultures with high **uncertainty avoidance** are concerned with security and tend to avoid conflict. People need consensus and struggle constantly against the threat of life's inherent uncertainty. Cultures with low uncertainty avoidance tolerate ambiguity better. People are more willing to take risks and more comfortable with individual differences. Conflict is seen as constructive, and people accept dissenting viewpoints. Norwegians and Australians value job mobility because they have low uncertainty avoidance; Japan and Italy are characterized by high uncertainty avoidance, and, not surprisingly, their cultures emphasize career stability.

Masculinity versus Femininity

In cultures characterized by traditional **masculinity**, assertiveness and materialism

individualism
A cultural orientation in which people belong to loose social frameworks, and their primary concern is for themselves and their families.

collectivism
A cultural orientation in which individuals belong to tightly knit social frameworks and depend strongly on extended families or clans.

power distance
The degree to which a culture accepts unequal distribution of power.

uncertainty avoidance
The degree to which a culture tolerates ambiguity and uncertainty.

masculinity
A cultural orientation in which assertiveness and materialism are valued.

are valued. Men should be assertive, tough, and decisive, whereas women should be nurturing, modest, and tender.[18] Money and possessions are important, and performance is what counts. Achievement is admired. Cultures characterized by traditional femininity emphasize relationships and concern for others. Men and women are expected to assume both assertive and nurturing roles. Quality of life is important, and people and the environment are emphasized.

Time Orientation

Cultures also differ in time orientation. A culture's values may be oriented toward the future (long-term orientation) or toward the past and present (short-term orientation).[19] In China, which has a long-term orientation, values such as thrift and persistence, which look toward the future, are emphasized. Russians generally have a short-term orientation and value respect for tradition (past) and meeting social obligations (present).

Developing Cross-Cultural Sensitivity

In today's multicultural environment, it is imperative that organizations help their employees recognize and appreciate cultural differences. One way companies do this is through cultural sensitivity training. IBM encourages its employees to develop knowledge of different cultures and awareness of global issues through its Global Citizens Portfolio. The portfolio consists of flexible spending accounts employees can use to enhance their training and in turn benefit the company.[20] Another way to develop sensitivity is by using cross-cultural task forces or teams. The Milwaukee-based GE Medical Systems Group (GEMS) has 19,000 employees working worldwide. GEMS has developed a vehicle for bringing managers from each of its three regions (the Americas, Europe, and Asia) together to work on a variety of business projects. The Global Leadership Program forms several work groups made up of managers from various regions and has them work on important projects, such as worldwide employee integration, to increase employees' sense of belonging throughout the GEMS international organization.[21] Because cultural differences are constantly in flux, it is important for managers to foster up-to-date knowledge of relevant cultural trends.

The globalization of business affects all parts of the organization, par-

ticularly human resource management. Human resource managers must adopt a global view of human resource planning, recruitment and selection, compensation, and training and development. They must possess a working knowledge of the legal systems in various countries as well as of global economics, culture, and customs. HR managers must not only prepare U.S. workers to live outside their native country but also help foreign employees interact with U.S. culture. Global human resource management is complex, but critical to organizations' success in the global marketplace.

LEARNING OUTCOME 3

The Diverse Workforce

Cultural differences contribute a great deal to the diversity of the workforce, but other forms of diversity are important as well. Diversity encompasses all forms of difference among individuals, including culture, gender, age, ability, religion, personality, social status, and sexual orientation. Diversity has garnered increasing attention in recent years, largely because of demographic changes in the working

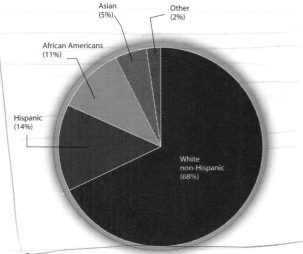

By the year 2020, the workforce will be more culturally diverse, more female, and older than ever.

Asian (5%)
Other (2%)
African Americans (11%)
Hispanic (14%)
White non-Hispanic (68%)

SOURCES: R. W. Judy and C. D'Amico, *Workforce 2020* (Indianapolis, Ind.: Hudson Institute, 1997); U.S. Department of Labor, "Usual Weekly Earnings Summary," *Labor Force Statistics from the Current Population Survey* (Washington D.C.: U.S. Government, 2002).

---

femininity
A cultural orientation in which relationships and concern for others are valued.

time orientation
Whether a culture's values are oriented toward the future (long-term orientation) or toward the past and present (short-term orientation).

diversity
All forms of difference among individuals, including culture, gender, age, ability, religion, personality, social status, and sexual orientation.

population. Managers feel that dealing with diversity is a paramount concern for two reasons. First, managers need to motivate diverse work groups. Second, managers must communicate with employees who have different values and language skills.

Several demographic trends are affecting organizations. By the year 2020, the workforce will be more culturally diverse, more female, and older than ever. Workforce demographic change and diversity are critical challenges for the study and management of organizational behavior.[22] The theories of motivation, leadership, and group behavior based on research in a workforce of one composition may not be applicable in a workforce of a very different composition.[23] This may be especially problematic if ethnic, gender, and/or religious differences lead to conflict between leaders and followers in organizations. Recent legislation and new technologies have helped more individuals with disabilities enter the workforce. Hence, learning to work together is an increasingly important skill, just as it is important to work with an open mind. Alcon Laboratories, the Swiss-owned and Fort Worth-based international company whose mission is to improve and preserve eyesight, offers diversity training to help employees learn to work together.

©Blend Images/Jupiter Images

[Can Women Work and Have a Life?]

How to balance work with other life commitments such as family and personal growth is a key issue on the minds of women and the companies they work for. Western women have typically adopted the provider role and are often still responsible for home management, child care, and sometimes care for their elderly parents.

Because of their multiple roles, women frequently experience conflicts between work and home. They struggle to manage logistics, avoid burnout, and find good mentors as well as time for themselves. Companies and governments in the United States and abroad are placing greater emphasis on support systems and alternative structures to help women create balance in their lives, and investors are increasingly looking to companies who offer flexibility and support. Flexible work schedules enabled by technology, child care, elder care, and work site health promotion programs assist working women in managing the stress of their lives.

SOURCES: D. L. Nelson and M. A. Hitt, "Employed Women and Stress: Implications for Enhancing Women's Mental Health in the Workplace," in J. C. Quick, L. R. Murphy, and J. J. Hurrell, Jr., eds., Stress and Well-Being at Work (Washington, D.C.: American Psychological Association, 1992): 164–177; S. Riss, "This Is How She Does It," Working Mother (June/July 2008) 19–23; E. McDargh, "Work-life Balance Issues Loom Large across the Globe: Work-life Balance Isn't Just Making News. It's Also Become a Criterion for Investment," Arkansas Business (May 12, 2008).

©Blend Images/Jupiter Images

Ethnic Diversity

The globalization of business is promoting cultural diversity in the workplace. Changing domestic demographics also affect organizations' cultural diversity. By 2020, minorities will constitute more than one-half of the new entrants to the U.S. workforce.

Strong shifts in the demographic makeup of society have important implications for organizations. African Americans and Hispanic Americans are overrepresented in declining occupations, thus limiting their opportunities. Further, African Americans and Hispanic Americans tend to live in a few large cities that are facing severe economic difficulties and high crime rates. Minority workers are less likely to be prepared because they are less likely to have had satisfactory schooling and on-the-job training, which will likely put them at a disadvantage within organizations. It need not be this way. For example, Coca-Cola has made substantial progress on diversity by monitoring its human resource systems, and companies such as Motorola already recognize and meet these needs by focusing on basic skills training.[24]

The globalization of business and changing demographic trends present organizations with a culturally diverse workforce,

Fast Fact

Women now own nearly 10.4 million of all American businesses, which employ more than 12.8 million people and generate $1.9 trillion in sales.

SOURCE: "Top Facts about Women-owned Businesses," Center for Women's Business Research, http://cfwbr.org/facts/index.php. Accessed 6/26/2008.

©Image 100/Jupiter Images

creating both challenge and risk. The challenge is to harness the wealth of differences provided by cultural diversity. The risk is that prejudices and stereotypes may prevent managers and employees from developing synergies to benefit the organization. Diversity of the workforce was a major factor in the innovation that drove the dot-com boom in Silicon Valley, illustrating that the benefits of a diverse workforce make good management of these challenges and risks important. [25]

Gender Diversity

The workforce now includes a substantial percentage of women. The number of women in the labor force increased from 31.5 million in 1970 to 65 million in 2008. This accounts for almost 60 percent of the overall expansion of the entire U.S. labor force for this period. In 2007, women made up more than 46 percent of the labor force.[26] In 2009, 70 percent of new workplace entrants were women and/or people of color.

Women are better prepared to contribute in organizations than ever before, because they earn 49 percent of all doctorates, 60 percent of master's degrees, and 58 percent of all undergraduate degrees.[27] But their share of authority and compensation is not increasing commensurately with their education and participation in the workforce. Not only has there been little recent increase in the number of women CEOs, but the number of women positioned to move into top jobs has also dropped. Half of the male workforce occupy line positions, compared to only one-quarter of women in business.[28] American Express is an exception to the rule. Rated one of the top companies for women in 2007 by *Pink* magazine, American Express not only places women in top positions, it trains them for advancement.[29] Nonetheless, median weekly earnings for women persist at a level of 81 percent of their male counterparts' earnings.[30] Because benefits are tied to compensation, women also receive fewer benefits. The **glass ceiling** is a transparent barrier that keeps women from rising above a certain level in organizations. In the United States, it has been rare to find women in positions above

Former United States Trade Representative Charlene Barshefsky currently sits on American Express's board of directors.

middle management.[31] Although growth in opportunities for women to attain executive positions has recently stagnated, the situation is improving for women in the boardroom. One study found no substantive increase in female corporate board members between 1996 and 2002, although this has increased in 2007.[32] The ultimate glass ceiling may well be the professional partnership. While women account for 30 percent of legal professionals, they account for only 17 percent of the partners.[33]

On a global basis, the leadership picture for women is improving. For example, the number of female political leaders has grown dramatically worldwide in recent decades. In the 1970s there were only five such leaders. In the 1990s, twenty-one female leaders came into power, and women around the world are leading major global companies. These global female business leaders do not come predominantly from the West. In addition, a large number of women have founded entrepreneurial businesses.

Removing obstacles to women's success presents a major challenge for organizations. Organizations must help the increasing numbers of female employees achieve their potential, or risk underutilizing the talents of half the U.S. workforce. They can do this by developing policies that promote equity in pay and benefits, encouraging benefit programs of special interest to women, and providing equal starting salaries for jobs of equal value. Corporations that shatter the glass ceiling share several practices. Upper managers demonstrate support for the advancement of women. Leaders incorporate practices into their diversity management programs to ensure that women perceive the organization as attractive.[34] Women are represented on standing committees addressing key strategic business issues and are targeted for participation in executive education programs. Systems are put in place to identify women with high potential for advancement.[35] Companies such as IBM and Ernst & Young work for diversity not only by offering excellent programs for advancing and developing women executives, but also judge supervisors based on their active support for such endeavors.[36]

Age Diversity

The graying of the U.S. workforce is another source of workplace diversity. Aging baby boomers (those individuals born between 1946 and 1964) contributed to the rise of the median age in the United States to thirty-six in the year 2000—six years older than at any other time in history. The number of middle-aged Americans is rising dramatically, while the number of younger workers and older workers (over age sixty-five) are declining. People over age sixty-five will comprise 13 percent of the population in 2010, and 20 percent of the population by 2030.[37]

This change in worker profile has profound implications for organizations. The job crunch among middle-aged workers will intensify as companies seek flatter organizations and

©Alex Wong/Getty Images

eliminate middle-management jobs. Older workers are often higher paid, and companies that employ large numbers of aging baby boomers may find these pay scales a handicap to competitiveness.[38] Paid volunteerism, however, can be a draw to younger generations.[39] Conversely, a more experienced, stable, reliable, and healthier workforce can pay dividends to companies. The baby boomers are well trained and educated, and their knowledge is a definite asset to organizations.

The aging workforce is increasing intergenerational contact at work.[40] As organizations flatten, workers traditionally segregated by old corporate hierarchies find themselves working together. Four generations are cooperating: *the silent generation* (people born from 1930 through 1945), a small group that includes most organizations' top managers; *the baby boomers*, whose substantial numbers give them a strong influence; *the baby bust generation*, popularly known as *Generation X* (those born from 1965 through 1976); and the subsequent generation, tentatively called *Generation Y*, *millenials*, or *the baby boomlet*.[41] The millenials often bring new challenges to the workplace because of their early access to technology and their continuing connection to parents.[42]

The differences in attitudes and values among these four generations can be substantial, and managers struggle to integrate their workers into a cohesive group. Most leadership positions are currently held by members of the silent generation. Baby boomers tend to regard the silent generation as complacent, strive for moral rights in the workplace, and take a more activist position regarding employee rights. The baby busters, newer to the workplace, are often impatient, want short-term gratification, and value a greater balance between family and work. They scorn the achievement orientation and materialism of the baby boomers. Members of Generation Y, on the other hand, place high importance on independence and creativity, and are less inclined to settle for work that is not in line with their values.

Younger workers may have false impressions of older workers, viewing them as resistant to change, unable to learn new work methods, less physically capable, and less

[Technology = Ability]

Individuals with disabilities face unique challenges in the workforce. Richard Saab became paralyzed from an aneurysm, forcing him to forego his job as a cook because he could no longer stand. Following his recovery, he wanted to cook again. The Florida Department of Vocational Rehabilitation was able to assist him by acquiring a standing wheelchair, which enabled him to assume a position as a line chef again. Development of new assistive technologies not only helps people avoid workplace injury, for example, from poor ergonomic design at computer workstations, but also help people with disabilities achieve their personal goals and contribute to the success of organizations.

SOURCE: "Standing Wheelchair for a Chef," http://www.workrerc.org. Accessed 6/26/2008.

creative than younger employees. Research indicates, however, that older employees are more satisfied with their jobs, more committed to the organization, and more internally motivated than their younger cohorts.[43] Research also indicates that direct experience with older workers reduces younger workers' negative beliefs.[44] Motivating aging workers and helping them maintain high levels of contribution to the organization is a key task for managers.

Ability Diversity

Employees with different abilities present yet another form of diversity. Individuals with disabilities are an underutilized human resource. An estimated 50 million individuals with disabilities live in the United States, and their unemployment rate is estimated to exceed 50 percent.[45] Nevertheless, they have entered the workforce in greater numbers since the Americans with Disabilities Act went

Yum! Brands is committed to attracting and retaining female and minority-group talent at all levels, from first-line operators to top executives.

into effect in the summer of 1992. The act defines a person with a disability as "anyone possessing a physical or mental impairment that substantially limits one or more major life activities."[46] Under this law, employers are required to make reasonable accommodations to permit workers with disabilities to perform jobs. The act's protection encompasses a broad range of illnesses that produce disabilities. Among these are acquired immune deficiency syndrome (AIDS), cancer, hypertension, anxiety disorders, dyslexia, blindness, and cerebral palsy, to name only a few.

Some companies recognized the value of employing workers with disabilities long before the legislation. In 1981, McDonald's created McJOBS, a corporate plan to recruit, train, and retain individuals with disabilities that has hired more than 9,000 mentally and physically challenged individuals.[47] Its participants include workers with visual, hearing, or orthopedic impairments; learning disabilities; and mental retardation. McJOBS holds sensitivity training sessions with managers and crew members before workers go onsite to help workers without disabilities understand what it means to be a worker with a disabling condition. Most McJOBS workers start part time and advance according to their own abilities and the opportunities available.

Valuing Diversity

Diversity involves more than culture, gender, age, ability, and personality. It also encompasses religion, social status, and sexual orientation. These diversity types lend heterogeneity to the workforce.

Managers must combat prejudice and discrimination to manage diversity. Prejudice is an attitude, while discrimination describes behavior. Both diminish organizational productivity. Organizations benefit when they ensure that good workers are promoted and compensated fairly. But the potential for unfair treatment also increases as the workforce becomes increasingly diverse. Combating stereotypes is essential. A recent study reveals that male bosses sometimes hold certain stereotypes that negatively influence their interaction with female employees of color.[48] Open communication can help clarify misperceptions and clear the way for advancement.

Diversity helps organizations in many ways. Some organizations recognize the potential benefits of aggressively working to increase the diversity of their workforces. Yum! Brands' Kentucky Fried Chicken (KFC) tries to attract and retain female and minority-group executives. A president of KFC's U.S. operations said, "We want to bring in the best people. If there are two equally qualified people, we'd clearly like to have diversity."[49]

In an effort to understand and appreciate diversity, Alcon Laboratories developed a diversity training class called Working Together. The course takes advantage of two key ideas. First, people work best when they are valued and when diversity is taken into account. Second, when people feel valued, they build relationships and work together as a team.[50] Even majority group managers may be more supportive of diversity training if they appreciate their own ethnic identity. One evaluation of diversity training found that participants preferred training with a traditional title and a broad focus.[51] Further, women react more positively to diversity training than men. Companies should measure the effects of training so they can monitor its positive payoffs.

Managing diversity helps companies become more competitive. But it takes more than simply being a good corporate citizen or complying with affirmative action.[52] Managing diversity requires a painful examination of employees' hidden assumptions. Biases and prejudices about people's differences must be uncovered and dealt with so that differences can be celebrated and used to their full advantage.

Diversity's Benefits and Problems

Diversity has the potential to enhance organizational performance. Table 2.2 summarizes the main benefits and problems with diversity at work. Organizations reap five main benefits from diversity. First, diversity management helps firms attract and retain the best available human talent. The companies topping the "Best Places to Work" lists are usually excellent at managing diversity. Second, diversity aids marketing efforts. Just as workforces are diversifying, so are markets. A diverse workforce can improve a company's marketing plans by drawing on insights from various employees' cultural backgrounds. Third, diversity promotes creativity and innovation. The most innovative companies, such as Hewlett-Packard, deliberately build diverse teams to foster creativity. Fourth, diversity improves problem solving. Diverse groups bring more expertise and experience to bear on problems and decisions and they encourage higher levels of critical thinking. Fifth, diversity enhances organizational flexibility because it makes an organization challenge old assumptions and become more adaptable. These five benefits add up to

TABLE 2.2 Diversity's Benefits and Problems

BENEFITS	PROBLEMS
• Attracts and retains the best talent	• Resistance to change
• Improves marketing efforts	• Lack of cohesiveness
• Promotes creativity and innovation	• Communication problems
• Results in better problem solving	• Interpersonal conflicts
• Enhances organizational flexibility	• Slower decision making

competitive advantage for companies with well-managed diversity.

We must also recognize diversity's potential problems. Five problems are particularly notable: resistance to change, lack of cohesiveness, communication problems, interpersonal conflicts, and slower decision making. People are attracted to and more comfortable with others like themselves. It stands to reason that workers may resist diversity efforts when they are forced to interact with others unlike themselves. Managers should be prepared for this resistance rather than naively assuming that everybody supports diversity. Another difficulty with diversity is the issue of cohesiveness, that invisible "glue" that holds a group together. Cohesive groups have higher morale and better communication, but diverse groups take longer to achieve cohesiveness, so they may also take longer to develop high morale.

Another obstacle to performance in diverse groups is communication. Culturally diverse groups may encounter special communication barriers. Misunderstandings can lower work group effectiveness by creating conflict and hampering decision making.[53]

Ethics, Character, and Personal Integrity

Managers frequently face ethical dilemmas and tradeoffs. Some organizations display good character and have executives known for their personal integrity. Merck & Company manages ethical issues well, and its emphasis on ethical behavior has consistently earned it a place on Business Ethics' list of top 100 corporate citizens.[54]

Despite many organizations' careful handling of ethical issues, unethical conduct sometimes occurs. The toughest problems for managers to resolve include employee theft, environmental issues, comparable worth of employees, conflicts of interest, and sexual harassment.[55]

Ethical theories help us understand, evaluate, and classify moral arguments; make decisions; and then defend conclusions about what is right and wrong. Ethical theories can be classified as consequential, rule-based, or character.

Consequential Theories of Ethics

Consequential theories of ethics emphasize the consequences or results of behavior. John Stuart Mill's utilitarianism, a well-known consequential theory, suggests that the consequences of an action determine whether it is right or wrong.[56] "Good" is the ultimate moral value, and we should maximize good effects for the greatest number of people.

But do good ethics make for good business?[57] Right actions do not always produce good consequences, and good consequences do not always follow right actions. And how do we determine the greatest good, whether short-term or long-term consequences? Using the "greatest number" criterion may mean that minorities (less than 50 percent) are excluded in evaluating the morality of actions. An issue that matters to a minority but not to the majority might be ignored. These are but two of the dilemmas raised by utilitarianism.

Corporations and business enterprises tend to subscribe to consequential ethics, partly due to the persuasive arguments of the Scottish political economist and moral philosopher Adam Smith.[58] He believed that the self-interest of human beings is God's providence, not the government's. Smith set forth a doctrine of natural liberty, presenting the classical argument for open-market competition and free trade. Within this framework, people should be allowed to pursue what is in their economic self-interest, and the natural efficiency of the marketplace would serve the well-being of society.

Rule-Based Theories of Ethics

Rule-based theories of ethics emphasize the character of the act itself, not its effects, in arriving at universal moral rights and wrongs.[59] Moral rights, the basis for legal rights, are associated with such theories. In a theological context, the Bible, the Talmud, and the Koran are rule-based guides to ethical behavior. Immanuel Kant worked toward the ultimate moral principle in formulating his categorical imperative, a universal standard of behavior.[60] Kant argued that individuals should be treated with respect and dignity and that they should not be used as a means to an end. He argued that we should put ourselves in the other person's position and ask if we would make the same decision if we were in that person's situation.

Character Theories of Ethics

Virtue ethics offer an alternative to understanding behavior in terms of self-interest or rules. Character theories of ethics emphasize the character of the individual and the intent of the actor instead of the character of the act itself or its consequences. These theories emphasize virtue-ethics and are based on an

consequential theory
An ethical theory that emphasizes the consequences or results of behavior.

rule-based theory
An ethical theory that emphasizes the character of the act itself rather than its effects.

character theory
An ethical theory that emphasizes the character, personal virtues, and intent of the individual.

ARISTOTLE

©Walter Bibikow/Photolibrary

Aristotelean approach to character. Aristotle shaped his vision around an individual's inner character and virtuousness rather than outward behavior. Thus, the good person who acted out of virtuous and right intentions was one with integrity and ultimately good ethical standards. Robert Solomon is the best known advocate of this Aristotelean approach to business ethics.[61] He advocates a business ethics theory centered on the individual within the corporation, emphasizing personal virtues as well as corporate roles. Solomon's six dimensions of virtue-ethics are community, excellence, role identity, integrity, judgment (phronesis), and holism. Further, the virtues summarize the ideals defining good character. These include honesty, loyalty, sincerity, courage, reliability, trustworthiness, benevolence, sensitivity, helpfulness, cooperativeness, civility, decency, modesty, openness, gracefulness, and many others.

Cultural Relativism

Cultural relativism contends that there are no universal ethical principles and that people should not impose their own ethical standards on others. Local standards guide ethical behavior. Cultural relativism encourages individuals to operate under the old adage "When in Rome, do as the Romans do." Unfortunately, people who adhere strictly to cultural relativism may avoid difficult ethical dilemmas by denying their own accountability.

Ethical Dilemmas Facing the Modern Organization

People need ethical theories to guide them through complex, difficult, and often confusing moral choices and ethical decisions. Contemporary organizations experience a wide variety of ethical and moral dilemmas. In this section, we address employee rights, sexual harassment, organizational justice, and whistle-blowing. We conclude with a discussion of social responsibility and codes of ethics.

Employee Rights

Managing the rights of employees at work creates many ethical dilemmas in organizations. Drug testing, free speech, downsizing and layoffs, and due process are but a few of the employee rights issues managers face.

These dilemmas include privacy issues related to technology. Many feel that computerized monitoring constitutes an invasion of privacy. Using employee data from computerized information systems presents many ethical concerns. New software allows employers to tap into their employees' address books and e-mail contacts to obtain new potential clients and discern who in the company might be best suited to approach them.[62] Safeguarding the employee's right to privacy while preserving access to the data for those who need it forces managers to balance competing interests.

The reality of AIDS in the workplace also illustrates the difficulties managers face in balancing various interests. Managers may face a conflict between the rights of HIV-infected workers and the rights of their coworkers who feel threatened. Laws protect HIV-infected workers. As mentioned earlier, the Americans with Disabilities Act (ADA) requires employees to treat HIV-infected workers as disabled individuals and to make reasonable accommodations for them. But ADA cannot encompass all of the ethical dilemmas involved.

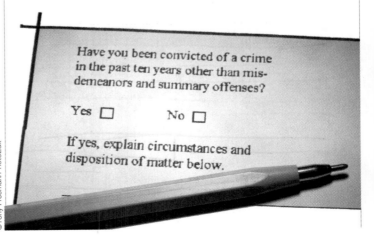

©Tony Freeman/PhotoEdit

Have you been convicted of a crime in the past ten years other than misdemeanors and summary offenses?

Yes ☐   No ☐

If yes, explain circumstances and disposition of matter below.

Confidentiality may also present challenges. Employers are not required to make concessions to coworkers, but they are obligated to educate, reassure, and provide emotional support to coworkers. Some employees with HIV or AIDS fear stigmatization or reprisals and do not want to reveal their condition to their coworkers. Management should discuss the ramifications of trying to maintain confidentiality and should assure the affected employee that every effort will be made to prevent negative consequences for him or her in the workplace.[63]

How does a manager protect the dignity of the HIV-infected employee and preserve the morale and productivity of the work group when so much prejudice and ignorance surround this disease? Many organizations, such as Wells Fargo, believe the answer is education.[64] Wells Fargo has written an AIDS policy to address confidentiality, employee socialization, coworker education, and counseling.

Sexual Harassment

According to the Equal Employment Opportunity Commission, sexual harassment is unwelcome verbal or physical sexual attention that affects an employee's job conditions or creates a hostile working environment.[65] Supreme Court rulings tend to blame companies when managers create a sexually hostile working environment. Some organizations are more tolerant of sexual harassment. Employees risk their jobs by complaining and are not taken seriously; perpetrators are rarely punished. Sexual harassment is more likely to occur in these organizations. Sexual harassment is also more likely to occur in male-dominated workplaces.[66] Managers can defend themselves by demonstrating that they took action to eliminate workplace harassment and that the complaining employee did not take advantage of company procedures to deal with harassment. Even the best sexual harassment policy, however, will not absolve a company when harassment leads to firing, demotions, or undesirable working assignments.[67]

There are three types of sexual harassment. *Gender harassment* includes crude comments or behaviors that convey hostility toward a particular gender. *Unwanted sexual attention* involves unwanted touching or repeated pressures for dates. *Sexual coercion* consists of implicit or explicit demands for sexual favors by threatening negative job-related consequences or promising job-related rewards.[68] Recent theory has focused attention on the aggressive behavior of sexual harassers.[69]

Sexual harassment costs the typical Fortune 500 company $6.7 million per year in absenteeism, turnover, and lost productivity. Valeant Pharmaceuticals International paid out millions to settle four sexual harassment complaints against former CEO Milan Panic. Plaintiffs may now sue for compensatory and punitive damages in addition to back pay. And these costs do not take into account the negative publicity sexual harassment cases may attract. Sexual harassment victims are less satisfied with their work, supervisors, and coworkers and may psychologically withdraw at work. They may suffer poorer mental health and even exhibit symptoms of post-traumatic stress disorder in conjunction with the harassment experience. Some victims report alcohol abuse, depression, headaches, and nausea.[70]

Several companies have created comprehensive sexual harassment programs. Atlantic Richfield (ARCO), owned by British Petroleum and a player in the male-dominated energy industry, has a handbook on preventing sexual harassment that includes phone numbers of state agencies where employees can file complaints. The openness seems to work. Lawsuits rarely happen at ARCO. When employees make sexual harassment complaints, the company investigates thoroughly. ARCO fired the captain of an oil tanker for sexually harassing coworkers.

Organizational Justice

Organizational justice also generates moral and ethical dilemmas at work. **Distributive justice** concerns the fairness of outcomes individuals receive. For example, during former President George H. W. Bush's 1992 visit, Japanese CEOs questioned the distributive justice of keeping American CEOs' salaries so high while many companies were struggling and laying off workers.

Procedural justice concerns the fairness of the process by which outcomes are allocated. The ethical questions in procedural justice examine the process by which an organization distributes its resources. Has the organization used the correct procedures in allocating resources? Have the right considerations, such as competence and skill, been brought to bear in the decision process? And have the wrong considerations, such as race and gender, been excluded from the decision process? One study of work-scheduling found that advance notice and consistency, two dimensions of procedural justice, reduced voluntary turnover.[71] Some research suggests cultural differences in the effects of distributive and procedural justice.[72]

Whistle-Blowing

Whistle-blowers are employees who inform authorities of wrongdoings by their companies or coworkers. Whistle-blowers

distributive justice
The fairness of outcomes that individuals receive in an organization.

procedural justice
The fairness of the process by which outcomes are allocated in an organization.

whistle-blower
An employee who informs authorities of the wrongdoings of his or her company or coworkers.

> # Whistle-blowing is a powerful influence on corporate America because committed organizational members sometimes engage in unethical behavior in an intense desire to succeed.

can be perceived as either "public heroes" or "vile wretches," depending on their situations. Those seen as heroes generally report serious and high magnitude ethical breaches widely perceived as abhorrent.[73] Others may see the whistle-blower as a wretch if they feel the act of whistle-blowing is more offensive than the situation reported.

Whistle-blowing is a powerful influence on corporate America because committed organizational members sometimes engage in unethical behavior in an intense desire to succeed. Organizations can manage whistle-blowing by explaining the conditions that are appropriate for disclosing wrongdoing. Clearly delineating wrongful behavior and the appropriate ways to respond are important organizational actions.

Social Responsibility

Corporate social responsibility is an organization's obligation to behave ethically in its social environment. Ethical conduct at the individual level can translate into social responsibility at the organizational level. Multiple stakeholders in society expect organizations to engage in socially responsible actions.

Current concerns include protecting the environment, promoting worker safety, supporting social issues, and investing in the community, among others. Some organizations, such as IBM, loan executives to inner-city schools to teach science and math. Some companies have even tried to build a brand around social responsibility, such as the Just Coffee Cooperative, which sponsors trips to coffee-producing regions in order to build customer loyalty to the cause and their brand.[74] Firms that are seen as socially responsible have a competitive advantage in attracting applicants.[75] American Apparel, however, tried to build a brand around the fact that they produce garments locally rather than in foreign sweatshops. As attractive as their ethics may be to customers, they found greater success using sex appeal to actually sell their product.[76]

Codes of Ethics

Most mature professions guide their practitioners' actions and behavior with codes of ethics. For example, the Hippocratic oath guides doctors. A profession's code of ethics becomes a standard against which members can measure themselves in the absence of internalized standards.

No universal code of ethics or oath exists for business as it does for medicine. However, Paul Harris and four business colleagues who founded Rotary International in 1905 addressed ethical and moral behavior. They developed the four-way test, shown in Figure 2.2, which is now used in more than 166 nations by 1.2 million Rotarians. Figure 2.2 focuses the questioner on key ethical and moral questions.

Beyond the individual and professional level, corporate culture is another excellent starting point for addressing ethics and morality. Sometimes regulations articulate a corporation's ethics. For example, the Joint Ethics Regulation (DOD 5500.7-R, August 1993) specifies the ethical standards that all U.S. military personnel must follow. In other cases, corporate ethics appear as a credo. Johnson & Johnson's credo, shown in Figure 2.3, helped hundreds of employees ethically address criminal tampering with Tylenol products.

Individual codes of ethics, professional oaths, and organizational credos must all be anchored in a moral, ethical framework. We must continue using ethical theories to question and improve our current standards. Although a universal right and wrong may exist, it would be hard to agree upon a single code of ethics to which all individuals, professions, and organizations can subscribe.

social responsibility
The obligation of an organization to behave ethically in its social environment.

FIGURE 2.2 The Four-Way Test

The Four-Way Test of What We Think, Say, or Do

1. Is it the TRUTH?

2. Is it FAIR to all concerned?

3. Will it build GOODWILL and better friendships?

4. Will it be BENEFICIAL to all concerned?

FIGURE **2.3** The Johnson & Johnson Credo

We believe our first responsibility is to the doctors, nurses, and patients, to mothers and all others who use our products and services. In meeting their needs everything we do must be of high quality. We must constantly strive to reduce our costs in order to maintain reasonable prices. Customers' orders must be serviced promptly and accurately. Our suppliers and distributors must have an opportunity to make a fair profit.

We are responsible to our employees, the men and women who work with us throughout the world. Everyone must be considered as an individual. We must respect their dignity and recognize their merit. They must have a sense of security in their jobs. Compensation must be fair and adequate, and working conditions clean, orderly, and safe. Employees must feel free to make suggestions and complaints. There must be equal opportunity for employment, development and advancement for those qualified. We must provide competent management, and their actions must be just and ethical.

We are responsible to the communities in which we live and work and to the world community as well. We must be good citizens—support good works and charities and bear our fair share of taxes. We must encourage civic improvements and better health and education. We must maintain in good order the property we are privileged to use, protecting the environment and natural resources.

Our final responsibility is to our stockholders. Business must make a sound profit. We must experiment with new ideas. Research must be carried on, innovative programs developed and mistakes paid for. New equipment must be purchased, new facilities provided, and new products launched. Reserves must be created to provide for adverse times. When we operate according to these principles, the stockholders should realize a fair return.

in workplace settings.[78] Great organizations avoid technology fads and bandwagons, instead pioneering the application of carefully selected technologies.[79]

The Internet has radically changed organizations' communication and work performance. By integrating computer, cable, and telecommunications technologies, businesses have learned new ways to compete. For example, Kmart takes advantage of the Internet through BlueLight.com for online retailing, thereby drastically reducing its investments in inventories. Networked organizations conduct business anytime and anywhere, which is essential in the global marketplace.

The Internet and electronic innovation have made surveillance of employees more widespread. However, companies need to balance the use of spyware, monitoring of employee e-mails and websites, and video monitoring systems with respect for employee rights to privacy. Managers with excellent interpersonal skills go beyond intense employee performance monitoring to ensure high productivity, commitment, and appropriate behavior from employees. Companies with clearly written policies spelling out their approach to monitoring employees walk the fine line between respecting employees' privacy and protecting the interests of the organization.

One fascinating technological change is the development of **expert systems**, computer-based applications that use a representation of human expertise in a specialized field of knowledge to solve problems. Expert systems can be used in many ways, including

LEARNING OUTCOME **6**

Technological Innovation and Today's Workforce

In addition to globalization, diversity, and ethics, a fourth challenge that managers face is technological innovation. **Technology** consists of the intellectual and mechanical processes used by an organization to transform inputs into products or services that meet its goals. Managers must adapt to rapidly changing technology and ensure its optimum use in their organizations. Their ability to incorporate new technologies into their organizations can make or break economic growth.[77] Although the United States still leads the way in developing new technologies, it lags behind in using them productively

technology

The intellectual and mechanical processes used by an organization to transform inputs into products or services that meet its goals.

expert system

A computer-based application that uses a representation of human expertise in a specialized field of knowledge to solve problems.

providing advice to nonexperts, providing assistance to experts, replacing experts, and serving as a training and development tool in organizations.[80] They are used in medical decision making, diagnosis, and medical informatics.[81] Anheuser-Busch has used an expert system to assist managers in ensuring that personnel decisions comply with antidiscrimination laws.[82]

Robots, another technological innovation, were invented in the United States. Although advanced research on robotics is still conducted here, Japanese organizations lead the world in the use of robotics. Organizations in the United States have fewer total robots than were added in 1989 alone in Japan.[83] Whereas Japanese workers are happy to let robots take over repetitive or dangerous work, American employees worry that they will be replaced by labor-saving robots.[84] The main reason for the reluctance of U.S. organizations to use robots is their slow payout. Robotics represents a big investment that does not pay off in the short term. Japanese managers are more willing to evaluate the effectiveness of robotics technology with a long-term horizon in view.

It is tempting to focus only on the positive side of technology, but a little realism is in order. Some firms that have been disappointed with costly technologies are electing to *de*-engineer: 42 percent of information technology projects are abandoned before completion, and half of all technology projects fail to meet managers' expectations. Pacific Gas and Electric (part of PG&E Corporation) spent tens of millions of dollars on a new IBM-based system. Then deregulation hit the utility industry, allowing customers to choose among utility companies. Keeping up with multiple suppliers and fast-changing prices was too much for the massive new system. It was scrapped in favor of a new project using the old first-generation computer system that is being updated and gradually replaced. Because some innovations fail to live up to

©Comstock Images/Jupiterimages

expectations, managers have to handle both revolutionary and evolutionary approaches to technological transitions.[85]

Alternative Work Arrangements

Technological advances have prompted the advent of alternative work arrangements, or the nontraditional work practices, settings, and locations that are now supplementing traditional workplaces. One alternative work arrangement is **telecommuting**, or electronically transmitting work from a home computer to the office. IBM was one of the first companies to experiment with the notion of installing computer terminals at employees' homes and having employees work at home. By telecommuting, employees gain flexibility, save the commute to work, and enjoy the comforts of being at home. Telecommuting also has disadvantages, however, including distractions and lack of opportunities to socialize with other workers. Despite these disadvantages, telecommuters still feel "plugged in" to the communication system at the office. Studies show that telecommuters often report higher satisfaction with office communication than do workers in traditional office environments.[86]

Telecommuting offers a number of advantages to both employers and employees, and an estimated 28 million Americans telecommute. Cost reductions are an obvious motivator for companies to encourage telecommuting. Since 1991, AT&T has gained $550 million in cash flow by eliminating office space and reducing overhead costs. Telecommuting also increases productivity by letting companies access workers with key skills regardless of their locations and gives them an advantage in hiring and keeping talented employees who find the flexibility of working at home very attractive. The environment also benefits from telecommuting, as less driving means cleaner air and reduces the contribution to global warming.[87]

Satellite offices comprise another alternative work arrangement. Large facilities are broken into a network of smaller workplaces located near employees' homes. Satellites are often located in comparatively inexpensive cities and suburban areas. They usually have simpler furnishings than the more centrally located offices. Satellites can save a company as much as 50 percent in real estate costs and can attract employees who do not want to work in a large urban area, thus broadening the pool of potential employees.[88]

These alternative work arrangements signal a trend toward *virtual offices*, in which people work anytime, anywhere, and with anyone. The concept suggests work occurring where people are, rather than people coming to work. Information technologies make connectivity, collaboration, and communication easy. Critical voice-mails and messages can be delivered to and from the central

> *42 percent of information technology projects are abandoned before completion, and half of all technology projects fail to meet managers' expectations.*

office, a client's office, the airport, the car, or home. Wireless Internet access and online meeting software such as WebEx allow employees to participate in meetings anywhere at any time.

Impact of Technology on Management

Technological innovation affects the very nature of the management job. Managers who once had to coax workers back to their desks from coffee breaks now find that they need to encourage workers mesmerized by new technology to take more frequent breaks.[89] Working with a computer can be stressful, both physically and psychologically. Long hours at computer terminals can cause eye strain, neck and back strain, and headaches. In addition, workers accustomed to the fast response time of the computer come to expect the same from their coworkers and scold coworkers when they fail to match the computer's speed and accuracy. New technology, combined with globalization and intensified business pressures, has created extreme workers, pushing up the ranks of workaholics.[90] These extreme workers pay a price in relationships, other dimensions of a full, rich life, and increased stress.

Computerized monitoring provides managers with a wealth of information about employee performance but holds great potential for misuse. The telecommunications, airline, and mail-order merchandise industries make wide use of systems that secretly monitor employees' interactions with customers. Employers praise such systems for improving customer service. Workers, however, react to

secret scrutiny with higher levels of depression, anxiety, and exhaustion. Bell Canada evaluated operators using a system that tabulated average working time with customers. Operators found the practice highly stressful and sabotaged the system by giving callers wrong directory assistance numbers rather than taking the time to look up the correct ones. Bell Canada now uses average working time scores for entire offices rather than for individuals.[91] If managed well, however, technology can benefit the company. Google, for example, gives its employees freedom to choose which technologies they use. While this strategy costs more, it leads to increased productivity.[92]

New technologies and rapid innovation place a premium on a manager's technical skills. Managers must develop technical competence in order to gain workers' respect. Computer-integrated manufacturing systems, for example, require managers to use participative management styles, open communication, and greater technical expertise to be effective.[93] In a world of rapid technological innovation, managers must focus on helping workers manage the stress of their work. They must take advantage of the wealth of information available to motivate, coach, and counsel workers rather than to stringently control or police them.

Helping Employees Adjust to Technological Change

Most workers understand the benefits of modern technologies. Innovation has improved working conditions and increased the availability of skilled jobs. Technology

©Laurent Davoust/iStockphoto.com

HOT *Trend: Intangible Assets*

Roughly 75 percent of *Fortune* 100's total market capitalization is in intangible assets, such as patents, copyrights, and trademarks. That means that managing intellectual property cannot be left to technology managers or corporate lawyers. How to manage sensitive information and intellectual property stored digitally is a key issue even for individual employees who must remain aware that the value of a computer drive includes the value of the data stored on it. Managers and companies with well-conceived strategies and policies for their intellectual property can use it for competitive advantage in the global marketplace.

SOURCE: M. Reitzig, "Strategic Management of Intellectual Property," *MIT Sloan Management Review* 45 (Spring 2004): 35–40; S. Evans, "Negligent Workers Put Data at Risk," Computer Business Review (December 11, 2007), http://www.computerbusinessreview.com/article_news.asp?guid=CF7991DF-8802-49F4-8A10-C150FE47368F. Acccessed 6/24/2008.

is also bringing disadvantaged individuals into the workforce. Microchips have dramatically increased opportunities for workers with visual impairments. Information can be decoded into speech using a speech synthesizer, into braille using a hard-copy printer, or into enlarged print visible on a computer monitor.[94] Engineers at Carnegie Mellon University have developed PizzaBot, a robot that individuals with disabilities can operate using a voice-recognition system. Despite these and other benefits of new technology in the workplace, however, employees may still resist change.

Technological innovations change employees' work environments, generating stress. Many workers react negatively to change that they feel threatens their work situation. Many of their fears center around loss—of freedom, of control, of the things they like about their jobs.[95] Employees may fear diminished quality of work life and increased pressure. Further, employees may fear being replaced by technology or being displaced into jobs of lower skill levels.

Managers can take several actions to help employees adjust to changing technology. Encouraging workers' participation in early phases of decisions regarding technological changes is important. Individuals who participate in planning for the implementation of new technology learn about the potential changes in their jobs and are less resistant to the change. Workers' input in early stages can smooth the transition into new ways of performing work.

Managers should also keep in mind the effects that new technology has on the skill requirements of workers. Many employees support changes that increase the skill requirements of their jobs. Increased skill requirements often lead to increased job autonomy, responsibility, and (potentially) pay. Whenever possible, managers should select technology that increases workers' skill requirements.

Providing effective training is essential. Training helps employees perceive that they control the technology rather than being controlled by it. The training should be designed to match workers' needs and should increase the workers' sense of mastery of the new technology.

A related challenge is to encourage workers to invent new uses for existing technology. **Reinvention** is the creative application of new technology.[96] Individuals who explore the boundaries of a new technology can personalize the technology, adapt it to their own job needs, and share this information with others in their work group.

Managers must lead organizations to adopt new technologies more humanely and effectively. Technological changes are essential for earnings growth and for expanded employment opportunities. The adoption of new technologies is a critical determinant of U.S. competitiveness in the global marketplace.

reinvention
The creative application of new technology.

> " Managers must lead organizations to adopt new technologies more humanely and effectively.

Emphasizing Cultures, ETHICS, & Norms

CHAPTER 3

OPENING CASE

Cartoons that Exploded

In September 2005, the Danish newspaper *Jyllands-Posten* (*Jutland Post*) published a dozen cartoons of the Muslim prophet Mohammed. These cartoons not only violated the Muslim norm against picturing the prophet, they also portrayed Mohammed in a highly negative, insulting light, especially those cartoons that pictured him as a terrorist. *Jyllands-Posten* knew that it was testing the limits of free speech and good taste. But it had no idea its cartoons would ignite such a ferocious explosion. For Denmark itself, this incident became the biggest crisis since the Nazi occupation during World War II. Beyond Denmark, publishers in a total of 22 countries, including Belgium, France, Germany, the Netherlands, and Norway, reprinted the cartoons to make a point about their right to do so in the name of freedom of expression. Muslims around the world were outraged; protests were organized; Danish flags were burned; and Western embassies in Indonesia, Iran, Lebanon, and Syria were attacked. A crowd of 50,000 in Kahrtoum, Sudan, chanted "Strike, strike, bin Laden!" At least ten people were killed in protests against the cartoons as police in Afghanistan shot into crowds besieging Western installations.

While mobs reacted in the street, Muslim governments also took action. Iran, Libya, Saudi Arabia, and Syria withdrew their ambassadors from Denmark in protest. The justice minister of the United Arab Emirates asserted, "This is cultural terrorism, not freedom of expression." However, Anders Rasmussen, the Danish prime minister, met with ambassadors from ten Muslim countries and indicated that however distasteful the cartoons were, the government could not apologize on behalf of the newspaper. The principle of freedom of speech is enshrined in Denmark (and the West generally), and even if the Danish government wanted to take action against the newspaper, there were no laws empowering it to do so.

© RIZWAN TABASSUM/AFP/Getty Images

LEARNING OBJECTIVES

After studying this chapter, you should be able to:

LO1 explain where informal institutions come from.

LO2 define culture and articulate its two main manifestations.

LO3 articulate three ways to understand cultural differences.

LO4 explain why understanding cultural differences is crucial for global business.

LO5 explain why ethics is important.

LO6 identify ways to combat corruption.

LO7 identify norms associated with strategic responses when firms deal with ethical challenges.

LO8 explain how you can acquire cross-cultural literacy.

While acknowledging the importance of freedom of speech, Western governments expressed sympathy to Muslims. French president Jacques Chirac issued a plea for "respect and moderation" in exercising freedom of expression. British foreign minister Jack Straw called the cartoons "insensitive." US president George W. Bush called on world governments to stop the violence and be "respectful." Carsten Juste, editor of *Jyllands-Posten*, who received death threats, said that the drawings "were not in violation of Danish law but offended many Muslims, for which we would like to apologize."

While Muslim feelings were hurt, Danish firms active in Muslim countries were devastated. Arla Foods, one of Denmark's (and Europe's) largest diary firms, had been selling to the Middle East for 40 years, had had production in Saudi Arabia for 20 years, and normally sold approximately $465 million a year to the region, including the best-selling butter in the Middle East. Arla's sales to the region plummeted to zero in a matter of days after the protests began. Arla lost $1.8 million every *day* and was forced to send home 170 employees. Other affected firms included Carlsberg (a brewer), Lego (a toy maker), and Novo Nordisk (an insulin maker). In addition, Carrefour, a French supermarket chain active in the re-

gion, voluntarily pulled Danish products from shelves in the Middle East and boasted about it to customers.

In response, Arla took out full-page advertisements in Saudi newspapers, reprinting the news release from the Danish Embassy in Riyadh saying that Denmark respected all religions. That failed to stop the boycott. Other Danish firms kept a low profile. Some switched "Made in Denmark" labels to "Made in European Union." Others used foreign subsidiaries to camouflage their origin. Danish shipping companies such as Maersk took down the Danish flag when docking in Muslim ports. Overall, although Muslim countries represented only approximately 3% of all Danish exports, a worst-case scenario would lead to 10,000 job losses, which would be a significant blow to a small country with a population of only 5.4 million.

Sources: A. Browne, "Denmark faces international boycott over Muslim cartoons," *Times Online*, 31 January 2006, available online at http://www.timesonline.co.uk; "Mutual incomprehension, mutual outrage," *Economist*, 11 February 2006, 29-31; E. Pfanner, "Danish companies endure snub by Muslim consumers," *New York Times*, 27 February 2006, 2; P. Reynolds, "A clash of rights and responsibilities," *BBC News*, 6 February 2006, available online at http://news.bbc.co.uk/ [accessed 29 June 2009].

While publishing the offending cartoons is legal in Denmark, is it ethical? Should the editor of *Jyllands-Posten*, the Danish prime minister, and managers at Arla have reacted differently? Why should many Danish firms, which have nothing to do with the cartoons, suffer major economic losses in Muslim countries? Why do non-Danish and non-Muslim firms such as Carrefour withdraw Danish products from their shelves in the Middle East? More fundamentally, what informal institutions govern individual and firm behavior in different countries?

This chapter continues our coverage on the institution-based view, which began with formal institutions in Chapter 2. Now we will focus on informal institutions represented by cultures, ethics, and norms. Cultures, ethics, and norms are not established by laws and regulations like formal institutions are, so they are less tangible. Yet, they too play an important part in shaping the success and failure of firms around the globe. Remember that the institution-based view involves two propositions. First, managers and firms rationally pursue their interests within a given institutional framework. Second, in situations where formal institutions are unclear or fail, informal institutions play a larger role in reducing uncertainty. The first proposition deals with both formal and informal institutions. But the second proposition hinges on the informal institutions we are about to discuss. As the Opening Case shows, informal institutions are about more than just basic customs such as how to present

business cards correctly and how to wine and dine properly. Informal institutions can make or break firms, which is why they deserve a great deal of our attention.

Ethnocentrism
A self-centered mentality held by a group of people who perceive their own culture, ethics, and norms as natural, rational, and morally right.

LO1 *Explain where informal institutions come from.*

WHERE DO INFORMAL INSTITUTIONS COME FROM?

Recall that any institutional framework consists of formal and informal institutions. While formal institutions such as politics, laws, and economics (see Chapter 2) are important, they make up a small (although important) part of the rules of the game that govern individual and firm behavior. As pervasive features of every economy, informal institutions can be found almost *everywhere*.

Where do informal institutions come from? They come from socially transmitted information and are a part of the heritage that we call cultures, ethics, and norms. Those within a society tend to perceive their own culture, ethics, and norms as "natural, rational, and morally right."[1] This self-centered mentality is known as **ethnocentrism**. For example, many Americans believe in "American exceptionalism," a view that holds the United States to be exceptionally well endowed to lead the world. The Chinese call China *zhong guo*, which literally means "the country in the middle" or "middle kingdom." Ancient Scandinavians called their country by a similar name (*midgaard*). Some modern Scandinavians, such as some Danes, believe in their freedom to publish whatever they please. Unfortunately, as shown in the Opening Case, those from other societies may beg to differ. In other words, common sense in one society may be uncommon elsewhere.

Recall from Chapter 2 that informal institutions are underpinned by the normative and cognitive pillars, while formal institutions are supported by the regulatory pillar. While the regulatory pillar clearly specifies the dos and don'ts, informal institutions, by definition, are more elusive. Yet, they are no less important. Thus it is imperative that we pay attention to three different informal institutions: culture, ethics, and norms.

LO2 *Define culture and articulate its two main manifestations.*

CULTURE

Out of many informal institutions, culture is probably the most frequently discussed. Before we can discuss its two major components—language and religion—first we must define culture.

Definition of Culture

Although hundreds of definitions of culture have appeared, we will use the definition proposed by the world's foremost cross-cultural expert, Geert Hofstede, a Dutch professor. He defines **culture** as "the collective programming of the mind which distinguishes the members of one group or category of people from another."[2] Before proceeding, it is important to make two points to minimize confusion. First, although it is customary to talk about American culture or Brazilian culture, no strict one-to-one correspondence between cultures and nation-states exists. Many subcultures exist within multiethnic countries such as Belgium, China, India, Indonesia, Russia, South Africa, Switzerland, and the United States. Second, culture has many layers, such as regional, ethnic, and religious. Even firms may have a specific organizational culture. Companies such as IKEA are well known for their distinctive corporate cultures. Acknowledging the validity of these two points, we will, however, follow Hofstede by using the term "culture" to discuss *national* culture unless otherwise noted. While this is a matter of expediency, it is also a reflection of the institutional realities of the world with about 200 nation-states.

Culture is made up of many elements. Our social structure, modes of communication, and education are all manifestations of the cultures in which we live. Although culture is too complex to dissect in the space we have here, we will highlight two major components of culture that impact global business: language and religion.

Language

Approximately 6,000 languages are spoken in the world. In terms of the number of native speakers, Chinese is the world's largest language (20% of the world population). English is a distant second (6% of the

©iStockphoto.com/Loïc Bernard

world population), followed closely by Hindi (5%) and Spanish (5%). Yet, the dominance of English as a global business language, or **lingua franca**, is unmistakable. This is driven by two factors. First, English-speaking countries contribute the largest share (approximately 40%) of global output.[3] Such economic dominance not only drives trade and investment ties between English-speaking countries and the rest of the world but also generates a constant stream of products and services marketed in English. Think about the ubiquitous Hollywood movies, *Economist* magazine, and Google's search engine.

Second, recent globalization has called for the use of one common language. For firms headquartered in English-speaking countries as well as Scandinavia and the Netherlands (where English is widely taught and spoken), using English to manage operations around the globe poses little difficulty. However, settling on a global language for the entire firm is problematic for firms headquartered in Latin countries (such as France) or Asian countries (such as Japan), in which English is not widely spoken. Yet, even in these firms, it is still difficult to insist on a language *other* than English as the global corporate *lingua franca*. Around the world, non-native speakers of English who can master English increasingly command a premium in jobs and compensation, and this fuels a rising interest in English. Think, for example, of the Taiwanese-born Hollywood director Ang Lee, Icelandic-born singer Björk, and Colombian-born pop star Shakira.

Culture
The collective programming of the mind which distinguishes the members of one group or category of people from another.

Lingua franca
A global business language.

©iStockphoto.com/iofoto

On the other hand, the dominance of English may also lead to a disadvantage. Although native English speakers have a great deal of advantage in global business, an expatriate manager who does not know the local language misses a lot of cultural subtleties and can only interact with locals fluent in English. Weak (or no) ability in foreign languages makes it difficult or even impossible to detect translation errors, which may result in embarrassments. For example, Rolls-Royce's Silver Mist was translated into German as "Silver Excrement." Coors Beer translated its slogan, "Turn it loose!" into Spanish as "Drink Coors and get diarrhea!" Chevrolet marketed its Nova car in Latin America with disastrous results—"No va" means "no go" in Spanish.[4] To avoid such embarrassments, you will be better off if you can pick up at least one foreign language during your university studies.

Religion

Religion is another major manifestation of culture. Approximately 85% of the world's population report having some religious belief. Exhibit 3.1 shows the geographical distribution of different religious heritages. The four leading religions are Christianity (approximately 1.7 billion adherents), Islam (1 billion), Hinduism (750 million), and Buddhism (350 million). Of course, not everybody claiming to be an adherent actively practices a religion. For instance, some Christians may go to church only *once every year*—at Christmas.

Because religious differences have led to numerous challenges, knowledge about religions is crucial even for *non*-religious managers. For example, in Christian countries, the Christmas season represents the peak in shopping and consumption. Half of toy sales for a given year in the United States occur during the month before Christmas. Since kids in America consume half of the world's toys and virtually all toys are made outside the United States (mostly in Asia), this means 25% of the world toy output is sold in one country in a month, thus creating severe production, distribution, and coordination challenges. For toy makers and stores, missing the boat from Asia, whose transit time is at least two weeks, can literally devastate an entire holiday season and probably the entire year. Overall, managers and firms ignorant of religious traditions and differences may end up with embarrassments and, worse, disasters, as the Opening Case illustrates. The hope is that historically and religiously sensitive managers and firms will avoid such blunders in the future.

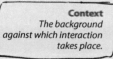

Context
The background against which interaction takes place.

Low-context culture
A culture in which communication is usually taken at face value without much reliance on unspoken conditions or assumptions.

High-context culture
A culture in which communication relies heavily on the underlying unspoken conditions or assumptions, which are as important as the words used.

LO3 Articulate three ways to understand cultural differences.

LO4 Explain why understanding cultural differences is crucial for global business.

CLASSIFYING CULTURAL DIFFERENCES

As you can now see, the world is full of many informal institutions. The web of cultures can be difficult to navigate. While it is important to understand the dynamics of a particular culture in a country where you might do business, it is also important to be able to step back, see the bigger picture, and be able to understand how cultures are *systematically* different. This section outlines three different ways to systematically understand cultural differences: (1) the context approach, (2) the cluster approach, and (3) the dimension approach. We will then link culture with different firm behavior.

The Context Approach

Of the three main approaches to cultural difference, the context approach is the most straightforward because it relies on a single dimension: context.[5] **Context** is the background against which interaction takes place. Exhibit 3.2 on page 38 outlines a spectrum of countries along the dimension of low versus high context. In **low-context cultures** such as North American and Western European countries, communication is usually taken at face value without much reliance on unspoken conditions or assumptions, which are features of context. In other words, "no" means "no." In **high-context cultures** such as Arab and Asian countries, on the other hand, communication relies heavily on unspoken conditions or assumptions, which are as important as the words used. "No" does not necessarily mean "no," and you must rely much more on the context in order to understand just what "no" means.

Why is context important? Failure to understand the differences in interaction styles may lead to misunderstandings. For example, in Japan, a high-context culture, negotiators prefer not to flatly say "no" to a business request. They will say something like "We will study it" or "We will get back to you later." Their negotiation partners are supposed to understand the context of these

© iStockphoto.com/Don Bayley

Chinese and Americans act differently at the negotiating table.

EXHIBIT 3.1 Religious Heritages of the World

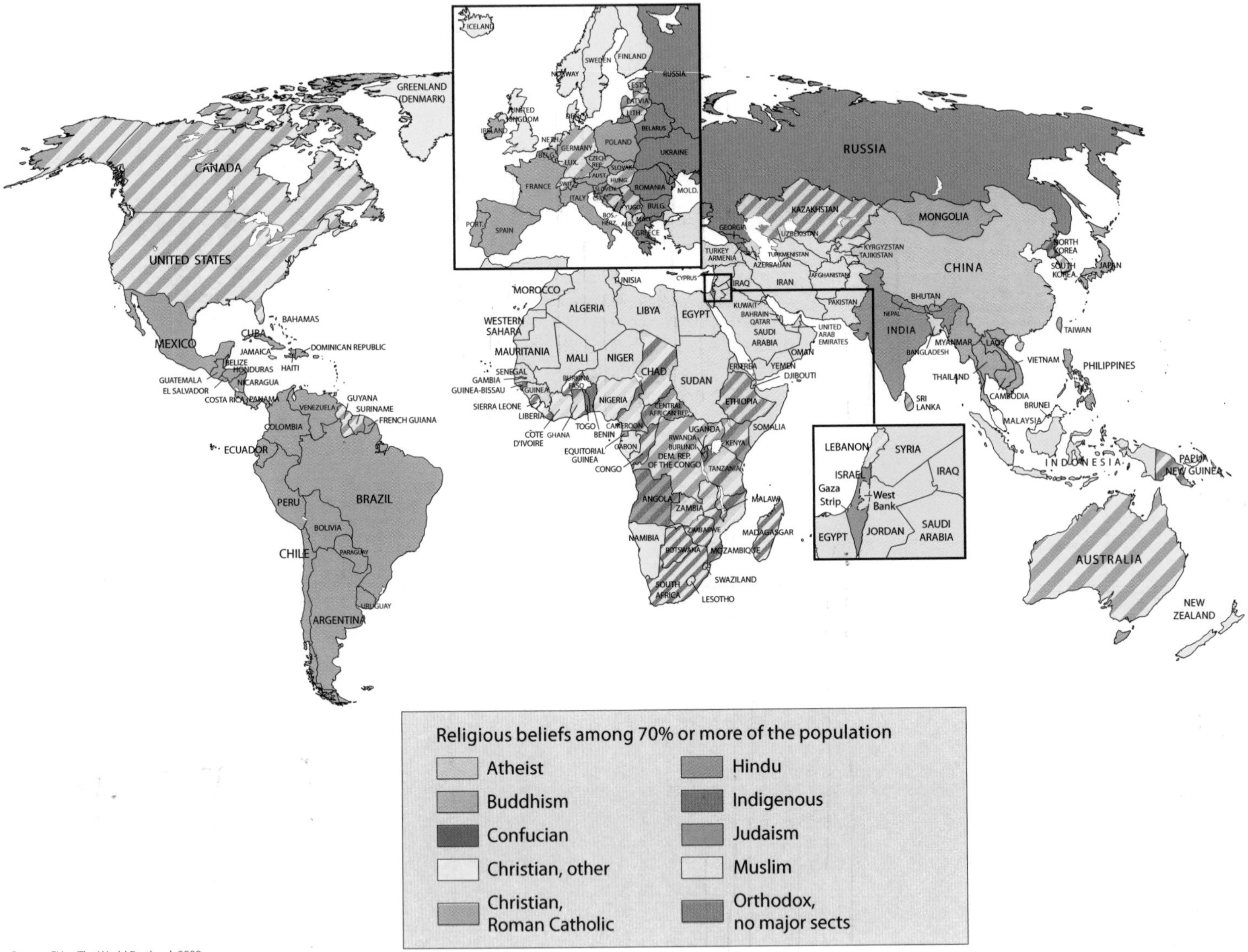

Religious beliefs among 70% or more of the population

Atheist
Buddhism
Confucian
Christian, other
Christian, Roman Catholic

Hindu
Indigenous
Judaism
Muslim
Orthodox, no major sects

Source: CIA—The World Factbook 2000.

Note: Confucianism, strictly speaking, is not a religion but a set of moral codes guiding interpersonal relationships.

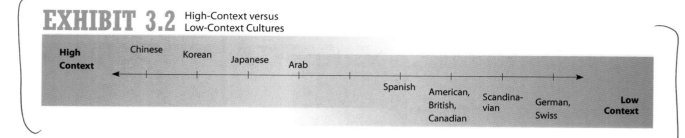

EXHIBIT 3.2 High-Context versus Low-Context Cultures

High Context — Chinese — Korean — Japanese — Arab — Spanish — American, British, Canadian — Scandinavian — German, Swiss — **Low Context**

unenthusiastic responses and interpret them as essentially "no," even though the word "no" is never explicitly said. By contrast, lawyers in the United States, a low-context culture, are included in negotiations to essentially help remove the context—a contract should be as straightforward as possible, and there should be no room for parties to read between the lines. But negotiators from high-context countries such as China often prefer *not* to involve lawyers until the very last phase of contract drafting. In high-context countries, initial rounds of negotiations are supposed to create the context for mutual trust and friendship. For individuals brought up in high-context cultures, decoding the context and acting accordingly becomes second nature. Straightforward communication and confrontation, typical in low-context cultures, often baffle them.

The Cluster Approach

The cluster approach groups countries that share similar cultures together as one **cluster**. There are three influential sets of clusters, illustrated in Exhibit 3.3. This table is the first time these three major systems of cultural clusters are compiled side by side. Viewing them together can allow us to see their similarities and differences. The first is the Ronen and Shenkar clusters, proposed by management professors Simcha Ronen and Oded Shenkar.[6] In alphabetical order, these clusters are Anglo, Arabic, Far Eastern, Germanic, Latin American, Latin European, Near Eastern, and Nordic. Ronen and Shenkar originally classified these eight clusters, which cover 44 countries. They classified Brazil, India, Israel, and Japan as independents. Upon consultation with Shenkar, my colleagues and I more recently added Central and Eastern Europe and sub-Saharan Africa as two new clusters.[7]

The second set of clusters is called the GLOBE clusters, named after the Global Leadership and Organizational Behavior Effectiveness project led by management professor Robert House.[8] The GLOBE project identifies ten clusters and covers 62 countries. Five of the clusters use identical labels as the Ronen and Shenkar clusters. The Anglo, Germanic Europe, Latin America, Latin Europe, and

Cluster
A group of countries that have similar cultures.

Civilization
The highest cultural grouping of people and the broadest level of cultural identity people have.

Nordic Europe clusters roughly (but not completely) correspond with the respective Ronen and Shenkar clusters. But Ronen and Shenkar's Latin America cluster does not include Brazil (which is regarded as an independent), whereas GLOBE includes Brazil. In addition, GLOBE has the clusters of Confucian Asia, Eastern Europe, Middle East, Southern Asia, and sub-Saharan Africa.

The third set of clusters is the Huntington civilizations, popularized by political scientist Samuel Huntington. Huntington includes eight civilizations, in theory covering *every* country. A **civilization** is "the highest cultural grouping of people and the broadest level of cultural identity people have."[9] Huntington divides the world into eight civilizations: African, Confucian (Sinic), Hindu, Islamic, Japanese, Latin American, Slavic-Orthodox, and Western. While this classification shares a number of similarities with the Ronen and Shenkar and GLOBE clusters, Huntington's Western civilization is a very broad cluster that is subdivided into Anglo, Germanic, Latin Europe, and Nordic clusters by Ronen and Shenkar and GLOBE. In addition to such an uncontroversial classification scheme, Huntington has advanced a highly controversial idea that Western civilization will clash with the Islamic and Confucian civilizations in the years to come. Incidents such as 9/11, the war in Iraq, and more recently the Danish cartoons discussed in the Opening Case have often been cited as evidence of such a clash.

For our purposes, we do not need to debate the validity of Huntington's provocative thesis of the "clash of civilizations"; we will leave that debate to your political science or international relations classes. However, we do need to appreciate the underlying idea that people and firms are more comfortable doing business with other countries within the same cluster/civilization. Having a common language, history, and religion as well as common customs within the same cluster/civilization reduces the liability of foreignness (see Chapter 1) when operating abroad. For example, Hollywood movies are more likely to succeed in English-speaking countries. Most foreign investors in China are from Hong Kong and Taiwan; they are not very "foreign." Conversely, the Danish firms discussed in the Opening Case suffered in Muslim countries in the aftermath of the cartoon incident because their high level of foreignness was a liability in a culturally distant cluster.

EXHIBIT 3.3 Cultural Clusters

Ronen and Shenkar Clusters	GLOBE Clusters	Huntington Civilizations
Anglo	Anglo	Western (1)
Arabic	Middle East	Islamic
Far East	Confucian Asia	Confucian (Sinic)
Germanic	Germanic Europe	Western (2)
Latin America	Latin America	Latin American
Latin Europe	Latin Europe	Western (3)
Near Eastern	Southern Asia	Hindu
Nordic	Nordic Europe	Western (4)
Central and Eastern Europe	Eastern Europe	Slavic-Orthodox
Sub-Saharan Africa	Sub-Saharan Africa	African
Independents: Brazil, India, Israel, Japan		Japanese

Sources: R. House, P. Hanges, M. Javidan, P. Dorfman, and V. Gupta, eds., *Culture, Leadership, and Organizations: The GLOBE Study of 62 Societies* (Thousand Oaks, CA: Sage, 2004); S. Huntington, *The Clash of Civilizations and the Remaking of World Order* (New York: Simon & Schuster, 1996); M. W. Peng, C. Hill, and D. Wang, "Schumpeterian dynamics versus Williamsonian considerations," *Journal of Management Studies* 37 (2000): 167-184; S. Ronen and O. Shenkar, "Clustering countries on attitudinal dimension," *Academy of Management Review* 10 (1985): 435-454. For Western civilization, Huntington does not use such labels as Western 1, 2, 3, and 4 as in the table. They were added to establish some rough correspondence with the respective Ronen and Shenkar and GLOBE clusters.

The Dimension Approach

While both the context and cluster approaches are interesting, the dimension approach is more influential. The reasons for such influence are probably twofold. First, insightful as the context approach is, it represents only one dimension. What about other dimensions? Second, the cluster approach has relatively little to offer regarding differences of countries *within* one cluster. For example, what are the differences between Italy and Spain, both of which belong to the same Latin Europe cluster according to Ronen and Shenkar and GLOBE? By focusing on multiple dimensions of cultural differences both within and across clusters, the dimension approach aims to overcome these limitations. While there are several competing frameworks, the work of Hofstede and his colleagues is by far the most influential and thus our focus here.

Hofstede and his colleagues have proposed five dimensions, shown in Exhibit 3.4 on page 40. First, **power distance** is the extent to which less powerful members within a country expect and accept that power is distributed unequally. For example, in high power distance Brazil, the richest 10% of the population receives approximately 50% of the national income, and everybody accepts this as the way it is. In low power distance Sweden, the richest 10% only get 22% of the national income.[10] Major differences occur even within the same cluster. For example, in the United States, subordinates often address their bosses on a first name basis, a reflection of a relatively low power distance. While your boss, Mary or Joe, still has the power to fire you, the distance appears to be shorter than if you have to address this person as Mrs. Y or Dr. Z. In low power distance American universities, all faculty members, including the lowest-ranked assistant professors, are commonly addressed as "Professor A." In high power distance British universities, only full professors are allowed to be called "Professor B" (everybody else is called "Dr. C" or "Ms. D" if D does not have a PhD). German universities are perhaps most extreme: Full professors with PhDs need to be honored as "Prof. Dr. X." I would be "Prof. Dr. Peng" if I were to teach at a German university.

Second, **individualism** refers to the idea that an individual's identity is fundamentally his or her own, whereas **collectivism** refers to the idea that an individual's identity is fundamentally tied to the identity of his or her collective group, be it a family, village, or company. In individualistic societies, led by the United States, ties between individuals are relatively loose and individual achievement and freedom are highly valued. In collectivist societies such as many countries in Africa, Asia, and Latin America, ties between individuals are relatively close and collective accomplishments are often sought after.

Power distance
The extent to which less powerful members within a culture expect and accept that power is distributed unequally.

Individualism
The idea that the identity of an individual is fundamentally his or her own.

Collectivism
The idea that an individual's identity is fundamentally tied to the identity of his or her collective group.

EXHIBIT 3.4 Hofstede Dimensions of Culture

To determine the cultural characteristics of a country, compare the number and vertical distance (higher means more) of that country on a particular cultural dimension (color coded and labeled on the right side of the exihibit) with those of other countries. For example, with a score of 80, Japan has the second highest long-term orientation; it is exceeded only by China, which has a score of 118. By contrast, with a score of 0, Pakistan has the weakest long-term orientation.

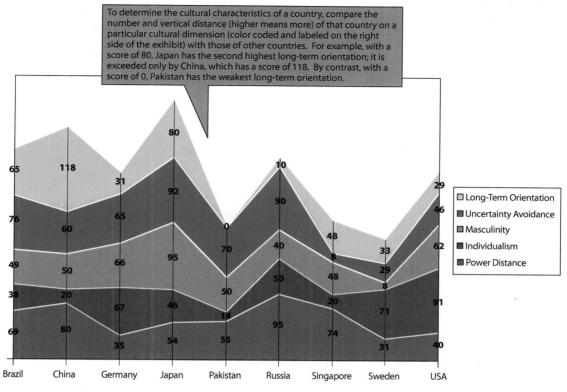

Legend:
- Long-Term Orientation
- Uncertainty Avoidance
- Masculinity
- Individualism
- Power Distance

Countries: Brazil, China, Germany, Japan, Pakistan, Russia, Singapore, Sweden, USA

Sources: G. H. Hofstede, "Cultural constraints in management theories," *Academy of Management Executive* 7, no. 1 (1993): 81-94 and G. Hosftede, *Cultures and Organizations: Software of the Mind* (New York: McGraw-Hill, 1997) 25, 26, 53, 84, 113, 166.

Third, the **masculinity** versus **femininity** dimension refers to sex role differentiation. In every traditional society, men tend to have occupations, such as politician, soldier, or executive, that reward assertiveness. Women, on the other hand, usually work in caring professions such as teacher and nurse in addition to being homemakers. High-masculinity societies (led by Japan) continue to maintain a sharp role differentiation along gender lines. In low-masculinity societies (led by Sweden), women are increasingly likely to become politicians, scientists, and soldiers (think about the movie *GI Jane*), and men frequently assume the role of nurses, teachers, and househusbands.

Fourth, **uncertainty avoidance** refers to the extent to which members in a culture accept or avoid ambiguous situations and uncertainty. Members of high uncertainty avoidance cultures (led by Greece) place a premium on job security and retirement benefits. They also tend to resist change, which often creates uncertainty. Low uncertainty avoidance cultures (led by Singapore) are characterized by a greater willingness to take risks and less resistance to change.

Masculinity
A relatively strong form of societal-level sex-role differentiation whereby men tend to have occupations that reward assertiveness and women tend to work in caring professions.

Femininity
A relatively weak form of societal-level sex-role differentiation whereby more women occupy positions that reward assertiveness and more men work in caring professions.

Uncertainty avoidance
The extent to which members of a culture accept or avoid ambiguous situations and uncertainty.

Part I: Laying Foundations

Finally, **long-term orientation** emphasizes perseverance and savings for future betterment. China, which has the world's longest continuous written history of approximately 4,000 years and the highest contemporary savings rate, leads the pack. On the other hand, members of short-term orientation societies (led by Pakistan) prefer quick results and instant gratification.

Overall, Hofstede's dimensions are interesting and informative. They are also largely supported by subsequent work.[11] It is important to note that Hofstede's dimensions are not perfect and have attracted some criticisms. However, it is fair to suggest that these dimensions represent a *starting point* for us as we try to figure out the role of culture in global business.

ate themselves, whereas collectivist Japanese firms tend to follow each other. Because entrepreneurs stick their necks out by founding new firms, individualistic societies tend to foster a relatively higher level of entrepreneurship.

Likewise, masculinity and femininity affect managerial behavior. The stereotypical manager in high-masculinity societies is "assertive, decisive, and aggressive," and the word "aggressive" carries positive connotations. In contrast, high-femininity societies generally consider "aggressive" a negative term, and managers are "less visible, intuitive rather than decisive, and accustomed to seeking consensus."[12]

Managers in low uncertainty avoidance countries such as Britain rely more on experience and training, whereas

Sensitivity to cultural differences does not guarantee success but can at least avoid blunders.

Culture and Global Business

A great deal of global business activity is consistent with the context, cluster, and dimension approaches to cultural differences. For instance, the average length of contracts is longer in low-context countries such as Germany than in high-context countries such as Vietnam where a lot of agreements are unspoken and not necessarily put in a legal contract.

Germany

Also, as pointed out by the cluster approach, firms are a lot more serious in preparation when doing business with countries in other clusters compared to how they deal with fellow countries within the same cluster.

Countless new books have recently been published on how to do business in China. Two decades ago, gurus wrote about how to do business in Japan. Evidently, there is a huge demand for English-speaking business people to read such books before heading to China and Japan. But has anyone ever seen a book in English on how to do business in Canada?

Hofstede's dimension approach can be illustrated by numerous real-world examples. For instance, managers in high power distance countries such as France and Italy have a greater penchant for centralized authority. Although widely practiced in low power distance Western countries, asking for feedback and participation from subordinates—known as empowerment—is often regarded as a sign of weak leadership and low integrity in high power distance countries such as Egypt, Russia, and Turkey.

Individualism and collectivism also affect business activities. Individualist US firms may often try to differenti-

managers in high uncertainty avoidance countries such as China rely more on rules. In addition, cultures with a long-term orientation are likely to nurture firms with long horizons. For example, Japan's Matsushita has a 250-year plan, which was put together in the 1930s.[13] While this is certainly an extreme case, Japanese and Korean firms tend to focus more on the long term. In comparison, Western firms often focus on relatively short-term profits (often on a *quarterly* basis).

Overall, there is strong evidence for the importance of culture. Sensitivity to cultural differences does not guarantee success but can at least avoid blunders. For instance, a Chinese manufacturer exported to the West a premium brand of battery called White Elephant without knowing the meaning of this phrase in Western culture. In another example, when a French manager was transferred to a US subsidiary and met his American secretary (a woman) for the first time, he greeted her with an effusive cheek-to-cheek kiss, a harmless "Hello" in France. However, the secretary later filed a complaint for sexual harassment.[14] More seriously, Mitsubishi Motors encountered major problems when operating in the United States. Although Japan leads the world in masculinity, the company's US facilities had more female participation in the labor force, as would be expected in a country with a relatively higher level of femininity. Yet, its North American division reportedly tolerated sexual discrimination and sexual harassment behaviors. In 1998, Mitsubishi paid $34 million to settle these charges in the United States.

Long-term orientation
A perspective that emphasizes perseverance and savings for future betterment.

ETHICS

Cross-cultural differences can be interesting. But they can also be unethical, all depending on the institutional frameworks in which firms are embedded. This is dealt with next.

Definition and Impact of Ethics

Ethics refers to the principles, standards, and norms of conduct that govern individual and firm behavior. Ethics is not only an important part of informal institutions but is also deeply reflected in formal laws and regulations. To the extent that laws reflect a society's minimum standards of conduct, there is a substantial overlap between what is ethical and legal as well as between what is unethical and illegal. However, in some cases, what is legal may be unethical, as the Opening Case illustrates.

Recent scandals have pushed ethics to the forefront of global business discussions. Numerous firms have introduced a **code of conduct**—a set of guidelines for making ethical decisions—but firms' ethical motivations are still subject to debate. Three views have emerged:

- A *negative view* suggests that firms may simply jump onto the ethics bandwagon under social pressure to *appear* more legitimate without necessarily becoming better.

- A *positive view* maintains that some (although not all) firms may be self-motivated to do it right regardless of social pressure.

- An *instrumental view* believes that good ethics may simply be a useful instrument to help make money.

Perhaps the best way to appreciate the value of ethics is to examine what happens after some crisis. As a reservoir of goodwill, the value of an ethical reputation is *magnified* during a time of crisis. One study found that any US firm engulfed in crisis (such as the *Exxon Valdez* oil spill) takes an average hit of 8% of their market value in the first week. After ten weeks, however, firms in the study with positive ethical reputations actually saw their stock value *rise 5%*, whereas the stock of those without such reputations dropped 15%.[15] Ironically, catastrophes may allow more ethical firms to shine. The upshot seems to be that ethics pays.

Ethics
The principles, standards, and norms of conduct that govern individual and firm behavior.

Code of conduct
A set of guidelines for making ethical decisions.

Ethical relativism
A perspective that suggests that all ethical standards are relative.

Ethical imperialism
The absolute belief that "there is only one set of Ethics (with a capital E), and we have it."

© Newscom

Managing Ethics Overseas

Managing ethics overseas is challenging because what is ethical in one country may be unethical elsewhere.[16] There are two schools of thought.[17] First, **ethical relativism** follows the cliché, "When in Rome, do as the Romans do." If Muslim countries discriminate against women, so what? Likewise, if industry rivals in China can fix prices, who cares? Isn't that what "Romans" do in "Rome"? Second, **ethical imperialism** refers to the absolute belief that "There is only one set of Ethics (with a capital E), and we have it." Americans are especially renowned for believing that their ethical values should be applied universally.[18] For example, since sexual discrimination and price fixing are wrong in the United States, they must be wrong everywhere. In practice, however, neither of these schools of thought is realistic. At the extreme, ethical relativism would have to accept any local practice, whereas ethical imperialism may cause resentment and backlash among locals.

Three middle-of-the-road guiding principles have been proposed by Thomas Donaldson, a business ethicist. These are shown in Exhibit 3.5. First, respect for human dignity and basic rights—such as concern for health, safety, and

EXHIBIT 3.5 Managing Ethics Overseas: Three Approaches

- Respect for human dignity and basic rights
- Respect for local traditions
- Respect for institutional context

Sources: T. Donaldson, "Values in tension: Ethics away from home," *Harvard Business Review* (September-October 1996): 4-11 and J. Weiss, *Business Ethics*, 4th ed. (Cincinnati: Thomson South-Western, 2006).

the need for education rather than working at a young age—should determine the absolute, minimal ethical thresholds for *all* operations around the world.

Second, firms should respect local traditions. If a firm bans giving gifts, it can forget about doing business in China and Japan, where gift giving is part of the business norm. While hiring employees' children and relatives instead of more qualified applicants is illegal in the United States under equal opportunity laws, it is routine practice for Indian companies and is expected to strengthen employee loyalty. What should US companies setting up subsidiaries in India do? Donaldson advises that such nepotism is not necessarily wrong, at least not in India.

Finally, respect for institutional context calls for a careful understanding of local institutions. Codes of conduct banning bribery are not very useful unless accompanied by guidelines for the scale and scope of appropriate gift giving/receiving. Citigroup allows employees to accept noncash gifts whose nominal value is less than $100. The *Economist* allows its journalists to accept any gift that can be consumed in a single day; a bottle of wine is acceptable, but a case of wine is not.[19] Overall, these three principles, although far from perfect, can help managers make decisions about which they may feel relatively comfortable.

Ethics and Corruption

Ethics helps to combat **corruption**, often defined as the abuse of public power for private benefits usually in the form of bribery, in cash or in kind.[20] Competition should be based on products and services, but corruption distorts that basis, causing misallocation of resources and slowing economic development. Transparency International (http://www.transparency.org), headquartered in Berlin, Germany, is probably the most influential anti-corruption nongovernmental organization (NGO). It found a strong correlation between a high level of corruption and a low level of economic development. In other words, corruption and poverty go together. Some evidence indicates that corruption discourages foreign direct investment (FDI). If the level of corruption in Singapore, which is very low, were to increase to the mid-range level in Mexico, it reportedly would have the same negative effect on FDI inflows as raising the tax rate by 50%.[21]

In the global fight against corruption, the Foreign Corrupt Practices Act (FCPA) was enacted by the US Congress in 1977 and bans bribery of foreign officials. Many US firms complain that the act has unfairly restricted them. They also point out that overseas bribery expenses were often tax deductible (!) in many EU countries such as Austria, France, and Germany until the late 1990s. Even with the FCPA, however, there is no evidence that US firms are inherently more ethical than others. The FCPA itself was triggered in the 1970s by investigations of many corrupt US firms. Even the FCPA makes exceptions for small

grease payments to get through customs abroad. Most alarmingly, the World Bank recently reported that despite over two decades of FCPA enforcement, US firms "exhibit systematically *higher* levels of corruption" than other firms in the Organization for Economic Co-operation and Development (OECD).[22]

Overall, the FCPA can be regarded as an institutional weapon in the global fight against corruption. Despite the FCPA's formal *regulatory* teeth, for a long time it had neither a *normative* pillar nor a *cognitive* pillar. Until recently, the norm among other OECD firms was to pay bribes first and get tax deductions later, a clear sign of ethical relativism. Only in 1997 did the OECD Convention on Combating Bribery of Foreign Public Officials commit all 30 member countries (essentially all developed economies) to criminalize bribery. The regulation went into force in 1999. A more ambitious campaign is the UN Convention against Corruption, signed by 106 countries in 2003 and activated in 2005. If every country criminalizes bribery and every firm resists corruption, their combined power will eradicate it.[23] But this will not happen unless FCPA-type legislation is institutionalized and *enforced* in every country.

LO7 *Identify norms associated with strategic responses when firms deal with ethical challenges.*

NORMS AND ETHICAL CHALLENGES

As an important informal institution, **norms** are the prevailing practices of relevant players—the proverbial "everybody else"—that affect the focal individuals and firms. How firms strategically respond to ethical challenges is often driven, at least in part, by norms. Four broad strategic responses are (1) reactive strategy, (2) defensive strategy, (3) accommodative strategy, and (4) proactive strategy. These are illustrated in Exhibit 3.6 on page 44.

A **reactive strategy** is passive. Firms do not feel compelled to act when problems arise, and denial is usually the first line of defense. In the absence of formal regulation, the need to take action is neither internalized through cognitive beliefs nor embodied in any practicable norm. For example, in the early 1970s, Ford marketed the Pinto car even though the company knew the gas tank had a fatal design flaw that made the car susceptible to exploding in rear-end collisions. Citing high costs, Ford decided against adding an $11-per-car improvement. Sure enough, accidents happened and people were burned and killed in

Corruption
The abuse of public power for private benefits, usually in the form of bribery.

Norms
The prevailing practices of relevant players that affect the local individuals and firms.

Reactive strategy
A passive response to an ethical challenge that often involves denial and belated action to correct problems.

EXHIBIT 3.6 Strategic Responses to Ethical Challenges

Strategic Responses	Strategic Behaviors	Examples in the Text
Reactive	Deny responsibility; do less than required	Ford Pinto safety (the 1970s)
Defensive	Admit responsibility but fight it; do the least that is required	Nike sweatshops (the early 1990s)
Accommodative	Accept responsibility; do all that is required	Ford Explorer rollovers (the 2000s)
Proactive	Anticipate responsibility; do more than is required	BMW recycling (the 1990s)

Pintos. Ford refused to recall the Pinto until 1978. Then, under intense formal pressures from the government and informal pressures from the media and consumer groups, Ford belatedly recalled all 1.5 million Pintos.

A **defensive strategy** focuses on regulatory compliance. In the early 1990s, media and activist groups charged Nike with running sweatshops, although there was no existing regulation prohibiting sweatshops. Nike's initial response was "We don't make shoes," because Nike did not directly own and manage the factories. Its contractors in Indonesia and Vietnam were in charge. This response, however, failed to convey that Nike felt any ethical responsibility. Only when several senators began to suggest legislative solutions—regulations with which Nike would need to comply—did Nike become more serious.

In an **accommodative strategy**, accepting responsibility becomes an organizational norm, and cognitive beliefs and values are increasingly internalized. These normative and cognitive values may be shared by a number of firms, leading to new industry norms. In other words, higher levels of ethical and moral responsibility, beyond simply the minimum of what is legally required, are accepted standards. In this fashion, Nike and the entire sportswear industry became more accommodative about the issue of sweatshops in the late 1990s.

Companies can change their strategic response. Ford evidently learned the painful lesson from its Pinto fire fiasco in the 1970s. When Ford Explorer vehicles equipped with Firestone tires had a large number of fatal rollover accidents in 2000, Ford aggressively initiated a speedy recall, launched a media campaign featuring its CEO, and discontinued the 100-year-old relationship with Firestone. While critics argue that Ford's accommodative strategy simply attempted to place the blame squarely on Firestone, the institution-based view (especially Proposition 1 in Chapter 2) suggests that such highly rational actions are to be expected. Even if Ford's public relations campaign was only window dressing designed to make the company look good to the public, it publicized a set of ethical criteria against which the company can be judged and opened doors for more scrutiny by concerned stakeholders. It is probably fair to say that Ford was a better corporate citizen in 2000 than it was in 1975.

Finally, firms that take a **proactive strategy** anticipate institutional changes and do more than is required. In 1990, the German government proposed a "take-back" policy, requiring automakers to design cars whose components can be taken back by the same manufacturers for recycling. With this policy in mind, BMW anticipated its emerging responsibility and not only designed easier-to-disassemble cars but also enlisted the few high-quality dismantler firms as part of an exclusive recycling infrastructure. Further, BMW actively participated in public discussions and succeeded in establishing its approach as the German national standard for automobile disassembly. Other automakers were thus required to follow BMW's lead. However, the other automakers had to fight over smaller, lower-quality dismantlers or develop in-house dismantling infrastructures from scratch.[24] Through such a proactive strategy, BMW set a new industry standard for environmentally friendly norms in both car design and recycling. Overall, while there is probably a certain element of window dressing in proactive strategies, the fact that proactive firms are going beyond the current regulatory requirements is indicative of the normative and cognitive beliefs held by many managers at these firms on the importance of doing the right thing.[25]

Defensive strategy
A response to an ethical challenge that focuses on regulatory compliance.

Accommodative strategy
A response to an ethical challenge that involves accepting responsibility.

Proactive strategy
A strategy that anticipates ethical challenges and addresses them before they happen.

Will you take me back, too?

Are Cultures Converging or Diverging?

Every culture evolves and changes. But what is the *direction* of change? This question is the center of a great debate.

CONVERGENCE In this age of globalization, one side of the debate argues that there is a great deal of convergence, especially toward more modern, Western values such as individualism and consumerism. As evidence, convergence gurus point out the worldwide interest in Western products such as Levi's jeans, iPods, and MTV, especially among the youth.[26]

DIVERGENCE Another side of the debate suggests that Westernization in consumption does not necessarily mean Westernization in values. In a most extreme example, on the night of September 10, 2001, the 9/11 terrorists drank American soft drinks, ate American pizzas, and enjoyed American movies—and then went on to kill thousands of Americans the next day.[27] More broadly, the popularity of Western brands in the Middle East does not change Muslim values, as the Opening Case illustrates. In another example, the increasing popularity of Asian foods and games in the West does

not necessarily mean that Westerners are converging toward Asian values (see In Focus). In short, the world may continue to be characterized by cultural divergence.

A middle-of-the-road group makes two points. First, the end of the Cold War, the rise of the Internet, and the ascendance of English as the language of business all offer evidence of some cultural convergence, at least on the surface and among the youth. For example, younger Chinese, Japanese, and Russian managers are typically more individualistic and less collectivistic than the average citizen of their respective countries. Second, deep down, cultural divergence may continue to be the norm. So perhaps a better term is "crossvergence," which acknowledges the validity of both sides of the debate. This idea suggests that when marketing products and services to younger customers around the world, a more global approach featuring uniform content and image may work, whereas local adaptation may be a must when dealing with older, more tradition-bound consumers.

LO8 Explain how you can acquire cross-cultural literacy.

MANAGEMENT SAVVY

The institution-based view emphasizes the importance of informal institutions—cultures, ethics, and norms—as the soil in which business around the globe either thrives or stagnates. How does this perspective answer our fundamental question: What determines the success and failure of firms around the globe? The institution-based view argues that firm performance is determined, at least in part, by the informal cultures, ethics, and norms governing firm behavior.

This emphasis on informal institutions suggests two broad implications for savvy managers around the globe. First, managers should enhance their **cultural intelligence**, defined as an individual's ability to understand and adjust to new cultures. Acquisition of cultural intelligence passes through three phases: awareness, knowledge, and skills.[28] *Awareness* refers to the recognition of both the pros and cons of your own cultural mental software and the appreciation of people from other cultures. *Knowledge* refers to the ability to identify the symbols, rituals, and taboos in other cultures. Knowledge is also known as cross-cultural literacy. While you may not share (or may disagree) with their values, you will at least have a road map of the informal institutions governing their behavior. Finally, *skills* are good practices based on awareness and knowledge of other cultures (Exhibit 3.7).

EXHIBIT 3.7 Implications for Action

- Be prepared.
- Slow down.
- Establish trust.
- Understand the importance of language.
- Respect cultural differences.
- Understand that no culture is inherently superior in all aspects.

While skills can be taught in a classroom, the most effective way to learn them is total immersion in a foreign culture. Even for gifted individuals, learning a new language and culture well enough to function at a managerial level will take at least several months of full-time studies. Most employers do not give their expatriates that much time to learn before sending them abroad. Most expatriates are thus inadequately prepared, and the costs for firms, individuals, and families are tremendous (see Chapter 13). This means that you, a student studying this book, are advised to invest in your own career by picking up at least one foreign language, spending one semester (or year) abroad, and reaching out to make some international friends who are taking classes with you and perhaps even sitting next to you. Such an investment during university studies will make you stand out among the crowd and propel your future career to new heights.

Cultural intelligence
An individual's ability to understand and adjust to new cultures.

IN FOCUS

Are We All "Asians" Now?

Around the world, Asian foods (such as tofu and sushi), martial arts (such as kung fu, taekwondo, and judo), toys (such as Pokemon), cartoons (such as *Astro Boy*), and belief systems (such as feng shui) are increasing in popularity. Asian business words such as *guanxi*, *keiretsu*, and *chaebol* now routinely appear in English publications without any bracketed explanations. The main pedestrian shopping street in Copenhagen, Denmark, has two competing Chinese restaurants, one called "Beijing" and another "Shanghai." Even at quintessentially American baseball parks, you can buy a box of sushi to accompany your beer.

School kids in the West can't get enough of toys, cartoons, comics, and video games originating from Japan—ranging from Hello Kitty for girls and Godzilla for boys. To combat declining reader interest in newspapers, especially among young readers, a number of US newspapers, including the *Los Angeles Times*, have introduced *manga*-style comics (Japanese comics with wide-eyed characters) to their Sunday funny pages. The top comic is *Peach Fuzz*, a playful chronicle of a nine-year-old girl and her pet ferret. (The sight of a ferret where Snoopy once reigned may lead some old-timers to exclaim: "Good grief!")

Until recently, the United States had been the only place that had muscle to generate cultural exports such as movies, music, and food. But the winds are shifting. Japan now sells approximately $15 billion in cultural exports, three times the value of its exports of TV sets. Publishers, toy makers, and game developers increasingly look east to spot new trends. Hasbro, a leading US toymaker, teamed with Shogakukan, a major *manga* publisher, to create *Duel Masters*, a new TV show and trading card game. Sony synched *Astro Boy* characters' lips with both Japanese and English to maximize their appeal.

Some have long argued that consumption of Western products, ranging from Coca-Cola to credit cards, would Westernize the world. Obviously, not everyone agrees. Now, if you are not ethnically Asian, ask yourself: If you carried a Samsung mobile phone, had fried rice and egg rolls for lunch, enjoyed *Peach Fuzz* comics, and practiced taekwondo for your exercise, are you really becoming more "Asian" in values and outlook?

Sources: "Can *manga* ferret out young readers," *Business Week*, 28 November 2005, 16; "Is Japanese style taking over the world," *Business Week*, 26 July 2004, 56-58; C. Robertson, "The global dispersion of Chinese values," *Management International Review* 40 (2000): 253-268; E. Tsang, "Superstition and decision-making," *Academy of Management Executive* 18, no. 4 (2004): 92-104.

Savvy managers should also be aware of the prevailing norms and their transitions globally. The norms around the globe in the 2000s are more culturally sensitive and more ethically demanding than, say, in the 1970s. This is not to suggest that every local norm needs to be followed. Failing to understand the changing norms or adapting to them in an insensitive and unethical way may lead to unsatisfactory or, worse, disastrous results, as the Opening Case illustrates. The best managers expect norms to shift over time and constantly decipher the changes in the informal rules of the game in order to take advantage of new opportunities. How BMW managers have proactively shaped the automobile recycling norms in Germany serves as a case in point. Firms that fail to realize the passing of old norms and adapt accordingly are likely to fall behind or even go out of business.

ETHICAL DILEMMA
CITIGROUP NEEDS TO CLEAN UP AROUND THE GLOBE

Citigroup is the world's largest financial services company with roots as far back as 1812. Currently, it does business in more than 100 countries and has been active in some for more than 100 years. A recent annual report proudly claimed that Citigroup had "the best international footprint of any US financial services company and the best US presence of any international financial services company." Yet, Citigroup recently found itself engulfed in a number of ethical crises around the globe. Most alarmingly, these new crises erupted *after* it was criticized for its failure to have a firewall separating analysts and investment bankers and for its involvement in the Enron bankruptcy in the United States in the early 2000s.

In London, on the morning of August 2, 2004, Citigroup's bond trading unit dumped $13.3 billion worth of European government bonds onto the market. Such a huge volume caused immediate chaos in the market and resulted in lower bond prices. Then, within about a half-hour, Citigroup's bond traders bought back a third of the bonds they just sold, raking in $24 million in profits. The traders were jubilant. Their actions were legal, but they broke an unwritten norm of the industry: Do not stimulate major turbulence in the thin summer trading. When a puzzled rival trader called to ask what was up, the Citigroup crew laughed and hung up. Nobody is laughing now. The profits were not worth the damage to its reputation. Citigroup angered governments, particularly in countries like Belgium and Italy, that relied on the international bond markets and offered Citigroup lucrative contracts to handle their deals. Overall, European regulators would no longer tolerate such behavior.

A worse disaster struck in Japan. In September 2004, regulators ordered Citigroup to shut down its private bank in Japan because of a series of abuses where Citigroup sold securities at unfair prices to clients. The Citigroup sales force pushed sales on many Japanese clients without explaining the underlying risk. Regulators charged the bank of fostering "a management environment in which profits are given undue importance by the bank headquarters." This drastic action followed repeated warnings in previous years. While Citigroup was still allowed to run a retail bank and a corporate bank in Japan, the damage to its reputation was significant.

The ramifications were profound. On the first page of the 2004 annual report, Chuck Prince, then Citigroup's CEO, apologized to shareholders. Around the world, Prince met with employees and stressed the importance of ethical integrity. Prince, a lawyer by training, had assumed his position to deal with the legal and ethical turbulence in the United States. Now he had his hands full

© LUCAS JACKSON/Reuters/Landov

around the world. In response to the European and Japanese scandals, a new Code of Conduct was implemented and a Global Compliance unit was established. Every employee would receive ethics training, and a toll-free ethics hotline was aggressively marketed to employees. Prince wrote in his letter to shareholders in the 2004 annual report:

These failures [in Europe and Japan] do not reflect the kind of company we are or want to be . . . We are already the most profitable and the largest financial institution in the world. We believe that when we add "most respected" to that resume, there is no limit to what we will accomplish.

But talk is cheap, say critics. Many have questioned whether the transformation pushed by Prince would be successful, especially since his forced resignation in November 2007. In October 2008, Citigroup reported that it cut 11,000 positions and suffered a $13 billion writedown during the third quarter of 2008. Still, it is not an accident that Citigroup has become a global industry leader in sales and profits. The competitive instinct permeates the corporate DNA. Yet, job number one for Citigroup remains: How can a firm become a more ethical firm without losing its competitive edge?

Sources: "Can Chuck Prince clean up Citi?," *Business Week*, 4 October 2004, 32-35; "For Citi, 'no more excuses'," *Business Week*, 3 April 2006, 134; *Citigroup 2004 Annual Report*; "Sayonara," *Economist*, 25 September 2004, 88; "A mixed week," *Economist*, 8 April 2006, 73; "Administrative actions on Citibank NA Japan branch," Financial Services Agency, 2004, available online at http://www.fsa.go.jp.

BY THE NUMBERS

approximate number of languages spoken in the world **6,000**

percent of global output produced in English-speaking countries **40**

percent of national income received by the richest 10 percent of Brazil's population **50**

percent of annual world toy output sold in the United States in December **25**

number of years covered by Matsushita's business plan **250**

MANAGING INDIVIDUALS AND A DIVERSE WORK FORCE

Workplace diversity as we know it today is changing. Exhibit 12.1 (on page 216) shows predictions from the U.S. Census Bureau concerning how the U.S. population will change over the next 40 years. The percentage of white, non-Hispanic Americans in the general population is expected to decline from 64.7 percent in 2010 to 46.3 percent by the year 2050. By contrast, the percentage of black Americans will increase (from 12.9 percent to 13.0 percent), as will the percentage of Asian Americans (from 4.7 percent to 7.8 percent). Meanwhile, the proportion of Native Americans will hold fairly steady (increasing from 1.0 to 1.2 percent). The fastest-growing group by far, though, is Hispanics, who are expected to increase from 16 percent of the total population in 2010 to 30.3 percent by 2050.[1]

Other significant changes have already occurred. For example, today women hold 46.5 percent of the jobs in the United States, up from 38.2 percent in 1970. Furthermore, white males, who composed 63.9 percent of the work force in 1950, hold just 38.2 percent of today's jobs.[2]

These rather dramatic changes have taken place in a relatively short time. And, as these trends clearly show, the work force of the near future will be increasingly Hispanic, Asian American, black American, and female. It will also be older, as the average baby boomer approaches the age of 70 around 2020. Since many boomers are likely to postpone retirement and work well into their 70s to offset predicted reductions in Social Security and Medicare benefits, the work force may become even older than expected.[3]

Learning Outcomes

1 describe diversity and explain why it matters.

2 understand the special challenges that the dimensions of surface-level diversity pose for managers.

3 explain how the dimensions of deep-level diversity affect individual behavior and interactions in the workplace.

4 explain the basic principles and practices that can be used to manage diversity.

© Thomas Northcut/Photodisc/Getty Images

Diversity and Why It Matters

D Diversity means variety. Therefore, **diversity** exists in an organization when there are a variety of demographic, cultural, and personal differences among the people who work there and the customers who do business there. For example, step into Longo Toyota in El Monte, California, one of Toyota's top-selling dealerships, and you'll find diversity in the form of salespeople who speak Spanish, Korean, Arabic, Vietnamese, Hebrew, and Mandarin Chinese. In fact, the 60 salespeople at Longo Toyota speak 30 different languages.[4] Surprisingly, this level of diversity was achieved without developing a formal diversity plan.[5]

 After reading the next section, you should be able to

1 describe diversity and explain why it matters.

Diversity a variety of demographic, cultural, and personal differences among an organization's employees and customers

M G M T

Exhibit 12.1

Percent of the Projected Population by Race and Hispanic Origin for the United States: 2010 to 2050

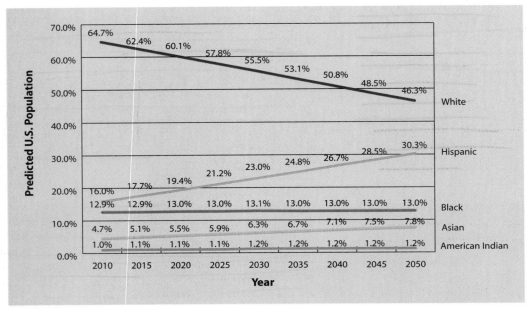

Note: The original race data from Census 2000 are modified to eliminate the "some other race" category. This modification is used for all Census Bureau projections products and is explained in the document entitled "Modified Race Data Summary File Technical Documentation and ASCII Layout" that can be found on the Census Bureau website at http://www.census.gov/popest/archives/files/MRSF-01-US1.html.

Sources: Population Division, U.S. Census Bureau, August 14, 2008; "Percent of the Projected Population by Race and Hispanic Origin for the United States: 2008 to 2050," U.S. Census Bureau, 14 August 2008, available at http://www.census.gov/population/www/projections/tablesandcharts/table_4.xls [accessed 4 November 2009].

1 Diversity: Differences That Matter

You'll begin your exploration of diversity by learning **1.1 that diversity is not affirmative action** and **1.2 how to build a business case for diversity.**

1.1 Diversity Is Not Affirmative Action

A common misconception is that workplace diversity and affirmative action are the same, yet these concepts differ in several critical ways, including their purpose, how they are practiced, and the reactions they produce. To start with, **affirmative action** refers to purposeful steps taken by an organization to create employment opportunities for minorities and women.[6] By contrast, diversity exists in organizations when there is a variety of demographic, cultural, and personal differences among the people who work there and the customers who do business there. So, one key difference is that affirmative action is more narrowly focused on demographics such as sex and race, while diversity has a broader focus that includes demographic, cultural, and personal differences. A second difference is that affirmative action is a policy for actively creating diversity, but diversity can exist even if organizations don't take purposeful steps to create it. For example, Longo Toyota achieved a high level of diversity without having a formal affirmative action program. Likewise, a local restaurant located near a university in a major city is likely to have a more diverse group of employees than one located in a small town. Affirmative action does not guarantee diversity. An organization can create employment opportunities for women and minorities yet not have a diverse work force.

A third important difference is that affirmative action is required by law for private employers with 50 or more employees while diversity is not. Affirmative action originated with Executive Order 11246 (https://www.dol.gov/ofccp/regs/compliance/aa.htm) but is also related to the 1964 Civil Rights Act, which bans discrimination in voting, public places, federal government programs, federally supported public education, and employment. Title VII of the Civil Rights Act (http://www.eeoc.gov/laws/statutes/titlevii.cfm) requires that workers have equal employment opportunities when being hired or promoted. More specifically, Title VII prohibits companies from discriminating in their employment practices on the basis of race, color, religion, sex, or national origin. Title VII also created the Equal Employment Opportunity Commission, or EEOC (http://www.eeoc.gov), to administer these laws. By contrast, there is no federal law or agency to oversee diversity. Organizations that pursue diversity goals do so voluntarily.

Affirmative action purposeful steps taken by an organization to create employment opportunities for minorities and women

> A common misconception is that workplace **diversity** and **affirmative action** are the same.

Fourth, affirmative action programs and diversity programs also have different purposes. The purpose of affirmative action programs is to compensate for past discrimination, which was widespread when legislation was introduced in the 1960s; to prevent ongoing discrimination; and to provide equal opportunities to all regardless of race, color, religion, sex, or national origin. Organizations that fail to uphold these laws may be required to

- hire, promote, or give back pay to those not hired or promoted;
- reinstate those who were wrongly terminated;
- pay attorneys' fees and court costs for those who bring charges against them; or
- take other actions that make individuals whole by returning them to the condition or place they would have been had it not been for discrimination.[7]

Consequently, affirmative action is basically a punitive approach.[8] By contrast, the general purpose of diversity programs is to create a positive work environment where no one is advantaged or disadvantaged, where "we" is everyone, where everyone can do his or her best work, where differences are respected and not ignored, and where everyone feels comfortable.[9] So, unlike affirmative action, which punishes companies for not achieving specific sex and race ratios in their work forces, diversity programs seek to benefit both organizations and their employees by encouraging organizations to value all kinds of differences.

Despite the overall success of affirmative action in making workplaces much fairer than they used to be, many people argue that some affirmative action programs unconstitutionally offer preferential treatment to females and minorities at the expense of other employees, a view accepted by some courts.[10] The American Civil Rights Institute successfully campaigned to ban race- and sex-based affirmative action in college admissions, government hiring, and government contracting programs in California (1996), Washington (1998), and Michigan (2006). Led by Ward Connerly, the Institute backed similar efforts in Arizona, Colorado, Missouri, Nebraska, and Oklahoma in 2008. Opponents like Connerly believe that affirmative action policies establish only surface-level diversity and, ironically, promote preferential treatment.[11]

Furthermore, research shows that people who have gotten a job or promotion as a result of affirmative action are frequently viewed as unqualified, even when clear evidence of their qualifications exists.[12] So, while affirmative action programs have created opportunities for minorities and women, those same minorities and women are frequently presumed to be unqualified when others believe they obtained their jobs as a result of affirmative action.

1.2 Diversity Makes Good Business Sense

Those who support the idea of diversity in organizations often ignore its

Generational Assets

A mix of older and younger workers may be critical to a company's success in our fast-paced, interconnected global marketplace. Gen-Xers and particularly millennials are flexible; learn new technologies and skills easily; are comfortable with crossing boundaries of space, time, and class; and tend to value collaboration. Baby boomers, while they can be slower to adapt to change, have experience and knowledge that are critical to a company's stability. The challenge? How to overcome generational differences in values, work methods, and communication styles within work groups. Capitalizing on the different strong points of each group and training employees on how to deal with these differences are essential for success.

Sources: W. Boddie, J. Contardo, and R. Childs, "The Future Workforce: Here They Come," *The Public Manager* 36 (Winter 2007), 25–28; E. White, "Age Is as Age Does; Making the Generation Gap Work for You," *The Wall Street Journal*, available online at http://online.wsj.com/article/SB121478926535514813.html [accessed 21 August 2008].

business aspects altogether, claiming instead that diversity is simply the right thing to do. Yet diversity actually makes good business sense in several ways: reducing costs, attracting and retaining talent, and driving business growth.[13]

Diversity helps companies *reduce costs* by decreasing turnover and absenteeism and enabling them to avoid expensive lawsuits.[14] In fact, turnover costs typically amount to more than 90 percent of employees' salaries. So, if an executive who makes $200,000 a year leaves an organization, it can cost approximately $180,000 to find a replacement; even the lowest-paid hourly workers can cost companies as much as $10,000 when they quit. Since turnover rates for black Americans average 40 percent higher than for whites, and since women quit their jobs at twice the rate men do, companies that manage diverse work forces well can cut costs by reducing the turnover rates of their employees.[15] And, with women absent from work 60 percent more often than men, primarily because of family responsibilities, diversity programs that address the needs of female workers can also reduce the substantial costs of absenteeism.[16]

Diversity programs also save companies money by helping them avoid discrimination lawsuits, which have increased by a factor of 20 since 1970 and quadrupled just since 1995. In one survey conducted by the Society for Human Resource Management, 78 percent of respondents reported that diversity efforts helped them avoid lawsuits and litigation costs.[17] Indeed, because companies lose two-thirds of all discrimination cases that go to trial, the best strategy from a business perspective is not to be sued for discrimination at all. When companies lose such lawsuits, the average individual settlement amounts to more than $600,000.[18] And settlement costs can be substantially higher in class-action lawsuits, in which individuals join together to sue a company as a group. In fact, the average class-action lawsuit costs companies $58.9 million for racial discrimination and $24.9 million for gender discrimination.[19]

Diversity also makes business sense by helping companies *attract and retain talented workers.*[20] Indeed, diversity-friendly companies tend to attract better and more diverse job applicants. Very simply, diversity begets more diversity. Companies that make *Fortune* magazine's list of the 50 best companies for minorities or are recognized by *Working Women* or *DiversityInc.* magazine have already attracted a diverse and talented pool of job applicants. But after being recognized for their efforts, they subsequently experience even bigger increases in both the quality and the diversity of people who apply for jobs. Research shows that companies with acclaimed diversity programs not only attract more talented workers but also have higher stock market performance.[21]

The third way that diversity makes business sense is by *driving business growth.* Diversity helps companies grow by improving their understanding of the marketplace. When companies have diverse work forces, they are better able to understand the needs of their increasingly diverse customer bases. A recent survey conducted by the Society for Human Resource Management found that tapping into "diverse customers and markets" was the number one reason managers gave for implementing diversity programs.[22] Former German Chancellor Willy Brandt put it this way: "If I'm selling to you, I speak your language. If I'm buying, dann müssen Sie Deutsch sprechen."[23]

Diversity also helps companies grow through higher-quality problem solving. Though diverse groups initially have more difficulty working together than homogeneous groups, diverse groups eventually establish a rapport and do a better job of identifying problems and generating alternative solutions, the two most important steps in problem solving.[24] In short, "diversity is no longer about counting heads; it's about making heads count," says Amy George, vice president of diversity and inclusion at PepsiCo.[25]

Diversity and Individual Differences

A survey that asked managers, "What is meant by diversity to decision makers in your organization?" found that they most frequently mentioned race, culture, sex, national origin, age, religion, and regional origin.[26] When managers describe workers this way, they are focusing on surface-level diversity. **Surface-level diversity** consists of differences that are immediately observable, typically unchangeable, and easy to measure.[27] In other words, independent observers can usually agree on dimensions of surface-level diversity, such as another person's age, sex, race/ethnicity, or physical capabilities.

Surface-level diversity differences such as age, sex, race/ethnicity, and physical disabilities that are observable, typically unchangeable, and easy to measure

Most people start by using surface-level diversity to categorize or stereotype other people. But those initial categorizations typically give way to deeper impressions formed from knowledge of others' behavior and psychological characteristics such as personality and attitudes.[28] When you think of others this way, you are focusing on deep-level diversity. **Deep-level diversity** consists of differences that are communicated through verbal and nonverbal behaviors and are recognized only through extended interaction with others.[29] Examples of deep-level diversity include personality differences, attitudes, beliefs, and values. In other words, as people in diverse workplaces get to know each other, the initial focus on surface-level differences such as age, race/ethnicity, sex, and physical capabilities is replaced by deeper, more complex knowledge of co-workers.

If managed properly, the shift from surface- to deep-level diversity can accomplish two things.[30] First, coming to know and understand co-workers better can result in reduced prejudice and conflict. Second, it can lead to stronger social integration. **Social integration** is the degree to which group members are psychologically attracted to working with each other to accomplish a common objective, or, as one manager put it, "working together to get the job done."

 After reading the next two sections, you should be able to

2 understand the special challenges that the dimensions of surface-level diversity pose for managers.

3 explain how the dimensions of deep-level diversity affect individual behavior and interactions in the workplace.

2 Surface-Level Diversity

Because age, sex, race/ethnicity, and physical disabilities are usually immediately observable, many managers and workers use these dimensions of surface-level diversity to form initial impressions and categorizations of co-workers, bosses, customers, or job applicants. Whether intentionally or not, sometimes those initial categorizations and impressions lead to decisions or behaviors that discriminate. Consequently, these dimensions of surface-level diversity pose special challenges for managers who are trying to create positive work environments where everyone feels comfortable and no one is advantaged or disadvantaged.

*Let's learn more about those challenges and the ways that **2.1 age, 2.2 sex, 2.3 race/ethnicity,** and **2.4 mental***

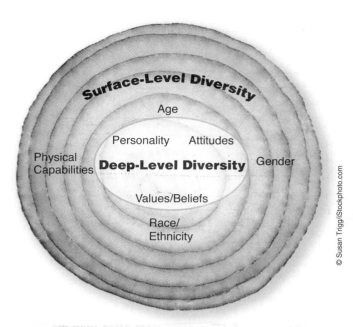

or physical disabilities can affect decisions and behaviors in organizations.

2.1 Age

Age discrimination is treating people differently (e.g., in hiring and firing, promotion, and compensation decisions) because of their age. According to the Society for Human Resource Management, 53 percent of 428 surveyed managers believed that older workers "didn't keep up with technology," and 28 percent said that older workers were "less flexible." When 57-year-old Sam Horgan, a former chief financial officer, was interviewing for a job, he was asked by a 30-something job interviewer, "Would you have trouble working with young bright people?"[31] It is also commonly assumed that older workers cost more, and some companies fear that older workers will require higher salaries and more health-care benefits.[32]

So, what's reality and what's myth? Do older employees actually cost more? In some ways, they do. The older people are and the longer they stay with a company, the more the company pays for salaries, pension plans, and vacation time. But older workers cost companies less,

Deep-level diversity differences such as personality and attitudes that are communicated through verbal and nonverbal behaviors and are learned only through extended interaction with others

Social integration the degree to which group members are psychologically attracted to working with each other to accomplish a common objective

Age discrimination treating people differently (e.g., in hiring and firing, promotion, and compensation decisions) because of their age

too, because they tend to show better judgment and care more about the quality of their work, and they are less likely to quit, show up late, or be absent, the cost of which can be substantial.[33] A survey by Chicago outplacement firm Challenger, Gray & Christmas found that only 3 percent of employees age 50 and over changed jobs in any given year, compared to 10 percent of the entire U.S. work force and 12 percent of workers ages 25 to 34. The study also found that while older workers make up about 14 percent of the work force, they suffer only 10 percent of all workplace injuries and use fewer health-care benefits than younger workers with school-age children.[34] As for the widespread belief that job performance declines with age, the scientific evidence clearly refutes this stereotype. Performance does not decline with age regardless of the type of job.[35]

What can companies do to reduce age discrimination?[36] To start with, managers need to recognize that age discrimination is much more pervasive than they probably think. Whereas "old" used to mean mid-50s, in today's workplace, "old" is closer to 40. When 773 CEOs were asked "At what age does a worker's productivity peak?" the average age they gave was 43. Thus, age discrimination may be affecting more workers because perceptions about age have changed. In addition, age discrimination is more likely to occur with the aging of baby boomers simply because there are millions more older workers than there used to be. And, because studies show that interviewers rate younger job candidates as more qualified (even when they aren't), companies need to train managers and recruiters to make hiring and promotion decisions on the basis of qualifications, not age. Companies also need to monitor the extent to which older workers receive training. The Bureau of Labor Statistics found that the number of training courses and number of hours spent in training drops dramatically after employees reach the age of 44.[37] Finally, companies need to ensure that younger and older workers interact with each other. One study found that younger workers generally hold positive views of older workers and that the more time they spent working with older co-workers, the more positive their attitudes became.[38]

2.2 Sex

Sex discrimination occurs when people are treated differently because of their sex. Sex discrimination and racial/ethnic discrimination (discussed in the next section) are often associated with the so-called **glass ceiling,** the invisible barrier that prevents women and minorities from advancing to the top jobs in organizations.

To what extent do women face sex discrimination in the workplace? In some ways, there is much less sex discrimination than there used to be. For example, whereas women held only 17 percent of managerial jobs in 1972, they now outnumber men, with 50.6 percent of managerial jobs, a percentage that surpasses their current representation in the work force (46.3 percent). Also, women own 40 percent of all U.S. businesses. Whereas women owned 700,000 businesses in 1977 and 4.1 million businesses in 1987, today they own 10 million! Finally, though women still earn less than men on average, the differential is narrowing, as shown in Exhibit 12.2. Women earned 79.9 percent of what men did in 2008, up from 63 percent in 1979.[39]

Although progress is being made, the glass ceiling is still in place, creating sex discrimination at higher levels in organizations, as shown in Exhibit 12.3. For instance, while the trends are upward, women were the top earners in their companies in just 6.2 percent of companies in 2008. Likewise, while there has been progress, only 15.7 percent of corporate officers (i.e., top management) are women, and the number is even lower for women of color. Indra K. Nooyi, PepsiCo's CEO, Andrea Jung, Avon's CEO, and Ursula Burns, Xerox's CEO, are the only women of color heading *Fortune* 500 companies.[40] Indeed, only 15 of the 500 largest companies in the United States have women CEOs. Angela Braly, CEO of WellPoint, is the only woman to run a *Fortune* 50

Sex discrimination treating people differently because of their sex

Glass ceiling the invisible barrier that prevents women and minorities from advancing to the top jobs in organizations

Exhibit 12.2

Women's Earnings as a Percentage of Men's, 1979–2008

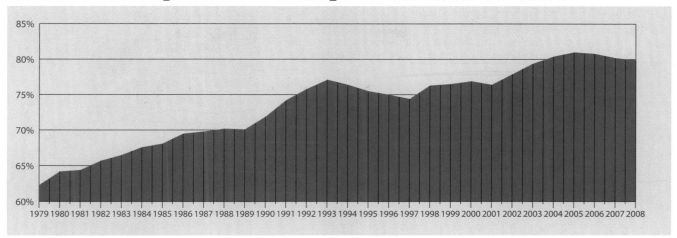

Sources: "Women's Earnings as a Percentage of Men's, 2008," U.S. Department of Labor, Bureau of Labor Statistics, 14 October 2009, available at http://www.bls.gov/opub/ted/2009/ted_20091014_data.htm [accessed on 7 November 2009].

Exhibit 12.3

Women at *Fortune* 500 and 1000 Companies

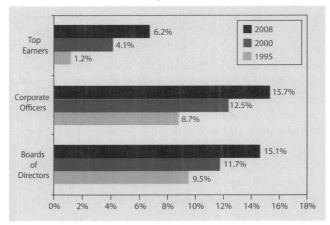

Sources: "Census of Women Corporate Officers and Top Earners" *Catalyst,* available at http://www. catalystwomen.org [accessed 26 May 2005]; "2003 Catalyst Census of Women Board Directors of the Fortune 1000," *Catalyst,* available at http://www.catalystwomen.org [accessed 26 May 2005]; "Catalyst 2008 Census of the Fortune 500 Reveals Women Gained Little Ground Advancing to Business Leadership Positions," *Catalyst,* 10 December 2008, available at http://www.catalyst.org [accessed 7 November 2009].

company.[41] Similarly, only 15.2 percent of the members of corporate boards of directors are women.[42]

Is sex discrimination the sole reason for the slow rate at which women have been promoted to middle and upper levels of management and seated on corporate boards? Some studies indicate that it's not.[43] In some instances, the slow progress appears to be due to career and job choices. Whereas men's career and job choices are often driven by the search for higher pay and advancement, women are more likely to choose jobs or careers that also give them a greater sense of accomplishment, more control over their work schedules, and easier movement in and out of the workplace.[44] Furthermore, women are historically much more likely than men to prioritize family over work at some time in their careers. For example, 96 percent of 600 female Harvard MBAs held jobs while they were in their 20s. That dropped to 71 percent in their late 30s when they had children, but then increased to 82.5 percent in their late 40s as their children became older.[45]

Beyond these reasons, however, it's likely that sex discrimination does play a role in women's slow progress into the higher levels of management. And even if you don't think so, many of the women you work with probably do. Indeed, one study found that more than 90 percent of executive women believed that the glass ceiling had hurt their careers.[46] In another study, 80 percent of women said they left their last organization because the glass ceiling had limited their chances for advancement.[47] A third study indicated that the glass ceiling is prompting more and more women to leave companies to start their own businesses.[48] In fact, discrimination is believed to be the most significant factor to explain the infrequency of women at top levels of management.[49]

So, what can companies do to make sure that women have the same opportunities for development and advancement as men? One strategy is *mentoring,* or pairing promising female executives with senior executives from whom they can seek advice and support. A vice president at a utility company says, "I think it's the single most critical piece to women advancing career-wise. In my experience you need somebody to help guide you and . . . go to bat for you."[50] In fact, 91 percent of female executives

IS THE MOMMY TRACK A LEGITIMATE CAREER PATH?

Diversity professionals have long pushed for equal treatment in the area of career/life balance. They assert that making special accommodations will undermine women's status in the firm and that men are also interested in career/life balance. But is equal treatment really necessary?

Jennifer Allyn, a managing director at PricewaterhouseCoopers (PwC), argues that most requests for flexible work accommodations come from women. At PwC, 93 percent of employees working reduced hours are women, and 75 percent of those say it's because of child-care needs. Allyn suggests formalizing career path options to accommodate various needs by offering

- flexible work schedules and hours,
- new roles and responsibilities to better fit family circumstances, or
- transition programs to accommodate extended leave periods

That way, people could manage advancement opportunities, and the firm could retain and develop key talent.

Sources: J. Allyn, "Reclaiming Mommy Track(s)," *Forbes*, 14 October 2009, available online at http://www.forbes.com/2009/10/14/mommy-track-flex-time-maternity-leave-forbes-woman-leadership-children.html [accessed 11 November 2009].

> Studies provide increasingly **strong** direct **evidence** of racial or ethnic discrimination in the workplace.

have had a mentor at some point and believe that their mentor was critical to their advancement.

Another strategy is to make sure that male-dominated social activities don't unintentionally exclude women. Nearly half (47 percent) of women in the work force believe that "exclusion from informal networks" makes it more difficult to advance their careers. By contrast, just 18 percent of CEOs thought this was a problem.[51] One final strategy is to designate a go-to person other than their supervisor that women can talk to if they believe that they are being held back or discriminated against because of their sex. Make sure this person has the knowledge and authority to conduct a fair, confidential internal investigation.[52]

2.3 Race/Ethnicity

Racial and ethnic discrimination occurs when people are treated differently because of their race or ethnicity. To what extent is racial/ethnic discrimination a factor in the workplace? Every year, the EEOC receives between 26,000 and 35,000 charges of race discrimination, which is more than any other type of discrimination

Racial and ethnic discrimination treating people differently because of their race or ethnicity

charge.[53] However, thanks to the 1964 Civil Rights Act and Title VII, there is much less racial and ethnic discrimination than there used to be. For example, eighteen *Fortune* 500 firms had a black American as CEO in 2007, whereas none did in 1988.[54] Nonetheless, strong racial and ethnic disparities still exist. For instance, whereas 12.9 percent of Americans are black, only 6.4 percent of managers and 3.9 percent of CEOs are black. Similarly, 16 percent of Americans are Hispanic, but only 7.3 percent of managers and 4.8 percent of CEOs are. By contrast, Asians, who constitute about 4.7 percent of the population, are better represented, holding 4.6 percent of management jobs and 4 percent of CEO jobs.[55]

What accounts for the disparities between the percentages of minority groups in the general population and their smaller representation in management positions? Some studies have found that the disparities are due to preexisting differences in training, education, and skills. When black Americans, Hispanics, Asian Americans, and whites have similar skills, training, and education, they are much more likely to have similar jobs and salaries.[56]

Other studies, however, provide increasingly strong direct evidence of racial or ethnic discrimination in the workplace. For example, one study directly tested hiring discrimination by sending pairs of black and white males and pairs of Hispanic and non-Hispanic males to apply for the same jobs. Each pair had résumés with identical qualifications, and all were trained to present themselves in similar ways to minimize differences during interviews. The researchers found that the white males got three times as many job offers as the black males and that the non-Hispanic males got three times as many offers as the Hispanic males.[57]

Another study, which used similar methods to test hiring procedures at 149 different companies, found that whites received 10 percent more interviews than blacks. Half of the whites interviewed received job offers, but only 11 percent of the blacks. And when job offers were made, blacks were much more likely to be offered lower-level positions, while whites were more likely to be offered jobs at higher levels than the jobs they had applied for.[58]

Critics of these studies point out that it's nearly impossible to train different applicants to give identical responses in job interviews and that differences in interviewing skills may have somehow accounted for the results. However, British researchers found similar kinds of discrimination when they sent letters of inquiry to prospective employers. As in the other studies, differences were minimized by making the letters identical except for the applicant's race. Employers frequently responded to letters from Afro-Caribbean, Indian, or Pakistani applicants by indicating that the positions had been filled. By contrast, they often responded to white, Anglo-Saxon applicants by inviting them to face-to-face interviews. Similar results were found with Vietnamese and Greek applicants in Australia.[59] In short, the evidence indicates that there is strong and persistent racial and ethnic discrimination in the hiring processes of many organizations.

What can companies do to make sure that people of all racial and ethnic backgrounds have the same opportunities?[60] Start by looking at the numbers. Compare the hiring rates of whites to the hiring rates for racial and ethnic applicants. Do the same thing for promotions within the company. See if nonwhite workers quit the company at higher rates than white workers. Also, survey employees to compare white and non-white employees' satisfaction with jobs, bosses, and the company, as well as their perceptions concerning equal treatment. Next, if the numbers indicate racial or ethnic disparities, consider employing a private firm to test your hiring system by having applicants of different races with identical qualifications apply for jobs in your company.[61] Although disparities aren't proof of discrimination, it's much better to investigate hiring and

MGMT FACT

TECHNOLOGY = ABILITY

Individuals with disabilities face unique challenges in the workplace. Richard Saab became paralyzed from an aneurysm and was forced to leave his job as a cook because he could no longer stand. Following his recovery, he wanted to cook again. The Florida Department of Vocational Rehabilitation was able to assist him by acquiring a standing wheelchair, which enabled him to assume a position as a line chef again. Development of new assistive technologies not only helps people avoid workplace injury (for example, from poor ergonomic design at computer workstations) but also helps people with disabilities achieve their personal goals and contribute to the success of organizations.

Source: "Standing Wheelchair for a Chef," available online at http://www.workrerc.org [accessed 26 June 2008].

promotion disparities yourself than to have the EEOC or a plaintiff's lawyer do it for you.

Another step companies can take is to eliminate unclear selection and promotion criteria. Vague criteria allow decision makers to focus on non-job-related characteristics that may unintentionally lead to employment discrimination. Instead, selection and promotion criteria should spell out the specific knowledge, skills, abilities, education, and experience needed to perform a job well. Finally, as explained in Chapter 11 on human resources management, it is also important to train managers and others who make hiring and promotion decisions.

2.4 Mental or Physical Disabilities

According to the Americans with Disabilities Act (http://www.ada.gov), a **disability** is a mental or physical impairment that substantially limits one or more major life activities.[62] One in every five Americans, or more than 54 million people, have a disability.[63] **Disability discrimination** occurs when people are treated differently because of their disabilities.

To what extent is disability discrimination a factor in the workplace? Although 79.7 percent of the overall U.S. population was employed in 2006, just 36.9 percent of people with disabilities had jobs. Individuals with sensory disabilities, such as blindness or deafness had the highest

Disability a mental or physical impairment that substantially limits one or more major life activities

Disability discrimination treating people differently because of their disabilities

> *Introverts and extraverts should be correctly matched to their jobs.*

employment rate (46.4 percent), while those with self-care disabilities, which inhibit their motor skills and their ability to care for their grooming needs, were the least well-represented in the work force (at 16.7 percent).[64] Furthermore, people with disabilities are disproportionately employed in low-status or part-time jobs, have little chance for advancement, and, on average, are twice as likely to live in poverty as people without disabilities.[65] Numerous studies also indicate that managers and the general public believe that discrimination against people with disabilities is common and widespread.[66]

What accounts for the disparities between the employment and income levels of people with and without disabilities? Contrary to popular opinion, it has nothing to do with how well people with disabilities can do their jobs. Studies show that as long as companies make reasonable accommodations for disabilities (e.g., changing procedures or equipment), people with disabilities perform their jobs just as well as other employees. They also have better safety records and are no more likely to be absent or quit their jobs.[67]

What can companies do to make sure that people with disabilities have the same opportunities as everyone else? Beyond educational efforts to address incorrect stereotypes and expectations, a good place to start is to commit to reasonable workplace accommodations such as changing work schedules, reassigning jobs, acquiring or modifying equipment, or providing assistance when needed. Accommodations for disabilities needn't be expensive. According to the Job Accommodation Network, 56 percent of accommodations don't cost anything at all, while the average cost of the rest is about $600.[68]

Finally, companies should actively recruit qualified workers with disabilities. Numerous organizations such as Mainstream, Kidder Resources, the American Council of the Blind (http://www.acb.org), the National Federation of the Blind (http://www.nfb.org), the National Association of the Deaf (http://www.nad.org), the Epilepsy Foundation of America (http://www.epilepsyfoundation.org), and the National Amputation Foundation (http://www.nationalamputation.org) actively work with employers to find jobs for qualified people with disabilities. Companies can also place advertisements in publications such as *Careers and the Disabled* that specifically target workers with disabilities.[69]

3 Deep-Level Diversity

As you learned in Section 2, people often use the dimensions of surface-level diversity to form initial impressions about others. Over time, however, as people have a chance to get to know each other, initial impressions based on age, sex, race/ethnicity, and mental or physical disabilities give way to deeper impressions based on behavior and psychological characteristics. When we think of others this way, we are focusing on deep-level diversity. *Deep-level diversity* is reflected in differences that can be recognized only through extended interaction with others. Examples include differences in personality, attitudes, beliefs, and values. In short, recognizing deep-level diversity requires getting to know and understand co-workers better. And that matters because it can result in less prejudice, discrimination, and conflict in the workplace. These changes can then lead to better *social integration*, the degree to which organizational or group members are psychologically attracted to working with each other to accomplish a common objective.

Stop for a second and think about your boss (or the boss you had in your last job). What words would you use to describe him or her? Is your boss introverted or extraverted? Emotionally stable or unstable? Agreeable or disagreeable? Organized or disorganized? Open or closed to new experiences? When you describe your boss or others in this way, what you're really doing is describing dispositions and personality.

A **disposition** is the tendency to respond to situations and events in a predetermined manner. **Personality** is the relatively stable set of behaviors, attitudes, and emotions displayed over time that makes people different from each other.[70] For example, which of your aunts or uncles is a little offbeat, a little out of the ordinary? What was that aunt or uncle like when you were small? What is she or he like now? Chances are she or he is pretty much the same wacky person. In other words, the person's core personality hasn't changed. For years, personality researchers studied thousands of different ways to describe people's personalities. In the last decade, however, personality research conducted in different cultures,

Disposition the tendency to respond to situations and events in a predetermined manner

Personality the relatively stable set of behaviors, attitudes, and emotions displayed over time that makes people different from each other

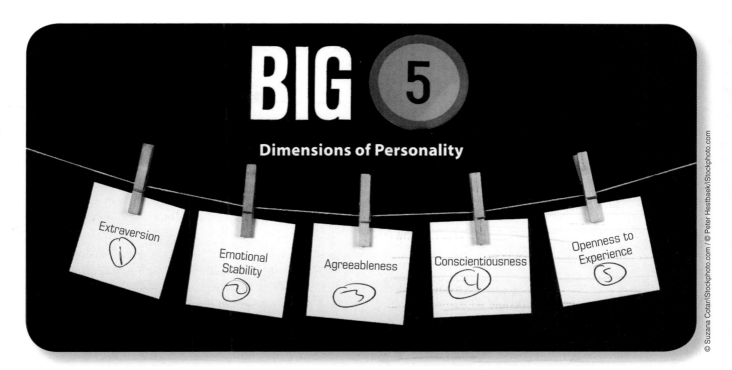

BIG 5

Dimensions of Personality

Extraversion

Emotional Stability

Agreeableness

Conscientiousness

Openness to Experience

different settings, and different languages has shown that five basic dimensions of personality account for most of the differences in people's behaviors, attitudes, and emotions. The *Big Five Personality Dimensions* are extraversion, emotional stability, agreeableness, conscientiousness, and openness to experience.[71]

Extraversion is the degree to which someone is active, assertive, gregarious, sociable, talkative, and energized by others. In contrast to extraverts, introverts are less active, prefer to be alone, and are shy, quiet, and reserved. For the best results in the workplace, introverts and extraverts should be correctly matched to their jobs.

Emotional stability is the degree to which someone is not angry, depressed, anxious, emotional, insecure, or excitable. People who are emotionally stable respond well to stress. In other words, they can maintain a calm, problem-solving attitude in even the toughest situations (e.g., conflict, hostility, dangerous conditions, or extreme time pressures). By contrast, emotionally un-

stable people find it difficult to handle the most basic demands of their jobs under only moderately stressful situations and become distraught, tearful, self-doubting, and anxious. Emotional stability is particularly important for high-stress jobs such as police work, fire fighting, emergency medical treatment, piloting planes, or commanding rockets.

Agreeableness is the degree to which someone is cooperative, polite, flexible, forgiving, good-natured, tolerant, and trusting. Basically, agreeable people are easy to work with and be around, whereas disagreeable people are distrusting and difficult to work with and be around.

Conscientiousness is the degree to which someone is organized,

Ninety-two studies across five occupational groups (professionals, police, managers, sales, and skilled/semiskilled jobs) with a combined total of 12,893 study participants indicated that, on average, conscientious people are inherently more motivated and are better at their jobs.[72]

Extraversion the degree to which someone is active, assertive, gregarious, sociable, talkative, and energized by others

Emotional stability the degree to which someone is not angry, depressed, anxious, emotional, insecure, and excitable

Agreeableness the degree to which someone is cooperative, polite, flexible, forgiving, good-natured, tolerant, and trusting

Conscientiousness the degree to which someone is organized, hardworking, responsible, persevering, thorough, and achievement oriented

hardworking, responsible, persevering, thorough, and achievement oriented. One management consultant wrote about his experiences with a conscientious employee: "He arrived at our first meeting with a typed copy of his daily schedule, a sheet bearing his home and office phone numbers, addresses, and his email address. At his request, we established a timetable for meetings for the next 4 months. He showed up on time every time, day planner in hand, and carefully listed tasks and due dates. He questioned me exhaustively if he didn't understand an assignment and returned on schedule with the completed work or with a clear explanation as to why it wasn't done."[73] Conscientious employees are also more likely to engage in positive behaviors, such as helping new employees, co-workers, and supervisors, and are less likely to engage in negative behaviors, such as verbally or physically abusing co-workers and stealing.[74]

Openness to experience is the degree to which someone is curious, broad-minded, and open to new ideas, things, and experiences; is spontaneous; and has a high tolerance for ambiguity. People in marketing, advertising, research, and other creative fields need to be curious, open to new ideas, and spontaneous. By contrast, openness to experience is not particularly important to accountants, who need to consistently apply stringent rules and formulas to make sense out of complex financial information.

Which of the Big Five Personality Dimensions has the largest impact on behavior in organizations? The cumulative results indicate that conscientiousness is related to job performance across five different occupational groups (professionals, police, managers, sales, and skilled or semiskilled jobs).[75] In short, people "who are dependable, persistent, goal directed, and organized tend to be higher performers on virtually any job; viewed negatively, those who are careless, irresponsible, low-achievement striving, and impulsive tend to be lower performers on virtually any job."[76] The results also indicate that extraversion is related to performance in jobs in areas such as sales and management, which involve significant interaction with others. In people-intensive jobs like these, it helps to be sociable, assertive, and talkative and to have energy and be able to energize others. Finally, people who are extraverted and open to experience seem to do much better in training. Being curious and open to new experiences as well as sociable, assertive, talkative, and full of energy helps people perform better in learning situations.[77]

Openness to experience the degree to which someone is curious, broad-minded, and open to new ideas, things, and experiences; is spontaneous; and has a high tolerance for ambiguity

How much should companies change their standard business practices to accommodate the diversity of their workers? What do you do when a talented top executive has a drinking problem that seems to affect his behavior only at company business parties (for entertaining clients), where he has made inappropriate advances toward female employees? What do you do when, despite aggressive company policies against racial discrimination, employees continue to tell racial jokes and publicly post cartoons displaying racial humor? And, since many people confuse diversity with affirmative action, what do you do to make sure that your company's diversity practices and policies are viewed as benefiting all workers and not just some workers?

No doubt about it, questions like these make managing diversity one of the toughest challenges that managers face. Nonetheless, there are steps companies can take to begin to address these issues.

After reading the next section, you should be able to

4 explain the basic principles and practices that can be used to manage diversity.

4 Managing Diversity

As discussed earlier, diversity programs try to create a positive work environment where no one is advantaged

IF YOU DON'T MEASURE SOMETHING, . . .

What Do You Think?

In Canada, McGregory Jackman, a bus driver for the York Region's VIVA public transportation system, was sent home for violating the organization's dress code by refusing to take off his kufi, a brimless cap often worn by Muslims as part of their religious observance. Said Jackman, "I just want to go back to work and take care of my family. I just want to be a Muslim and do my job."

Source: N. Keung, "Bus Driver in Headgear Battle," *The Toronto Star*, 25 March 2008, A07.

Should Jackman be allowed to wear his kufi as prescribed by his religious beliefs, or is his employer correct for insisting that all bus drivers follow the dress code?

IT DOESN'T COUNT.

or disadvantaged, where "we" is everyone, where everyone can do his or her best work, where differences are respected and not ignored, and where everyone feels comfortable. *Let's see how companies can move toward those goals by learning about **4.1 different diversity paradigms, 4.2 diversity principles,** and **4.3 diversity training and practices.***

4.1 Diversity Paradigms

There are several different methods or paradigms for managing diversity: the discrimination and fairness paradigm, the access and legitimacy paradigm, and the learning and effectiveness paradigm.[78] The *discrimination and fairness paradigm*, which is the most common method of approaching diversity, focuses on equal opportunity, fair treatment, recruitment of minorities, and strict compliance with the equal employment opportunity laws. Under this approach, success is usually measured by how well companies achieve recruitment, promotion, and retention goals for women, people of different racial/ethnic backgrounds, and other underrepresented groups. According to a recent workplace diversity practices survey conducted by the Society for Human Resource Management, 77 percent of companies with more than 500 employees systematically collect measurements on diversity-related practices.[79] For example, one manager says "If you don't measure something, it doesn't count. You measure your market share. You measure your profitability. The same should be true for diversity. There has to be some way of measuring whether you did, in fact, cast your net widely, and whether the company is better off today in terms of the experience of people of color than it was a few years ago. I measure my market share and my profitability. Why not this?"[80] The primary benefit of the discrimination and fairness paradigm is that it generally brings about fairer treatment of employees and increases demographic diversity. The primary limitation is that the focus of diversity remains on the surface-level dimensions of sex, race, and ethnicity.[81]

The *access and legitimacy paradigm* focuses on the acceptance and celebration of differences to ensure that the diversity within the company matches the diversity found among primary stakeholders such as customers, suppliers, and local communities. This is related to the *business growth* advantage of diversity discussed earlier in the chapter. The basic idea behind this approach is to create a demographically diverse work force in order to attract a broader customer base. Consistent with this goal, Ed Adams, vice president of human resources for Enterprise Rent-a-Car, says, "We want people who speak the same language, literally and figuratively, as our customers. We don't set quotas. We say [to our managers], 'Reflect your local market.'"[82] The primary benefit of this approach is that it establishes a clear business reason for diversity. Like the discrimination and fairness paradigm, however, it focuses only on the surface-level diversity dimensions of sex, race, and ethnicity. Furthermore, employees who are assigned responsibility for customers and stakeholders on the basis of their sex, race, or ethnicity may eventually feel frustrated and exploited.

Whereas the discrimination and fairness paradigm focuses on assimilation (having a demographically representative work force), and the access and legitimacy paradigm focuses on differentiation (having demographic differences inside the company match those of key customers and stakeholders), the *learning and effectiveness paradigm* focuses on integrating deep-level diversity differences, such as personality, attitudes, beliefs, and values, into the actual work of the organization. Aetna's 28,000 employees are diverse not only in terms of sex, ethnicity and race, but also age, sexual orientation, work style, perspective, education, skills, and other characteristics. Raymond Arroyo, head of diversity at Aetna, says, "Diversity at Aetna means treating individuals individually, leveraging everyone's best, and maximizing the powerful potential of our workforce." He adds, "Part of a top diversity executive's role in any organization is to integrate diversity into every aspect of a business, including the workforce, customers, suppliers, products, services, and even into the community a business serves."[83]

The learning and effectiveness paradigm is consistent with achieving organizational plurality. **Organizational plurality** is a work environment where (1) all members are empowered to contribute in a way that maximizes the benefits to the organization, customers, and themselves, and (2) the individuality of each member is respected by not segmenting or polarizing people on the basis of their membership in a particular group.[84]

The learning and effectiveness diversity paradigm offers four benefits.[85] First, it values common ground. Dave Thomas of the Harvard Business School explains: "Like the fairness paradigm, it promotes equal opportunity for all individuals. And like the access paradigm, it acknowledges cultural dif-

Organizational plurality a work environment where (1) all members are empowered to contribute in a way that maximizes the benefits to the organization, customers, and themselves, and (2) the individuality of each member is respected by not segmenting or polarizing people on the basis of their membership in a particular group

How to Create a Learning and Effectiveness Diversity Paradigm

1. Understand that a diverse work force will embody different perspectives and approaches to work. Value variety of opinion and insight.
2. Recognize both the learning opportunities and the challenges that the expression of different perspectives presents for your organization.
3. Set high standards of performance for everyone.
4. Create an organizational culture that stimulates personal development.
5. Encourage openness and a high tolerance for debate. Support constructive conflict on work-related matters.
6. Create an organizational culture in which workers feel valued.
7. Establish a clear mission and make sure it is widely understood. This keeps discussions about work differences from degenerating into debates about the validity of individual perspectives.
8. Create a relatively egalitarian, nonbureaucratic structure.

Source: D. A. Thomas and R. J. Ely, "Making Differences Matter: A New Paradigm for Managing Diversity," *Harvard Business Review* 74 (September–October 1996): 79–90.

ferences among people and recognizes the value in those differences. Yet this new model for managing diversity lets the organization internalize differences among employees so that it learns and grows because of them. Indeed, with the model fully in place, members of the organization can say, 'We are all on the same team, with our differences—not despite them.'"[86]

Second, this paradigm makes a distinction between individual and group differences. When diversity focuses only on differences between groups, such as females versus males, large differences within groups are ignored.[87] For example, think of the women you know at work. Now, think for a second about what they have in common. After that, think about how they're different. If your situation is typical, the list of differences should be just as long as the list of commonalities if not longer. In short, managers can achieve a greater understanding of diversity and their employees by treating them as individuals and by realizing that not all black Americans, Hispanics, women, or white males want the same things at work.[88]

Third, because the focus is on individual differences, the learning and effectiveness paradigm is less likely to lead to the conflict, backlash, and divisiveness sometimes associated with diversity programs that focus only on group differences. Ray Haines, a consultant who has helped companies deal with the aftermath of diversity programs that became divisive, says, "There's a large amount of backlash related to diversity training. It stirs up a lot of hostility, anguish, and resentment but doesn't give people tools to deal with [the backlash]. You have people come in and talk about their specific ax to grind."[89] Not all diversity programs are divisive or lead to conflict. But, by focusing on individual rather than group differences, the learning and effectiveness paradigm helps to minimize these potential problems.

Finally, unlike the other diversity paradigms that simply focus on the value of being different (primarily in terms of surface-level diversity), the learning and effectiveness paradigm focuses on bringing different talents and perspectives *together* (i.e., deep-level diversity) to make the best organizational decisions and to produce innovative, competitive products and services. Video game designer Will Wright believes that his teams work best when they consist of diverse individuals. He will try to find older, more experienced veterans and mix them with younger employees, might be highly talented and motivated and less set in their ways. He'll also try to add in some individuals who might be somewhere in between. When he's able to achieve this diverse balance in his teams, Will has found that members work together very well and create significant value.[90]

4.2 Diversity Principles

Diversity paradigms are general approaches or strategies for managing diversity. Whatever diversity paradigm a manager chooses, diversity principles will help managers do a better job of *managing company diversity programs.*[91]

Begin by *carefully and faithfully following and enforcing federal and state laws regarding equal opportunity employment.* Diversity programs can't and won't succeed if the company is being sued for discriminatory actions and behavior. Faithfully following the law will also reduce the time and expense associated with EEOC investigations or lawsuits. Start by learning more at the EEOC web site (http://www.eeoc.gov). Following the law also means strictly and fairly enforcing company policies.

Treat group differences as important but not special. Surface-level diversity dimensions such as age, sex, and race/ethnicity should be respected but should not be treated as more important than other kinds of differences (i.e., deep-level diversity). Remember, the shift

Diversity Principles
1. Carefully and faithfully follow and enforce federal and state laws regarding equal employment opportunity.
2. Treat group differences as important but not special.
3. Find the common ground.
4. Tailor opportunities to individuals, not groups.
5. Reexamine, but maintain, high standards.
6. Solicit negative as well as positive feedback.
7. Set high but realistic goals.

Source: L. S. Gottfredson, "Dilemmas in Developing Diversity Programs," in *Diversity in the Workplace*, ed. S. E. Jackson & Associates (New York: Guildford Press, 1992).

from surface- to deep-level diversity helps people know and understand each other better, reduces prejudice and conflict, and leads to stronger social integration, as people want to work together and get the job done. Also, *find the common ground.* Respecting differences is important. But it's just as important, especially with diverse work forces, to actively find ways for employees to see and share commonalities.

Tailor opportunities to individuals, not groups. Special programs for training, development, mentoring, or promotions should be based on individual strengths and weaknesses, not on group status. Instead of making mentoring available for just one group of workers, create mentoring opportunities for everyone who wants to be mentored.

Solicit negative as well as positive feedback. Diversity is one of the most difficult management issues. No company or manager gets it right from the start. Consequently, companies should aggressively seek positive and negative feedback about their diversity programs. One way to do that is to use a series of measurements to see if progress is being made.

Set high but realistic goals. Just because diversity is difficult doesn't mean that organizations shouldn't try to accomplish as much as possible. The general purpose of diversity programs is to try to create a positive work environment where no one is advantaged or disadvantaged, where "we" is everyone, where everyone can do his or her best work, where differences are respected and not ignored, and where everyone feels comfortable. Even if progress is slow, companies should not abandon these goals.

4.3 Diversity Training and Practices

Organizations use diversity training and several common diversity practices to manage diversity. There are two basic types of diversity training programs. **Awareness training** is designed to raise employees' awareness of diversity issues, such as the big 5 personality dimensions discussed in this chapter, and to get employees to challenge underlying assumptions or stereotypes they may have about others. As a starting point in awareness training, some companies have begun using the Implicit Association Test (IAT), which measures the extent to which people associate positive or negative thoughts (i.e., underlying assumptions or stereotypes) with blacks or whites, men or women, homosexuals or heterosexuals, young or old, or other groups. For example, test takers are shown black or white faces that they must instantly pair with various words. Response times (shorter responses generally indicate stronger associations) and the pattern of associations indicates the extent to which people are biased. Most people are, and strongly so. For example, 88 percent of whites have a more positive mental association toward whites than toward blacks, but, surprisingly, 48 percent of blacks also show the same bias. Taking the IAT is a good way to increase awareness of diversity issues. To take the IAT and to learn more about the decade of research behind it, go to http://implicit.harvard.edu.[92] By contrast, **skills-based diversity training** teaches employees the practical skills they need for managing a diverse work force such as flexibility and adaptability, negotiation, problem solving, and conflict resolution.[93]

Companies also use diversity audits, diversity pairing, and minority experiences for top executives to better manage diversity. **Diversity audits** are formal assessments that measure employee and management attitudes, investigate the extent to which people are advantaged or disadvantaged with respect to hiring and promotions, and review companies' diversity-related policies and procedures. For example, the results of a formal diversity audit prompted BRW, an architecture and engineering firm, to increase job advertising in minority publications, set up a diversity committee to make recommendations to upper management, provide diversity training for all employees, and rewrite the company handbook to make a stronger statement about the company's commitment to a diverse work force.[94]

Earlier in the chapter you learned that *mentoring*, pairing a junior employee with a senior employee, is a common strategy for creating learning and promotional opportunities for women. Diversity pairing is a special kind of mentoring. In **diversity pairing**, people of different cultural backgrounds, sexes, or races/ethnicities are paired for mentoring. The hope is that stereotypical beliefs and attitudes will change as people get to know each other as individuals.[95] For more than 20 years, Xerox has been fostering a culture where women and minorities are prepared and considered for top positions. CEO Ursula Burns, the first African American woman to lead a major U.S. company, worked as special assistant to Xerox's president of marketing and customer operations, Wayland Hicks, in 1990 and later with former CEO Paul A. Allaire. When Anne Mulcahy took over in 2001, Burns was gradually given control of day-to-day operations while Mulcahy repaired Xerox's financial position and customer service.[96]

Finally, because top managers are still overwhelmingly white and male, a number of companies believe that it is worthwhile to *have top executives experience what it is like to be in the minority*. This can be done by having top managers go to places or events where nearly everyone else is of a different sex or racial/ethnic background. At Hoechst Celanese (which has now split into two companies), top managers joined two organizations in which they were a minority. For instance, the CEO, a white male, joined the boards of Hampton University, a historically African American college, and Jobs for Progress, a Hispanic organization that helps people prepare for jobs. Commenting on his experiences, he said, "The only way to break out of comfort zones is to be exposed to other people. When we are, it becomes clear that all people are similar." A Hoechst vice president who joined three organizations in which he was in the minority said, "Joining these organizations has been more helpful to me than 2 weeks of diversity training."[97]

Awareness training training that is designed to raise employees' awareness of diversity issues and to challenge the underlying assumptions or stereotypes they may have about others

Skills-based diversity training training that teaches employees the practical skills they need for managing a diverse work force, such as flexibility and adaptability, negotiation, problem solving, and conflict resolution

Diversity audits formal assessments that measure employee and management attitudes, investigate the extent to which people are advantaged or disadvantaged with respect to hiring and promotions, and review companies' diversity-related policies and procedures

Diversity pairing a mentoring program in which people of different cultural backgrounds, sexes, or races/ethnicities are paired together to get to know each other and change stereotypical beliefs and attitudes

Career Management

After reading this chapter, you should be able to do the following:

1 Explain occupational and organizational choice decisions.

2 Identify foundations for a successful career.

4 Explain the major tasks facing individuals in the establishment stage of the career model.

5 Identify the issues confronting individuals in the advancement stage of the career model.

6 Describe how individuals can navigate the challenges

> ## "Whether we approach it as managers or as employees, career management is an integral activity in our lives."

A **career** is a pattern of work-related experiences that spans the course of a person's life.[1] The two elements in a career are the objective element and the subjective element.[2] The objective element of the career is the observable, concrete environment. For example, you can manage a career by getting training to improve your skills. In contrast, the subjective element involves your perception of the situation. Rather than getting training (an objective element), you might change your aspirations (a subjective element). Thus, both objective events and the individual's perception of those events are important in defining a career.

Career management is a lifelong process of learning about self, jobs, and organizations, setting personal career goals, developing strategies for achieving the goals, and revising the goals based on work and life experiences.[3] Whose responsibility is career management? It is tempting to place the responsibility on individuals, and it is appropriate. However, it is also the organization's duty to form partnerships with individuals in managing their careers. Careers are made up of exchanges between individuals and organizations. Inherent in these exchanges is the idea of reciprocity, or give and take.

[handwritten note: individuals AND organizations are responsible for career management]

Whether we approach it as managers or as employees, career management is an integral activity in our lives. There are three reasons why it is important to understand careers:

> If we know what to look forward to over the course of our careers, we can take a proactive approach to planning and managing them.

> As managers, we need to understand the experiences of our employees and colleagues as they pass through the various stages of careers over their life spans.

> Career management is good business. It makes good financial sense to have highly trained employees keep up with their fields so that organizations can protect valuable investments in human resources.

7 Explain how individuals withdraw from the workforce.

8 Explain how career anchors help form a career identity.

©Jason Mckeown/iStockphoto.com

career
The pattern of work-related experiences that spans the course of a person's life.

career management
A lifelong process of learning about self, jobs, and organizations; setting personal career goals; developing strategies for achieving the goals, and revising the goals based on work and life experiences.

Occupational and Organizational Choice Decisions

The time of the fast track to the top of the hierarchical organization is past. Also gone is the idea of lifetime employment in a single organization. Today's environment demands leaner organizations. The paternalistic attitude that organizations take care of employees no longer exists. Individuals now take on more responsibility for managing their own careers. The concept of the career is undergoing a paradigm shift, as shown in Table 17.1. The old career is giving way to a new career characterized by discrete exchange, occupational excellence, organizational empowerment, and project allegiance.[4] Moreover, one recent study found that both individuals and organizations are actively involved in the management of the new career of employees. As such, the new career involves a type of participatory management technique on the part of the individual, but the organization responds to each

TABLE 17.1 The New versus Old Career Paradigms

NEW CAREER PARADIGM	OLD CAREER PARADIGM
Discrete exchange means: • explicit exchange of specified rewards in return for task performance • basing job rewards on the current market value of the work being performed • engaging in disclosure and renegotiation on both sides as the employment relationship unfolds • exercising flexibility as each party's interests and market circumstances change	**The mutual loyalty contract meant:** • implicit trading of employee compliance in return for job security • allowing job rewards to be routinely deferred into the future • leaving the mutual loyalty assumptions as a political barrier to renegotiation • assuming employment and career opportunities are standardized and prescribed by the firm
Occupational excellence means: • performance of current jobs in return for developing new occupational expertise • employees identifying with and focusing on what is happening in their adopted occupation • emphasizing occupational skill development over the local demands of any particular firm • getting training in anticipation of future job opportunities; having training lead jobs	**The one-employer focus meant:** • relying on the firm to specify jobs and their associated occupational skill base • employees identifying with and focusing on what is happening in their particular firm • forgoing technical or functional development in favor of firm-specific learning • doing the job first to be entitled to new training: making training follow jobs
Organizational empowerment means: • strategic positioning is dispersed to separate business units • everyone is responsible for adding value and improving competitiveness • business units are free to cultivate their own markets • new enterprise, spinoffs, and alliance building are broadly encouraged	**The top-down firm meant:** • strategic direction is subordinated to "corporate headquarters" • competitiveness and added value are the responsibility of corporate experts • business unit marketing depends on the corporate agenda • independent enterprise is discouraged, and likely to be viewed as disloyalty
Project allegiance means: • shared employer and employee commitment to the overarching goal of the project • a successful outcome of the project is more important than holding the project team together • financial and reputational rewards stem directly from project outcomes • upon project completion, organization and reporting arrangements are broken up	**Corporate allegiance meant:** • project goals are subordinated to corporate policy and organizational constraints • being loyal to the work group can be more important than the project itself • financial and reputational rewards stem from being a "good soldier" regardless of results • social relationships within corporate boundaries are actively encouraged

individual's needs and thus is more flexible in its career development programs.[5]

Discrete exchange occurs when an organization gains productivity while a person gains work experience. It is a short-term arrangement that recognizes that job skills change in value and that renegotiation of the relationship must occur as conditions change. This contrasts sharply with the mutual loyalty contract of the old career paradigm in which employee loyalty was exchanged for job security.

Occupational excellence means continually honing skills that can be marketed across organizations. The individual identifies more with the occupation (I am an engineer) than the organization (I am an IBMer). In contrast, the old one-employer focus meant that training was company specific rather than preparing the person for future job opportunities. A recent research study that focused on ethnographic data (interviews and stories) was conducted among software engineers in three European firms and two U.S. firms. Software engineers did not have much regard for their immediate supervisors, the organization, or formal dress codes. The only thing they did believe in was occupational excellence so that they could be better at what they do. In this regard, the authors of the study note that software engineers represent a unique group in terms of career development and that they fit well within the model of the "new career."[6]

Organizational empowerment means that power flows down to business units and in turn to employees. Employees are expected to add value and help the organization remain competitive by being innovative and creative. The old top-down approach meant that control and strategizing were only done by the top managers, and individual initiative might be viewed as disloyalty or disrespect.

Project allegiance means that both individuals and organizations are committed to the successful completion of a project. The firm's gain is the project outcome; the individual's gain is experience and shared success. On project completion, the project team breaks up as individuals move on to new projects. Under the old paradigm, corporate allegiance was paramount. The needs of projects were overshadowed by corporate policies and procedures. Work groups were long term, and keeping the group together was often a more important goal than project completion.

Preparing for the World of Work

When viewed from one perspective, you might say that we spend our youth preparing for the world of work. Educational experiences and personal life experiences help an individual develop the skills and maturity needed to enter a career. Preparation for work is a developmental process that gradually unfolds over time.[8] As the time approaches for beginning a career, individuals face two difficult decisions: occupational choice and organizational choice.

Occupational Choice

In choosing an occupation, individuals assess their needs, values, abilities, and preferences and attempt to match them with an occupation that provides a fit. Personality plays a role in the selection of occupation. John Holland's theory of occupational choice contends that there are six types of personalities and that each personality is characterized by a set of interests and values.[9]

Holland also states that occupations can be classified using this typology. For example, realistic occupations include mechanic, restaurant server, and mechanical engineer. Artistic occupations include architect, voice coach, and interior designer. Investigative occupations include physicist, surgeon, and economist. Real estate agent, human resource manager, and lawyer are enterprising occupations. The social occupations include counselor, social worker, and member of the clergy. Conventional occupations include word processor, accountant, and data entry operator.

HOT Trend: Job Hopping

In today's business environment, job hopping and company hopping are becoming more the norm. In fact, college graduates typically change jobs four times in their first ten years of work, a number that is projected to increase. At that rate, you could easily hold twenty different jobs in a typical career. The stigma associated with frequent job changes has largely disappeared, and some recruiters now view a résumé littered with different companies and locations as a sign of a smart self-promoter. The key is to know "why" you are making each job move, including both what it will cost and gain for you. By presenting your job-hopping career path as a growth process, rather than a series of impulsive changes, you may set yourself apart in the minds of recruiters.[7]

©iStockphoto.com

HOLLAND'S SIX TYPES

>>

1 *Realistic:* stable, persistent, and materialistic.

2 *Artistic:* imaginative, emotional, and impulsive.

3 *Investigative:* curious, analytical, and independent.

4 *Enterprising:* ambitious, energetic, and adventurous.

5 *Social:* generous, cooperative, and sociable.

6 *Conventional:* efficient, practical, and obedient.

Holland's typology has been used to predict career choices with a variety of international participants, including Australians, Germans, Indians, Mexicans, New Zealanders, Pakistanis, South Africans, and Taiwanese.[10]

An assumption that drives Holland's theory is that people choose occupations that match their own personalities. People who fit Holland's social types are those who prefer jobs that are highly interpersonal in nature. They may see careers in physical and math sciences, for example, as not affording the opportunity for interpersonal relationships.[11] To fulfill the desire for interpersonal work, they may instead gravitate toward jobs in customer service or counseling in order to better match their personalities.

Although personality is a major influence on occupational choice, it is not the only influence. There are a host of other influences, including social class, parents' occupations, economic conditions, and geography.[12] Once a choice of occupation has been made, another major decision individuals face is the choice of organizations.

Organizational Choice and Entry

Several theories of how individuals choose organizations exist, ranging from theories that postulate very logical and rational choice processes to those that offer seemingly irrational processes. Expectancy theory, discussed in Chapter 5, can be applied to organizational choice.[13] According to the expectancy theory view, individuals choose organizations that maximize positive outcomes and avoid negative outcomes. Job candidates calculate the probability that an

organization will provide a certain outcome and then compare the probabilities across organizations.

Other theories propose that people select organizations in a much less rational fashion. Job candidates may satisfice, that is, select the first organization that meets one or two important criteria and then justify their choice by distorting their perceptions.[14]

The method of selecting an organization varies greatly among individuals and may reflect a combination of the expectancy theory and theories that postulate less rational approaches. Entry into an organization is further complicated by the conflicts that occur between individuals and organizations during the process. Figure 17.1 illustrates these potential conflicts. The arrows in the figure illustrate four types of conflicts that can occur as individuals choose organizations and organizations choose individuals. The first two conflicts (1 and 2) occur between individuals and organizations. The first is a conflict between the organization's effort to attract candidates and the individual's choice of an organization. The individual needs complete and accurate information to make a good choice, but the organization may not provide it. The organization is trying to attract a large number of qualified candidates, so it presents itself in an overly attractive way.

The second conflict is between the individual's attempt to attract several organizations and the organization's need to select the best candidate. Individuals want good offers, so they do not disclose their faults. They describe their preferred job in terms of the organization's opening instead of describing a job they would really prefer.

Conflicts 3 and 4 are conflicts internal to the two parties. The third is a conflict between the organization's desire to recruit a large pool of qualified applicants and the organization's need to select and retain the best candidate. In recruiting, organizations tend to give only positive information, and this results in mismatches between the indi-

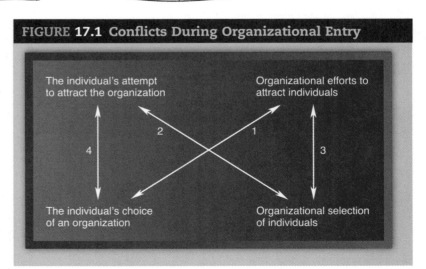

FIGURE 17.1 Conflicts During Organizational Entry

The individual's attempt to attract the organization

Organizational efforts to attract individuals

The individual's choice of an organization

Organizational selection of individuals

SOURCE: Figure in L. W. Porter, E. E. Lawler III, and J. R. Hackman, *Behavior in Organizations*, New York: McGraw-Hill, Inc., 1975, p. 134. Reproduced with permission of The McGraw-Hill Companies.

vidual and the organization. The fourth conflict is internal to the individual; it is between the individual's desire for several job offers and the need to make a good choice. When individuals present themselves as overly attractive, they risk being offered positions that are poor fits in terms of their skills and career goals.[15]

The organizational choice and entry process is very complex due to the nature of these conflicts. Partial responsibility for preventing these conflicts rests with the individual. Individuals should conduct thorough research of the organization through published reports and industry analyses. Individuals also should conduct a careful self-analysis and be as honest as possible with organizations to ensure a good match. The job interview process can be stressful, but also fun.

Partial responsibility for good matches also rests with the organization. One way of avoiding the conflicts and mismatches is to utilize a realistic job preview.

Realistic Job Previews The conflicts just discussed may result in unrealistic expectations on the part of the candidate. People entering the world of work may expect, for example, that they will receive explicit directions from their boss, only to find that they are left with ambiguity about how to do the job. They may expect that promotions will be based on performance and find that promotions are based mainly on political considerations. Some new hires expect to be given managerial responsibilities right away; however, this is not often the case.

Giving potential employees a realistic picture of the job they are applying for is known as a **realistic job preview (RJP)**. When candidates are given both positive and negative information, they can make more effective job choices. Traditional recruiting practices produce unrealistically high expectations, which produce low job satisfaction when these unrealistic expectations hit the reality of the job situation. RJPs tend to create expectations that are much closer to reality, and they increase the numbers of candidates who withdraw from further consideration.[16] This occurs because candidates with unrealistic expectations tend to look for employment elsewhere. The Idaho State Police Department's online employment site provides an RJP, which begins with these words: ". . . you should put aside the images you have seen on television or in the movies and read carefully about the tasks an Idaho State Police Trooper performs."[17] It goes on to provide an exhaustive list of tasks ranging from the exciting (manhunts and serving warrants) to the mundane (inspecting heavy trucks), as well as noting that troopers currently work rotating ten-hour shifts. While the site concludes with a

> ## With today's emphasis on ethics, organizations need to do all they can to be seen as operating consistently and honestly.

summary of the rewards that accompany the job, it clearly notes that the work is at times tedious and far less glamorous than might be expected.

RJPs can also be thought of as inoculation against disappointment. If new recruits know what to expect in the new job, they can prepare for the experience. Newcomers who are not given RJPs may find that their jobs don't measure up to their expectations. They may then believe that their employer was deceitful in the hiring process, become unhappy and mishandle job demands, and ultimately leave the organization.[18]

Job candidates who receive RJPs view the organization as honest and also have a greater ability to cope with the demands of the job.[19] RJPs perform another important function: uncertainty reduction.[20] Knowing what to expect, both good and bad, gives a newcomer a sense of control that is important to job satisfaction and performance.

With today's emphasis on ethics, organizations need to do all they can to be seen as operating consistently and honestly. Realistic job previews are one way in which companies can provide ethically required information to newcomers. Ultimately, RJPs result in more effective matches, lower turnover, and higher organizational commitment and job satisfaction.[21] There is much to gain, and little to risk, in providing realistic job information.[22]

In summary, the needs and goals of individuals and organizations can clash during entry into an organization. To avoid potential mismatches, individuals should conduct a careful self-analysis and provide accurate information about themselves to potential employers. Organizations should present realistic job previews to show candidates both the positive and negative aspects of the job, along with the potential career paths available to the employee.

Foundations for a Successful Career

In addition to planning and preparation building a career takes attention and self-examination. One way you can build a successful career is by becoming your own career coach. Another is by developing your emotional intelligence, which is an important attribute if you want to climb the corporate ladder.

> **realistic job preview (RJP)**
> Both positive and negative information given to potential employees about the job they are applying for, thereby giving them a realistic picture of the job.

Becoming Your Own Career Coach

The best way to stay employed is to see yourself as being in business for yourself, even if you work for someone else. Know what skills you can package for other employers and what you can do to ensure that your skills are state of the art. Organizations need employees who have acquired multiple skills and are adept at more than one job. Employers want employees who have demonstrated competence in dealing with change.[23] To be successful, think of organizational change not as a disruption to your work but instead as the central focus of your work. You will also need to develop self-reliance, as discussed in Chapter 7, to deal effectively with the stress of change. Self-reliant individuals take an interdependent approach to relationships and are comfortable both giving and receiving support from others.

The people who will be most successful in the new career paradigm are individuals who are flexible, team oriented (rather than hierarchical), energized by change, and tolerant of ambiguity. Those who will become frustrated in the new career are individuals who are rigid in their thinking and learning styles and who have high needs for control. A commitment to continuous, lifelong learning will prevent you from becoming a professional dinosaur.[24] An intentional and purposeful commitment to taking charge of your professional life will be necessary in managing the new career.

Behaving in an ethical manner, standing by your values, and building a professional image of integrity are also very important. Major corporations such as Google conduct extensive reference checks on their applicants—not just with the references supplied by the applicants, but also with friends of friends of such references. Behaving ethically is not just a benefit to your job application. An ethical foundation can also help you withstand pressures that might endanger your career. One study suggests that executives succumb to the temptation of fraud because they feel pressure to keep

up with inflated expectations and changes in cultural norms, short-term versus long-term orientations, the composition of the board of directors, and senior leadership in the organization.[25]

Emotional Intelligence and Career Success

Almost 40 percent of new managers fail within the first eighteen months on the job. What are the reasons for the failure? Newly hired managers flame out because they fail to build good relationships with peers and subordinates (82 percent of failures), are confused or uncertain about what their bosses expect (58 percent of failures), lack internal political skills (50 percent of failures), and are unable to achieve the two or three most important objectives of the new job (47 percent of failures).[26] You'll note that these failures are all due to a lack of human skills.

In Chapter 13, we introduced the concept of emotional intelligence (EI) as an important determinant of conflict management skills. Daniel Goleman argues that emotional intelligence is a constellation of the qualities that mark a star performer at work. These attributes include self-awareness, self-control, trustworthiness, confidence, and empathy, among others. Goleman's belief is that emotional competencies are twice as important to people's success today as raw intelligence or technical know-how. He also argues that the further up the corporate ranks you go, the more important emotional intelligence becomes.[27] Employers, either consciously or unconsciously, look for emotional intelligence during the hiring process. In addition to traditionally recognized competencies such as communication and social skills, interns with higher levels of emotional intelligence are rated as more hireable by their host firms than those with lower levels of EI.[28] Neither gender seems to have cornered the market on EI. Both men and women who can demonstrate high levels of EI are seen as particularly gifted and may be promoted more rapidly.[29]

L'Oréal has found emotional intelligence to be a profitable selection tool. Salespeople selected on the basis of emotional competence outsold those selected using the old method by an average of $91,370 per year. As an added bonus for the firm, these salespeople also had 63 percent less turnover during the first year than those selected in the traditional way.[30]

©Andersen Ross/Brand X Pictures/Jupiterimages

Emotional intelligence is important to career success in many cultures. A recent study in Australia found that high levels of emotional intelligence are associated with job success. EI improves one's ability to work with other team members and to provide high-quality customer service, and workers with high EI are more likely to take steps to develop their skills. This confirms U.S. studies that identify high emotional intelligence as an important attribute for the upwardly mobile worker.[31]

The good news is that emotional intelligence can be developed and does tend to improve throughout life. Some companies are providing training in emotional intelligence competencies. American Express began sending managers through an emotional competence training program. It found that trained managers outperformed those who lacked this training. In the year after completing the course, managers trained in emotional competence grew their businesses by an average of 18.1 percent compared to 16.2 percent for those businesses whose managers were untrained.[32]

LEARNING OUTCOME 3

The Career Stage Model

A common way of understanding careers is viewing them as a series of stages through which individuals pass during their working lives.[33] Figure 17.2 presents the career stage model which will form the basis for our discussion in the remainder of this chapter.[34] The career stage model shows that individuals pass through four stages in their careers: establishment, advancement, maintenance, and withdrawal. It is important to note that the age ranges shown are approximations; that is, the timing of the career transitions varies greatly among individuals.

Establishment is the first stage of a person's career. The activities that occur in this stage center around learning the job and fitting into the organization and occupation. Advancement is a high achievement-oriented stage in which people focus on increasing their competence. The maintenance stage finds the individual trying to maintain productivity while evaluating progress toward career goals. The withdrawal stage involves contemplation of retirement or possible career change.

Along the horizontal axis in Figure 17.2 are the corresponding life stages for each career stage. These life stages are based on the pioneering research on adult development conducted by Levinson and his colleagues. Levinson conducted extensive biographical interviews to trace the life stages of men and women. He interpreted his research in two books, *The Seasons of a Man's Life* and *The Seasons of a Woman's Life*.[35] Levinson's life stages are characterized by an alternating pattern of stability and transition.[36] Throughout the discussion of career stages that follows, we weave in the transitions of Levinson's life stages. Work and personal life are inseparable, and to understand a person's career experiences, we must also examine the unfolding of the person's personal experiences.

You can see that adult development provides unique challenges for the individual and that there may be considerable overlap between the stages. Now let us examine each career stage in detail.

establishment

The first stage of a person's career in which the person learns the job and begins to fit into the organization and occupation.

advancement

The second, high achievement-oriented career stage in which people focus on increasing their competence.

maintenance

The third stage in an individual's career in which the individual tries to maintain productivity while evaluating progress toward career goals.

withdrawal

The final stage in an individual's career in which the individual contemplates retirement or possible career changes.

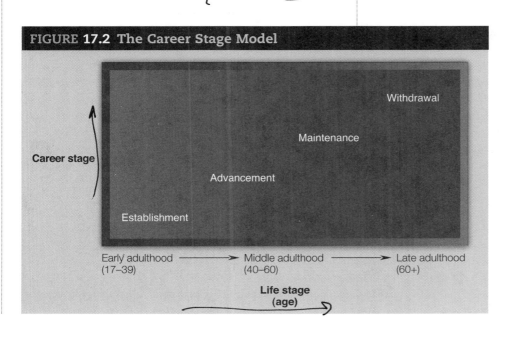

FIGURE 17.2 The Career Stage Model

Career stage

Withdrawal

Maintenance

Advancement

Establishment

Early adulthood (17–39) → Middle adulthood (40–60) → Late adulthood (60+)

Life stage (age)

The Establishment Stage

During the establishment stage, the individual begins a career as a newcomer to the organization. This is a period of great dependence on others, as the individual is learning about the job and the organization. The establishment stage usually occurs during the beginning of the early adulthood years (ages eighteen to twenty-five). During this time, Levinson notes, an important personal life transition into adulthood occurs: the individual begins to separate from his or her parents and becomes less emotionally and financially dependent. Following this period is a fairly stable time of exploring the adult role and settling down.

The transition from school to work is a part of the establishment stage. Many graduates find the transition to be a memorable experience. The following description was provided by a newly graduated individual who went to work at a large public utility:

We all tried to one-up each other about jobs we had just accepted . . . bragging that we had the highest salary, the best management training program, the most desirable coworkers, the most upward mobility . . . and believed we were destined to become future corporate leaders. . . . Every Friday after work we met for happy hour to visit and relate the events of the week. It is interesting to look at how the mood of those happy hours changed over the first few months . . . at first, we jockeyed for position in terms of telling stories about how great these new jobs were, or how weird our bosses were. . . . Gradually, things quieted down at happy hour. The mood went from "Wow, isn't this great" to "What in the world have we gotten ourselves into?" There began to be general agreement that business wasn't all it was cracked up to be.[37]

Establishment is thus a time of big transitions in both personal and work life. At work, three major tasks face the newcomer: negotiating effective psychological contracts, managing the stress of socialization, and making a transition from organizational outsider to organizational insider.

Psychological Contracts

A psychological contract is an implicit agreement between the individual and the organization that specifies what each is expected to give and receive in the relationship.[38] Individuals expect to receive salary, status, advancement opportunities, and challenging work to meet their needs. Organizations expect to receive time, energy, talents, and loyalty in order to meet their goals. Working out the psychological contract with the organization begins with entry, but the contract is modified as the individual proceeds through the career.

Psychological contracts exist between individuals also.[39] During the establishment stage, newcomers form attachment relationships with many people in the organization. Working out effective psychological contracts within each relationship is important. Newcomers need social support in many forms and from many sources. Table 17.2 shows the type of psychological contracts, in

[Mending a Breach]

When an employee's psychological contract with the organization is broken, the employee usually attempts to cope with or resolve the breach. She might do so by retaliating against the organization through absenteeism, neglect of duties, or even more deviant behavior such as theft. A recent study, however, found that conscientious individuals will respond differently than those with low conscientiousness to psychological breaches. While conscientious employees are likely to respond by lowering task performance, nonconscientious employees are more likely to experience a drop in organizational loyalty and job satisfaction. Nonconscientious workers are more likely to withdraw from the organization or quit. It is important that organizations recognize these distinctions. Though psychological breaches should be avoided at all costs, when they are inescapable, organizations need to understand how to intervene to reduce some of the negative impacts. Understanding how different individuals react to psychological breaches may aid in that pursuit.

SOURCE: K. A. Orvis, N. M. Dudley, and J. M. Cortina "Conscientiousness and Reactions to Psychological Contract Breach" *Journal of Applied Psychology* (2008): 1183–1193.

psychological contract

An implicit agreement between an individual and an organization that specifies what each is expected to give and receive in the relationship.

the form of social support, that newcomers may work out with key insiders in the organization.

One common newcomer concern, for example, is whose behavior to watch for cues to appropriate behavior. Senior colleagues can provide modeling support by displaying behavior that the newcomer can emulate. This is only one of many types of support that newcomers need. Newcomers should contract with others to receive each of the needed types of support so that they can adjust to the new job. Organizations should help newcomers form relationships early and should encourage the psychological contracting process between newcomers and insiders. Broken or breached psychological contracts can have detrimental outcomes. When a breach occurs, employees might experience negative emotional reactions that can lead to loss of trust, reduced job satisfaction, lower commitment to the organization, and higher turnover intentions.[40] The influence of a broken psychological contract is often felt even after an employee leaves a job. Laid-off employees who feel that a psychological contract breach has occurred are not only unhappy with their former firms but may also be both more cynical and less trusting of their new employers.[41]

The Advancement Stage

The advancement stage is a period when many individuals strive for achievement. They seek greater responsibility and authority and strive for upward mobility. Usually around age thirty, an important life transition occurs.[42] Individuals reassess their goals and feel the need to make changes in their career dreams. The transition at age thirty is followed by a period of stability during which the individual tries to find a role in adult society and wants to succeed in the career. During this stage, several issues are important: exploring career paths, finding a mentor, working out dual-career partnerships, and managing conflicts between work and personal life.

Career Paths and Career Ladders

Career paths are sequences of job experiences

career path
A sequence of job experiences that an employee moves along during his or her career.

TABLE 17.2 Newcomer–Insider Psychological Contracts for Social Support

TYPE OF SUPPORT	FUNCTION OF SUPPORTIVE ATTACHMENTS	NEWCOMER CONCERN	EXAMPLES OF INSIDER RESPONSE/ACTION
Protection from stressors	Direct assistance in terms of resources, time, labor, or environmental modification	What are the major risks/threats in this environment?	*Supervisor* cues newcomer to risks/threats.
Informational	Provision of information necessary for managing demands	What do I need to know to get things done?	*Mentor* provides advice on informal political climate in organization.
Evaluative	Feedback on both personal and professional role performances	How am I doing?	*Supervisor* provides day-to-day performance feedback during first week on new job.
Modeling	Evidence of behavioral standards provided through modeled behavior	Whom do I follow?	Newcomer is apprenticed to *senior colleague*.
Emotional	Empathy, esteem, caring, or love	Do I matter? Who cares if I'm here or not?	*Other newcomers* empathize with and encourage individual when reality shock sets in.

SOURCE: Table from D. L. Nelson, J. C. Quick, and J. R. Joplin, "Psychological Contracting and Newcomer Socialization: An Attachment Theory Foundation," from *Journal of Social Behavior and Personality* 6 (1991): 65. Reprinted with permission.

along which employees move during their careers.[43] At the advancement stage, individuals examine their career dreams and the paths they must follow to achieve those dreams. For example, suppose a person's dream is to become a top executive in the pharmaceutical industry. She majors in chemistry in undergraduate school and takes a job with a nationally recognized firm. After she has adjusted to her job as a quality control chemist, she reevaluates her plan and decides that further education is necessary. She plans to pursue an MBA degree part time, hoping to gain expertise in management. From there, she hopes to be promoted to a supervisory position within her current firm. If this does not occur within five years, she will consider moving to a different pharmaceutical company. An alternate route would be to try to transfer to a sales position, from which she might advance into management.

The career paths of many women have moved from working in large organizations to starting their own businesses. Currently, there are 10.6 million women-owned firms in the United States, comprising almost half of all privately held firms in the country. What is the motivation for this exodus to entrepreneurship? The main reasons are to seek additional challenge and self-fulfillment and to have more self-determination and freedom.[44]

A **career ladder** is a structured series of job positions through which an individual progresses in an organization. For example, at Southwestern Bell, it is customary to move through a series of alternating line and staff supervisory assignments to advance toward upper management. Supervisors in customer service might be assigned next to the training staff and then rotate back as line supervisors in network services to gain experience in different departments.

Some companies use the traditional concept of career ladders to help employees advance in their careers. Other organizations take a more contemporary approach to career advancement. Sony encourages creativity from its engineers by using nontraditional career paths. At Sony, individuals have the freedom to move on to interesting and challenging job assignments without notifying their supervisors. If they join a new project team, their current boss is expected to let them move on. This self-promotion philosophy at Sony is seen as a key to high levels of innovation and creative new product designs. There has been heightened interest in international assignments by multinational corporations in response to globalization and global staffing issues. One challenge in this regard has been that most expatriate assignments are not successful and organizations have been facing the challenge of properly training and preparing individuals for such assignments. Alternative international work assignments (e.g., commuter work assignments, virtual assignments, short-term assignments, and so on) can be used to help individuals gain international work experience in preparation for higher levels in the organization.[45]

Another approach used by some companies to develop skills is the idea of a career lattice—an approach to building competencies by moving laterally through different departments in the organization or by moving through different projects. Top management support for the career lattice is essential, because in traditional terms an employee who has made several lateral moves might not be viewed with favor. However, the career lattice approach is an effective way to develop an array of skills to ensure one's employability.[46]

Exploring career paths is one important activity in advancement. Another crucial activity during advancement is finding a mentor.

Finding a Mentor

A **mentor** is an individual who provides guidance, coaching, counseling, and friendship to a protégé. Mentors are important to career success because they perform both career and psychosocial functions.[47]

The career functions provided by a mentor include sponsorship, facilitating exposure and visibility, coaching, and protection. Sponsorship means actively helping the individual get job experiences and promotions. Facilitating exposure and visibility means providing opportunities for the protégé to develop relationships with key figures in the organization in order to advance. Coaching involves providing advice in both career and job performance. Protection is provided by shielding the protégé from potentially damaging experiences. Career functions are particularly important to the protégé's future success. One study found that the amount of career coaching received by protégés was related to more promotions, and higher salaries four years later.[48]

The mentor also performs psychosocial functions. Role modeling occurs when the mentor displays behavior for the protégé to emulate. This facilitates social learning. Acceptance and confirmation

©Somos/Veer/Jupiterimages

career ladder

A structured series of job positions through which an individual progresses in an organization.

mentor

An individual who provides guidance, coaching, counseling, and friendship to a protégé.

> ## "Positive regard and appreciation from the junior colleague provide a sense of satisfaction for the mentor.

are important to both the mentor and protégé. When the protégé feels accepted by the mentor, it fosters a sense of pride. Likewise, positive regard and appreciation from the junior colleague provide a sense of satisfaction for the mentor. Counseling by a mentor helps the protégé explore personal issues that arise and require assistance. Friendship is another psychosocial function that benefits both mentor and protégé alike.

There are characteristics that define good mentoring relationships. In effective mentoring relationships, there is regular contact between mentor and protégé that has clearly specified purposes. Mentoring should be consistent with the corporate culture and the organization's goals. Both mentors and protégés alike should be trained in ways to manage the relationship. Mentors should be held accountable and rewarded for their role. Mentors should be perceived (accurately) by protégés as having considerable influence within the organization.[49] While it may be tempting to go after the "top dog" as your mentor, personality compatibility is also an important factor in the success or failure of a mentoring relationship. Mentors who are similar to their protégés in terms of personality traits such as extraversion, and whose expectations are largely met by the relationship, are more likely to show interest in continuing the arrangement.[50] Cigna Financial Advisors takes a proactive approach to integrating new employees. As part of the company's Partnership Program, all new hires work for up to twenty-seven months under the oversight of an experienced, successful mentor. This relationship provides the new hires with hands-on instruction in how to sell more effectively, and it increases sales levels for the mentors themselves. Cigna demonstrates its commitment to this approach by hiring no more new producers than it can assign to individual mentors.[51]

Mentoring programs are also effective ways of addressing the challenge of workforce diversity. The mentoring process, however, presents unique problems, including the availability of mentors, issues of language and acculturation, and cultural sensitivity, for minority groups such as Hispanic-Americans. Negative stereotypes can limit minority members' access to mentoring relationships and the benefits associated with mentoring.[52] To address this problem, companies can facilitate access to mentors in organizations. Informal mentoring programs identify

pools of mentors and protégés, provide training in the development of effective mentoring and diversity issues, and then provide informal opportunities for the development of mentoring relationships. Network groups are another avenue for mentoring. Network groups help members identify with those few others who are like them within an organization, build relationships with them, and build social support. Network groups enhance the chance that minorities will find mentors.[53] Lucent Technologies, for example, has several Employee Business Partner groups that serve networking functions. Some of these groups are HISPA, for Hispanic Americans; 4A, which is for Asian Americans; ABLE, for African Americans; LUNA, for Native Americans; and Equal!, for gay, lesbian, and bisexual individuals. These groups serve as links to their respective communities within Lucent. Networks also increase the likelihood that individuals have more than one mentor. Individuals with multiple mentors, such as those gained from mentoring networks, have even greater career success than those with only one mentor.[54]

Some companies have formal mentoring programs. PricewaterhouseCoopers (PwC) also uses the mentoring model to help its interns. Each intern is assigned both a peer mentor to help with day-to-day questions and an experienced mentor to help with larger issues such as career path development. As an international firm, PwC also employs similar methods overseas. In PwC's Czech Republic operations, a team of two mentors—one of whom is called a "counselor"—fills the same guidance role as the two mentors generally fill for U.S. employees.[55]

Mentoring has had a strong impact in shaping the identities of the Big Four accounting firms. In one study, every partner who was interviewed reported having at least one mentor who played a critical role in his/her attainment of the partnership and beyond. Protégés' identities are shaped through mentoring, and their work goals, language, and even lifestyles reflect the imperatives of the Big Four firm.[56] Protégés are schooled on partners' "hot buttons" (what not to talk about), what to wear, to "tuck in the tie," and not to cut the grass without wearing a shirt.

Although some companies have formal mentoring programs, junior employees more often are left to negotiate their own mentoring relationships. The barriers to finding a mentor include lack of access to mentors, fear of initiating a mentoring relationship, and fear that supervisors or coworkers might not approve of the mentoring relationship. Individuals may also be afraid to initiate a mentoring relationship because it might be misconstrued as a sexual advance by the potential mentor or others. This is a fear of potential mentors as well. Some are unwilling to develop a relationship because of their own or the protégé's gender. Women report more of these barriers than men, and individuals who lack previous experience report more barriers to finding a mentor.[57] There are other gender differences found in mentoring relationships. Male protégés report receiving less psychological support than female protégés. Additionally, male mentors report giving more career development support, whereas female mentors report giving more psychological support.[58]

Organizations can encourage junior workers to approach mentors by providing opportunities for them to interact with senior colleagues. The immediate supervisor is not always the best mentor for an individual, so exposure to other senior workers is important. Seminars, multilevel teams, and social events can serve as vehicles for bringing together potential mentors and protégés.

Mentoring relationships go through a series of phases: initiation, cultivation, separation, and redefinition. There is no fixed time length for each phase, because each relationship is unique. In the initiation phase, the mentoring relationship begins to take on significance for both the mentor and the protégé. In the cultivation phase, the relationship becomes more meaningful, and the protégé shows rapid progress because of the career and psychosocial support provided by the mentor. Protégés influence mentors as well.

In the separation phase, the protégé feels the need to assert independence and work more autonomously. Separation can be voluntary, or it can result from an involuntary change (the protégé or mentor may be promoted or transferred). The separation phase can be difficult if it is resisted, either by the mentor (who is reluctant to let go of the relationship) or by the protégé (who resents the mentor's withdrawal of support). Separation can proceed smoothly and naturally or can result from a conflict that disrupts the mentoring relationship.

The redefinition phase occurs if separation has been successful. In this phase, the relationship takes on a new identity as the two parties consider each other colleagues or friends. The mentor feels pride in the protégé, and the protégé develops a deeper appreciation for the support from the mentor.

Why are mentors so important? Aside from the support they provide, research shows that mentors are important to the protégé's future success. For example, studies have demonstrated that individuals with mentors have higher promotion rates and higher incomes than individuals who do not have mentors.[59] Professionals who have mentors earn between $5,600 and $22,000 more per year than those who do not.[60] Individuals with mentors also are better decision makers.[61] It is not just the presence of the mentor that yields these benefits. The quality of the relationship is most important.[62]

Dual-Career Partnerships

During the advancement stage, many individuals face another transition. They settle into a relationship with a life partner. This lifestyle transition requires adjustment in many respects—learning to live with another person, being concerned with someone besides yourself, dealing with an extended family, and many other demands. The partnership can be particularly stressful if both members are career oriented.

The two-career lifestyle has increased in recent years due in part to the need for two incomes to maintain a preferred standard of living. **Dual-career partnerships** are relationships in which both people have important career roles. This type of partnership can be mutually beneficial, but it can also be stressful. Often these stresses center around stereotypes that providing income is a man's responsibility and taking care of the home is the woman's domain. Among married couples, working women's satisfaction with the marriage is affected by how much the husband helps with child care. Men who adhere to traditional gender beliefs may be threatened when the wife's income exceeds their own. Beliefs about who should do what in the partnership complicate the dual-career issue.[63]

One stressor in a dual-career partnership is time pressure. When both partners work outside the home, there may be a time crunch in fitting in work, family, and leisure time. Yet another potential problem is jealousy. When one partner's career blooms before the other's, the partner may feel threatened.[64] Another issue to work out is whose career takes precedence. For example, what happens if one partner is transferred to another city? Must the other partner make a move that might threaten his or her own career in order to be with the individual who was transferred? Who, if anyone, will stay home and take care of a new baby?

Working out a dual-career partnership takes careful planning and consistent communication between the partners. Each partner must serve as a source of social support for the other. Couples can also turn to other family members, friends, and professionals for support if the need arises.

Work–Home Conflicts

An issue related to dual-career partnerships that is faced throughout the career cycle, but often first encountered in the advancement phase, is the conflicts between work and personal life. Experiencing a great deal of work–home conflict negatively affects an individual's overall quality of life. Work–home conflicts can lead to emotional exhaustion. Dealing with customer complaints all day, failed sales calls, and missed deadlines can magnify negative

dual-career partnership
A relationship in which both people have important career roles.

events at home, and vice versa.[65] Responsibilities at home can clash with responsibilities at work, and these conflicts must be planned for. For example, suppose a child gets sick at school. Who will pick up the child and stay home with him? Couples must work together to resolve these conflicts. Even at Eli Lilly and Co., only 36 percent of workers said it is possible to get ahead in their careers and still devote sufficient time to family. This is surprising, because Lilly has a reputation as one of the world's most family-friendly workplaces.[66] A recent study found that an individual's work-home conflict can lead to unfavorable critique and discouragement of goal attainment by that individual's partner, leading to mutual feelings of exhaustion and negativity.[67]

Work–home conflicts are particular problems for working women.[68] Women have been quicker to share the provider role than men have been to share responsibilities at home.[69] When working women experience work–home conflict, their performance declines, and they suffer more strain. Work–home conflict is a broad topic. It can be narrowed further into work–family conflict, in which work interferes with family, versus family–work conflict, in which family or home life interferes with work.[70] Individuals who believe that men and women should share work and home lives equally experience more guilt from work–home conflict than traditionalists, who tend to feel more guilt when home life interferes with work.[71] Cultural differences arise in these types of conflicts. One study showed that while Americans experience more family–work conflict, Chinese experience more work–family conflict.[72] For example, women in management positions in China were very positive about future advancements and carried a strong belief in their ability to succeed. This, in turn, caused them to reevaluate their personal and professional identities. Such an identity

ADVANCEMENT AND MIDLIFE

>>

People in the advancement stage are also dealing with developmental and life-stage changes. The midlife transition, which takes place approximately between ages forty and forty-five, is often a time of crisis. Levinson points out three major changes that contribute to the midlife transition:

> People realize that their lives are half over and that they are mortal.
> Age forty is considered by people in their twenties and thirties to be "over the hill" and not part of the youthful culture.
> People reassess their dreams and evaluate how close they have come to achieving those dreams.

Midlife transition can add a layer of stress to the challenges employees face during the advancement stage.

transformation is marked by happiness associated with career advancement, even though many women foresaw emotional costs with such career advancement. This study indicated that female Chinese managers experience work–family conflict in part because the Chinese culture emphasizes close social ties and *guanxi*.[73]

Ways to Manage Work–Home Conflict

To help individuals deal with work–home conflict, companies can offer **flexible work schedules**.[74] Programs such as flextime, discussed in Chapter 14, give employees freedom to take care of personal concerns while still getting their work done. Company-sponsored child care is another way to help. Companies with on-site day-care centers include Johnson & Johnson, Perdue Farms, and Campbell's Soup. Mitchell Gold, an award-winning furniture maker, believes that treating people right must come first. Its 2,700-square-foot on-site day-care center is education based rather than activity based and operates at

©Corbis/Jupiterimages

flexible work schedule

A work schedule that allows employees discretion in order to accommodate personal concerns.

break-even rates to make it more accessible. The day-care facility was named the county's "Provider of the Year" in 2003.[75] Whereas large companies may offer corporate day care, small companies can also assist their workers by providing referral services for locating the type of child care the workers need. For smaller organizations, this is a cost-effective alternative.[76] At the very least, companies can be sensitive to work–home conflicts and handle them on a case-by-case basis with flexibility and concern.

A program of increasing interest that organizations can provide is eldercare. Often workers find themselves part of the sandwich generation. They are expected to care for both their children and their elderly parents. Inclusion in this extremely stressful role is reported more often by women than men.[77] The impact of caring for an aging loved one is often underestimated. But 17 percent of those who provide care eventually quit their jobs due to time constraints, and another 15 percent cut back their work hours for the same reason.[78] Caring for an elderly dependent at home can create severe work–home conflicts for employees and also takes a toll on the employee's own well-being and performance at work. This is most often the case if the organization is not one that provides a supportive climate for discussion of eldercare issues.[79] Harvard University has taken steps to help its faculty and staff deal with eldercare issues by contracting with Parents in a Pinch, Inc., a firm that specializes in nanny services and now also offers eldercare.[80]

John Beatrice is one of a handful of men making work fit their family, rather than trying to fit family around career. John remembers his father working most of the night so he could be at John's athletic events during the day, and John wants the same for his family. So while job sharing, flexible scheduling, and telecommuting have traditionally been viewed as meeting the needs of working mothers, John and other men are increasingly taking advantage of such opportunities. In John's case, flexible work hours at Ernst & Young allow him to spend part of his mornings and afternoons coaching a high school hockey team. In John's assessment, flexible work hours actually lead him to work more hours than he would otherwise, and he's happier about doing it. Not surprisingly, John's employer also benefits from the arrangement. After nineteen years, John is more loyal than ever and still loves what he does.[81]

Alternative work arrangements such as flextime, compressed workweeks, work-at-home arrangements, part-time hours, job sharing, and leave options can help employees manage work–home conflicts. Managers must not let their biases get in the way of these benefits. Top managers may be less willing to grant alternative work arrangements to men than to women, to supervisors than to subordinates, and to employees caring for elderly parents rather than children. It is important that family-friendly policies be applied fairly.[82]

eldercare
Assistance in caring for elderly parents and/or other elderly relatives.

[KPMG Provides Help for the Sandwich Generation]

Many midlife workers find themselves taking care of both their children and their elderly parents. Accounting firm KPMG recognized this precarious position and took steps to address the needs of its sandwiched employees by implementing progressive scheduling practices that promote a healthy work–life balance. Compressed work weeks, flextime, and telecommuting are all available, and if employees' babysitting arrangements fall through, KPMG offers a back-up child-care service. KPMG also has a shared leave program in which employees can donate personal vacation time to colleagues facing family emergencies like sudden illness or the death of a loved one.

Most unique of the new initiatives is the three-part eldercare benefit. First, KPMG provides an online information and referral service that connects employees with aging and health-related resources and facilities. Second, the firm underwrites up to twenty days of facility-based or in-home care for elderly relatives per year. As with the shared leave program, employees can donate unused care days to colleagues. Third, if an employee needs to take a break from work to plan for eldercare or to tend to an elderly relative, he or she can request a leave of absence or use paid time-off days.

The payoffs for providing such benefits are many. The programs led to reduced turnover and an award from Catalyst (the leading nonprofit organization promoting inclusive workplaces for women). Employees reported greater productivity, a boost in morale, and reduced stress and work–home conflict. Certainly, KPMG's novel efforts to accommodate the sandwich generation have proven worthwhile.

Sources: http://www.catalyst.org/file/280/difinalpracticekpmg_pdf.pdf; https://www.web1.lifebenefits.com/MMG/resources/aware_newsletter/aware0408/ef_print.html.

©Kelly Cline/iStockphoto.com

4 KEYS TO A SUCCESSFUL MENTORING PROGRAM

>> Kathy Kram notes that there are four keys to the success of a formal mentoring program:

1 > Participation should be voluntary. No one should be forced to enter a mentoring relationship, and careful matching of mentors and protégés is important.

2 > Support from top executives is needed to convey the intent of the program and its role in career development.

3 > Training should be provided to mentors so they understand the functions of the relationship.

4 > A graceful exit should be provided for mismatches or for people in mentoring relationships who have fulfilled their purpose.[83]

LEARNING OUTCOME 6

The Maintenance Stage

Maintenance may be a misnomer for this career stage, because some people continue to grow in their careers, although the growth is usually not at the rate it was earlier. A career crisis at midlife may accompany the midlife transition. A senior product manager at Borden found himself in such a crisis and described it this way: "When I was in college, I had thought in terms of being president of a company. . . . But at Borden I felt used and cornered. Most of the guys in the next two rungs above me had either an MBA or fifteen to twenty years of experience in the food business. My long-term plans stalled."[84]

Some individuals who reach a career crisis are burned out, and a month's vacation will help, according to Carolyn Smith Paschal, who owns an executive search firm. She recommends that companies give employees in this stage sabbaticals instead of bonuses. This would help rejuvenate them.

Some individuals reach the maintenance stage with a sense of achievement and contentment, feeling no need to strive for further upward mobility. Whether the maintenance stage is a time of crisis or contentment, however, there are two issues to grapple with: sustaining performance and becoming a mentor.

Sustaining Performance

Remaining productive is a key concern for individuals in the maintenance stage. This becomes challenging when one reaches a **career plateau**, a point where the probability of moving further up the hierarchy is low. Some people handle career plateauing fairly well, but others may become frustrated, bored, and dissatisfied with their jobs.

To keep employees productive, organizations can provide challenges and opportunities for learning. Lateral moves are one option. Another option is to involve the employee in project teams that provide new tasks and skill development. The key is keeping the work stimulating and involving. Individuals at this stage also need continued affirmation of their value to the organization. They need to know that their contributions are significant and appreciated.[85]

Becoming a Mentor

During maintenance, individuals can make a contribution by sharing their wealth of knowledge and experience with others. Opportunities to be mentors to new employees can keep senior workers motivated and involved in the organization. It is important for organizations to reward mentors for the time and energy they expend. Some employees adapt naturally to the mentor role, but others may need training on how to coach and counsel junior workers.

Maintenance is a time of transition, like all career stages. It can be managed by individuals who know what to expect and plan to remain productive, as well as by organizations that focus on maximizing employee involvement in work. According to Levinson, during the latter part of the maintenance stage, another life transition occurs. The age fifty transition is another time of reevaluating the dream and working further on the issues raised in the midlife transition. Following the age fifty transition is a fairly stable period. During this time, individuals begin to plan seriously for withdrawing from their careers.

LEARNING OUTCOME 7

The Withdrawal Stage

The withdrawal stage usually occurs later in life and signals that a long period of continuous employment will soon come to a close. Older workers may face discrimination and stereotyping. They may be viewed by others as less productive, more resistant to change, and less motivated. However, older workers are one of the most undervalued groups in the workforce. They can provide continuity in the midst of change and can serve

career plateau
A point in an individual's career in which the probability of moving further up the hierarchy is low.

as mentors and role models to younger generations of employees.

Discrimination against older workers is prohibited under the Age Discrimination in Employment Act. (Go to eeoc.gov/policy/adea.html to read the provisions of this 1967 act.) Organizations must create a culture that values older workers' contributions. With their level of experience, strong work ethic, and loyalty, these workers have much to contribute. In fact, older workers have lower rates of tardiness and absenteeism, are more safety conscious, and are more satisfied with their jobs than are younger workers.[86]

Planning for Change

The decision to retire is an individual one, but the need for planning is universal. A retired sales executive from Boise Cascade said that the best advice is to "plan no unplanned retirement."[87] This means carefully planning not only the transition but also the activities you will be involved in once the transition is made. All options should be open for consideration. One recent trend is the need for temporary top-level executives. Some companies are hiring senior managers from the outside on a temporary basis. The qualities of a good temporary executive include substantial high-level management experience, financial security that allows the executive to choose only assignments that really interest her, and a willingness to relocate.[88] Some individuals at the withdrawal stage find this an attractive option.

Planning for retirement should include not only financial planning but also a plan for psychologically withdrawing from work. The pursuit of hobbies and travel, volunteer work, or more time with extended family can all be part of the plan. The key is to plan early and carefully, as well as to anticipate the transition with a positive attitude and a full slate of desirable activities.

Retirement

There are several retirement trends right now, ranging from early retirement to phased retirement to never retiring. Some adults are choosing a combination of these options, leaving their first career for some time off before reentering the workforce either part time or full time doing

phased retirement
An arrangement that allows employees to reduce their hours and/or responsibilities in order to ease into retirement.

bridge employment
Employment that takes place after a person retires from a full-time position but before the person's permanent withdrawal from the workforce.

Some retirement-agers may go through a second midlife crisis. People are living longer and staying more active. Vickie Ianucelli, for example, bought a condo on a Mexican beach, celebrated a birthday in Paris, bought herself a 9.5-karat ring, and got plastic surgery. And, it's her second midlife crisis. She's a psychologist who is also a 60-plus grandmother of two.[89]

something they enjoy. For more and more Americans, the idea of a retirement spent sitting beside the swimming pool sounds, for lack of a better word, boring. Factors that influence the decision of when to retire include company policy, financial considerations, family support or pressure, health, and opportunities for other productive activities.[90]

During the withdrawal stage, the individual faces a major life transition that Levinson refers to as the late adulthood transition (ages sixty to sixty-five). One's own mortality becomes a major concern and the loss of one's family members and friends becomes more frequent. The person works to achieve a sense of integrity in life—that is, the person works to find the encompassing meaning and value in life.

Retirement need not be a complete cessation of work. Many alternative work arrangements can be considered, and many companies offer flexibility in these options. **Phased retirement** is a popular option for retirement-age workers who want to gradually reduce their hours and/or responsibilities. There are many forms of phased retirement, including reduced workdays or workweeks, job sharing, and consulting and mentoring arrangements. Many organizations cannot afford the loss of large numbers of experienced employees at once. In fact, although 50 percent of all U.S. workers are officially retired by age sixty, only 11 percent fully withdraw from work. This means there is an increase in **bridge employment**, which is employment that takes place after a person retires from a full-time position but before the person's permanent withdrawal from the workforce. Bridge employment is related to retirement satisfaction and overall life satisfaction.[91]

Some companies are helping employees transition to retirement in innovative ways. Retired individuals can continue their affiliation with the organization by serving as mentors to employees who are embarking on retirement planning or other career transitions. This helps diminish the fear of loss some people have about retirement, because the retiree

©Workbook Stock/Jupiterimages/Getty Images

has an option to serve as a mentor or consultant to the organization.

Lawrence Livermore National Labs (LLNL) employs some of the best research minds in the world. And when these great minds retire from full-time work, they have numerous opportunities to continue contributing. LLNL's retiree program Web site lists a wide variety of requests, ranging from guiding tours and making phone calls to providing guidance on current research and helping researchers make contact with other researchers.[92] Programs like this one help LLNL avoid the typical knowledge drain that takes place when seasoned veteran employees retire.

Now that you understand the career stage model, you can begin to conduct your own career planning. It is never too early to start.

FIVE CAREER ANCHORS

1 *Technical/functional competence.* Individuals who hold this career anchor want to specialize in a given functional area (for example, finance or marketing) and become competent. The idea of general management does not interest them.

2 *Managerial competence.* Adapting this career anchor means individuals want general management responsibility. They want to see their efforts have an impact on organizational effectiveness.

3 *Autonomy and independence.* Freedom is the key to this career anchor, and often these individuals are uncomfortable working in large organizations. Autonomous careers such as writer, professor, or consultant attract these individuals.

4 *Creativity.* Individuals holding this career anchor feel a strong need to create something. They are often entrepreneurs.

5 *Security/stability.* Long-term career stability, whether in a single organization or in a single geographic area, fits people with this career anchor. Some government jobs provide this type of security.

Career Anchors

Much of an individual's self-concept rests upon a career. Over the course of the career, career anchors are developed. **Career anchors** are self-perceived talents, motives, and values that guide an individual's career decisions described above.[93] Edgar Schein developed the concept of career anchors based on a twelve-year study of MBA graduates from the Massachusetts Institute of Technology (MIT). Schein found great diversity in the graduates' career histories but great similarities in the way they explained the career decisions they had made.[94] From extensive interviews with the graduates, Schein developed the five career anchors (see box above).

Career anchors emerge over time and may be modified by work or life experiences.[95] The importance of knowing your career anchor is that it can help you find a match between you and an organization. For example, individuals with creativity as an anchor may find themselves stifled in bureaucratic organizations. Textbook sales may not be the place for an individual with a security anchor because of the frequent travel and seasonal nature of the business.

career anchors
A network of self-perceived talents, motives, and values that guide an individual's career decisions.

BY THE NUMBERS

11% of retirees fully withdraw from work

17% of workers responsible for eldercare in their families quit their jobs

10.6 million women-owned businesses in the United States

$91,370 more in average sales for L'Oréal employees with high emotional competence than for those without

6 personalities in Holland's typology

CHAPTER 2
Leading Strategically

Knowledge Objectives

Reading and studying this chapter should enable you to:

1. Define and explain strategic leadership.

2. Explain how vision and mission create value.

3. Define the meaning of a top management team and the value of having a heterogeneous top management team.

4. Explain the importance of managerial succession.

5. Define human capital and social capital and describe their value to the firm.

6. Describe an entrepreneurial culture and its contribution to a firm.

7. Explain the importance of managerial integrity and ethical behavior.

8. Discuss why firms should have a control system that balances the use of strategic controls and financial controls.

Changes in Corporate Governance Have Reformed the Role of the CEO in Strategic Leadership

The role of the chief executive officer (CEO), especially in the United States, has been changing due to increased scrutiny by boards of directors and corporate governance trends in general. One of the most visible changes has been the division of the CEO role from that of the chairperson of the board of directors. Historically, many CEOs resisted sharing power by insisting on holding both roles simultaneously. For example, in 2002, 73 percent of public companies had combined roles whereas by 2007, 55 percent had a nonemployee chairperson of the board. Furthermore, the chairperson being independent of the board has created a situation such that "the age of the imperial CEO" is declining. Where the roles are separate, boards often have separate planning meetings in which board members might examine important strategy or executive succession issues. Additionally, in such boards, members are more likely to engage investors in concerns around executive pay and takeover defenses. Much of the unease regarding corporate governance has been due to the enactment of the Sarbanes-Oxley Act of 2002, which was a response to the accounting scandals such as those by Enron and WorldCom in 2001.

© Kevin Winer/Getty Images

However, because of the separation of the board chairperson and CEO roles, questions arise as to how these roles should be carried out in regard to important strategic issues. The basic question is "Who has the power to formulate strategy?" Interestingly, U.S. executives have been looking to Great Britain, which forced major public companies to divorce the two roles in 1992 during a period of corporate governance reform. As such, the board chairperson in large British companies usually comes from outside company ranks. Increasingly, boards of U.S. firms have likewise been naming former CEOs with no affiliation to the focal company to fill the chairperson role, which is now the case in 7.2 percent of S&P companies.

Critics, however, have warned that this new breed of chairpersons may be tempted to get involved in management issues that are reserved for the actual CEO, creating confusion for shareholders as to who is actually in charge. Often, under the new board reforms, the board will have an outside director who is not part of the firm's employment structure historically. Although this person will not necessarily be the board chair, he/she can hold independent meetings without executives from the board and can consult with other outsider directors regarding issues that pertain to strategy and management succession without political influence from the current CEO. Accordingly, these new changes and other changes associated with the Sarbanes-Oxley Act of 2002 mean more power sharing in important issues related to strategy of the overall firm.

Examples of recent companies that have divided the roles and have hired a strong external chairperson of the board are Walt Disney Company, Marsh & McLennan Cos., and Bristol Meyers Squibb Co. Some of these companies were seeking to reassure stockholders after a scandal or bad corporate report that they would pursue better corporate governance procedures. These changes in corporate governance have led to a decrease in the CEO's power and an increase in power sharing among board members and the CEO in regard to overall strategic responsibilities and direction of the company. Thus, the CEO is not only accountable to shareholders, but also more accountable to a chairperson or a lead outside director who can consult with an increasing number of independent outside directors on boards regarding important strategic issues.

Power sharing has also occurred because firms have more diffuse supply chains as well as numerous and often complex strategic alliances or joint ventures with numerous partner firms. As such, strategic leaders find that they must manage with more involvement of employees and of managers of these complex partnering arrangements. In essence, this situation requires less top-down strategic leadership and more power sharing and joint decision making with middle managers, strategic partners, and supplier and customer firms in regard to important strategic decisions.

In summary, strategic leadership is more diffuse because of corporate governance as well as other strategic partnering arrangements that are necessary to manage a large firm both domestically and globally. Consequently, strategy becomes more of a dynamic process that involves continual evaluation rather than a set solution to establish long-term sustainable competitive advantage. Thus, strategy has become a process of continual creation and recreation rather than a stable set of characteristics that differentiate the company from its competitors.

Sources: R. M. Kanter, 2008, Transforming giants, *Harvard Business Review*, 86(1): 43–52; J. S. Lublin, 2008, When chairman and CEO roles get a divorce, *Wall Street Journal*, January 14, B1; S. Mishra, 2008, Counting progress; The state of boards five years after Sarbanes-Oxley, *The Corporate Governance Advisor*, January/February, 12; C. A. Montgomery, 2008, Putting leadership back into strategy, *Harvard Business Review*, 86(1): 54–60; S. E. Needleman, 2008, Corporate governance (a special report); Too many cooks? Companies are tapping outside CEOs to run their boards; It makes sense—but it could be a recipe for conflict, *Wall Street Journal*, January 14, R4; K. Elsayed, 2007, Does CEO duality really affect corporate performance? *Corporate Governance: An International Review*, 15: 1203–1204.

Strategic leadership involves developing a vision for the firm, designing strategic actions to achieve this vision, and empowering others to carry out those strategic actions. As defined in Chapter 1, *strategic leaders* are the individuals practicing strategic leadership. Strategic leaders hold upper-level organizational positions. As Focusing on Strategy indicated, today's strategic leaders are involving people throughout the firm as well as other governance participants (board of director members and other stakeholders (suppliers and customers) in strategic management. Thus, any person in the firm (and outside) responsible for designing strategic actions and ensuring that they are carried out in ways that move the firm toward achievement of the vision is essentially playing the role of a strategic leader.

Is strategic leadership important? A substantial amount of research suggests that it is.[1] Richard Clark became CEO of Merck, a large pharmaceutical firm, in mid-2005 shortly after the drug Vioxx was recalled, which led to a number of lawsuits and a dramatic drop in Merck's share price. Clark immediately began to reshape the company's strategy and rebuild Merck's reputation. Working with other leaders (for example, chief scientist Peter Kim and former legal counsel Ken Frazier), Clark sought to unite Merck operationally by seeking "a more integrated approach." Clark is quoted as saying, "From the moment we begin talking about a particular drug franchise, I want researchers, marketers, and manufacturing people sitting in the same room."[2] Besides having a stronger purpose and developing a more integrated approach internally and through its partners, it also had to rebuild its reputation given the Vioxx disaster. It helped that by late 2007, of the 20 Vioxx cases that had gone to trial, Merck won 12 (although two of those verdicts have been set aside) and lost five. This winning record helped to restore investor confidence. Although Merck's problems may not be over, without the strategic leadership of CEO Richard Clark and other top executives, Merck's situation would likely be much worse.

In this chapter, we examine important strategic leadership actions: establishing the firm's vision and mission, developing a management team and planning for succession, managing the resource portfolio, building and supporting an entrepreneurial culture, promoting integrity and ethical behavior, and using effective organizational controls. These strategic leadership actions are displayed in Figure 2.1. We begin with a discussion of how vision and mission are used to direct the firm's future.

strategic leadership

developing a vision for the firm, designing strategic actions to achieve this vision, and empowering others to carry out those strategic actions

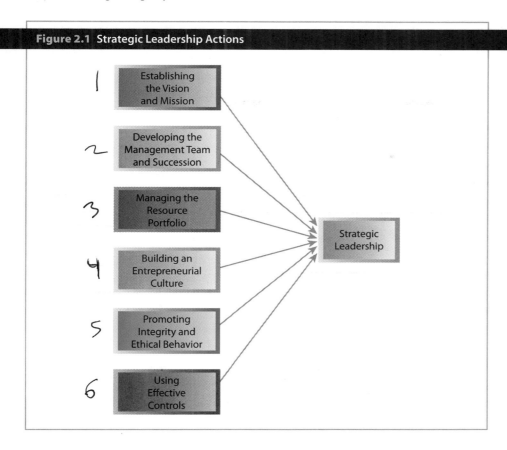

Figure 2.1 Strategic Leadership Actions

Establishing the Vision and Mission

Most strategic plans are designed for a 3- to 5-year time period, but a vision is usually targeted for a longer time, generally 10 to 20 years. As explained in Chapter 1, the *vision* contains at least two components—a statement describing the firm's DNA and the "picture" of the firm as it is hoped to exist in a future time period. The second part of the vision is *mission,* which defines the firm's core intent and the business or businesses in which it intends to operate. The mission flows from the vision and compared to the vision is more concrete in nature.

Visions can differ greatly across firms depending on the strategic leaders' intentions. For example, Steven Jobs, CEO of Apple, continues to develop visions of new products and markets. He developed not only Apple, but also Pixar—an extremely successful animation company that teamed with Disney to make the movie *Finding Nemo*. He created the Mac revolution with the Apple Macintosh computer; reshaped the music industry with Apple's iPod and iTunes online music venture; and more recently introduced the iPhone and Apple TV Take Two, a revamped version of the company's living-room media server. These new products are part of Jobs's vision to dramatically change the computer, music, cell phone, and media industries.[3]

Other firms have simpler visions even though they still may be difficult to achieve. For example, some firms may envision being among the most admired firms for their performance and effective management. A number of organizations now rank firms on a regular basis. For example, *Fortune* publishes a list of the world's most admired companies based on an annual survey; the top 20 firms for 2005, 2006, and 2007 are shown in Table 2.1. Although *Fortune*'s ranking includes only U.S. firms, the ranks change over time as some firm's strategies fall out of favor or strategic leaders make errors of strategic judgment. For example, Dell has been having a hard time relative to competitors such as Hewlett-Packard. Similarly, Wal-Mart's reputation has declined as it finds itself on the negative side

Table 2.1 *Fortune*'s Most Admired Companies Ranking

2008	2007	2006
1. Apple	1. General Electric	1. General Electric
2. Berkshire Hathaway	2. Starbucks	2. FedEx
3. General Electric	3. Toyota Motor	3. Southwest Airlines
4. Google	4. Berkshire Hathaway	4. Procter & Gamble
5. Toyota	5. Southwest Airlines	5. Starbucks
6. Starbucks	6. FedEx	6. Johnson & Johnson
7. FedEx	7. Apple	7. Berkshire Hathaway
8. Procter & Gamble	8. Google	8. Dell
9. Johnson & Johnson	9. Johnson & Johnson	9. Toyota Motor
10. Goldman Sachs Group	10. Procter & Gamble	10. Microsoft
11. Target	11. Goldman Sachs Group	11. Apple Computer
12. Southwest Airlines	12. Microsoft	12. Wal-Mart Stores
13. American Express	13. Target	13. United Parcel Service
14. BMW	14. 3M	13. Home Depot
15. Costco Wholesale	15. Nordstrom	15. PepsiCo
16. Microsoft	16. United Parcel Service	15. Costco Wholesale
17. United Parcel Service	17. American Express	17. American Express
18. Cisco Systems	18. Costco Wholesale	18. Goldman Sachs Group
19. 3M	19. PepsiCo	19. International Business Machines
20. Nordstrom	20. Wal-Mart Stores	20. 3M

Source: A. Fisher, 2008, America's most admired companies, *Fortune*, March 17, 65; A. Fisher, 2007, America's most admired companies, *Fortune*, March 19, 88; A. Fisher & T. Demos, 2006, America's most admired companies, *Fortune*, March 6, 65.

of much media attention. On the other hand, General Electric has been able to maintain a strong reputation, most likely due to strong strategic leadership.

An effective strategic leader not only can develop a vision of the future, but also can inspire stakeholders to commit to achieving it. It is especially important for the leader to gain the support of the company's shareholders and employees. If the shareholders do not support the vision, they may pressure the board of directors to change it or find new strategic leaders. Similarly, employee commitment to the vision is needed because they must help implement the strategy designed to achieve the vision. Consider the case of Porsche. Company officials believe that they have a clear strategy in place to develop a group of new models through 2012. The firm's vision entails growth and maintenance of its strong brand image by introducing these new products. More specifically, CEO Wendelin Wiedeking has an "emphasis on turning out high performance cars that are as durable as Japanese sedans."[4] This vision has helped establish Porsche's brand as the number one rank in J.D. Power & Associates' survey of initial quality in the automobile industry. Wiedeking has also maintained a Japanese-like focus on reducing costs such that Porsche cars have the "performance of an exotic car but the reliability of a Honda." In 2009, Porsche plans to introduce a new four-door coupe, the Panamera. To make sure that the new model meets the standards of its vision and image, marketers and engineers communicate almost daily about quality, seeking to make sure that even minor problems are ironed out before the company starts delivery.

As we mentioned earlier, and as exemplified by Porsche, strategic leaders often use their team of managers as well as others in the firm to help make major decisions, especially to define and implement a vision for the firm. This team also helps formulate the firm's strategy. Next, we examine the teams of managers that strategic leaders use in the decision process.

Developing the Top Management Team and Succession

Top Management Team

Because of the complexity of their roles, most strategic leaders form teams to help them complete their work. A **top management team** is the group of managers charged with the responsibility to develop and implement the firm's strategies. Generally, the top management team is composed of officers of the company with the title of vice president and higher.[5]

Typically, when people select individuals for a team to work with, they prefer to choose people who think like them and are more likely to agree with them. Although such a team can facilitate making fast decisions (because members of the team more easily agree), these teams are more prone to making mistakes. A team of people with similar backgrounds (a *homogeneous team*) may achieve a quick consensus about issues but may lack sufficient knowledge and information needed to make an effective decision. Additionally, because they "think alike," they may overlook important issues and make errors in judgment. Therefore, to be most effective, strategic leaders need a management team composed of members who see and think differently. The team members may have different types of education (such as engineering, chemistry, and business) or varying amounts and types of experience (working in different functional areas, companies, or industries). We refer to this type of group as a *heterogeneous team*. A heterogeneous team is likely to take more time to make decisions but also likely to make better decisions. However, such teams may hinder strategic expansion if they have problems relating socially to one another.[6]

Historically, Nissan included only Japanese employees in its management teams. However, in 2000, it was nearly bankrupt when Carlos Ghosn took over as CEO of the Japanese-centered company. Ghosn was born in Brazil; reared in Lebanon; and attended school in Paris, France. As such, he had a broad understanding of global issues and was able to help Nissan recover dramatically. He also was promoted to be the CEO of Renault, which has a joint venture with Nissan. Part of Ghosn's success at Nissan was due to the diversity of the management team that he brought in to help revive Nissan. Although Nissan subsequently stumbled, it has had recent successes with the subcompact Versa. In the future, with his diverse management team, he seeks to put an electric car on the road by 2011 and eventually partner with a Detroit car maker through an auto alliance with Renault and/or Nissan. But even though he is as popular as a rock star at industry events, he won't succeed as a one-person team. So he needs to continue to develop his top management team.[7]

Management Succession

In addition to forming the management team, strategic leaders must develop people who can succeed them. In fact, having people with skills to take over a job when needed is important to a firm's success. Some companies use sophisticated leadership screening systems to select people with the skills needed to perform well as a strategic leader.[8] The people selected then normally participate in an intensive management development program to further hone their leadership skills. The "ten-step talent" management development program at General Electric (GE) is considered one of the most effective programs for developing strategic leaders. Because of the quality of its programs, General Electric "is famous for developing leaders who are dedicated to turning imaginative ideas into leading products and services."[9]

Obviously, a change in CEO is a critical succession event in firms. The effects of CEO succession can be different based on whether the new CEO is from inside or outside the firm. The majority of CEO successions are from the inside, with a person groomed for the position by the former CEO or the board of directors. "Hiring from the inside" motivates employees because they believe that they have opportunities to receive promotions and more challenging jobs if they perform well. A recent inside CEO succession was announced at PepsiCo. Having worked for PepsiCo since 1994, Indra Nooyi proved herself worthy to the board and was

top management team

the group of managers charged with the responsibility to develop and implement the firm's strategies

© Sean Gallup/Getty Images

nominated and promoted to CEO in late 2006. She had served as a CFO and helped integrate the acquisition of Quaker Oats and the Gatorade brands.[10]

Most new CEOs selected for the job in an inside succession are unlikely to change in any drastic way the strategies designed under the leadership of the former CEO.[11] However, when the firm is performing poorly, it is more common to select an outside successor.

When new CEOs are chosen from outside the organization, the board often does so with the desire to change the firm's strategies. A change in strategies may be desired because the firm is performing poorly or because opportunities and threats in the competitive landscape require adjustments to avoid performing poorly in the future.[12] For example, Lou Gerstner helped to provide significant change at IBM when he was recruited from a consumer goods firm to become CEO of IBM. Gerstner transformed IBM into a successful performer again with a major change in its strategy.[13] Under Gerstner, IBM moved from a strategy based on selling separate pieces of hardware to a strategy calling for the firm to emphasize its service solutions and consulting services.

At times, it is more difficult to determine whether a succession is from the inside or outside. For example, in 2008, John Donahoe was selected to be the new CEO of eBay Inc. to replace Meg Whitman who planned to retire. Donahoe was recruited in 2005 to become the president of eBay's main auction business unit. He was a managing partner of Bain Consulting Company and thus came to eBay as an outsider. However, he is considered an insider given that he has been managing the core auction business for several years. Thus, it is hard to tell at times whether a successor is an insider or an outsider.[14] Interestingly, research shows that companies perform significantly better when they appoint insiders to the job of CEO. However, this research also suggests that many companies do not have succession plans; as such, when it comes time to find a new CEO, many firms turn to outsiders.

Of course as already noted, both insiders and outsiders have strengths and weaknesses depending on the conditions of the firm. Nonetheless, utilizing a strong succession plan and developing a strong set of training programs for managers firms can develop internal candidates who have a strong outside perspective. These executives in training can spend much of their time away from the main operations of the organization, that is, away from headquarters and working with new businesses that are different from the dominant business. They can be appointed CEOs of these business units and thus have the opportunity to manage the whole business. They can also be mentored to preserve their outside perspective and learn how to turn their new ideas into successful businesses that are protected from the dominant culture in the organization. Ultimately they can be CEOs who have an understanding of the inside approach to management, but also have the ability to transform the dominant organization in new ways should this be required.[15]

As discussed next, managing the firm's resource portfolio is another critical component of strategic leadership.

Managing the Resource Portfolio

Resources are the basis for a firm's competitive advantages and strategies (see Chapter 4). Even though we often think of tangible resources such as buildings, manufacturing plants, offices, machinery, and computers as being important,

[handwritten margin note: - have succession plan / develop training program]

intangible resources may be more important. Indeed, recent estimates suggest that as much as 75 percent of a firm's value may be contained in its intangible resources.[16] Intangible resources include human capital, social capital, and organizational capital (such as the organizational culture). Additionally, financial capital is a critically important resource.

Intellectual property can be an especially valuable intangible resource in high-technology companies. For example, TiVo, a company that popularized digital video recorders (DVRs), lost much of its value when more generic DVRs were produced and undercut its success. However, because TiVo was a first mover in this market of 20 million users, the Patent and Trademark Office recognizes TiVo's patent on "time-warp" technology, which allows users to record one program while watching another. Because TiVo sees itself as a technology company, it has been creating partnerships and licenses with firms such as NBC Universal and cable companies such as Comcast and Cox that pay a premium to download TiVo's software on their generic DVRs. Previously, where others had been copying its technology, TiVo filed lawsuits in order to protect its intellectual property. For instance it filed a suit against EchoStar Communications, a satellite television producer. TiVo continues to move from a focus on hardware to an increased emphasis on software and processing advertising data as part of its strategy to facilitate advertising media expenditures through DVR systems. Additionally, it is seeking to help the television industry move to a media-on-demand strategy that will allow content delivery directly to people's television sets and to their PCs.[17]

A firm's intellectual property such as TiVo's is developed by its human capital. **Human capital** includes the knowledge and skills of those working for the firm. Employees' knowledge and skills are critical for all organizations. According to Ed Breen, CEO of Tyco International Ltd., "Companies compete with their brains as well as their brawn. Organizations today must not only outgun and outhustle competitors, they must also outthink them. Companies win with ideas."[18] To outthink competitors, a firm must depend on the knowledge of its workforce (managers and nonmanagerial employees) and continuously invest in developing their knowledge and skills. Such organizations are focused on learning. Knowledge can be acquired in training programs or through experience on the job. Learning from failure is a quality that leaders will experience repeatedly. The difference between some people and others is that some "fail better than others." In other words, it is not whether you fail but how you fail and what you learn from it that really matters.[19] It is the strategic leader's responsibility to help the firm learn faster and persevere better than others when mistakes are made.

Effective strategic leaders base their strategies on the organization's human capital.[20] They do so because the human capital in the organization must have the skills and motivation needed to implement chosen strategies. As such, leaders must help develop skills throughout the firm's workforce, motivate employees to use their skills when working to implement strategies, and reward them for doing so.[21] Steven K. Green, chairperson of the board of directors of the large global bank HSBC, suggests, "If we don't create the proper climate internally and live up to our brand name, we won't be able to achieve our strategic objective—managing for corporate growth."[22]

Another important resource is social capital. **Social capital** includes all internal and external relationships that help the firm provide value to customers and ultimately to its other stakeholders. *Internal social capital* refers to the relationships among people working inside the firm. These relationships help each organizational unit effectively complete its work while contributing to the overall value of the firm's human capital. "Most companies continue to assume that innovation comes from that individual genius, or best sequestered teams that vanish from sight and then return with big ideas, but the truth is most innovations are created through networks—groups of people working in concert."[23]

External social capital refers to relationships between those working within a firm and others (individuals and organizations) outside the firm. Such relationships

human capital

includes the knowledge and skills of those working for the firm

social capital

includes all internal and external relationships that help the firm provide value to customers and ultimately to its other stakeholders

*Strong external relations
broader resource pool*

are essential because they provide access to needed resources. Few firms have all of the resources they need. Furthermore, most firms cannot do everything well. It may be better to outsource some activities to partner companies who can perform those activities exceptionally well, thereby increasing the quality of the focal firm's ability to produce products. External social capital can also help firms enter new markets. New companies may seek the financial support and expertise of venture capitalists, whereas more established companies often develop alliances with reliable suppliers or joint ventures with highly competent partners. In a sense, strategic leaders serve as key points of effective linkages for their firm in a network of relationships with other organizations. Some relationships involve strong ties where trust exists between the parties and reciprocity is expected, whereas other relationships represent weaker ties that serve more informational roles and allow strategic leaders to stay on top of the latest developments—even outside their industry—that may affect their firm (such as technology developments). So both strong and weak ties are important in strategic leaders' networks.[24]

The most effective social capital occurs when partners trust each other (strong ties). Effective strategic leaders have well-developed relational skills that help them establish trusting relationships with others inside and outside the organization. Andrea Jung, CEO of Avon Products, suggests that compassion is one of the key characteristics of effective leaders. As such, she believes that leaders should treat people fairly, with dignity and respect. In so doing, leaders are leading with their heart as well as their head.[25] One analysts suggested that leaders of today such as Jung need "the essential qualities of what we now call a Cross-Enterprise Leader—a leader adept at building, fostering and influencing a complex web of relationships across all levels—from employees, partners and suppliers to customers, citizens, and even competitors."[26]

Other resources such as financial capital are also important. In fact, firms with strong human capital and social capital are more likely to build a good base of financial capital.[27] Some also believe that an organization's culture can be a valuable resource. We discuss that topic next.

Building an Entrepreneurial Culture

Strategic leaders are concerned about the organization's culture because it can have major effects on employees' actions. An organizational culture is based on the core values of an organization, largely espoused by its leaders. When these values support opportunities to innovate, an entrepreneurial culture may develop. An **entrepreneurial culture** encourages employees to identify and exploit new opportunities. It encourages creativity and risk taking but also tolerates failure. Championing innovation is rewarded in this type of culture.[28] Building an entrepreneurial culture is of particular importance to strategic leaders.

Because of the pressure to be innovative yet profitable, many leaders try to focus their firm's innovation to increase the chances of success. For example, as explained in Understanding Strategy: Learning from Success, General Mills recently focused on innovative activities designed to provide foods that are healthier and products that meet government agency health standards.[29] As this example illustrates, such an approach has improved its new product growth rates and profitability.

Innovation is important in high-technology industries such as computers and in creative industries such as music and film animation. Steve Jobs is an appropriate strategic leader for Apple with his emphasis on creativity and innovation. However, 3M operates in several different industries with lower technology, such as adhesives (i.e., Scotch tape), traffic signs, and sandpaper. Yet the firm has been a pioneer, being the first to introduce products in its markets, such as the Post-it note. Therefore, an entrepreneurial culture is important in both firms.

entrepreneurial culture

encourages employees to identify and exploit new opportunities

General Mills Creates Wealth with a Focus on Healthier Products

In 2007, Kendall Powell replaced Steve Sanger as the CEO at General Mills. Powell has had a 28-year career at General Mills. As such, his promotion is seen as an inside succession. He managed the Yoplait Yogurt and Big G cereal divisions. He was also the chief executive for Cereal Partners Worldwide, a Switzerland-based joint venture with Nestle SA. His most recent position was president and chief operating officer (COO), to which he was appointed in June 2006. Powell's appointment is part of the company's long-time succession plan.

In his most recent role as COO, he worked at developing the company's long-term growth strategies, which included "broadening the channels through which the company sells its products, expanding overseas, and bringing more innovation to the business." For instance, half of its sales in Cascadian Farm and Muir Glen, which are organic brands, were sold through natural and organic specialty stores such as Whole Foods Market. Additionally, a new line of Pillsbury miniature desserts will be sold in convenience stores. General Mills has also been expanding internationally by reaching out to new consumers, such as with the Chinese brand Wanchai Ferry. The company has also been pushing to develop new innovative products such as Fizzix, a carbonated yogurt.

Probably one of the biggest changes has been its success in pursuing healthier product lines. Susan Crockett, who runs the company's Bell Institute of Health and Nutrition, an internal group of scientists who study and conduct health research, has been pushing the company to pursue healthier products. In this effort, the division heads, as well as Sanger and Powell, have found that they had to compensate managers for meeting more healthy product goals. The consumer trend in the food industry is toward healthier packaged food products. Also, Kellogg's, Kraft Foods, Campbell Soup Company, and Sara Lee have all been pushed by regulators and consumer advocates to increase nutrition in their products.

© Susan Van Etten

At General Mills, the company found that its fastest-growing sales were in products that carried some type of U.S. Food and Drug Administration approval health claim. In the mid-1990s, General Mills "established a goal of having its products preferred by 60 percent of consumers in market tests." In 2004, it established an additional goal that 20 percent of its sales should include products that "meet certain nutritional standards." A measurable goal was set such that divisions could meet these objectives by "a 10 percent reduction in fat, sugar, or sodium content; a 10 percent increase in healthful ingredients, including vitamins and fiber; or by meeting FDA guidelines that allow the product to carry labels such as 'reduced sodium' or 'lower fat.' " Interestingly, the company met its goals ahead of schedule and in 2006, the top executives set another standard that 20 percent more of its sales should meet the more stringent healthful product standards by 2010. Executives attribute the progress toward these healthy goals to linking 25 percent of the annual bonuses to these health and wellness objectives.

For example, to get children to eat more vegetables, the Green Giant brand spent two years on focused research with parents and developed a product that included "10 ounces of vegetables" in small packages. Although it costs more money to put the vegetables into individual microwavable trays, the company was convinced by the consumer research it carried out to create a "just for one" advertising campaign. Although it experienced some failures with this innovative approach, 34 percent of its products now meet its new standards for healthier products. Overall, the company reformulated more than 200 products and introduced at least 100 new ones. Even more important, significant firm sales growth and profits have come from these new lines.

Sources: J. Jargon, 2008, General Mills sees wealth via health: New recipe for profit, sales growth: More whole grains, less salt, fat, *Wall Street Journal*, February 25, A9; J. Jargon, 2007, General Mills taps Powell as next CEO: Successor to Steve Sanger is seeing continual plans for long-term growth, *Wall Street Journal*, September 25, B8; J. Birchall, 2007, General Mills's chief executive to bow out, *Financial Times*, September 25, 22.

The preceding discussions suggest the importance of innovation and strategic leadership. Even though the type and focus of innovation may vary, it is important in nearly all industries. As a result, building an entrepreneurial culture is a vital task for strategic leaders. Strategic leaders also must demonstrate ethical behavior. Next, we discuss the importance of integrity and ethical behavior for strategic leaders.

Promoting Integrity and Ethical Behavior

Strategic leaders not only develop standards for behavior among employees, but also serve as role models in meeting and exceeding those standards. Even though quality of performance is an important criterion, showing integrity and behaving ethically are also essential. So strategic leaders should determine the boundaries of acceptable behavior; establish the tone for organizational actions; and ensure that ethical behaviors are expected, praised, and rewarded. Lack of integrity and unethical behavior can be serious and extremely costly for a firm and for the person lacking integrity and behaving unethically. In fact, extraordinary unethical behavior can even lead to a firm's demise; Enron is a well-known example.

Recently, cases in which strategic leaders acted opportunistically in managing their firms have been a major concern. Acting opportunistically means that managers are making decisions that are in their own best interests rather than in the firms' best interests. Enron and Tyco are examples of what happens when leaders allow opportunistic behavior.

Because of opportunistic behavior in a number of companies, significant emphasis has been placed on how firms govern themselves (*corporate governance*). Corporate governance begins with the board of directors, whose members are responsible for overseeing managerial activities and approving (or disapproving) managerial decisions and actions. As illustrated in the opening Focusing on Strategy, the outcry from shareholders and the public in general has placed pressure on board members to be more diligent in examining managerial behavior. Legislation (such as Sarbanes-Oxley) passed in the United States requires greater managerial responsibility for the firm's activities and outcomes. Institutional owners in particular have pressured boards to enact better governance practices. For example, they generally want more independent outsiders than inside officers on the board. They believe that independent outside board members will be more objective and are less likely to agree with the CEO if he/she takes actions that appear not to be in the firm's best interests. In this way, managers' opportunistic actions can be curtailed.[30]

© Benoit Tessier/Reuters/Landov

related-party transactions

paying a person who has a relationship with the firm extra money for reasons other than his or her normal activities on the firm's behalf

One form of potential opportunism, **related-party transactions**, involves paying a person who has a relationship with the firm extra money for reasons other than his or her normal activities on the firm's behalf. For example, Apple CEO Steve Jobs was reimbursed $1.2 million for costs he incurred while using his personal jet on company business. Two directors for Ford Motor Company, William Clay Ford and Edsel Ford, receive hundreds of thousands of dollars in consulting fees in addition to their compensation for serving as directors. Many of these transactions are legitimate, but some can be for questionable purposes as well. The Securities and Exchange Commission has started to carefully scrutinize related-party deals because of the opportunity for unethical behavior. Related-party deals were curtailed in the United States by Sarbanes-Oxley.[31]

Often worse than opportunistic actions by managers are fraudulent and other unlawful activities in which managers and companies' representatives engage. As an example, Jerome Kerviel was a night trader who pursued secret deals at the French Bank, Societe Generale, which cost the company

$7 billion. Kerviel was adept at covering his tracks and was able to slip through several of the banks security firewalls. Even more critical is that many of his coworkers thought that there was something wrong, but none of them spoke to a manager about their concerns. A system to detect these problems is essential, but it functions best when individuals are encouraged to report such activities in order to prevent fraudulent behavior.[32]

Only leaders who demonstrate integrity and values respected by all constituents of the company will be able to sustain effective outcomes over time. Those who engage in unethical or unlawful activities may go unrecognized or undetected for a time, but eventually they will fail. People working under the leader often demonstrate the same values in their actions that are evident in the leader's behavior. Thus, if the leader engages in unethical activities, the followers are likely to do the same. As a consequence, the leader will suffer from the poor performance that results from his/her own and others' unethical behaviors. However, when the leader displays integrity and strong positive ethical values, the firm's performance will be enhanced over time because the followers will do the same.[33] Opportunism and unethical activities evident in several companies in recent times clearly show the importance of having effective control systems, which are discussed next.

Using Effective Controls

Controls are necessary to ensure that standards are met and that employees do not misuse the firm's resources. Control failures are evident in such dismal outcomes as exemplified by Enron and Tyco. Unfortunately, in both of these cases, the strategic leaders with responsibility for implementing the controls violated them, and the weak governance in both firms was unable to identify and correct the problems until they became excessive and external entities expressed concern about them. However, the potential value of controls goes beyond preventing fraud and managerial opportunism. Properly formed and used controls guide managerial decisions, including strategic decisions. Effective strategic leaders ensure that their firms create and use both financial controls and strategic controls as guides in the strategic management process.

Financial controls focus on shorter-term financial outcomes. These controls help the firm stay on the right path in terms of generating sales revenue, maintaining expenses within reason, and remaining financially solvent. Of course, a prime reason for financial controls is to generate an adequate profit. However, if financial controls are overly emphasized to increase current profits, managers are likely to limit their expenditures more than is necessary. Too many expense reductions in certain categories (such as R&D) can damage the firm's ability to perform successfully in the future. Money spent on R&D helps the firm develop products that customers will want to buy.

Alternatively, **strategic controls** focus on the content of strategic actions rather than on their outcomes. Strategic controls are best employed under conditions of uncertainty. For example, a firm may employ the correct strategy but the financial results may be poor because of a recession or unexpected natural disasters or political actions (such as the 9/11 terrorist attacks). To use strategic controls, the strategic leader or board must have a good understanding of the industry and markets in which the firm or its units operate in order to evaluate the accuracy of the strategy. Using strategic controls encourages managers to adopt longer-term strategies and to take acceptable risks while maintaining the firm's profitability in the current time period. As Understanding Strategy: Learning from Failure indicates, firms without good strategic controls often have significant growth stalls. For example, Dell and Starbucks recently brought back their former CEO's Michael Dell and Howard Schultz, respectively, to reverse problems of slow growth and execution. Four major reasons that pertain to strategic controls are given as reasons for such growth stalls.

financial controls

focus on shorter-term financial outcomes

strategic controls

focus on the content of strategic actions rather than on their outcomes

Understanding Why Growth Stalls and What to Do About It

Recently, two firms that were experiencing stalled growth brought back the former CEO to help save the company. Howard Schultz and Michael Dell were instituted as CEOs at Starbucks and Dell, respectively. In the past, Charles Schwab at Charles Schwab, Inc., Steve Jobs at Apple, and Eli Calloway at Calloway Golf were recruited back to help reestablish a growth trajectory in these firms. Although they may not be the only person in a firm who can solve the problem, former CEOs do help, as the history of these firms seems to indicate.

However, a more important question is "What occurred in these firms that led to the stall in growth and success?" Usually growth stalls because a firm has difficulties in

© Susan Van Etten

perceiving problems through its strategic and financial control systems. Recent research analyzed points of problems for more than 500 firms that had stalls in their track record of growth. By far, the most important category of factors was labeled "Premium-position captivity: The inability of the firm to respond effectively to new, low-cost competitive challenges or to a significant shift in consumer valuation of product features." In other words, because a firm is captivated by its long history of success, it may find it difficult to evolve relative to external market changes. For instance, Eastman Kodak found it difficult to change to a digital imaging strategy given its strong base of competence and resources invested in film imaging through a chemical base. Levi Strauss faltered in the jean segment, being unable to recognize the threat of the rise of house brand and designer brand jeans.

The second most frequent cause for stalled growth is the breakdown of innovation management systems. At 3M, the company was so focused on creating new products for new strategies that it was unable to execute a strong manufacturing set of competencies and process innovations when it was forced to compete on price. Thus, at times, it is not only the amount of R&D

spending, but also the focus of the R&D spending. 3M needed to put more focus on process innovations.

A third major cause is premature abandonment of a core product or strategy. An interesting example is the failure of Kmart, which at one point did have a strong position in large-box, low-price retailing. Kmart pursued a strategy of acquisition in a number of disparate businesses including PayLess Drug Stores, The Sports Authority, and Office Max. Alternatively, Wal-Mart was investing significantly in its logistical capabilities. As such, Wal-Mart was able to gain a significant advantage in its inbound logistics costing and inventory management, which enabled it to have a better pricing capacity in the discount retailing segment compared to Kmart.

Another category that affects growth is human resource talent. When the human resource talent falls short, companies suffer. Hitachi had a narrow set of functional managers within its strong engineering culture. However, over time, more top executives with MBAs and other functional backgrounds such as marketing were needed as market changes in telecommunication and information system sectors became important. Thus, the top management team did not have the capabilities required to manage in a different market.

In order to meet these challenges, strong strategic controls as well as financial controls are necessary. But flexibility and a balanced approach in all areas are necessary to meet a more dynamic environment that will continuously challenge strategic leaders.

Sources: J. Adamy, 2008, Starbucks shares rise as CEO returns, *Wall Street Journal*, January 9, A12; J. Birchall, 2008, Starbucks chief plans revamp to restore "coffee authority," *Financial Times*, January 31, 21; H. Greenberg, 2008, Why investors should applaud a CEO's encore performance, *Wall Street Journal*, January 12–13, B3; M. S. Olson, D. van Bever, & S. Verry, 2008, When growth stalls, *Harvard Business Review*, 86(3): 50–61; D. Sewer, 2008, Starbucks fix, *Fortune*, February 4, 14; 2008, Come back kids and the risks of a repeat performance, *Financial Times*, January 16, 14.

The most effective system of controls is balanced using strategic *and* financial controls as illustrated. Controlling financial outcomes is important while simultaneously looking to the longer term and evaluating the content of the strategies used. To obtain the desired balance in control systems, many firms use a **balanced scorecard,**[34] which provides a framework for evaluating the simultaneous use of financial controls and strategic controls.

A balanced scorecard focuses on four areas—*financial* (profit, growth, and shareholder risk), *customers* (value received from the firm's products), *internal business processes* (asset utilization, inventory turnover), and *learning and growth* (a culture that supports innovation and change). In addition to helping implement a balanced control system, the balanced scorecard allows leaders to view the firm from the eyes of stakeholders such as shareholders, customers, and employees. The company's management system is the important link between strategy and operational execution. The company must necessarily begin with a strategic statement and then translate this statement into specific objectives and initiatives that serve as a guide for all employees, especially top management. The plan should map out operations and execution as well as the resources necessary to achieve the objectives. Through the control systems implemented, managers and employees monitor and learn from the strategy performance results and execution of the plan. Periodic assessment and updating of the strategic plan are necessary as emerging strategies show potential and necessitate adaptation and change. Thus, continuous strategic assessment and analysis are required to refine the vision and mission of the corporation that will guide the changes in strategy and execution.[35]

balanced scorecard

provides a framework for evaluating the simultaneous use of financial controls and strategic controls

SUMMARY

The primary purpose of this chapter is to explain strategic leadership and emphasize its value to an organization. In doing so, we examined the following topics:

- **Strategic leadership** involves developing a vision for the firm, designing strategic actions to achieve this vision, and empowering others to carry out those strategic actions. Establishing the firm's vision (and mission), developing a management team and planning for succession, managing the resource portfolio, building and supporting an entrepreneurial culture, promoting integrity and ethical behavior, and using effective organizational controls are the actions of strategic leadership.
- Strategic leaders, those practicing strategic leadership, develop a firm's vision and mission. The vision contains at least two components—a statement describing the firm's DNA and the "picture" of the firm as it is hoped to exist in the future. The mission of the firm focuses on the markets it serves and the goods and services it provides and defines the firm's core intent and the business or businesses in which it intends to operate.
- A **top management team** is the group of managers responsible for developing and implementing the firm's strategies. A heterogeneous team usually develops more-effective strategies than a homogeneous team because it holds a greater diversity of knowledge, considers more issues, and evaluates more alternatives.
- Managerial succession is important for the maintenance of the firm's health. Individuals should be developed and prepared to undertake managerial roles throughout the firm's hierarchy.
- **Human capital** includes the knowledge and skills of those working for the firm. Employees' knowledge and skills are an important

resource to all organizations. Another important resource is social capital. **Social capital** includes all internal and external relationships that help the organization provide value to customers and ultimately to its other stakeholders. Strategic leaders must help develop the skills within the firm's workforce, motivate employees to use those skills to implement strategies, and reward them when they successfully use their skills.

- Strategic leaders shape an organization's culture. In the current competitive environment, all firms need to be innovative to remain competitive. Therefore, building an entrepreneurial culture is of particular importance to strategic leaders. An **entrepreneurial culture** encourages employees to identify and exploit new opportunities. It encourages creativity and risk taking and tolerates failures as a result.
- Strategic leaders develop standards for behavior among employees and serve as role models for meeting those standards. Integrity and ethical behavior are essential in today's business environment. Lack of integrity and unethical behavior can be serious and highly costly—to the firm and to individuals lacking integrity and behaving unethically. Ethical strategic leaders guard against managerial opportunism and fraudulent actions.
- Effective controls guide managerial decisions, including strategic decisions. **Financial controls** focus on shorter-term financial outcomes, whereas **strategic controls** focus on the content of the strategic actions rather than their outcomes. An effective control system balances the use of financial controls and strategic controls. The **balanced scorecard** approach is a useful technique that can help balance these two types of control.

KEY TERMS

balanced scorecard, 35
entrepreneurial culture, 30
financial controls, 33

human capital, 29
related-party transactions, 32
social capital, 29

strategic controls, 33
strategic leadership, 24
top management team, 27

DISCUSSION QUESTIONS

1. What is strategic leadership? Describe the major actions involved in strategic leadership.
2. How do a vision and a mission create value for a company?
3. What is a top management team? Why does a heterogeneous top management team usually formulate more effective strategies?
4. Why is it important to develop managers for succession to other managerial jobs?

5. What do the terms *human capital* and *social capital* mean? What is the importance of human capital and social capital to a firm?
6. How can a strategic leader foster an entrepreneurial culture, and why is such a culture valuable to a firm?
7. Why are managerial integrity and ethical behavior important to a firm?
8. Why should strategic leaders develop a control system that balances strategic controls and financial controls?

STRATEGY TOOLBOX

Introduction

Strategic management is the study of how business leaders take their organizations to new heights. A key player in this process is the Chief Executive Officer (CEO). Chapter 2 provides the foundation for the strategic analysis the CEO must perform. With that in mind, we offer for the Strategy Toolbox a "CEO Strategy Checklist" for completion of this awesome responsibility.

"CEO Strategy Checklist"

Key Question	Assessment
Develop—Do we have a strategy that leads to differentiation in the market?	Low – Medium – High
Understand—Could our employees articulate our mission and vision?	Low – Medium – High
Accept—Do our employees believe in our organizational strategy?	Low – Medium – High
Implement—Are our employees making decisions consistent with our strategies?	Low – Medium – High
Modify—Do we have adequate feedback mechanisms to track progress?	Low – Medium – High

Was There Strategic Leadership Failure at Boeing?

Boeing has historically been a global leader in manufacturing commercial airplanes. However, in 2001, Airbus had more orders than Boeing for the first time in their competitive history. In 2006, however, Boeing regained its supremacy with 1,044 versus 790 orders for commercial aircraft. The main turnaround in this battle for competitor orders has been most visible in the super jumbo category with Airbus's A380 versus Boeing's 787 Dreamliner. Boeing's 787 Dreamliner design focused on long-range efficient flight, capable of transporting 250 passengers, whereas Airbus's strategy focused on long-haul flights with the A380 offering 550-plus seats. In their diverging strategies, Airbus focused on flying to larger airports that use the hub-and-spoke system, whereas Boeing concentrated more on a point-to-point system in which smaller airports are more abundant. In reality, the Airbus A380 aircraft, because of its size and weight, is currently able to land at only about 35 airports. The Boeing aircraft, on the other hand, can land at many more airports around the world and the number is growing in emerging economies such as Eastern Europe where smaller airports desire international connections.

Airbus won the competitor battle that occurred between 2001 and 2005 because it focused on the midsized market as well, using the A320 strategy, which competes with Boeing's 737 and 757 aircraft. The A320 was more efficient than the aircraft used by Boeing, and Boeing did not respond to customer demands to create new, efficient aircraft. In fact, it had slowed its innovation process in regard to new models. Besides the lack of new models, the commercial aircraft business was sluggish; new orders ebbed significantly due to the complications associated with the terrorist attacks and the subsequent recession. It was a bleak time for Boeing relative to Airbus.

One analyst described Boeing's problems as a flawed strategy, lax controls, a weak board, and shortcomings in leadership. Philip Condit ascended to CEO in 1996 and became board chairperson in 1997. His time as CEO and board chair was characterized by a number of mergers and acquisitions as well as a struggle with increasing competition with Airbus. Condit was forced to resign in 2003 amidst corruption charges involving his freezing of a contract with the U.S. Air Force. Condit was described as a brilliant engineer with excellent problem-solving skills and a capability to envision elegant designs. Such good decision-making skills and creativity are valuable in a formal leadership role. However, as CEO, Condit did not seem to display those skills.

Some described Condit as indecisive and isolated from Boeing's operations. Condit and his management team failed to understand the determination of the firm's major competitor, Airbus, which by 2003, for the first time ever, had more orders for aircraft than Boeing. Condit and his team also had lapses in judgment, and their actions raised questions of unethical actions. For example, controversial allegations were made about inappropriate contact with Pentagon officials to obtain knowledge about a lower Airbus bid on a contract. In turn, the official providing the information was allegedly offered a job at Boeing. Additionally, the Pentagon placed an indefinite ban on bids by Boeing for military satellite launches because the company possessed documents about rival Lockheed's activities, helping Boeing win contracts.

Harry Stonecipher was the president and COO until 2003, when he filled the shoes of recently resigned Philip Condit as CEO. In 2005, however, Stonecipher resigned at the request of the board after news of a "consensual relationship" with a female board member (violating Boeing's Code of Conduct). The ethical lapses in governance and the defense contract business were especially harmful. In mid-2005, James McNerney was hired from 3M to be Boeing's CEO and to inject the firm with a fresh culture. The new top management team moved quickly to overcome the ethical problems and restore stakeholder confidence. Boeing now has an Ethics and Business Conduct section on its Web site. Included in this section is an Ethics Challenge that employees are encouraged to take.

The new top management team also decided to speed the development of the 787 Dreamliner. In making its decision to move ahead with the 787 Dreamliner versus a more jumbo aircraft comparable to the A380, Boeing made a more concerted effort in connecting and getting input from its airline customers, as well as the ultimate customers, the passengers. Overwhelmingly, the passengers in particular, and thereby the airlines, preferred smaller aircraft that would enable them to get to smaller airports quickly, without as many transfers on a point-to-point system. Additionally, Boeing followed up with the ultimate creditors, the leasing agents who fund airplanes for many airlines, and asked what they would prefer as far as risks were concerned. Again, the leasing agents preferred a smaller aircraft to reduce their risks in financing versus the large super jumbo A380. Boeing's orders for the 787 have been exceeding those for the Airbus A380.

Interestingly, much of the 787 will be produced through a large outsourcing program. Engineers in Everett, Washington, where Boeing is based, will in effect "snap together the parts" that are produced by "risk-sharing partners from Japan, Italy and elsewhere in the United States." This approach is made possible by a switch "to carbon-fibre reinforced plastic for large parts such as the fuselage and wings." The material creates an aircraft that is light and strong and will thereby improve fuel efficiency and cut maintenance costs associated with metal corrosion. "The plastic pieces are built in huge sections, baked in an oven, and shipped from partner plants for final assembly in Everett."

In pursuing this approach, Boeing sought to balance financial controls (to improve its performance today) with strategic controls (to develop innovative products and processes, associated with the 787 Dreamliner) in order to create improved success.

Sources: K. Done, 2008, Boeing bullish in spite of setbacks over Dreamliner, *Financial Times*, January 31, 17; D. Cameron, 2007, "Green" plastic airliner takes off: In the spotlight Boeing 787 Dreamliner, *Financial Times*, July 2, 32; G. Colvin, 2007, Boeing prepares for takeoff, *Fortune*, June 11, 133; C. Matlac & S. Holmes, 2007, Airbus revs up the engines, *BusinessWeek*, March 5, 41; J. Newhouse, 2007, Boeing versus Airbus: The Inside Story of the Greatest International Competition in Business, Toronto, Canada: Alfred A. Knoph; L. Wayne, 2007, A U.S. star turn for the jumbo of jets, *New York Times*, March 20, C1; D. Q. Wilber, 2007, Boeing's 2006 jet orders surpass Airbus, *Washington Post*, January 18, D03; M. Duffy, 2003, How Boeing got lost, *Time*, December 15: 49; S. Holmes, 2003, Boeing: What really happened, *BusinessWeek*, December 15: 33–38.

Questions

1. What are the strategic leadership failures in Boeing that you can identify?
2. Will the actions of Boeing's new top management team resolve the firm's problems? Why or why not?
3. If you were Boeing's CEO, what additional actions would you take to continue to improve the firm's position?

EXPERIENTIAL EXERCISES

Exercise One: Building an Entrepreneurial Culture

In the chapter, building an entrepreneurial culture, one of the important strategic leadership actions, was discussed. An entrepreneurial culture encourages employees to identify and exploit new opportunities, encourages creativity and risk taking, and tolerates failures.

In Small Groups

Each group should choose one of the following five firms. These firms were identified in a recent issue of *Fast Company* as the top five of the 50 most innovative companies in the world. Your group should investigate what the firm does to build an entrepreneurial culture.

- Google
- Apple
- Facebook
- General Electric
- Ideo

Answer the following questions:

1. Does the firm do what was suggested in the chapter? For example, does it encourage risk taking? Does it tolerate failures?
2. What are some examples of how the firm encourages employees to identify or exploit new opportunities? How does the firm encourage risk taking?
3. Does the firm have some other ways of building an entrepreneurial culture that are not discussed in the chapter?

Whole Class

The groups should then compare answers to the questions. What are the similarities and differences in how these innovative companies build an entrepreneurial culture?

Exercise Two: Codes of Ethics

Many types of organizations try to define expectations and deal with the behavior of their leaders, employees, agents, and perhaps even business partners by establishing codes of ethics. The content of codes can vary greatly and is often linked to the mission of the organization. Explore www.e-businessethics.com, especially the Ethics Links. Be prepared to discuss the prevalence and importance of ethics dialogues across various business, government, and professional organizations.

BIZ FLIX

Backdraft: Strategic Leadership

Watch the scene from the film *Backdraft* to see dramatic examples of the strategic leadership discussions in this chapter. Use the discussion questions that follow as guides to your viewing of the scene.

Two brothers follow their late father, a legendary Chicago firefighter, and join the department. Stephen "Bull" McCaffrey (Kurt Russell) joins first and rises to the rank of lieutenant. Younger brother Brian (William Baldwin) joins later and becomes a member of Bull's Company 17. Sibling rivalry tarnishes their work relationship, but they continue to fight Chicago fires successfully. Add a plot element about a mysterious arsonist, and you have the basis for an extraordinary film. The intense, unprecedented special effects give the viewer an unparalleled experience of what it is like to fight a fire. Chicago firefighters applauded the realism of the fire scenes.

The scene comes from the "Time to Move On" sequence that appears about 50 minutes into the film. A woman has told the firefighters that her baby is in the burning building. The film continues after this scene with many more dramatic moments in a Chicago firefighter's life.

What to Watch for and Ask Yourself

1. Does Stephen have a vision for how to fight the fire in the burning building? Does he design strategic actions to reach that vision?
2. Does Stephen empower Brian to help reach his vision for fighting the fire? Why or why not?
3. Risk is often part of strategic leadership. What risks does Stephen take? Does he appear to take excessive risks in trying to rescue the child from the fire?

ENDNOTES

1. L. Bassi & D. McMurrer, 2007, Maximizing your return on people, *Harvard Business Review*, 85(3): 115–23; E. F. Goldman, 2007, Strategic thinking at the top, *MIT Sloan Management Review*, 48(4): 75–81.
2. J. Simons, 2008, From scandal to stardom: How Merck healed itself, *Fortune*, February 18, 94–98.
3. S. Levy, 2008, Hot air from Apple, *Newsweek*, January 28, 61.
4. G. Edmondson, 2007, Pedal to the metal at Porsche: It boasts the speediest growth in the industry, *BusinessWeek*, September 3, 68.
5. A. M. L. Raes, U. Glunk, M. G. Heijltjes, & R. A. Roe, 2007, Top management team and middle managers, *Small Group Research*, 38: 360–386; I. Goll, R. Sambharya, & C. L. Tucci, 2001, Top management team composition, corporate ideology, and firm performance, *Management International Review*, 41(2): 109–129.
6. H. G. Barkema & O. Shvyrkov, 2007, Does top management team diversity promote or hamper foreign expansion? *Strategic Management Journal*, 28: 663–680; M. Jensen & E. Zajac, 2004, Corporate elites and corporate strategy: How demographic preferences and structural position shape the scope of the firm, *Strategic Management Journal*, 25: 507–524; L. Markoczy, 2001, Consensus formation during strategic change, *Strategic Management Journal*, 22: 1013–1031.
7. K. Naughton, 2007, A rock star's rebirth: Carlos Ghosn made history saving Nissan. Then the company stumbled. Now he is trying for a comeback, *Newsweek*, December 24, 50.
8. A. Karaevli, 2007, Performance consequences of new CEO "outsiderness": Moderating effects of pre- and post-succession contexts, *Strategic Management Journal*, 28: 681–706; W. Shen & A. Cannella, 2002, Revisiting the performance consequences of CEO succession: The impacts of successor type, post succession, senior executive turnover, and departing CEO tenure, *Academy of Management Journal*, 45: 717–734.
9. D. Ulrich & N. Smallwood, 2007, Building a leadership brand, *Harvard Business Review*, 85(7/8): 93–100.
10. B. Morris, 2008, The Pepsi challenge: Can this snack and soda giant go healthy? CEO Indra Nooyi says yes, but Cola wars and corn prices will test her leadership, *Fortune*, March 3, 55–64.
11. W. Shen & A. A. Cannella, 2003, Will succession planning increase shareholder wealth? Evidence from investor reactions to relay CEO successions, *Strategic Management Journal*, 24: 191–198.
12. L. Greiner, T. Cummings, & A. Bhambri, 2002, When new CEOs succeed and fail: 4-D theory of strategic transformation, *Organizational Dynamics*, 32: 1–16.
13. T. Foremski, 2004, Motorola's new boss aims for Zander-du, *Financial Times*, www.ft.com, May 9.
14. C. Holahan, 2008, eBay's new tough love CEO; John Donahoe will concentrate on winning back users, even at investor's expense, *BusinessWeek*, February 4, 58.
15. J. L. Bower, 2007, Solve the succession crisis by growing inside-outside leaders, *Harvard Business Review*, 85(11): 90–96.
16. G. Kristandl & N. Bontis, 2007, Constructing a definition for intangibles using the resource-based view of the firm, *Management Decision*, 45(9): 1510–1524; M. Reitzig, 2004, Strategic management of intellectual property, *MIT Sloan Management Review*, 45(3): 35–40.
17. N. Aspan, 2007, TiVo shifts to help companies it once threatened, *New York Times*, www.nytimes.com, December 10.
18. B. Breen, 2004, Hidden asset, *Fast Company*, March, 93.
19. S. Brown, 2008, Learning from failure, *Director*, February, 31; S. Finkelstein, 2003, *Why Smart Executives Fail: And What You Can Learn from Their Mistakes*, New York: Penguin Group.
20. B. A. Ready & J. A. Conger, 2007, Make your company a talent factory, *Harvard Business Review*, 85(6): 68–77.
21. J. Champ, 2003, The hidden qualities of great leaders, *Fast Company*, November, 139.
22. B. A. Ready & J. A. Conger, 2007, Make your company a talent factory, 71.
23. R. Cross, A. Hargadon, S. Parise, & R. J. Thomas, 2008, Innovation: Together we innovate, *Wall Street Journal*, September 15–16, R6.
24. D. W. Yiu & C.-M. Lau, 2008, Corporate entrepreneurship as resource capital configuration in emerging markets, *Entrepreneurship Theory and Practice*, 32: 37–57; J. Nahapiet & S. Ghoshal, 1998, Social capital, intellectual capital and the organizational advantage, *Academy of Management Review*, 23: 242–266; R. D. Ireland, M. A. Hitt, & D. Vaidyanath, 2002, Alliance management as a source of competitive advantage, *Journal of Management*, 28: 413–446.
25. A. Jung, 2004, You will stand on our shoulders (keynote address at the WWIB Conference), Knowledge @ Wharton, http://knowledge.wharton.upenn.edu, November 5.
26. C. Stephenson, 2008, Dorothy Gale: A compassionate leader, *Financial Times*, January 28, 5.
27. Yiu & Lau, Corporate entrepreneurship as resource capital configuration in emerging markets; R. A. Baron & G. D. Markman, 2003, Beyond social capital: The role of entrepreneurs' social competence in their financial success, *Journal of Business Venturing*, 18: 41–60.
28. S. D. Anthony, N. W. Johnson, & J. B. Sinfield, 2008, Institutionalizing innovation, *MIT Sloan Management Review*, 49(2): 45-50; R. D. Ireland, M. A. Hitt, & D. Sirmon, 2003, A model of strategic entrepreneurship: The construct and its dimensions, *Journal of Management*, 29: 963–989.
29. J. Jargon, 2008, General Mills sees wealth via health: New recipe for profit, sales growth: More whole grains, less salt, fat, *Wall Street Journal*, February 25, A9.
30. S. Mishra, 2008, Counting progress: The state of boards five years after Sarbanes-Oxley, *The Corporate Governance Advisor*, January/February, 12; R. E. Hoskisson, M. A. Hitt, R. A. Johnson, & W. Grossman, 2002, Conflicting voices: The effects of ownership heterogeneity and internal governance on corporate strategy, *Academy of Management Journal*, 45: 697–716.
31. E. A. Gordon, E. Henry, T. J. Louwers, & B. J. Reed, 2007, Are you auditing related-party transactions: A literature overview and research synthesis, *Accounting Horizons*, 21(1): 81–102.
32. J. Welch & S. Welch, 2008, Miscreants among us: Most rogues like SocGen's Jerome Kerviel don't go unnoticed—just unreported, *Business Week*, February 18, 84.
33. D. Pastoriza, M. A. Arino, & J. E. Ricart, 2008, Ethical managerial behavior as an antecedent of organizational social capital, *Journal of Business Ethics*, 78: 329–341.
34. R. S. Kaplan & D. P. Norton, 2008, Mastering the management system, *Harvard Business Review*, 86(1): 62–77.
35. Ibid.

W. EARL SASSER

HEATHER BECKHAM

Thomas Green:
Power, Office Politics, and a Career in Crisis

Another long day at the office had drawn to a close. Thomas Green felt the pulsing in his temples that usually preceded a migraine. As he stepped outside Dynamic Displays' corporate headquarters in Boston, the brisk air made him catch his breath. It was now February 5, 2008. Green could not believe that in five short months his dream promotion had turned into a disaster. When Green had been promoted to his new position in September, he was a rising star. Now, he would be lucky to celebrate his one-year anniversary with the company. His boss, Frank Davis, had sent the division vice president, Shannon McDonald, two scathing emails criticizing Green's performance. Green and Davis had yet to see eye to eye on work styles or market trends. Tension had also risen when Green did not enthusiastically endorse the sales forecasts made by Davis. Green felt the forecasts were either overly optimistic or outright fabrications.

Before he left for the day, Green had reread the series of emails regarding his performance and was certain that Davis was setting him up to be dismissed. Davis's most recent email had made it clear to Green that his position as a senior market specialist was in jeopardy. He did not have much time to rectify the situation. McDonald had emailed a formal request to him that afternoon, asking for his perspective on his performance and how he was going to improve the situation. With this in mind, Green started his commute home and began to analyze what went wrong and what he could do to save his job.

Company and Industry Background

Dynamic Displays was founded in 1990 as a provider of self-service options to banks via Automated Teller Machines (ATMs). In 1994, Dynamic Displays launched a new division aimed at the travel and hospitality industry, and deployed their first self-service check-in kiosk for Discover Airlines. In 2007, Dynamic Displays' Travel and Hospitality Division had 60% market share with over 1,500 self-service kiosks in use at more than 75 airports. Customers included regional, national, and international airline carriers, as well as various hotels and car-rental agencies. Eighty percent of the Travel and Hospitality Division's 2007 revenue came from airline carrier clients, 15% from hotels, and 5% from car-rental agencies. The company was a full service provider, offering hardware, software, engineering, and maintenance support.

Kiosks were an attractive option for airlines to quickly and easily check in passengers while reducing processing costs. Dynamic Displays' kiosks not only reduced costs but also improved customer service, shortened passenger wait times, and provided valuable information to these travelers. In 2006, Forrester Research estimated the average cost for an airline passenger to check in through an agent was $3.02, versus a range of $0.14 to $0.32 for kiosk check-in.[1] This impressive savings was realized by allowing the repetitive tasks of selecting or changing seat assignments and printing and distributing boarding passes to be handled by the passengers themselves. Airlines reduced headcount or assigned the agents to more value-added tasks, such as solving complex customer service issues and ensuring compliance with safety and security standards. The cost savings were particularly important for the airline industry during a period when margins were razor thin and fuel costs were continuing to climb.

Airlines were also aggressively promoting another self-service option for travelers. Web check-in allowed passengers to complete the entire check-in process via the internet from a remote location, utilizing their personal or office computer. Cost savings using online check-in was of even greater benefit because the airline did not have to purchase and install a kiosk, and passengers printed their own boarding passes using their own paper. According to a 2006 Forrester report, airport kiosks were a mature application with 75% of U.S. leisure passengers using kiosk in 2006. Web check-in on the other hand, was still experiencing dramatic growth, increasing from less than 45% of U.S. leisure passengers in 2005 to 64% in 2006.[2]

Thomas Green: Path to Senior Market Specialist

Thomas Green was born in 1979 in Brunswick, Georgia, the son of a postman and a school secretary. At the University of Georgia, he worked in a warehouse and washed cars while earning a bachelor's degree in Economics. His first full-time job was in sales for National Business Solutions in Atlanta. Green enjoyed impressive success in the Banking Division, focusing on ATM sales to regional banks in the Southeast. In March 2007, Dynamic Displays recruited Green for an account executive position in the Southeast territory for the Travel and Hospitality Division. To Green, Dynamic Displays seemed to present a great chance for a fast climb up the managerial ladder.

Green hit the ground running at Dynamic Displays. In his first four months as an account executive, he completed a contract for one of the largest airline carriers, Journey Airlines, to accelerate rollout of kiosks in 20 airports and purchase upgraded software for kiosks in the majority of their locations.

Green had told a close friend, "I wanted to come in and dazzle them at Dynamic Displays. This was no easy feat. But I wanted more than an account executive position. I had heard there was a lot of opportunity for fresh talent at corporate headquarters and I made it my mission to get noticed immediately."

Senior executives at Dynamic Displays quickly took notice of Green's performance and were eager to strengthen his relationship with the company. In July 2007, Green attended a week-long training session at corporate headquarters. Shannon McDonald, the division vice president, and Mary Jacobs,

---

[1] Harteveldt and Epps, "Self-Service Check-In Clicks with Travelers," *Forrester Report*, February 23, 2007

[2] Ibid.

the national sales director, made a concerted effort to get to know him better. Green and McDonald were both University of Georgia alumni and Georgia natives. They had an instant connection, and McDonald seemed to take Green under her wing. McDonald had several informal meetings with Green, and by the end of the week Green became aware of an open position for a senior market specialist. Green aggressively campaigned to be considered for this position. Over the next month, Green made several trips to corporate headquarters to meet with McDonald. Green discussed his various client relationships, and McDonald agreed that in a short time he had developed unique insights into their markets. Following a dinner meeting at which Green offered lengthy explanations of the client opportunities he perceived and his strategies for winning them, McDonald promoted him to the position of senior market specialist.

McDonald told Green, "Tom, you are obviously a bright and ambitious account executive. You have a great rapport with your clients. You have made a strong case for your promotion and I'm willing to take a chance on you. I think this group needs a fresh perspective. However, I do have a couple of reservations about your lack of managerial experience. You have only held sales roles, and the senior market specialist position is very different. This new job will require you to think strategically as well as tactically, and you will have to coordinate between several different functions and layers of corporate management. I am hoping you compensate for your lack of experience by seeking out guidance from some of our more seasoned managers." *mentor*

Green was assigned to work out of corporate headquarters in Boston. The division's organizational structure is shown in **Exhibit 1**. The promotion had been a giant step upward for Green; an account executive interested in joining the marketing team usually moved first to a market specialist position and then put in a number of years in the field before reaching "senior" status. The other senior market specialists in the division were in their forties. Green was 28. His salary was now $125,000, a 50% increase over his previous salary.

Senior market specialists were responsible for identifying industry trends, evaluating new business opportunities, and establishing sales goals. In addition, specialists developed general market and specific client strategies to help the account executives obtain a sale. Green directly supervised the two market specialists in his region. Green reported to Frank Davis, the marketing director. Davis had recently been promoted from the position that Green assumed (see **Exhibit 2** for relevant bios).

After Green's Promotion

Green's promotion became effective on September 10, 2007. McDonald stopped by Green's office that first day and told Green, "Tom, you are walking into a tricky situation with Frank Davis. Frank had expected to choose the new senior market specialist and it would not have been you. You'll have to deal with any fallout that might result from that. You are getting an unusual opportunity with this promotion. Don't let me down."

Green used most of his first week to review 2006 and 2007 year-to-date sales. He spent the next week with his boss, Frank Davis, making a rapid tour of major airline industry clients. At the end of the week, Davis told Green, "We had some good meetings this week and the clients responded well to your ideas. However, I think we would have been more effective if we had been able to provide the clients with some market data. When you are on your own I expect you to spend a significant amount of time preparing for client meetings and developing supporting detail for your proposals. I know you will need a little time to get up to speed on your new position, but I expect you to start developing some new market strategies for your region soon."

Green next visited clients, market specialists, and account executives in New York, Atlanta, and Orlando. In addition to the travel, Green's personal life was very busy. He was searching for a house in Boston, arranging to move belongings there, and still trying to maintain a relationship with his girlfriend in Atlanta.

On October 8, Green attended the 2008 Budget Plan meeting in which Davis presented sales projections for the upcoming year. This was the first time Green had been exposed to the planning and forecasting process. Since Davis had held Green's position when the estimates were due, the numbers for the Eastern region had been developed without input from Green. At the meeting, Davis assigned 2008 performance commitments for all senior marketing specialists and their teams. Performance reviews would be based upon their ability to meet or exceed the objectives. Green was surprised by the numbers that Davis was proposing. Davis estimated 10% growth in the Eastern region.

According to Green, "Frank Davis was way off base with his pro forma numbers. I had been talking with our account execs and there was no way we could achieve double-digit growth in 2008. The sales goals Frank set for my region were totally unrealistic. In the meeting I expressed my concern that my goals would be impossible to meet. I couldn't believe I was the only one with the guts to speak up. After the meeting, Frank stopped me in the hall and told me about all these big opportunities for the market. I listened politely, but the time I'd spent out on the road with clients gave me every reason to doubt Frank's expectations."

Davis was visibly upset that Green openly challenged him at the meeting. Davis commented to McDonald, "Thomas's negative attitude is not what we need on this team. Corporate expects this division to be a growth engine for the company. We've realized a 10% CAGR over the past 5 years. The market indicators are positive, and with the right sales strategy my projections are attainable. The hotel and car-rental markets are virtually untapped right now. Thomas's problem is that he's too conservative in his outlook. He is thinking like an account exec who is only concerned with the sales target. In the senior market specialist position, he has to think outside the box and develop strategies to capture that aggressive growth target."

Meeting with Frank Davis

It was customary for employees at Dynamic Displays to have an informal evaluation in the first or second month after a promotion. When Green saw a meeting with Davis regarding his performance pop up on his Outlook calendar, he was not the least bit worried. On October 15, 2007, Green met with Davis to discuss his performance to date. Quite to Green's surprise, Davis had prepared a list of problems he had encountered with Green's work in the first month after his promotion.

Davis sternly looked Green in the eye and began. "Thomas, you have not done a good job of keeping me informed of your schedule. For example, this past Thursday, I was trying to locate you and your Outlook calendar said you were in Orlando. I needed you to send me some information on one of our accounts. You didn't answer your cell phone. I ended up calling the account exec in Orlando and was told you had left the previous day. To make matters worse, I had asked you to deliver on that same day a brief report on that new kiosk opportunity in Tampa—and I didn't receive it."

Flabbergasted, Green responded, "I decided to go to Atlanta a day early because I had run out of good opportunities in Orlando. I was able to get a meeting with the VP of purchasing at a client in Atlanta and thought that would be more productive than sitting around Orlando talking to nobodies."

Davis continued, "On September 20, I asked you to check why VIP Hotel Group had not purchased any of our kiosks. After three reminders, I still have not received a good answer from you. In the same vein, two weeks ago, I requested the status of the regional jet division of Journey Airlines. I have not received any update from you yet. I also asked for organizational charts on two clients in Charlotte and Raleigh. Do you remember your reply? You said, 'What's the value of charts like that? I have that information in my head.' Thomas, we can make good use of those charts—they can help us lay out a strategy for getting to the decision makers in a company. I expect the charts on my desk by end of the week."

Davis and Green spent the next two hours going over various incidents and discussing a plan to improve the situation.

Later, Green told a manager outside his group, "I can't shake this nagging suspicion that Frank's criticisms of my performance are a direct result of my questioning the validity of his forecasts in the Budget Plan meeting. I was blindsided by his negative assessment of my work. Frank spent two hours picking apart my work style. You would think he would be concerned with bigger issues than how often I update my Outlook calendar."

A few days after the meeting, Davis wrote an email to McDonald, who had promoted Green, outlining the points covered in the meeting and copied Green on the communication (**Exhibit 3**).

Three Months Later: Trouble Continues

After the October 15 meeting, Green met with the national sales director and director of software development. Green was focused on developing a new up-selling and cross-selling software program that would allow airline passengers to upgrade seating; have meals, magazines, or books delivered to the flight; and book hotel rooms or cars at their destination. According to Green, "The only way for us to capture growth is if we can convince the airlines that our products have revenue-generating opportunity and other advantages over web check-in. However, these programs may take months to develop and will not impact our sales in 2008."

Green spent most of November, December, and January working independently on his special software project and traveling to meet with his market specialists and various clients. According to one of the market specialists who accompanied Green to several meetings, "Thomas is great when it comes to selling the clients on his ideas. He is very charismatic and can think quickly on his feet. I can tell he has put a lot of thought into his strategies and I really like working for him. However, the clients are starting to ask me for hard data to back up his claims of cost savings. They are also requiring memos and presentations to bring to their superiors that justify the expenditure. Thomas doesn't really work that way. He would rather talk through the issues face to face."

During this time, Green avoided interactions with Davis whenever he could. Green continued to tell people outside the group he did not agree with his boss's projections for 2008. Green stated, "With the continued financial distress in the airline industry and preference for web check-in, I don't foresee a lot of growth in spending next year. Davis is holding firm with his upbeat projections. I deliberately steer clear of him. I know my mood is terrible. The excitement's gone from work. I must say, though, I've had a couple of good chats with managers from another part of Dynamic Displays, and they're supportive. They told me to stand my ground. "

On January 28, Davis held another performance review meeting with Green, focusing on the continuing deficiencies in Green's work and attitude. After the meeting, Davis sent an email to McDonald outlining his issues with Green (**Exhibit 4**). Green was not copied on this email, but someone sent him a copy by interoffice mail. McDonald met with Davis the following day to flesh out the issue. Davis told McDonald, "I am truly disappointed with Thomas's work. He is an intelligent and capable young man, but I do not believe he is making a strong effort."

In response to Davis's complaints, McDonald sent a short email to Green (**Exhibit 5**) asking for his point of view on the situation.

Green told a close friend, "It's clear that Frank intends to get rid of me. He's just putting his argument together."

Green's Next Move

As Green entered I-93 on the way to his new home in North Andover, he replayed in his head the series of events and subsequent emails. Green recognized that he had not paid much attention to office politics when he'd taken on his job. He had met one-on-one with McDonald only twice since he moved to the corporate headquarters. He had been preoccupied with the job itself, and with living up to McDonald's expectations. Now it seemed as though he had no allies in the company. McDonald's email today struck a nerve. Because McDonald sponsored his promotion, Green had taken for granted that she would watch out for him. If Davis was indeed trying to fire him, Green wondered who McDonald would side with.

Several questions persisted in Green's mind. What steps should he take next? Set up a meeting with McDonald? Write McDonald a detailed memo? Do what Davis tells him and keep his mouth shut, even though he was convinced that the forecasts were inflated? Was it his responsibility to expose Davis's overstated projections? Maybe contact a head hunter and start looking for another job? He had to sort through before he responded to McDonald's email. Next week, his first mortgage payment was due and the new furniture he'd picked out was scheduled to be delivered. This was certainly not a good time to be out of work, for 2008 was shaping up to be a very stressful year for Thomas Green.

Exhibit 1   Abbreviated Organization Chart, Travel and Hospitality Division of Dynamic Displays, 2007

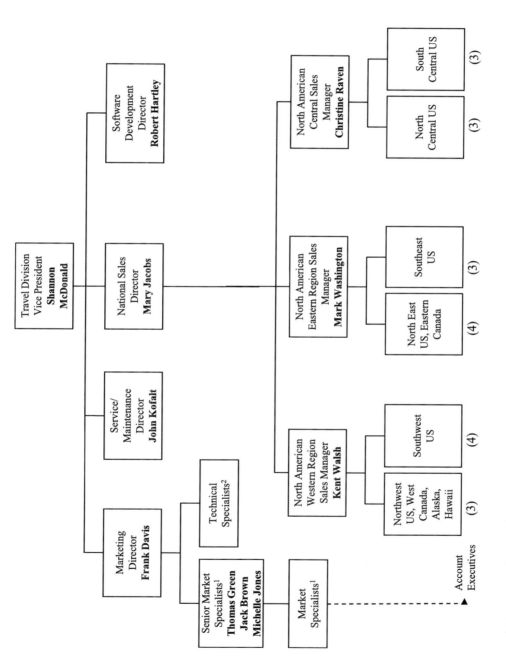

[1] There were three senior market specialists (one for each region) and six market specialists (one for each territory). Thomas Green was the market specialist for Eastern Region

[2] There were six technical specialists (one for each territory)

Exhibit 2   Relevant Bios

Thomas Green (Age 28) – Senior Market Specialist

Thomas Green began his career as an account executive for National Business Solutions in Atlanta, Georgia. He spent six years as an account executive in the Banking Division, selling ATMs to regional banks throughout the Southeast. In March 2007 he joined Dynamic Displays as an account executive in their Travel and Hospitality Division. He is currently the division's senior market specialist for the Eastern region of North America. Green graduated summa cum laude from University of Georgia with a bachelor's degree in Economics in 2001.

Frank Davis (Age 45) – Marketing Director

Frank Davis is a 17-year veteran of Dynamic Displays. He joined the company in 1990 as an account executive with the Financial Services Solutions Division. He has also held positions as an account executive, market specialist, and senior market specialist with the Travel and Hospitality Division. Frank Davis is currently the marketing director for the Travel and Hospitality Division. Prior to joining Dynamic Displays, Davis worked as a sales representative for Advanced Telecommunications Services selling PBX phone systems to large corporations. He holds a bachelors degree in history from New York University (1986) and an Executive MBA from Suffolk University, Sawyer Business School (2002).

Shannon McDonald (Age 42) – Division Vice President

Reporting to the Dynamic Displays Chairman, Chief Executive Officer and President, Sam Costello, Shannon McDonald was promoted to Division Vice President in November of 2006 and is responsible for all aspects of the Travel and Hospitality Business. Previously, McDonald was the director of national sales for the Travel and Hospitality Division (2000-2006). She was responsible for driving Dynamic Displays' self-service business with the largest airline carriers in the United States. Ms. McDonald has also held positions as a strategic consultant with Chicago Consulting Group's Travel and Tourism practice and as a marketing analyst with Quest Airlines. She holds a bachelors degree in marketing from the University of Georgia (1987) and an MBA from Northwestern's Kellogg School of Management (1992).

Exhibit 3 10/19/07 Email Regarding Green's Performance

FROM: "FRANK DAVIS" <FDAVIS@dynamicdisplays.com >

TO: "SHANNON MCDONALD" <smcdonald@dynamicdisplays.com >

CC: "THOMAS GREEN" <TGREEN@dynamicdisplays.com >

SENT: FRIDAY, OCTOBER 19, 2007 3:48:32 pM

SUBJECT: THOMAS GREEN

Since Thomas assumed the position of senior market specialist on September 10, 2007, numerous incidents of poor judgment and questionable behavior have concerned me. Thomas and I talked about most of these incidents as they occurred. However, I concluded that we needed to have an overarching discussion about his performance and to develop a strategy for improving his work style. At that meeting, held October 15, 2007, we reviewed a range of problems. Among them:

1. Thomas fails to inform me of his plans and keep me updated on his schedule.

2. He does not follow up when information is requested of him.

3. Thomas's lack of enthusiasm is troubling. He has a right and an obligation to question aspects of our plans if he finds them illogical or unfeasible, but the kind of negativity he displayed in the Budget Plan meeting on October 8 is dangerous to the organization and unacceptable to me.

Thomas seemed to accept my criticisms in a thoughtful manner and assured me he will do what is necessary to succeed in his position. He and I plan to discuss his overall performance again in mid-November. Meanwhile, he'll be expected to take the following corrective measures:

1. Plan to make focused calls when dealing with market specialists, account executives, and clients. Have a specific communication strategy going into a call, and have all sales collateral and other necessary materials available. Stop making calls purely for the purpose of meeting people.

2. Update Outlook calendar regularly and always return calls from our office promptly.

3. Provide feedback to my requests in a timely manner. Thomas says he now recognizes that my requests are not merely "reminders"; they are a call for information that I genuinely need.

4. Demonstrate a more positive attitude both inside and outside the company.

Frank R. Davis
Travel and Hospitality Marketing Director
Dynamic Displays
212-314-1420

Exhibit 4   1/30/08 Email Regarding Green's Performance

FROM: "FRANK DAVIS" <FDAVIS@dynamicdisplays.com >

TO: "SHANNON MCDONALD" <smcdonald@dynamicdisplays.com >

SENT: WEDNESDAY, January 30, 2008 4:28:12 pM

SUBJECT: THOMAS GREEN

On October 19, 2007, I sent you an email communicating my concerns with Thomas's attitude and job performance. On January 28, 2008, Thomas and I had another meeting on this subject.   I would like to summarize that conversation.

Thomas wastes a great deal of time complaining about the problems of selling to our current and prospective clients and far too little time developing strategic marketing approaches and effective sales tactics.   I informed him that his job is to sell the accounts, not to agree with our clients' assertions about alleged disadvantages of our products or the current excess capacity in the industry.

I told Thomas his lack of effort and enthusiasm are not consistent with the standards of Dynamic Displays and could lead to an outcome he likely would not find pleasant. Thomas then said he felt I was micromanaging his activities.   It was here that I think we uncovered the root of the problem.   I inquired as to what new or even slightly imaginative marketing approaches he documented in the past five months.   His answer was, "None that are documented." When I see no new targets and no thoughtful, creative marketing, I feel I must micromanage, and I communicated this to Thomas.

I then pulled up several Power Point presentations, spreadsheet models, and associated emails that Michelle Jones, the Western Region senior market specialist, had used to shape her region's strategy and to support their selling efforts. As we paged through her work, Thomas stated that all those email updates and fancy presentations and models were "political" and didn't match up well with his personal approach to selling. I told him this was not only good politics, but also proved to his boss that he was working effectively.

Thomas ultimately conceded the mistakes and personal shortcomings that I explained to him.. He pledged to develop creative marketing approaches and keep me updated on his progress. I hope these promises materialize in the next 30 days. If not, I recommend we part ways with Thomas Green and quickly seek out a competent replacement for this extremely important position.

Frank R. Davis
Travel and Hospitality Marketing Director
Dynamic Displays
212-314-1420

Exhibit 5   2/5/08 Email from McDonald to Green

FROM: "SHANNON MCDONALD" <smcdonald@dynamicdisplays.com >

TO: "THOMAS GREEN" <TGREEN@dynamicdisplays.com >

CC: "FRANK DAVIS" <FDAVIS@dynamicdisplays.com >

SENT: TUESDAY, FEBRUARY 5, 2008 8:38:53 AM

SUBJECT: PERFORMANCE

Frank Davis has explained to me his point of view on your performance. I think all of us want to improve the current situation, which is regrettable. At this point I would like to get your perspective on your recent performance and to understand your ideas about specific areas that need improvement.

I look forward to resolving this issue ASAP. I would be glad to discuss this matter with you in detail, but first I would like to receive your statement in writing.

Shannon A. McDonald
Travel and Hospitality Group Vice-President
Dynamic Displays
212-314-1415

W11022

WHERE HAVE YOU BEEN?: An Exercise To Assess Your Exposure To The Rest Of The World's Peoples

INSTRUCTION

1. On each of the attached worksheets, note the total number and names of those countries you have visited, and the corresponding percentage of world population which each country represents. Sum the relevant regional totals on P. 11.

2. If used as part of a group or class analysis, estimate the grand total for the entire group. Then consider the following questions:

3. Why is there such a high variability in individual profiles (i.e., high exposure vs. low exposure)?

4. What are the implications of each profile for one's career?

5. What would it take to get you to personally change your profile?

REGION: AFRICA

1)	NIGERIA	152.2	2.2
2)	ETHIOPIA	88.0	1.3
3)	EGYPT	80.5	1.2
4)	CONGO (DEM. REP)	70.9	1.0
5)	SOUTH AFRICA	49.1	0.7
6)	SUDAN	43.9	0.6
7)	TANZANIA	41.9	0.6
8)	KENYA	40.0	0.6
9)	ALGERIA	34.6	0.5
10)	UGANDA	33.4	0.5
11)	MOROCCO	31.6	0.5
12)	GHANA	24.3	0.4
13)	MOZAMBIQUE	22.1	0.3
14)	MADAGASCAR	21.3	0.3
15)	CÔTE d'IVOIRE	21.1	0.3
16)	CAMEROON	19.3	0.3
17)	BURKINA FASO	16.2	0.2
18)	NIGER	15.9	0.2
19)	MALAWI	15.5	0.2
20)	MALI	13.8	0.2
21)	ZAMBIA	13.5	0.2
22)	ANGOLA	13.1	0.2
23)	SENEGAL	12.3	0.2
24)	ZIMBABWE	11.7	0.2
25)	RWANDA	11.1	0.2
26)	TUNISIA	10.6	0.2
27)	CHAD	10.5	0.2
28)	GUINEA	10.3	0.2
29)	SOMALIA	10.1	0.1
	Subtotal Africa	938.8	13.7

REGION: AFRICA (CONTINUED)

Country	2010 (July) Population (in millions)	% of World Total
30) BURUNDI	9.9	0.1
31) BENIN	9.1	0.1
32) TOGO	6.6	0.1
33) LIBYA	6.5	0.1
34) ERITREA	5.8	0.1
35) SIERRA LEONE	5.3	0.1
36) CENTRAL AFRICAN REPUBLIC	4.9	0.1
37) CONGO, REP.	4.1	0.1
38) LIBERIA	3.7	0.1
39) MAURITANIA	3.2	0.0
40) NAMIBIA	2.1	0.0
41) BOTSWANA	2.0	0.0
42) LESOTHO	1.9	0.0
43) GAMBIA, THE	1.8	0.0
44) GUINEA-BISSAU	1.6	0.0
45) GABON	1.6	0.0
46) SWAZILAND	1.4	0.0
47) MAURITIUS	1.3	0.0
48) COMOROS	0.8	0.0
49) EQUATORIAL GUINEA	0.7	0.0
50) DJIBOUTI	0.7	0.0
51) CAPE VERDE	0.5	0.0
52) MAYOTTE (FR)	0.2	0.0
53) SÁO TOMÉ and PRINCIPE	0.2	0.0
54) SEYCHELLES	0.1	0.0
Total Africa	1,014.8	14.8

REGION: NORTH AMERICA AND CARIBBEAN

Country	2010 (July) Population (in millions)	% of World Total
1) USA	310.2	4.6
2) MEXICO	112.5	1.7
3) CANADA	33.8	0.5
4) GUATEMALA	13.6	0.2
5) CUBA	11.5	0.2
6) DOMINICAN REPUBLIC	9.8	0.1
7) HAITI	9.7	0.1
8) HONDURAS	8.0	0.1
9) EL SALVADOR	6.1	0.1
10) NICARAGUA	6.0	0.1
11) COSTA RICA	4.5	0.1
12) PUERTO RICO (U.S.)	4.0	0.1
13) PANAMA	3.4	0.1
14) JAMAICA	2.9	0.0
15) TRINIDAD AND TOBAGO	1.2	0.0
16) BAHAMAS, THE	0.3	0.0
17) BARBADOS	0.3	0.0
18) BELIZE	0.3	0.0
19) NETHERLANDS ANTILLES	0.2	0.0
20) ST. LUCIA	0.2	0.0
21) ARUBA (NETH.)	0.1	0.0
22) ANTIGUA AND BARBUDA	0.1	0.0
23) BERMUDA (UK)	0.1	0.0
24) DOMINICA	0.1	0.0
25) GRENADA	0.1	0.0
26) ST. VINCENT & THE GRENADINES	0.1	0.0
27) VIRGIN ISLANDS (U.S.)	0.1	0.0
28) CAYMAN ISLANDS	0.1	0.0
29) ST. KITTS AND NEVIS	0.1	0.0
Total North America and Caribbean	539.4	7.9

REGION: SOUTH AMERICA

Country	2010 (July) Population (in millions)	% of World Total
1) BRAZIL	201.1	3.0
2) COLOMBIA	44.2	0.7
3) ARGENTINA	41.3	0.6
4) PERU	29.9	0.4
5) VENEZUELA	27.2	0.4
6) CHILE	16.8	0.2
7) ECUADOR	14.8	0.2
8) BOLIVIA	10.0	0.1
9) PARAGUAY	6.4	0.1
10) URUGUAY	3.5	0.1
11) GUYANA	0.8	0.0
12) SURINAME	0.5	0.0
Total South America	396.5	5.8

REGION: WESTERN EUROPE

Country	2010 (July) Population (in millions)	% of World Total
1) GERMANY	82.3	1.2
2) FRANCE	64.8	1.0
3) UNITED KINGDOM	62.4	0.9
4) ITALY	58.1	0.9
5) SPAIN	46.5	0.7
6) NETHERLANDS	16.8	0.2
7) GREECE	10.8	0.2
8) PORTUGAL	10.7	0.2
9) BELGIUM	10.4	0.2
10) SWEDEN	9.1	0.1
11) AUSTRIA	8.2	0.1
12) SWITZERLAND	7.6	0.1
13) DENMARK	5.5	0.1
14) FINLAND	5.3	0.1
15) NORWAY	4.7	0.1
16) IRELAND	4.7	0.1
17) LUXEMBOURG	0.5	0.0
18) MALTA	0.4	0.0
19) ICELAND	0.3	0.0
20) JERSEY	0.1	0.0
21) ANDORRA	0.1	0.0
22) ISLE OF MAN	0.1	0.0
23) GUERNSEY	0.1	0.0
24) GREENLAND (DEN.)	0.1	0.0
25) FAROE ISLANDS (DEN.)	0.1	0.0
26) LIECHTENSTEIN	-	-
27) MONACO	-	-
28) SAN MARINO	-	-
Total Western Europe	409.7	6.0

REGION: EASTERN EUROPE

Country	2010 (July) Population (in millions)	% of World Total
1) RUSSIA	139.4	2.1
2) UKRAINE	45.4	0.7
3) POLAND	38.5	0.6
4) ROMANIA	22.0	0.3
5) CZECH REPUBLIC	10.2	0.2
6) HUNGARY	10.0	0.1
7) BELARUS	9.6	0.1
8) SERBIA	7.4	0.1
9) BULGARIA	7.2	0.1
10) SLOVAKIA	5.5	0.1
11) BOSNIA and HERZEGOVINA	4.6	0.1
12) CROATIA	4.5	0.1
13) MOLDOVA	4.3	0.1
14) LITHUANIA	3.6	0.1
15) ALBANIA	3.0	0.0
16) LATVIA	2.2	0.0
17) MACEDONIA	2.1	0.0
18) SLOVENIA	2.0	0.0
19) KOSOVO	1.8	0.0
20) ESTONIA	1.3	0.0
21) MONTENEGRO	0.7	0.0
Total Eastern Europe	325.3	4.7

REGION: CENTRAL ASIA and INDIAN SUBCONTINENT

Country	2010 (July) Population (in millions)	% of World Total
1) INDIA	1,173.1	17.3
2) PAKISTAN	184.4	2.7
3) BANGLADESH	156.1	2.3
4) AFGHANISTAN	29.1	0.4
5) NEPAL	29.0	0.4
6) UZBEKISTAN	27.9	0.4
7) SRI LANKA	21.5	0.3
8) KAZAKHSTAN	15.5	0.2
9) AZERBAIJAN	8.3	0.1
10) TAJIKISTAN	7.5	0.1
11) KYRGYZSTAN	5.5	0.1
12) TURKMENISTAN	4.9	0.1
13) GEORGIA	4.6	0.1
14) MONGOLIA	3.1	0.0
15) ARMENIA	3.0	0.0
16) BHUTAN	0.7	0.0
17) MALDIVES	0.4	0.0
Total Central Asia and Indian Subcontinent	1,674.6	24.4

REGION: MIDDLE EAST

Country	2010 (July) Population (in millions)	% of World Total
1) TURKEY	77.8	1.1
2) IRAN	76.9	1.1
3) IRAQ	29.7	0.4
4) SAUDI ARABIA	25.7	0.4
5) YEMEN	23.5	0.3
6) SYRIA	22.2	0.3
7) ISRAEL	7.4	0.1
8) JORDAN	6.4	0.1
9) UNITED ARAB EMIRATES	5.0	0.1
10) WEST BANK AND GAZA	4.1	0.1
11) LEBANON	4.1	0.1
12) OMAN	3.0	0.0
13) KUWAIT	2.8	0.0
14) CYPRUS	1.1	0.0
15) QATAR	0.8	0.0
16) BAHRAIN	0.7	0.0
Total Middle East	291.2	4.3

REGION: ASIA PACIFIC

Country	2010 (July) Population (in millions)	% of World Total
1) CHINA (EXCL. HK & MACAU)	1,330.1	19.7
2) INDONESIA	243.0	3.6
3) JAPAN	126.8	1.9
4) PHILIPPINES	99.9	1.5
5) VIETNAM	89.6	1.3
6) THAILAND	67.1	1.0
7) BURMA	53.4	0.8
8) SOUTH KOREA	48.6	0.7
9) MALAYSIA	28.3	0.4
10) TAIWAN	23.0	0.3
11) NORTH KOREA	22.8	0.3
12) AUSTRALIA	21.5	0.3
13) CAMBODIA	14.5	0.2
14) HONG KONG (SAR - CHINA)	7.1	0.1
15) LAOS	6.4	0.1
16) PAPUA NEW GUINEA	6.1	0.1
17) SINGAPORE	4.7	0.1
18) NEW ZEALAND	4.3	0.1
19) TIMOR-LESTE	1.2	0.0
20) FIJI	0.9	0.0
21) SOLOMON ISLANDS	0.6	0.0
22) MACAU (SAR-CHINA)	0.6	0.0
23) BRUNEI	0.4	0.0
24) FRENCH POLYNESIA (FR.)	0.3	0.0
25) NEW CALEDONIA (FR.)	0.3	0.0
26) GUAM (U.S.)	0.2	0.0
27) SAMOA	0.2	0.0
28) VANUATU	0.2	0.0
29) AMERICAN SAMOA (U.S.)	0.1	0.0
30) KIRIBATI	0.1	0.0
31) MARSHALL ISLANDS	0.1	0.0
32) MICRONESIA, FED. STS	0.1	0.0
33) NORTHERN MARIANA ISLANDS	0.1	0.0
34) TONGA	0.1	0.0
35) PALAU	-	-
Total Asia Pacific	2,202.7	32.1

SUMMARY

Region	# of Countries	Which You Have Visited	2010 (July) Population (millions)	Region's % of World Population	% of Population You Have Been Exposed To
AFRICA	54	0	1,014.8	14.8	0
NORTH AMERICA and CARIBBEAN	29	1	539.4	7.9	4.6
SOUTH AMERICA	12	0	396.5	5.8	0
WESTERN EUROPE	28	4	409.7	6.0	3.1
EASTERN EUROPE	21	1	325.3	4.7	.2
CENTRAL ASIA and INDIAN SUBCONTINENT	17	0	1,674.6	24.4	0
MIDDLE EAST	16	0	291.2	4.3	0
ASIA PACIFIC	35	0	2,202.7	32.1	0
GRAND TOTAL	212	6	6,854.2	100.0	7.9

Harvard Business Review ▨

www.hbr.org

Should Michael go
to China?

Five commentators offer
expert advice.

Into the Fray

by M. Ellen Peebles

Reprint R0501A

Rumors are flying and knives are out at Lafleur SA after a key executive resigns. Michael just wants to work hard and get ahead—does he have to play politics, too?

HBR CASE STUDY

Into the Fray

by M. Ellen Peebles

"Psst, psst, psst." That's all Michael Feldstein heard as he walked down the hall toward his office. "Psst, psst, psst." "What did people talk about before last week?" he asked himself. "What more can we possibly say about it?"

"It" was the sudden and mysterious resignation of Lucien Beaumont, Lafleur SA's president of U.S. operations. Everyone was imagining the worst. Financial misdeeds? Illness? An illicit affair? The rumors were flying fast and furious, each more lurid than the next. Less entertaining, though even more distracting, was the speculation about who would get Lucien's job—and what would happen to everybody else, once that question was settled. Everyone wanted to back the right horse.

It wasn't a simple race. Lafleur was a major international beverage company that had grown rapidly through acquisitions. Michael, the global category director for rums and a contender for the newly open position, was a

relative newcomer; he'd joined the company two years earlier, when Lafleur acquired New York–based Campos Beverage. In his eyes, Michael's chief competitor was Danielle Harcourt, the global category director for vodkas and liqueurs, who had moved to New York from the company's Paris headquarters just after the Campos acquisition. She had been at Lafleur 15 years and was practiced at what could be called either networking or office politics, depending on where you sat.

But there were other possible candidates. The company had a fast-growing sports and health drink division that was getting a lot of media attention, and the director in that category—he'd started in orange juice and had risen quickly through the ranks—was turning heads in Paris. The spirits business was still doing well, but growth was beginning to taper off, and Lafleur was looking for new sources of revenue.

HBR's cases, which are fictional, present common managerial dilemmas and offer concrete solutions from experts.

Or the job could go to an outsider. Charles Brooke, the CFO at Cazares Laird International, one of Lafleur's competitors, had just lost out on the COO job at Cazares's U.S. business. He was highly regarded in the industry—and unhappy about having been passed over. Charles had a strong background in the wine business, which was a relative weakness at Lafleur. And then there was Genevieve Basset, a former Lafleur employee, who was running a small spirits company based in the United States but who had maintained good relationships with Lafleur managers in Paris and New York.

Still, Michael believed he had a good shot at Lucien's job. The only P&L experience he had was running Campos's U.S. operations for a few months just before Lafleur acquired the company, but he had a richly varied background. He'd started at Campos in sales, shifted to marketing, done a stint in production, and taken a turn in finance. He'd been classified as a "high potential" early in his career, and although Lafleur did not have an official program for high potentials, Campos had offered a rigorous training curriculum emphasizing on-the-job learning as well as focused skill development. As a result, Michael was one of the company's more well-rounded executives, and his brands were consistently turning a profit to boot. Knight Rum was, in fact, Lafleur's top performer. Michael could do the job—but could he convince the top brass in Paris of that?

Dismissing the various scenarios from his mind, Michael turned to his computer and got to work. "If I keep producing," he reasoned, "it'll be obvious that I have the chops for the job."

The Rumors

Outside Michael's office, the atmosphere was considerably less focused. Twenty-four months after the Campos acquisition, the dust was beginning to settle and cost cutting was in the air. The company had announced plans for a restructuring—a guaranteed morale and productivity killer, as people tried to guess who would stay and who would go. Lucien's departure had only served to fan the flames. People were sniping at one another, and alliances began to form, divided on who should get Lucien's job and who would stand to benefit as a result. Many employees began to meticulously

document their work; others publicly scorned the scorekeeping but made casual digs in meetings or in the hallway.

Francesca Reynard, category manager for U.S. rums and one of Michael's direct reports, was in her office talking quietly with her assistant, Nora Ash. Nora was worried about her job, and the stress was getting to her. "The word is that Lafleur people are going to be favored in the restructuring," she confided. "In the copy room yesterday, I overheard someone saying that the Campos people never really tried to fit in; we're a bunch of 'stuffed shirts.' They didn't know I was there, or maybe they just didn't know I came from Campos."

"I would be shocked if the decisions were made along those lines," Francesca said. "But I can't make any promises. You're right: Things are a little crazy around here right now. All I can do is hope that you'll hang in there. The work you're doing is great."

After Nora left, Francesca reflected on the conversation. It was true that a cultural divide remained between acquirer and acquired. Mistrust was rampant, and the tension in the office was thick. She opened her e-mail to compose a message to Michael; she wanted to pick his brain about a new campaign. To be honest, she wanted to probe his thoughts on the restructuring as well. The two were old friends. But before she had a chance to type the message, she noticed an e-mail from Danielle Harcourt—a first. It was curiously casual.

"Hi, Francesca," the message read. "Do you want to have lunch tomorrow? I'd love to hear what you're working on—wondering what you've got planned. I've got some ideas. D."

The Competitor

Before heading home that evening, Michael stopped in at a party celebrating the expansion of a line of rum-inspired malt beverages. Lafleur had introduced Silver Knight the previous year; now it was adding vanilla-flavored White Knight, cranberry-flavored Red Knight, and low-carb Knight Light. When he stepped into the room, Michael could hear glasses clinking, jumbled conversation, and periodic laughter. "Lords" and "ladies" strolled the floor, offering samples and handing out "Tonight's the Knight" T-shirts in red, white, and silver. Michael ordered a soda water and

M. Ellen Peebles (epeebles@hbsp.harvard.edu) is a senior editor at HBR. Her case study, "And Now, a Word from Our Sponsor," appeared in the October 2003 issue.

canned the crowd.

Before long he spotted Albert Joffroy, a buddy of his from finance, chatting with a few people from the Paris office whom Michael recognized but didn't know by name. As he approached, he noticed Danielle standing with the group as well, holding a glass of red wine. The French contingent was moving on just as Michael arrived, and he heard one woman from the back say to Danielle, "See you next week!" Michael looked quizzically at Danielle.

"Oh, I'm heading back to the mother ship for a visit," she said. "I'll have some meetings, see some old friends, eat and drink a lot." She looked at her watch. "I have to run!" she said. "I'll see you in the office tomorrow." With that, he disappeared into the crowd.

"Interesting timing," Michael said thoughtfully, glancing at Albert.

Albert leaned in. "You didn't hear it from me, but I guess she wants to talk to Pierre about some new ideas for how we position our premium brands." Pierre Hoffman was Lafleur's CEO.

Michael raised his eyebrows. "Premium vodkas?"

"Premium brands."

"How do you know all this?"

Albert shrugged. He had a particular talent for wheedling information out of people. And he'd known Danielle for some time; they had worked together in Paris.

Michael thought for a moment. "Interesting timing," he repeated. He looked at the drink in his hand and momentarily wished it were something stronger. "She doesn't know anything about rum. Pierre knows I know what I'm doing. My numbers speak for themselves. I don't think I have anything to worry about."

"That's where you're wrong, my naive friend. Yes, numbers matter, but they don't speak. Danielle—she speaks."

"If you're suggesting that I get political and start trying to elbow my way into Pierre's office ahead of Danielle, you're talking to the wrong guy. That's just not how I work."

Albert was shaking his head. "It's not politics, Michael. It's corporate life. You think you're above the fray, but nobody is. Roll up your sleeves! Get in there!"

The Family

A couple of hours later Michael entered his darkened house, tripped over his 12-year-old son's trumpet case by the front door, and righted himself just in time to stumble over his nine-year-old daughter's backpack. He flipped on the hall light and shook his head, marveling at the disorder.

Upstairs, Michael's wife, Karen, was half asleep, a mystery novel slipping out of her grip. She was the general counsel at a regional clothing company, having given up a partnership-track position at a law firm as a concession to her family and the demands of Michael's career. She roused when Michael entered the room.

"Hey you," she said. "How was the party?"

"The usual," Michael said. "Sort of."

"What does that mean?"

"I found out that Danielle's flying to Paris next week, and I'm not so sure her intentions are good."

"Huh?" Karen slowly sat up and pushed her glasses back up to the bridge of her nose.

"Albert seems to think she's got an eye on my brands—well, actually, on Lucien's job, in the end. He also lectured me on office politics. Apparently, I'm not playing the game right. It's all just so stupid and unnecessary. Pierre likes me, so why should I waste the time and energy on making sure he knows my every move?"

Karen stretched and sat up further, now fully awake. "Politics…It's everywhere, Michael. It may seem silly to you, but you do have to know what's going on. Danielle's probably not thinking of it as 'stealing' your brands; she's just trying to play it smart. You have to do the same. But be yourself—even Albert may have his own agenda."

The Opportunity

As Michael entered the building the next morning, he saw Danielle walking toward him. Then she stopped. She put her head down, turned abruptly, and, before long, was out of sight. "Is she avoiding me?" he wondered, staring after her. He shook off the thought. "I'm being paranoid." Still, he regretted not having made any effort to connect with Danielle before now—before she posed a direct threat. He remembered that she'd invited him to lunch soon after the acquisition, and he'd turned down the invitation because of another commitment. He knew he should

"Yes, numbers matter, but they don't speak. Danielle—she speaks."

have returned the courtesy, but time had slipped away and somehow he'd never gotten around to it.

Michael strode into his office, flicked on the light, threw his coat on a chair, and turned on his computer. He had 25 new e-mails. The first one summarized the latest financials. The numbers on the Knight line were even better than he'd hoped. The next one was from Francesca.

"Michael, do you have any time to talk about a new duty-free promotion for Knight?" she wrote. "P.S. Danielle wants to have lunch with me today. She wants to talk about my work. Is there something I should know?"

Michael sat back in his chair. He lifted his head from his computer screen and muttered, "What a—" before he stopped himself. He realized Albert was there, leaning on the door frame and wearing a bemused expression.

"A what?" Albert asked.

"I'm starting to think you were right," Michael said. "Danielle's making a play for my job."

"There's no question about that. The question is, What are you going to do about it?"

Just then, Michael's assistant tapped on the door. Pierre Hoffman was on the line. Surprised, Michael quickly picked up his phone as Albert retreated. "Pierre! Hello!" he said.

Michel! Comment ça va? How is your golf game?" came the booming voice of Lafleur's chief executive.

"Could be better," Michael answered, leaning back and thinking to himself, "Hey, I'm not so bad off. I play golf with the CEO."

"Listen," Pierre said. "I have a proposition for you. You know that company we acquired in China—in Beijing? Marcel Rousseau—you know him?—he was going to run China, but he's leaving Lafleur to join a start-up. A start-up! Who would have thought? Anyway, we need somebody smart and experienced to take over—and I think you're the one."

A few seconds passed in silence. "China?" Michael responded.

Of course, the dialogue inside Michael's head had begun right away. China? He supposed it would be a feather in his cap if the office took off. It was the kind of international experience his résumé lacked. It would probably be very attractive financially. And then there was the lure of escaping New York, where politics were consuming the office. But

he would effectively be handing Danielle hi[s] job—and maybe Lucien's, too. Senior manag[-]ers were increasingly groomed in New Yor[k] these days, and he'd be off the radar screen en[-]tirely. Would he ever get to Paris?

And could he make it in China? The compe[-]tition was formidable. Soft-drink giant Ali[a] had moved in two years earlier and had taker[n] the youth market by storm. Several of Lafleur'[s] most impressive competitors were making sig[-]nificant inroads in the wine and spirits mar[-]kets. Then, of course, there was Michael's fam[-]ily. Karen had already sacrificed a lo[t] professionally. And how would the kids fee[l] about leaving their schools—and their friends[?]

But—China! A chance for the kids to learn a[] new language and experience a different cul[-]ture. His head was spinning.

"Are you asking me or telling me?" he aske[d] Pierre. "It sounds exciting, but I don't kno[w] how my wife will take it."

"I'm not telling you," Pierre said. "I thin[k] you're the man for the job, and I hope yo[u] think so, too."

The Dilemma

His mind full, Michael called his wife at he[r] office. "Are you sitting down?"

"Oh God, what is it?"

"Pierre called. He wants me—he wants us— to move to China."

Dead silence.

"Karen? Are you there?"

"China. China?! You've got to be kidding me. Please tell me you're kidding, Mike."

"No, I'm not kidding. And yes, China."

Karen sighed. "China. I'm late to a meeting I can't think about this right now. Can we tal[k] tonight?"

• • •

That evening, Michael and Karen plante[d] themselves in their living room and hashe[d] things out. The truth was, Karen didn't want t[o] go to China. She was willing to look past he[r] own interests if Michael truly wanted to go[,] but her career would suffer a major setback[.] Again. She also questioned the wisdom of th[e] move—was Pierre merely trying to sideline[] Michael for the time being? Karen and[] Michael agreed there were good argument[s] both for and against taking the kids oversea[s.] For his part, Michael was torn.

The next morning he walked into the office[] and found an e-mail from Danielle. "I have[]

"It's not politics, Michael. It's corporate life. You think you're above the fray, but nobody is. Roll up your sleeves! Get in there!"

ome thoughts about the Knight line, Michael," she wrote. "Do you have a few minutes to talk in the next couple of days? I'm going to Paris next week, and I'd like to run some things past you before I go, if you have a moment."

Michael stared at his desk. He didn't feel like fighting. He just wanted to do his job—that's what he was paid to do, and it's what he liked to do. His career was going well in New York, but would moving to China take him to the next level? In the end, would either path get him to Paris?

Should Michael go to China? • Five commentators offer expert advice.
See **Case Commentary**

Case Commentary

by Nancy Clifford Widmann and Amy Dorn Kopelan

Should Michael go to China?

Michael Feldstein should go to China.

The issue isn't whether Michael *can* do Lucien Beaumont's job, or even whether he *should* get it given his qualifications. It's pretty clear he's not going to get it, and the opportunity in China is a great one.

The clearest indication that he won't get the job is coming from the CEO himself. Most likely Pierre Hoffman already knows whom he's going to put into Lucien's position, and if he'd chosen Michael, China wouldn't be on the table. There are several contenders for the job. They're all successful, and they're all talented; at the level of business Michael has reached, *everyone* is talented. The winners play a better game of politics, and Michael hasn't shown himself to be terribly adept in this area. What's more, a couple of Michael's competitors are from the purchasing company, which more often than not gets to appoint the key players. Acquirers usually don't do it immediately following a deal because it's demotivating, but as jobs open up, they tend to put their own people in place. The fact is, Michael was acquired, and now he's at a disadvantage no matter how talented he is, especially because he has made little effort to build relationships with his new colleagues.

All that said, Michael has every reason to feel optimistic about his future with the company. China is strategic to Lafleur's future—an important source of new revenue—and Pierre wouldn't be offering him the job if he weren't confident in Michael's abilities and concerned about losing him. That puts Michael in a wonderful bargaining position. He should sit down with the CEO in Paris and reach a written agreement on certain terms before he accepts the job.

First, he should put a time limit on the contract; two years is about right. He may want to extend the contract at some point, but initially he needs the option to leave China and be considered for a job at headquarters. Second, he should get a clear definition of what will constitute success over the course of the contract, whether it's a certain percentage increase in sales, a measure of brand recognition, or a given market share. And he should not simply ask Pierre how he defines success but also propose his own measures.

Third, Michael needs to negotiate a certain number of trips per year to both New York and Paris. This will help him maintain his visibility in the more established offices and ensure that he remains on the radar screen should other senior management positions open up. Fourth, he should negotiate a job for his wife at a multinational corporation in China. His children are at an age where they can relocate relatively easily, but his wife isn't. She's sacrificed a lot already, and he needs to find a way to make it worth her while to go. And finally, he should consider requesting that certain trusted members of his current staff go along with him.

Once he's got his contract nailed down in cold, hard terms, he needs to repair his relationship with Danielle Harcourt. She was smart enough to reach out to him early on, and it wasn't reciprocated. But now that she no longer poses a threat, they can be great allies. Michael needs a peer in New York with whom he can touch base regularly. If Danielle gets Lucien's job—and it looks as though she's a serious contender—she can learn a lot from Michael about the Campos businesses. Michael should not get on that plane until he has Danielle in his camp.

Once he gets to China, Michael needs to promote his accomplishments. Whether it's by hiring a publicist or a personal manager or working through a PR agency, he needs to make sure that people in the industry—not just within Lafleur—are tuned into what he's doing. He needs exposure in trade magazines and in the general media so industry players can see that he's a pioneer in this new market. Search firms will start paying attention, as will Lafleur's competitors. Regardless of how his career works out at Lafleur, Michael's star will be much brighter because of his experience in China.

Nancy Clifford Widmann (widmannnc@ aol.com) is an executive coach based in New York. *Amy Dorn Kopelan* (bedlamcpw@earthlink.net) is the CEO of Bedlam Entertainment, a conference management company based in New York. They are coauthors (with organizational psychologist and consultant Elaine Eisenman) of the book, *I Didn't See It Coming*, forthcoming from Harvard Business School Press.

Michael is in a wonderful bargaining position.

by Fred Hassan

Should Michael go to China?

Many people working in multinationals find themselves, at some point in their careers, in the situation Michael is facing. I know because I've been through it.

Foreign companies will often insist that a U.S. employee go overseas and run a small business before that person can come back and run the parent's U.S. operation; they want to be sure that the person running the U.S. is "one of their own." If Lafleur were based in the United States, the dynamics would be different, and it might be less attractive for Michael to move: U.S.-based multinationals have a harder time bringing expats home and an even harder time reabsorbing them into their succession plans. Foreign companies seem to do a better job.

With that as a backdrop, the first thing Michael and his wife have to decide is whether they both want him to build a career at Lafleur. If he's not so sure about staying with the company, and if he wants to build his professional capability as a marketeer, he should stay in New York and look for opportunities outside of Lafleur. But if he's going to continue to move up at this company, he's probably going to need to go overseas; if not now, then at some point. It's important that Karen be part of the goal-setting process and willing to make the necessary commitments. When people move into different environments, they tend to rely heavily on their partners for strength and support. If Karen is unhappy about the move, the job becomes more risky for Michael. It's very important to have balance between personal life and work life. Michael should not sacrifice one for the other.

Assuming that accepting the China job is consistent with Michael's ultimate ambitions, there are significant advantages to it. First, he'll have the chance to be a "mini-CEO." He'll be in charge of sales, marketing, manufacturing, new product development, government relations—all the aspects of a general management role. Second, once he's successfully done the work in China (at the CEO's request) he'll

become an insider at Lafleur. And third, no matter what happens with Lafleur, he'll have broadened his and his family's world view.

Now, the question of politics is a separate one. Rather than look at China as an opportunity to run away, Michael needs to grow up. In any large organization, you are going to see a lot of complicated power dynamics. If and when he gets to Paris—which is what he seems to want—ambitions may be even more apparent; it's headquarters, after all.

Management is more art than science, and dealing with the human side of an enterprise is a very large part of a manager's career progression. Having a capacity for empathy is very important to a leader's success. Michael thinks he should be rewarded for keeping his head down and getting his job done. He thinks he shouldn't have to deal with Danielle—that she's a distraction. But just because he plays golf with the CEO and produces strong business results doesn't mean he's going to do well at Lafleur.

Like Michael, I had to weigh the opportunities available to me at a multinational. I was working for a global Swiss company, initially at U.S. headquarters in New Jersey. I made two significant moves, both of which forced me into totally different environments. The first was within the United States—from New Jersey to one of the company's divisions in Lincoln, Nebraska. In New Jersey, I had been primarily involved in corporate planning and finance; in Nebraska, I was more involved in operations. The second move was to go to a country in Asia to manage a problem subsidiary. I got to be a mini-CEO—at the age of 35—and it was an opportunity to show that I could make a difference. After those two assignments, the company made me head of U.S. operations, which would not have happened had I not gotten the broader experience and made the most of my opportunities.

Fred Hassan is the chairman and CEO of Schering-Plough, a health care company based in Kenilworth, New Jersey.

If Michael's going to continue to move up at his company, he's probably going to need to go overseas.

Case Commentary

by Allan Cohen

Should Michael go to China?

Michael's focused on the wrong things. Instead of defining healthy competition as bad and avoiding a colleague like Danielle—who has reached out to him more than once—he needs to, first, think about what he really wants to do with his career and his life and, second, gain a greater appreciation for the social alliances that make an organization run. You can call those aspects of organizational life "politics," but they aren't necessarily nasty and can be quite productive.

Does Michael really want Lucien's job—is advancement in that direction really that important right now—or is his frenzied desire for it just an automatic response to a sudden opening? Does Michael really want to manage outside of his sales and marketing expertise and become a general manager, a position in which networking and relationship building are even more essential than they are in his current position? There's no shame in deciding not to seek a promotion, even if it seems like the next logical move.

In making this calculation, Michael has to consider the needs of his family. He and Karen should define and discuss their individual and collective needs and aspirations. If Michael continues up the ladder at Lafleur, he will inevitably have to travel a lot. Is that what he wants, given that he has young children? The couple should also investigate what, if anything, Karen could do in China to further her learning and career connections.

Michael isn't the first manager to wish that office politics would simply go away. Any large organization will have its politics—many different units and people, each pursuing goals that may be at odds with one another. This process is natural and not necessarily destructive. And the further you advance within an organization, the more political your job becomes. The time horizons needed to judge your individual contributions become longer, and other factors come into play in assessing your performance—intangibles such as trustworthiness, initiative, the talent for coping with ambiguity, and the ability to look beyond functional interests. People can play tough—as some at Lafleur may be doing—but unless they are lying outright, deliberately trying to make others look bad, or applying illegitimate pressure on people, they aren't being underhanded or acting inappropriately. If behavior gets vicious, use the sunshine law: Get as much as possible out in the open. Despite the discomfort felt by some at Lafleur, it doesn't seem like the company is at that point.

What's more, any large organization will have a grapevine and unofficial speculation. When a key player is suddenly removed without explanation, in the wake of an acquisition and an announced but unexplained restructuring, anxiety levels soar. Michael and others are interpreting events and behaviors—including Danielle's legitimate ambitions—as ominous and threatening. Danielle and Michael are both looking for ways to get ahead, but while he frets and looks for excuses, she is coming up with new ideas and connecting with people in many different directions. His belief that his numbers should do the talking is not unusual but it restricts him to a very limited view of how organizations select higher-level managers. Doing a good job is the price of admission for advancement but not a guaranteed pass. Smart managers know that a network of connections—providing support, information, and resources—is critical to their success. Even if Danielle gets the promotion Michael wants, wouldn't it be better to be on good terms with her? He may need her support in the future.

The chance to lead a business in China is a stellar career-development opportunity for Michael and a real test of his abilities. He will have to work without clear guidelines, improvise, negotiate across cultural barriers, and create from scratch rather than carry out others' plans. If he doesn't build the proper connections, he will fail. It is just such crucibles—taking on jobs beyond your proven skills and somehow finding ways to deliver—that forge leaders' abilities and reputations.

Allan Cohen (cohen@babson.edu) is the Edward A. Madden Distinguished Professor in Global Leadership at Babson College, based in Babson Park, Massachusetts. The revised and updated version of his book, *Influence Without Authority,* will be published in April by Wiley.

Smart managers know that a network of connections is critical to their success.

Case Commentary

by Gary B. Rhodes

Should Michael go to China?

To make this decision, Michael needs more information. For one, he needs to know more about the China job before he can think about his future. What are Lafleur's expectations for growth in China? How much authority and control would he have over personnel, budget, and other operating decisions? If we can assume that Pierre is a straight shooter, I would want to hear more from him about how he thinks going to China would strengthen Michael's ability to compete for a top-level job in this company.

Michael's also making some assumptions about his current position that might not pan out. He believes that since he's been asked to go to China he has no chance at Lucien's job. He should check that out with Pierre before he makes any decisions, especially since he seems to have a relationship with Pierre that would allow him some degree of candor.

He's also making some assumptions about Danielle's motives. We don't know that she has the inside track on Lucien's job, and neither does Michael. We don't know why she's asked to meet with Michael. Based on feedback from a colleague, he's decided her intentions are not good, and he's gone so far as to validate that with his wife. He needs to give Danielle the benefit of the doubt and learn more about what makes her tick.

All that said, if Michael wants to get ahead at Lafleur, he needs to go to China. To be a successful global executive, you have to have lived somewhere other than your homeland. We don't know the extent of Danielle's experience, but we know she's done some managing in at least two cultures, which may work to her advantage. That's not playing politics; such experience is what it takes to be effective in a global company. China will pose some unique challenges for Michael because the cultural differences are so great. But this is a region that promises significant growth opportunities in nearly every industry, so he's in an enviable position.

I've worked with people in Michael's position, and I've seen people struggle with this very decision. In one case, my client was competing for a COO job. One contender had global experience, having lived and managed abroad. My client held a more strategic position within the local organization but hadn't worked in other countries. When he didn't get the coveted job at headquarters, he went overseas. He didn't end up in the general management job he was shooting for, but he got impressive experience nonetheless, which led to a great position as an executive vice president for production and quality control, a first-rate job in its own right. Perhaps even more important, he rounded out his résumé so he will be more attractive to potential employers. It was a strategic career move in the long run. Now he has more options than he ever had in the past, and, in today's economy, such options matter more than any current position.

Finally, it's important to note that the dynamic that Michael considers "politics" is merely a normal state of affairs and not necessarily an unhealthy aspect of organizational life. He seems reluctant to talk to people directly, and he's making decisions based on hearsay rather than fact. I would recommend that he have a straight-up conversation with Danielle, since he's not giving her the benefit of the doubt. Every organization has its political aspects, and if Michael wants to get ahead, he has to learn how to participate in that world and how to pursue his own agenda in an intelligent way.

At the end of the day, it doesn't matter whether Michael thinks his agenda is political or not. The hard lesson for him—as it is for all of us—is that performance alone is not enough. Performance is essential, but it is never a ticket to the top job.

> *The dynamic that Michael considers "politics" is merely a normal state of affairs and not necessarily an unhealthy aspect of organizational life.*

Gary B. Rhodes is a senior fellow at the Center for Creative Leadership, based in Greensboro, North Carolina.

Reprint R0501A
Case only R0501X
Commentary only R0501Z
To order, call 800-988-0886
or 617-783-7500 or go to www.hbr.org

To Order

For reprints, *Harvard Business Review* OnPoint orders, and subscriptions to *Harvard Business Review:* Call 800-988-0886 or 617-783-7500. Go to www.hbr.org

For customized and quantity orders of reprints and *Harvard Business Review* OnPoint products: Call Frank Tamoshunas at 617-783-7626, or e-mail him at ftamoshunas@hbsp.harvard.edu

Harvard Business Review

www.hbr.org

U.S. and Canada
800-988-0886
617-783-7500
617-783-7555 fax

Charlotte Beers at Ogilvy & Mather Worldwide (A)

It was December 1993, and during the past year and a half, Charlotte Beers had found little time for reflection. Since taking over as CEO and chairman of Ogilvy & Mather Worldwide in 1992, Beers had focused all her efforts on charting a new course for the world's sixth-largest advertising agency. The process of crafting a vision with her senior management team had been—by all accounts—painful, messy, and chaotic. Beers, however, was pleased with the results. Ogilvy & Mather was now committed to becoming "the agency most valued by those who most value brands."

During the past year, the agency had regained, expanded, or won several major accounts. Confidence and energy appeared to be returning to a company the press had labeled "beleaguered" only two years earlier. Yet, Beers sensed that the change effort was still fragile. "Brand Stewardship," the agency's philosophy for building brands, was not well understood below the top tier of executives who had worked with Beers to develop the concept. Internal communication efforts to 272 worldwide offices were under way, as were plans to adjust O&M's structures and systems to a new set of priorities. Not the least of the challenges before her was ensuring collaboration between offices on multinational brand campaigns. The words of Kelly O'Dea, her Worldwide Client Service president, still rang in her ears. "We can't lose momentum. Most change efforts fail after the initial success. This could be the prologue, Charlotte . . . or it could be the whole book."

Ogilvy & Mather

In 1948, David Ogilvy, a 38-year-old Englishman, sold his small tobacco farm in Pennsylvania and invested his entire savings to start his own advertising agency. The agency, based in New York, had financial backing from two London agencies, Mather & Crowther and S.H. Benson. "I had no clients, no credentials, and only $6,000 in the bank," Ogilvy would later write in his autobiography, "[but] I managed to create a series of campaigns which, almost overnight, made Ogilvy & Mather famous."[1]

Ogilvy's initial ads—for Rolls-Royce, Schweppes, and Hathaway Shirts—were based on a marketing philosophy that Ogilvy had begun developing as a door-to-door salesman in the 1930s, and later, as a pollster for George Gallup. Ogilvy believed that effective advertising created an indelible image of the product in consumers' minds and, furthermore, that campaigns should always be intelligent, stylish, and "first class." Most of all, however, David Ogilvy believed that advertising must sell. "We sell—or else" became his credo for the agency. In 1950, Ogilvy's campaign for Hathaway featured a distinguished man with a black eye patch, an idea that increased sales by 160%

---

[1] David Ogilvy, *Blood, Beer, and Advertising* (London: Hamish Hamilton, 1977).

Research Associate Nicole Sackley prepared this case under the supervision of Professor Herminia Ibarra as the basis for class discussion rather than to illustrate either effective or ineffective handling of an administrative situation.

and ran for 25 years. Other famous campaigns included Maxwell House's "Good to the Last Drop" launched in 1958 and American Express's "Don't Leave Home Without It," which debuted in 1962.

Gentlemen with Brains

David Ogilvy imbued his agency's culture with the same "first class" focus that he demanded of creative work. Employees were "gentlemen with brains," treating clients, consumers, and one another with respect. "The consumer is not a moron," admonished Ogilvy. In a distinctly British way, collegiality and politeness were highly valued: "We abhor ruthlessness. We like people with gentle manners and see no conflict between adherence to high professional standards in our work and human kindness in our dealings with others."[2]

At Ogilvy's agency, gentility did not mean blandness. Ogilvy took pride in his agency's "streak of unorthodoxy." He smoked a pipe, refused to fly, and peppered his speeches with literary references and acerbic wit. He once advised a young account executive, "Develop your eccentricities early, and no one will think you're going senile later in life." In a constant stream of letters, he made his dislikes clear: "I despise toadies who suck up to their bosses. . . . I am revolted by pseudo-academic jargon like *attitudinal*, *paradigms*, and *sub-optimal*." He also exhorted his staff to achieve brilliance through "obsessive curiosity, guts under pressure, inspiring enthusiasm, and resilience in adversity." No one at Ogilvy & Mather ever forgot the full-page announcement he placed in the *New York Times*: "Wanted: Trumpeter Swans who combine personal genius with inspiring leadership. If you are one of these rare birds, write to me in inviolable secrecy."

In 1965, Ogilvy & Mather merged with its partner agencies in Britain to form Ogilvy & Mather International.[3] "Our aim," wrote David Ogilvy, "is to be One Agency Indivisible; the same advertising disciplines, the same principles of management, the same striving for excellence." Each office was carpeted in the same regal Ogilvy red. Individual offices, however, were run independently by local presidents who exercised a great deal of autonomy.

David Ogilvy retired in 1975. Succeeding the legendary founder proved daunting. "The next four chairmen," commented one longtime executive, "did not have his presence. David is quirky; they were straightforward, middle-of-the-road, New York." Ogilvy's successors focused on extending the network offices internationally and building direct response, marketing research, and sales promotion capabilities. Revenues soared in the 1970s, culminating in record double-digit gains in the mid-1980s (see Exhibit 1). The advertising industry boomed, and Ogilvy & Mather led the pack. Nowhere was the agency's reputation greater than at its New York office, heralded in 1986 by the press as "the class act of Madison Avenue."

Advertising Industry Changes

The booming economy of the 1980s shielded the advertising industry from the intensifying pressures of global competition. Companies fought for consumer attention through marketing, and advertising billings grew—on average, between 10% and 15% per annum. Brand manufacturers—challenged by the growth of quality generic products and the diverse tastes of a fragmented mass market—created multiple line extensions and relied on agencies' creative powers to differentiate them. As business globalized, so did agencies. Responding to clients' demands for global communications and a range of integrated services, agencies expanded rapidly, many merging to achieve economies of scale as "mega-agencies" with millions in revenues worldwide.

---

[2]David Ogilvy, *Confessions of an Advertising Man* (New York: Atheneum, 1963).
[3]Dictionary of Company Histories, 1986.

After the stock market crash of 1987, companies reconsidered the value added by large advertising budgets. Increasingly, many chose to shift resources from expensive mass media and print campaigns towards direct mail, cable, telemarketing, and sales promotion. Fixed fees began to replace the agencies' historical 15% commission on billings. Long-standing client-agency relations were severed as companies sought the best bargains. Viewed by some as ad factories selling a commodity product, the mega-agencies were challenged by new, "boutique" creative shops. The globalization of media and pressures for cost efficiencies encouraged companies to consolidate product lines and to sell them in more markets worldwide. They, in turn, directed agencies to transport their brands around the world. The advertising agency of the 1990s—often a loose federation of hundreds of independent firms—was asked to launch simultaneous brand campaigns in North America, Europe, and the emerging markets of Asia, Latin America, and Africa.

Organizational Structure

By 1991, Ogilvy's 270 offices comprised four regions. The North American offices were the most autonomous, with office presidents reporting directly to the Worldwide CEO. Outside North America, presidents of local offices—sometimes majority stakeholders (see **Exhibit 2**)—reported to country presidents, who in turn reported to regional chairmen. Europe was coordinated centrally, but—with significant European multinational clients and a tradition of high creativity—the region maintained its autonomy from New York. To establish a presence in Latin America, Ogilvy obtained minority ownership in locally owned agencies and formed partnerships with local firms. The last region to be fully formed was Asia/Pacific, with the addition of Australia, India, and Southeast Asia in 1991 (see **Exhibit 3** for organization chart).

Between and across regions, "worldwide management supervisors" coordinated the requirements of multinational clients such as American Express and Unilever. WMSs served as the point of contact among multiple parties: client headquarters, clients' local subsidiaries, and the appropriate Ogilvy local offices. They were also responsible for forming and managing the core multi-disciplinary account team. More important, they facilitated the exchange of information throughout the network, attempting to ensure strategic unity and avoid operating at cross-purposes.

Over time, Ogilvy & Mather came to pride itself as "the most local of the internationals, the most international of the locals." Local delivery channels and the need for consumer acceptance of multinational products required specialized local knowledge and relationships. Local and global clients also served as magnets for each other: without local accounts, country offices were unable to build sufficient critical mass to service multinational clients well; without multinational accounts to draw top talent, the agency was less attractive to local clients.

With a "light center and strong regions," most creative and operating decisions were made locally. The role of Worldwide Headquarters in New York, staffed by 100 employees, was limited largely to ensuring consistency in financial reporting and corporate communications. Key capital allocation and executive staffing decisions were made by the O&M Worldwide board of directors, which included regional chairmen and presidents of the most powerful countries and offices such as France, Germany, the United Kingdom, New York, and Los Angeles.

The Ogilvy offices represented four core disciplines: sales promotion, public relations, advertising, and direct marketing.[4] Sales promotion developed point-of-purchase materials such as in-store displays and flyers. Public relations offices worked to promote clients' corporate reputation and product visibility. Advertising focused on mass marketing, establishing the core of a client's brand image through the development and production of television commercials, print campaigns,

---

[4]The number of Ogilvy offices by discipline in 1994 were as follows: 83 Advertising, 60 Direct Response, 12 Promotional, 23 Public Relations, and 92 in other areas, including highly specialized market research firms.

and billboards. Direct Marketing created and delivered targeted advertising—from mail order catalogues to coupons and television infomercials—designed to solicit a direct response from consumers. While the latter three resided within the regional structure, O&M Direct was an independent subsidiary. In the late 1980s, the Ogilvy board of directors decided to focus on advertising and direct marketing, the firm's chief competitive strengths. Unlike advertising, Direct's business in the 1980s remained chiefly local, but expanded explosively. By 1991, O&M Direct had received numerous industry accolades and was ranked the largest direct marketing company in the world.

"Beleaguered" Ogilvy & Mather

As clients demanded lower costs and greater service, Ogilvy & Mather—like many large agencies at the time—was slow to make adjustments. In 1988, Ogilvy was ranked the sixth-largest advertising firm in the world. As one executive remembered:

> Everything was going well. All we had to do was wake up in the morning and we were plus 15%. So why did we need to change? Our vision was "just keep doing the same thing, better." We failed either to recognize or acknowledge what were the first real indications that life around here was about to change fundamentally.

In May 1989, WPP Group Plc, a leading marketing services company, acquired Ogilvy & Mather for $864 million.[5] WPP, led by Harvard Business School-trained Martin Sorrell, had already purchased the J. Walter Thompson agency for $550 million two years earlier.[6] The takeover was hostile, with agency executives—including CEO Kenneth Roman—opposed. "It was a shock," explained one long-time executive. "We were a proud company with a constant stock market growth, the masters of our destiny. Suddenly, we were raided." Within months of the takeover, CEO Roman resigned. "Ken had absolutely nothing in common with WPP. There was a lack of trust, an air of conflict, adversaries, and invasion," remembered another. A number of top creative and account executives followed Roman, leaving Ogilvy & Mather for other agencies.[7]

Graham Phillips, a 24-year Ogilvy veteran, was appointed Roman's successor. One executive who worked with Phillips described him as "a brilliant account guy and a very good manager who identified our need to become a total communications company. But few would describe him as an inspirational leader."

In 1989, the agency lost major advertising assignments from Unilever and Shell. In 1990, Seagram's Coolers and Nutrasweet withdrew their multinational accounts.[8] Account losses in 1991 proved particularly damaging to the New York office, the agency's center and standard-bearer. "If New York thrives, the world thrives. If New York fails, the world fails," went a familiar company adage. New York's client defections were explained by one executive as a failure in leadership: "The office was run by czars with big accounts. People got used to a highly political way of working and work deteriorated." In 1991, Campbell Soup withdrew $25 million in business, Roy Rogers $15 million, and American Express—the account for which Ogilvy had won "Print Campaign of the Decade"—pulled out $60 million.[9] "Losing American Express had symbolism far beyond what the actual business losses were," recalled one Ogilvy executive. "People who were loyal Ogilvy

---

[5]Christie Dugas, "The Death of Ogilvy and an Era," *Newsday*, May 17, 1989.
[6]Ibid.
[7]"Change Comes to Fabled Ogilvy," *New York Times*, April 12, 1992.
[8]"Beers Succeeds Phillips at O&M Worldwide," *Adweek*, April 13, 1992.
[9]"Operation Winback," *Advertising Age*, February 1993.

employees, believers for years, disengaged. They threw up their hands and said, 'This place is falling apart.'"

Despite declines in revenue, the agency found itself unable to adapt to clients' changing demands. Budgets were not reduced at local offices, even as large clients pushed Ogilvy to streamline and centralize their accounts. "We were a high-cost operation in a low-cost world. There was a lack of financial discipline, a lack of focus on cost, and a lack of structured decision making on business issues," noted one executive. Another faulted the firm's tradition of local autonomy and failure to institute systems for managing collaboration: "We were spending a lot of money at the creative center without cutting back locally—building costs at both ends."

Recalling the atmosphere at the time, another executive concluded, "A shaken confidence permeated the whole company. We talked about change and what we needed to do ad nauseam, but nothing was happening. We tried to work within the old framework when the old ways of working were irrelevant."

At the end of 1991, Phillips stepped down as CEO, telling the press: "I have taken Ogilvy through a very difficult period in the industry. I had to let go people whom I had worked with for 27 years, and that wears you down." In April, Charlotte Beers was appointed CEO and chairman of Ogilvy & Mather Worldwide, the first outsider ever to lead the company.

Charlotte Beers

The daughter of a cowboy, Beers grew up in Texas, where she began her career as a research analyst for the Mars Company. In 1969, she moved to Chicago as an account executive with J. Walter Thompson. Once there, she cultivated success with clients Sears, Kraft, and Gillette, combining a Southern Texan charm with sharp business acumen. Beers rose quickly to senior vice president for Client Services.

At Thompson, Beers was known for her passionate interest—unusual in account executives—in the philosophy of marketing. Commented Beers, "I try never to discuss with clients only the stuff of business. I focus on advertising as well—on the ideas." Once described on a performance evaluation as "completely fearless," Beers earned a reputation for her ability to win over clients. Colleagues retold the story of how Beers impressed a roomful of Sears executives in the early 1970s by taking apart, then reassembling, a Sears power drill without skipping a beat in her pitch for a new advertising campaign.

In 1979, Beers became COO of the Chicago agency Tatham-Laird & Kudner. Her success in winning the mid-sized agency several new brands with Proctor & Gamble helped turn the firm around. Accounts with Ralston-Purina and Stouffer Foods followed. Beers was elected CEO in 1982 and chairman of the board in 1986. In 1987, she became the first woman ever named chairman of the American Association of Advertising Agencies. One year later, she led TLK through a merger with the international agency Eurocome-RSCG. Tatham's billings had tripled during Beers's tenure, to $325 million.

Beers Takes Over

Beers's appointment, recalled O&M veterans, created initial apprehension. Commented one executive, "She was from a smaller agency in Chicago and had not managed multiple offices. O&M is a worldwide company, and she had never worked outside the United States. And, she was not from Ogilvy." Added another, "This is an organization that rejects outsiders."

Her approach quickly made an impression with Ogilvy insiders. "It was clear from day one that Charlotte would be a different kind of leader. Full of life. Eyes open and clearly proud of the brand she was now to lead. Here was somebody who could look around and see the risks, but wasn't afraid to turn the corner even though it was dark out," said one executive. "We had leaders before, who said all the right things, were terribly nice, did a good job, but they didn't inspire. Charlotte has an ability to inspire—Charlotte has presence." Commented another executive, "She is delightfully informal, but you always know that she means business." Within two months of her appointment, Beers dismissed a top-level executive who had failed to instigate necessary changes.

Activate the Assets

"When I took over," recalled Beers, "all the press reports talked about 'beleaguered' Ogilvy. My job was to remove, 'beleaguered' from our name." In her first six weeks, Beers sent a "Hello" video to all 7,000 of Ogilvy's employees. It began:

> Everybody wants to know my nine-point plan for success and I can't tell you that I know yet what it is. I'm building my own expectations and dreams for the agency—but I need a core of people who have lived in this company and who have similar dreams to help me. That's going to happen fast, because we are rudderless without it. David [Ogilvy] gave us a great deal to build on, but I don't think it's there for us to go backwards. It's there to go forward.

Beers concluded that people had lost sight of Ogilvy's still impressive assets—its vast network of offices worldwide, its creative talent, and its distinguished list of multinational clients. "We must," she told senior executives, "activate the assets we already have." In her second month at Ogilvy, Beers observed a major client presentation by the heads of five O&M offices:

> It was a fabulous piece of thinking. We had committed enormous resources. But in the end, they didn't tell the clients why it would work. When the client said, "We'll get back to you," they didn't demand an immediate response, so I intervened. "You saw a remarkable presentation, and I think you need to comment." Ogilvy had gotten so far from its base, that talented people lacked the confidence to speak up.

For Beers, her early interactions with a key client symbolized the state of the company. "He kept retelling the tale of New York's downfall: how we blew a major account in Europe and how our groups fought among one another. The fourth time I heard this story," remembered Beers, "I interrupted. 'That's never going to happen again, so let's not talk about it anymore. Let's talk about what we can accomplish together.'"

Beers spent much of her first months at Ogilvy talking to investors and clients. For Wall Street, she focused on the quality of Ogilvy's advertising. "I refused to do a typical analyst report," she said. "When the Wall Street analysts asked me why I showed them our ads, I told them it was to give them reason to believe the numbers would happen again and again." Clients voiced other concerns. "I met with 50 clients in six months," recalled Beers, "and found there was a lot of affection for Ogilvy. Yet, they were also very candid. Clients stunned me by rating us below other agencies in our insight into the consumer." Beers shared these perceptions with senior managers: "Clients view our people as uninvolved, distant, and reserved. We have organized ourselves into fiefdoms, and that has taken its toll. Each department—Creative, Account, Media, and Research—are often working as separate entities. It's been a long time since we've had some famous advertising."

To restore confidence both internally and externally, Beers maintained that the agency needed a clear direction. "I think it's fair to say Ogilvy had no clear sense of what it stood for. I wanted to give people something that would release their passion, that would knit them together. I wanted the extraneous discarded. I wanted a rallying point on what really matters."

For Beers, what mattered was brands. "She is intensely client- and brand-focused," explained one executive. "You can't go into her office with financial minutia. You get about two seconds of attention." Beers believed that clients wanted an agency that understood the complexity of managing the emotional as well as the logical relationship between a consumer and a product. "I became confident that I knew what clients wanted and what Ogilvy's strengths were. It was my job to be the bridge." Beers, however, was as yet unsure what form that bridge would take or how it would get built. One of her early challenges was to decide whom to ask for help in charting this new course:

> I knew I needed their involvement, and that I would be asking people to do much more than they had been, without the benefits of titles and status. I avoided calling on people on the basis of their titles. I watched the way they conducted business. I looked to see what they found valuable. I wanted people who felt the way I did about brands. I was looking for kindred spirits.

The "Thirsty for Change" Group

Over the next few months, Beers solicited ideas for change from her senior managers, asking them to give candid evaluations of disciplines and regions, as well as of one another. In a style that managers would describe as "quintessential Charlotte," Beers chose to meet with executives one-on-one and assigned them tasks without regard to their disciplinary backgrounds. She commented, "I was slow to pull an executive committee together. I didn't know who could do it. It was a clumsy period, and I was account executive on everything— everything came to me." At first, some found the lack of structure unnerving. Noted one executive, "People weren't quite sure what their roles were. It caused discomfort. We began to wonder, 'Where do I fit? Who is whose boss?'" Another added, "She was purposely vague in hopes that people would stretch themselves to new configurations." Several executives, though cautious, found Beers's talk of change inspiring and responded with their ideas.

By May 1992, Beers had identified a group whom she described as "thirsty for change." Some were top executives heading regions or key offices; others were creative and account directors who caught her eye as potential allies. Her selection criterion was "people who got it"—those who agreed on the importance of change. All had been vocal about their desire to move Ogilvy forward. She sent a memo inviting them to a meeting in Vienna, Austria, that month:

Date: May 19, 1992   **HIGHLY CONFIDENTIAL**
From: Charlotte Beers

To: LUIS BASSAT, President, Bassat, Ogilvy & Mather—Spain
          BILL HAMILTON, Creative Director—O&M New York
          SHELLY LAZARUS, President—O&M New York
          KELLY O'DEA, Worldwide Client Service Director, Ford and AT&T—London
          ROBYN PUTTER, President and Creative Director—O&M South Africa
          HARRY REID, CEO—O&M Europe, London
          REIMER THEDENS, Vice Chairman—O&M Europe, Frankfurt
          MIKE WALSH, President—O&M, United Kingdom, London
          ROD WRIGHT, Chairman—O&M Asia/Pacific, Hong Kong

Will you please join me . . . in re-inventing our beloved agency? I choose you because you seem to be truth-tellers, impatient with the state we're in and capable of leading this revised, refreshed agency. We want to end up with a vision for the agency we can state . . . and excite throughout the company. Bring some basics to Vienna, like where we are today and where we'd like to be in terms of our clients and competition. But beyond the basics, bring your dreams for this great brand.

Brand Stewardship

The Vienna meeting, recalled Beers, "put a diversity of talents in a climate of disruption." Having never met before for such a purpose, members were both tentative with each other and elated to share their perspectives. Two common values provided an initial glue: "We agreed to take no more baby steps. And it seemed clear that brands were what we were going to be about."

Beers asked Rod Wright, who had led the Asia/Pacific region through a vision formulation process, to organize and facilitate the meeting. Wright proposed a conceptual framework, based on the McKinsey "7-S" model,[10] to guide discussion of the firm's strengths and weaknesses. He also hoped to generate debate. "We don't have passionate arguments in this company. We avoid conflict, and debates go off line. When you use a framework, it's easier to depersonalize the discussion."

Reactions to the discussion ranged from confusion to disinterest. "It was theoretical mumbo-jumbo," commented one participant, "I tend to be far more pragmatic and tactical." Added another, "I don't have much patience for the theoretical bent. I wanted to get on with it." Wright admitted, "They rolled their eyes and said, 'You mean we've got to do all that?'" Beers agreed: "The B-school approach had to be translated." As the discussion unfolded, the group discovered that their personalities, priorities, and views on specific action implications diverged widely.

One debate concerned priorities for change. Shelly Lazarus diagnosed a firm-wide morale problem. She argued for restoring confidence with a pragmatic focus on bottom-line client results and counseled against spending much energy on structural changes. Mike Walsh agreed but insisted that the group take time to articulate clearly its vision and values. But Kelly O'Dea had become frustrated with Ogilvy's geographical fragmentation and argued that anything short of major structural changes would be insufficient.

Participants were also divided on whether the emerging brand focus was an end or a starting point. The "creatives" in the group[11]—Luis Bassat, Bill Hamilton, and Robyn Putter—flanked by Beers, Lazarus and Walsh were interested primarily in finding an effective vehicle for communicating O&M's distinctive competency. An eloquent statement, they felt, would sell clients and inspire employees. The others—O'Dea, Wright, Harry Reid, and Reimer Thedens—wanted a vision that provided guidelines for an internal transformation. Summarized Wright, "One school of thought was looking for a line which encapsulates what we do: our creative credo. The other was looking for a strategy, a business mission to guide how we run the company."

Yet another discussion concerned the route to competitive advantage. Bassat, Putter and Hamilton, commented one participant, felt that Ogilvy had lost sight of the creative product in its rush to worry about finances—"we'd become too commercial." A recommitment to better, more imaginative advertising, they believed, would differentiate the firm from its competitors. Reid and Thedens, architects of a massive re-engineering effort in Europe, insisted on financial discipline and tighter operations throughout the company as the only means of survival in the lean operating environment of the 1990s. Wright and Thedens added the O&M Direct perspective. Convinced that media advertising by itself was becoming a commodity product, each pressed for a commitment to brand building through a broader, more integrated range of communication services.

---

[10]Wright's model included 10 issue categories: shared values, structures, stakeholders, staff, skills, strategy, suggestions, solutions, service systems, and a shared vision.

[11]Within advertising and direct marketing, "creatives" develop the art and copy for each media outlet of a brand campaign.

At the close of the meeting, remembered one attender, "There was a great deal of cynicism. 'Was this just another chat session?' we asked ourselves. But, we also had a sense that Charlotte felt right. She fit."

In August 1992, the group reassembled at the English resort Chewton Glen. Members presented Beers with their respective lists of priorities requiring immediate attention. Taken together, there were 22 "to do" items ranging from "examine the process by which we develop and present creative ideas" to "improve our delivery of services across geographical divisions." Beers recalled, "No one can focus on 22 things! I was so depressed, I stayed up all night and wrote a new list." She delivered her thoughts the next day:

I think we have hit bottom and are poised for recovery. Poised but not assured. Our job is to give direction for change. So here is where I start. For 1993, we have three—and only three—strategies. They are:

1. *Client Security.* Let's focus our energy, resources and passion on our present clients. It takes three years to replace the revenue from a lost client. Under strategy one, there's a very important corollary: We must focus particularly on multinational clients. This is where we have our greatest opportunity for growth and where our attitudes, structure, and lack of focus have been obstacles.

2. *Better Work, More Often.* Without it, you can forget the rest. Our work is not good enough. Maybe it will never be, but that's O.K.—better to be so relentless about our work that we are never satisfied. You tell me there's nothing wrong with our credo, "We Sell, or Else," but you also say we need some fresh thinking on how to get there. We must have creative strategies that make the brand the central focus.

3. *Financial Discipline.* This has been a subject of high concentration but not very productively so. We simply have not managed our own resources very well, and that must change.

These 1993 strategies were linked to the emerging vision by a declaration: "The purpose of our business is to build our clients' brands." One participant recalled, "The idea of brand stewardship was still embryonic. Charlotte clearly understood it in her own mind but was just learning how to communicate it. She used us as guinea pigs to refine her thinking." But some expressed concern: "There was no disagreement that the 1993 strategy was correct. It was fine for the short-term but we needed a long-term strategy."

Through the fall of 1992, group members worked to communicate the strategy—dubbed the "Chewton Glen Declaration"—to the next level of managers. Beers directed her energy toward clients, working vigorously to win new and lost accounts. She spoke about the emotional power of brands, warning them of the abuse inflicted by agencies and brand managers who failed to understand the consumers' relationship with their products. Ogilvy & Mather, Beers told clients, was uniquely positioned to steward their brands' growth and development. Clients were intrigued. By October, O&M boasted two major successes: Jaguar Motor cars' entire U.S. account and the return of American Express's $60 million worldwide account.[12] The press hailed, "Ogilvy & Mather is back on track."

---

[12]"Operation Winback," *Advertising Age*, February 1993.

Worldwide Client Service

The Chewton Glen mandate to focus on multinationals heightened the need for better global coordination. Although Ogilvy had pioneered multinational account service in the 1970s, the firm in the 1990s remained "segregated into geographic and discipline fiefdoms" that hampered the development and delivery of brand campaigns worldwide. Noted O'Dea, "What most clients began to seek was the best combination of global efficiencies and local sensitivity, but we were not set up to facilitate that. We had the local strength, but international people were commandos with passports and begging bowls, totally dependant on the goodwill of local agencies and their own personal charisma."

In the fall of 1992, Beers asked O'Dea to head a new organization, Worldwide Client Service, that would "tap the best brains from anywhere in the world for each account." O'Dea envisioned dozens of virtual organizations, each focused on a multinational client, with multiple "centers" located wherever their respective clients maintained international headquarters. Under WCS, members of multinational account teams became "dual citizens," reporting both to their local office presidents and WCS supervisors. One WCS director noted, "International people coordinating multinational accounts used to be regarded by the local offices as staff. We thought we were line; the clients treated us like line; but internally, we had no real authority. What WCS did was give us teeth by giving us line responsibility for our accounts—tenure, profits, growth, and evaluation of local offices."

WCS brand teams were structured to mirror their clients' organizations. Some WCS directors served largely as consultants, while others ran highly centralized operations, with a core team responsible for the entire creative and client development process. "We had to reinvent ourselves in the client's footprint," remarked the WCS account director for Kimberly-Clark. His counterpart at Unilever agreed but noted that current trends favored centralization. "Speed, cost-efficiency, and centralization are our clients' priorities. What matters is not just having good ideas, but getting those ideas to as many markets as possible, as **fast** as possible."

By 1993, O'Dea began to travel the world presenting the possibilities of transnational teams without borders. "Good sell-ins had to be done. Office heads had to understand that there were no choices—global accounts had to be managed horizontally. We'd be dead if we didn't do it," said Reid.

Tools for Brand Stewardship

"The first six months were high excitement, high energy, and a steep learning curve," said Beers. "That was followed by 12 months of disappointment and frustration. It didn't look as if we were getting anywhere." In December 1992, Beers asked Robyn Putter and Luis Bassat, two of the firm's top creative talents, for help in developing the emerging notion of "Brand Stewardship." They answered: "If we are to be successful, we must 'audit' our brands. We must ask the kinds of questions that will systematically uncover the emotional subtleties and nuances by which brands live." Beers took their insight directly to existing and prospective clients. One manager remembered:

> Clients immediately bought into Brand Stewardship. That created pressure to go public with it before we had every "i" dotted and "t" crossed. We didn't have a codified process, but Charlotte would talk to clients and we'd have to do it. Clients came to O&M offices saying, "I want a brand audit." And, our offices responded with, 'What's a brand audit?' One client asked us for permission to use the term. We had to move quickly, or risk losing ownership of the idea.

Beers responded by asking a group of executives to elaborate the notion of a brand audit. Led by Walsh, they produced a series of questions designed to unveil the emotional as well as the logical significance of a product in the users' lives: "What memories or associations does the brand bring to mind? What specific feelings and emotions do you experience in connection with using this brand? What does this brand do for you in your life that other brands cannot?" The insights gathered from these questions—which became the brand audit—would, in Beers's words, "guide each brand team to the rock-bottom truth of the brand." Focusing on two of Ogilvy's global brands— Jaguar and Dove—Beers's working group struggled to articulate in a few words and images each brand's unique "genetic fingerprint." The result was O&M's first BrandPrintsϑ:

- A Jaguar is a copy of absolutely nothing—just like its owners.
- Dove stands for attainable miracles.

Crafting a Vision

As the "technology" of brand stewardship developed, the senior team continued to wrestle with the formulation of a vision statement. Some argued, "We have the vision—it's Brand Stewardship." Others maintained that Brand Stewardship was but a tool to be used in attaining a yet undefined, future state. Further, as O'Dea explained, "Nearly everyone had had some contact with Brand Stewardship and WCS but they viewed them as separate and isolated actions without a strategic context."

The solution to the impasse, for some, was to include a larger group in the vision formulation. "We needed to decide collectively what we were going to be. If you have 30 people deciding and 30 people who have bought into the vision, then they have no reason not to go out and do it," reasoned Wright. Walsh agreed: "You get the 30 most influential people in the company to open their veins together—which hasn't happened in a very long time." Others, including Beers, worried about losing control of the end result. Advocates for a larger group prevailed, and the entire O&M Worldwide board of directors along with eight other local presidents attended the next meeting in July 1993 at the Doral Arrowwood, a conference center in Westchester, New York.

The purpose of the meeting, explained one of the organizers, was to get final agreement on the vision and where brand stewardship fit in. Feedback from clients on brand stewardship and WCS was used to guide the initial discussion. Participants' recollections of the three-day event ranged from "ghastly" to "painful" and "dreadful." Noted Lazarus, "It seemed an endless stream of theoretical models. Everyone was frustrated and grumpy."

The turning point, Beers recalled, took place at the end of a grueling first day, when one person voiced what many were thinking: "He said, 'There's nothing new here. I don't see how Brand Stewardship can be unique to Ogilvy.' This was very helpful. One of the negatives at Ogilvy is all the real debates unfold outside the meeting room." The next morning, Beers addressed the group: "Certainly, the individual pieces of this thinking are not new. But to practice it would be remarkable. I have heard that in any change effort, one-third are supporters, one-third are resisters, and one-third are apathetic. I'm in the first group. Where are you?"

With Beers's challenge precipitating consensus, attenders split into groups to tackle four categories of action implications. One group, which included Beers, was charged with crafting the specific wording of the vision. A second began to develop a statement of shared values that would integrate traditional Ogilvy principles with the emerging values of the new philosophy. "That was hard to agree on," recalled Wright. "At issue was how much of the past do we want to take forward." The third group worked on a strategy for communicating the vision to all levels and offices throughout the company. Plans for a Brand Stewardship handbook, regional conferences, and a training program were launched. A fourth group was asked to begin thinking about how to realign titles, structures, systems, and incentives to support the new vision.

After heated brainstorming and drawing freely from the other three groups to test and refine their thinking, Walsh remembered that, finally, "there it was: **'To be the agency most valued by those who most value brands.'"** Summing up the meeting, one attender said, "There had been an amazing amount of distraction, irrelevance, and digression. I didn't think we could pull it together, but we did." (See **Exhibit 4** for the final version of the Vision and Values statement.)

Moving Forward

Through the fall of 1993, Beers and her senior team worked relentlessly to spread the message of Brand Stewardship throughout the agency. It was a slow, sometimes arduous, process. By the end of the year, they had identified several issues that they felt required immediate attention.

Spreading the Gospel

Compared to clients' enthusiasm, reactions to Brand Stewardship within the agency were initially tepid. Across disciplines, employees below the most senior level lacked experience with, and knowledge of how to use, the principles of Brand Stewardship. O'Dea remarked, "Brand Stewardship has not seeped into everyday practice. Only a minority of the O&M population truly understands and embraces it. Others are aware of Brand Stewardship, but not deeply proficient. Many are still not true believers."

Account executives who misunderstood the concept were at a loss when their clients demanded it. Planners expressed confusion about how to use Brand Stewardship to develop a creative strategy.[13] Recalled one executive, "People didn't understand such basic things as the difference between a BrandPrint∂ and an advertising strategy."

Greater familiarity with the process did not always mitigate opposition. Admitted Beers, "We didn't always have much internal support. It did not sound like anything new." Another problem was that a brand audit might suggest a change of advertising strategy. "Doing an audit on existing business can be seen as an indictment of what we have been doing," noted one executive. Lazarus concluded:

> It will only be internalized throughout the organization with experience. I did a Brand Stewardship presentation recently with some of our account people. The client was mesmerized. They wanted the chairman of the company to see the presentation. Now, that had an effect on the people who were with me. I can bet you that when they make the next presentation, Brand Stewardship will be their focal point.

Perhaps the greatest resistance came from the creative side. "We've got to get greater buy-in from the creative people," noted Walsh. Their initial reactions ranged from viewing the BrandPrint∂ as an infringement on their artistic license—"I didn't believe in recipe approaches. They can lead to formulaic solutions," said one early convert—to the tolerant skepticism reported by another: "The

---

[13]Account executives managed the agency's contact with clients, bringing in new accounts and coordinating information flow between other functions and the client. Planners worked with account executives to establish creative marketing strategies.

creatives tell me, 'If it helps you get new business, that's great, but why are you in my office talking about this? I have a deadline and don't see what this has to do with creating advertising.' But you can't develop a good BrandPrint without cross-functional involvement."

Others questioned the relevance of Brand Stewardship for O&M Direct. While clear to Beers that Brand Stewardship clarified the rewards to clients from integrating advertising and direct marketing, some were slow to see this potential. Dispelling the popular notion that direct encourages short-term sales while advertising builds brands over the long-term, Thedens argued, "You can't send a message by mail that contradicts what you show on television. Both disciplines sell and both build the brand."

One executive concluded that the biggest problem was insufficient communication: "Anyone who heard it firsthand from Charlotte bought in. From the moment she opens her mouth to talk about brands, you know she has a depth of understanding that few people have. The problem is that, until recently, she has been the only missionary. Although the senior team had started "taking the show on the road," Walsh felt they were too few for the magnitude of the task: "The same six or seven people keep getting reshuffled. The result is that follow-through is not good." O'Dea, however, pointed out that the new missionaries had different tribes to convert. He emphasized the importance of translating the vision into a new role for each employee:

> We need to move beyond a vision that is useful to the top five percent of account and creative people, to one that has meaning for everyone at Ogilvy. The Information Systems staff should see themselves as brand stewards, because without information technology, we can't respond with appropriate speed. I want the Media people to say, "I will not buy airtime on these T.V. shows because they don't fit the BrandPrint." Creatives at O&M Direct developing coupon designs must be as true to the BrandPrint as creatives in advertising. Everyone must see themselves as co-stewards of the vision.

Local/Global Tensions

Success in 1993 winning several, large multinational accounts created further challenges for the embryonic WCS. Their goal of helping clients to develop a consistent brand image globally created tension in the firm's traditional balance of power. WCS pressed local agencies to give priority to brands with high global development potential over local accounts. For local agencies, however, local accounts often provided the most stable revenue stream and greatest profit. Further, in their zeal to exercise their newfound "line" responsibility, WCS supervisors were viewed at times as overstepping the bounds of their authority.

While tension had always existed between the centers and local markets, the increasingly centralized brand campaigns exacerbated conflicts. "Local agencies were used to always giving the client what they wanted," explained one WCS supervisor, "I had to start telling them to stop over-servicing the client." Some balked. Local expertise had always been one of Ogilvy's greatest competitive strengths. As one senior executive explained, "Certain local offices have not responded well to some of the advertising created centrally. One downside of global work is that it can end up being middle-of-the-road. When this happens, it's bad for an office's creative image locally."

But with costs escalating both centrally and locally, many felt that "the local barons" had to be reigned in. "How do we help our clients globalize," asked Walsh, "when our local management will conspire to keep them geographically oriented?"

For smaller agencies, issues of creative pride and autonomy were especially salient. Under the new system, the central WCS team developed the BrandPrint and advertising campaign with input from local offices. Local offices then tailored execution to regional markets. But while large offices usually served as the center for at least one global account, smaller offices, explained one WCS director, "are more often on the receiving end now. They begin to feel like post boxes. How do you attract good people to smaller offices if they never get to run big accounts?"

Beers felt that maintaining flexibility was key. "Some of our competitors—McCann Erickson is a good example—are excellent at running highly centralized campaigns. For us to view WCS that way would be a mistake. WCS should build upon, not diminish, our local strength." Creative and execution roles, she explained further, should shift according to the locus of the best ideas or relevant resources:

> I want to continue to cultivate the tension between local and center. The easiest thing would be to have far more dominance centrally. It is more efficient, and the clients like it, because they invariably wish they had more control at the center. The reality is that nothing substitutes for full-blown, local agencies where the people are talented enough to articulate the heart of the brand, to interpret it in a sophisticated way, and—if necessary—to change it. If you have messengers or outlets, you will never execute well. The best ideas have unique, local modifications. One brand campaign we tested, for example, was an absolute win around the world, except in Asia, where the humor did not translate well. Our creative director in Asia worked with the idea, and it became the print campaign we use globally.

Also on her mind was the brewing controversy about how to split fees and allocate costs between WCS and local offices. Agency compensation on large accounts consisted frequently of fixed fees that were negotiated up front. With new clients, it could be difficult to estimate the range of Ogilvy services needed and the extent of local adaptation that would be required. Agencies in more distant markets were asked to contribute—sometimes without compensation—when the need for additional local work was discovered. Local presidents complained that, although WCS accounts pulled their people away from local accounts with clear-cut billable time, their portion of multinational fees was small. WCS, on the other hand, maintained that they were being forced to absorb more than their fair share of local costs.

Beers recounted one specific incident that unfolded in December. "Kelly told me that one of our offices had refused to do any more work for a client, because they did not have any fees. I said to him, 'I think you ought to talk to them about our new way of working and how much promise there is in it. Give them more information. If they still can't see their way, have them come to me.' You ask for collaboration," she concluded, "but occasionally you act autocratically."

As conflicts continued to erupt, senior management was divided on the solution. "We have highly individual personalities running our offices. With 272 worldwide," one account director observed, "it's been like herding cats." Debate swirled around the degree of management structure required. Lazarus advocated common sense resolutions between the global account director and local agency presidents: "In our business, the quality of the work that gets done all comes down to the people who are doing it, not to bureaucratic structures. If you create the right environment and you have the right people, you don't need a whole structure." Others, O'Dea and his WCS corps included, insisted that organizational changes were necessary to make Brand Stewardship a reality agencywide. Walsh agreed: "What we don't have is a structure, working practices, remuneration, praise of people—all based on Brand Stewardship." Referring to the trademark Ogilvy color, Beers offered her perspective:

> We have to make Ogilvy "redder." The finances should follow our goal of killing geography as a barrier to serving the brand. ... Let's get the emotional content high and the structure will follow. We have people in the company who would prefer it the other way, but I want to get it done in my lifetime. So much of

what happens at Ogilvy is cerebral, thoughtful and slow. We can't afford to move at a "grey" pace.

At the end of 1993, yet another issue had come to the fore. With large multinational accounts, some WCS heads controlled billings that easily surpassed those of many countries in the network. The agency, however, had always accorded the greatest prestige and biggest bonuses to presidents of local offices, countries, and regional chairmen. Brand Stewardship now required top-notch brand stewards and organizations centered around products and processes rather than Ogilvy office locations. "I ask people to collaborate, but I don't pay them for it. This company has never asked its feudal chiefs to consider the sum," observed Beers. She pondered how to attract the best and the brightest to WCS posts, knowing she would be asking them to leave the safety of turf to head brand-focused, virtual organizations.

The "thirsty for change" veterans believed another hurdle would be learning to work better as a team. Said Lazarus, "I don't think we make a lot of group decisions. We talk about it, but decisions tend to get made by Charlotte and by the specific individuals who are affected." But implementation revived many of the debates of the first Vienna meeting. "I think we are all still very guarded," explained Walsh. "As each meeting goes by, it's a bit like a lump of ice slowly melting—our edges getting smoother all the time." Lazarus hoped that team members would grow "comfortable enough to disagree openly with one another." Battling a culture she had once described as "grotesquely polite" was still on Beer's list of priorities as she considered the group she had assembled to help carry the change forward.

By December 1993, Charlotte Beers assessed the year's progress: "Clients love Brand Stewardship. Competitors are trying to copy it. And internally, we lack consensus." She wondered what course of action in 1994 would provide the best stewardship of the Ogilvy brand.

Exhibit 1   Selected Financial and Organization Data

1984-1988

	1984	**1985**	**1986**	**1987**	**1988**
Revenues (in thousands)	$428,604	$490,486	$560,132	$738,508	$838,090
Net income (in thousands)	25,838	30,247	26,995	29,757	32,950
Operating profit (in thousands)	49,191	45,355	47,764	57,933	65,922

Source: The Ogilvy Group Annual Report, 1988.

1989-1993[a]

	1989	**1990**	**1991**	**1992**	**1993**
Total annual billings (in thousands)[b]	$4,089,000	$4,563,700	$5,271,000	$5,205,700	$5,814,100
Revenues (in thousands)	592,600	653,700	757,600	754,800	740,000
Percent change in net income[c]	NA	4.7	-2.8	1.9	5.3
Operating margin	NA	6.4	4.1	4.9	7.6

Source: *Advertising Age.*

[a]Financial information for 1989-1993 is not comparable to 1984-1988 due to the restructuring of the company following sale to WPP Group, plc. It is the policy of WPP Group, plc not to release revenue and net income information about its subsidiaries.

[b]Represents an estimate by Advertising Age of the total value of all advertising and direct marketing campaigns run in a given year.

[c]The percent increase or decrease is given from an undisclosed sum at base year 1989.

Exhibit 2   Percent of Regional Offices Owned by O&M Worldwide

	# of Offices	**100%**	**>50%**	**<50%**	**0%**
North America	40	80	20	0	0
Europe	97	63	24	8	5
Asia/Pacific	66	57	36	7	0
Latin America	48	25	6	21	48

Exhibit 3   Ogilvy & Mather Worldwide Organization Chart, 1991

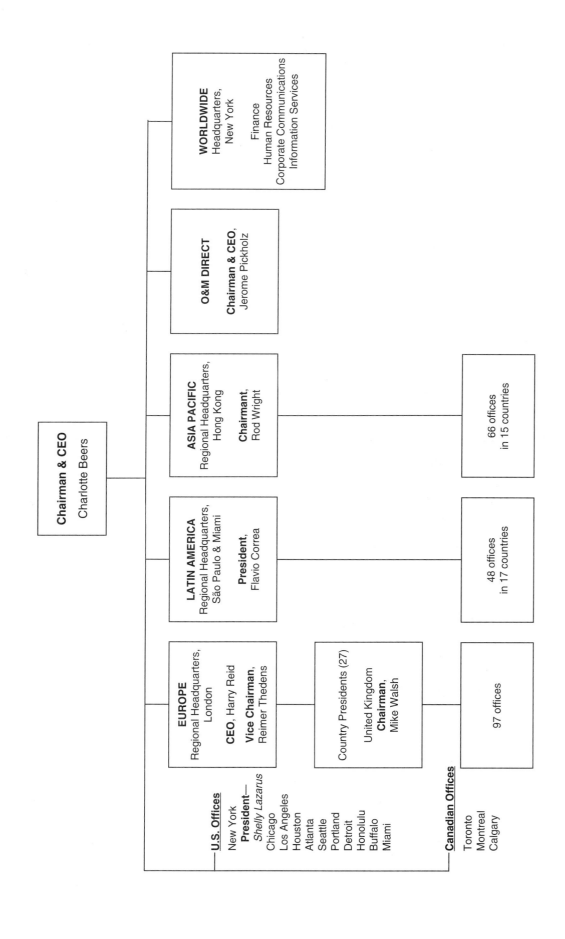

Chairman & CEO
Charlotte Beers

EUROPE
Regional Headquarters,
London

CEO, Harry Reid
Vice Chairman,
Reimer Thedens

Country Presidents (27)

United Kingdom
Chairman,
Mike Walsh

U.S. Offices

New York
President—
Shelly Lazarus
Chicago
Los Angeles
Houston
Atlanta
Seattle
Portland
Detroit
Honolulu
Buffalo
Miami

Canadian Offices

Toronto
Montreal
Calgary

97 offices

LATIN AMERICA
Regional Headquarters,
São Paulo & Miami

President,
Flavio Correa

48 offices
in 17 countries

ASIA PACIFIC
Regional Headquarters,
Hong Kong

Chairmant,
Rod Wright

66 offices
in 15 countries

O&M DIRECT

Chairman & CEO,
Jerome Pickholz

WORLDWIDE
Headquarters,
New York

Finance
Human Resources
Corporate Communications
Information Services

Exhibit 4   Statement of Vision and Values, 1993

To our people, our clients, and our friends—

The winds of change are blowing through Ogilvy & Mather. We are raising the sights of everybody in the company to a sweeping new vision:

TO BE THE AGENCY MOST VALUED BY THOSE WHO MOST VALUE BRANDS

Not that we have ever been unmindful of the importance of brands. Quite the contrary. Our new thrust gets a big boost from ingrained Ogilvy & Mather strengths. Its roots lie in the teachings of David Ogilvy that reverberate through our halls. We have always aimed to create great campaigns with the spark to ignite sales and the staying power to build enduring brands.

What's new is a restructuring of resources, an arsenal of modern techniques, and an intensity of focus that add up to a major advance in the way we do business. We call it BRAND STEWARDSHIP — the art of creating, building, and energizing profitable brands.

The new techniques and procedures of Brand Stewardship have already proved their value for many important brands. As I write they are being put to work for others. In March we will launch them formally — in print, on tape, and throughout the Ogilvy & Mather network.

This will affect the working habits of every professional in the agency, to the benefit, I am convinced, of every brand we work for. I predict that it will bring out the best in all of you — creatively and in every other aspect of your work — and add a lot to the pleasure and satisfaction you get out of your jobs.

As a first formal step the Board of Directors is putting forward the new statement of Shared Values on the facing page. You may notice that several of the points are taken from principles that have guided the company since its start — principles that were most recently set on paper in 1990 when David Ogilvy brought our Corporate Culture up to date.

Thus the Shared Values perform two functions: they *expand* our culture to reflect inexorable change, and in the same breath they *reinforce* its timeless standards.

All vital cultures — national, artistic, corporate — tend to evolve as conditions change, preserving valuable old characteristics as new ones come into the spotlight. In just that way these Shared Values now take their place at the forefront of the dynamic culture of Ogilvy & Mather.

Charlotte Beers
Chairman, Ogilvy, Mather & Worldwide

The market in which we compete is not a static one. To progress toward our new Vision will demand restless challenge and frequent change. The values we share, however, the way we do things day-to-day, will remain constant.

We work not for ourselves, not for the company, not even for a client. We work for Brands.

We work with the client, as Brand Teams. These Teams represent the collective skills of our clients and ourselves. On their performance, our client will judge the whole agency.

We encourage individuals, entrepreneurs, inventive mavericks: with such members, teams thrive. We have no time for prima donnas and politicians.

We value candor, curiosity, originality, intellectual rigor, perseverance, brains — and civility. We see no conflict between a commitment to the highest professional standards in our work and to human kindness in our dealings with each other.

We prefer the discipline of knowledge to the anarchy of ignorance. We pursue knowledge the way a pig pursues truffles.

We prize both analytical and creative skills. Without the first, you can't know where to go; without the second, you won't be able to get there.

The line between confidence and arrogance is a fine one. We watch it obsessively.

We respect the intelligence of our audiences:
"The consumer is not a moron."

We expect our clients to hold us accountable for our Stewardship of their Brands. Only if we have built, nourished, and developed prosperous Brands, only if we have made them more valuable both to their users and to their owners, may we judge ourselves successful.

ETHICS AND SOCIAL RESPONSIBILITY

Today, it's not enough for companies to make a profit. We also expect managers to make a profit by doing the right things. Unfortunately, no matter what managers decide to do, someone or some group will be unhappy with the outcome. Managers don't have the luxury of choosing theoretically optimal, win-win solutions that are obviously desirable to everyone involved. In practice, solutions to ethical and social responsibility problems aren't optimal. Often, managers must be satisfied with a solution that just makes do or does the least harm. Rights and wrongs are rarely crystal clear to managers charged with doing the right thing. The business world is much messier than that.

What Is Ethical and Unethical Workplace Behavior?

Ethics is the set of moral principles or values that defines right and wrong for a person or group. Unfortunately, numerous studies have consistently produced distressing results about the state of ethics in today's business world. A Society for Human Resources Management survey found that only 27 percent of employees felt that their organization's leadership was ethical. This may be a misperception due to opaque

Ethics the set of moral principles or values that defines right and wrong for a person or group

Learning Outcomes

1 identify common kinds of workplace deviance.

2 describe the U.S. Sentencing Commission Guidelines for Organizations and explain how they both encourage ethical behavior and punish unethical behavior by businesses.

3 describe what influences ethical decision making.

4 explain what practical steps managers can take to improve ethical decision making.

5 explain to whom organizations are socially responsible.

6 explain for what organizations are socially responsible.

7 explain how organizations can choose to respond to societal demands for social responsibility.

8 explain whether social responsibility hurts or helps an organization's economic performance.

© Giorgio Majno/Photographer's Choice/Getty Images

company policies, since 45 percent of HR professionals showed confidence in their leadership's ethics.[1] Nonetheless, the frequency of ethical violations speaks for itself. In a study of 1,324 randomly selected workers, managers, and executives across multiple industries, 48 percent of the respondents admitted to actually committing an unethical or illegal act in the past year, including cheating on an expense account, discriminating against coworkers, forging signatures, paying or accepting kickbacks, and looking the other way when environmental laws were broken.[2]

Other studies contain good news. When people believe their work environment is ethical, they are six times more likely to stay with that company than if they believe they work in an unethical environment.[3]

According to Dwight Reighard, the chief HR officer at HomeBanc Mortgage Corp. in Atlanta, "People want to work for leaders they trust."[4] In short, much needs to be done to make workplaces more ethical, but—and this is very important—most managers and employees want this to happen.

 After reading the next two sections, you should be able to

1   identify common kinds of workplace deviance.

2   describe the U.S. Sentencing Commission Guidelines for Organizations and explain how they both encourage ethical behavior and punish unethical behavior by businesses.

1 Workplace Deviance

Ethical behavior conforms to a society's accepted principles of right and wrong. Depending on which study you look at, however, one-third to three-quarters of all employees admit that they have stolen from their employers, committed computer fraud, embezzled funds, vandalized company property, sabotaged company projects, faked injuries to receive workers' compensation benefits or insurance, or "called in sick" to work when they weren't really sick. Experts estimate that unethical behaviors like these, which researchers call *workplace deviance* may cost companies nearly $1 trillion a year, or roughly 7 percent of their revenues.[5]

Workplace deviance is unethical behavior that violates organizational norms about right and wrong. As Exhibit 4.1 shows, workplace deviance can be categorized by how deviant the behavior is, from minor to serious, and by the target of the deviant behavior, either the organization as a whole or particular people in the workplace.[6]

Company-related deviance can affect both tangible and intangible assets. One kind of workplace deviance, called **production deviance,** hurts the quality and quantity of work produced. Examples include leaving early, taking excessively long work breaks, intentionally working more slowly, or wasting resources. **Property deviance** is unethical behavior aimed at company property or products. Examples include sabotaging, stealing, or damaging equipment or products and overcharging for services and then pocketing the difference. For example, Karin Wilson, who owns the Page and Palette bookstore in Fairhope, Alaska, found that her bookkeeper was using the bookstore's company credit card to pay off her personal credit card and also wrote checks to herself instead of paying publishers for books. In all, Wilson estimates that her bookkeeper made off with $150,000.[7] Employee stealing is more widespread than you'd think. A survey of 24 large retailers employing 2.3 million workers found that 1 out of 28 employees were caught stealing each year.[8]

Theft of company merchandise by employees, called **employee shrinkage,** is another common form of property deviance. Employee shrinkage costs U.S. retailers more than $15.8 billion a year, and typically reduces store profits by 2 to 3 percent, and takes many forms.[9] "Sweethearting" occurs when employees discount or don't ring up merchandise their family or friends bring to the cash register. In "dumpster diving," employees unload trucks, stash merchandise in a dumpster, and then retrieve it after work.[10]

Whereas production and property deviance harm companies, political deviance and personal aggression are unethical behaviors that hurt particular people within companies. **Political deviance** is using one's influence to harm others in the company. Examples include making decisions based on favoritism rather than performance, spreading rumors about coworkers, and blaming others for mistakes they didn't make. **Personal aggression** is hostile or aggressive behavior toward others. Examples include sexual harassment, verbal abuse, stealing from coworkers, and personally threatening coworkers. One of the fastest-growing kinds of personal aggression is workplace violence. More than 2 million Americans are victims of some form of workplace violence each year. According to a U.S. Bureau of Labor Statistics (BLS)

Ethical behavior
behavior that conforms to a society's accepted principles of right and wrong

Workplace deviance
unethical behavior that violates organizational norms about right and wrong

Production deviance
unethical behavior that hurts the quality and quantity of work produced

Property deviance
unethical behavior aimed at the organization's property or products

Employee shrinkage
employee theft of company merchandise

Political deviance
using one's influence to harm others in the company

Personal aggression
hostile or aggressive behavior toward others

Exhibit 4.1

Types of Workplace Deviance

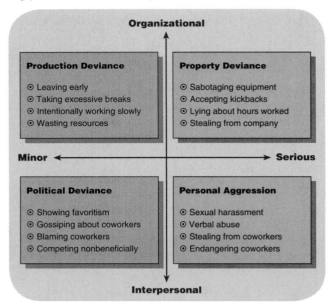

Source: Republished with permission of Academy of Management, P.O. Box 3020, Briar Cliff Manor, NY, 10510-8020. "A Typology of Deviant Workplace Behaviors" (Figure), S. L. Robinson & R. J. Bennett. *Academy of Management Journal*, 1995, Vol. 38. Reproduced by permission of the publisher via Copyright Clearance Center, Inc.

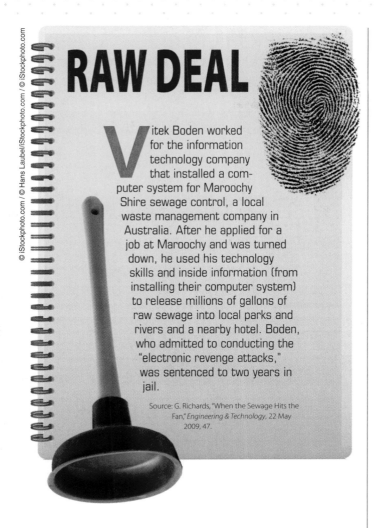

RAW DEAL

Vitek Boden worked for the information technology company that installed a computer system for Maroochy Shire sewage control, a local waste management company in Australia. After he applied for a job at Maroochy and was turned down, he used his technology skills and inside information (from installing their computer system) to release millions of gallons of raw sewage into local parks and rivers and a nearby hotel. Boden, who admitted to conducting the "electronic revenge attacks," was sentenced to two years in jail.

Source: G. Richards, "When the Sewage Hits the Fan," *Engineering & Technology*, 22 May 2009, 47.

survey of 7.4 million U.S. companies, 5.4 percent of all employees experience an incident of workplace violence each year.[11] Between 650 and 1,000 people are killed in such incidents each year.[12]

2 U.S. Sentencing Commission Guidelines for Organizations

Historically, if management was unaware of an employee's unethical activities, the company could not be held responsible. Since 1991, however, when the U.S. Sentencing Commission Guidelines for Organizations were established, companies can be prosecuted and punished *even if management doesn't know about the unethical behavior*. Penalties for unethical behavior can be substantial, with maximum fines approaching $300 million![13] An amendment made in 2004 outlines much stricter requirements for ethics training and emphasizes creating a legal and ethical company culture.[14]

Let's examine **2.1 to whom the guidelines apply and what they cover** and **2.2 how, according to the guidelines, an organization can be punished for the unethical behavior of its managers and employees.**

2.1 Who, What, and Why

Nearly all businesses are covered by the U.S. Sentencing Commission's guidelines. This includes nonprofits, partnerships, labor unions, unincorporated organizations and associations, incorporated organizations, and even pension funds, trusts, and joint stock companies. If your organization can be characterized as a business (remember, nonprofits count, too), then it is subject to the guidelines.[15]

The guidelines cover offenses defined by federal laws such as invasion of privacy, price fixing, fraud, customs violations, antitrust violations, civil rights violations, theft, money laundering, conflicts of interest, embezzlement, dealing in stolen goods, copyright infringements, extortion, and more. But it's not enough merely to stay within the law. The purpose of the guidelines is not just to punish companies *after* they or their employees break the law, but also to encourage companies to take proactive steps such as ethics training that will discourage or prevent white-collar crime *before* it happens. The guidelines also give companies an incentive to cooperate with and disclose illegal activities to federal authorities.[16]

2.2 Determining the Punishment

The guidelines impose smaller fines on companies that take proactive steps to encourage ethical behavior or voluntarily disclose illegal activities to federal authorities. Essentially, the law uses a carrot-and-stick approach. The stick is the threat of heavy fines that can total millions of dollars. The carrot is a substantial reduction in the fine, but only if the company has

> Penalties for unethical behavior can be **substantial**, with maximum fines approaching $300 million!

Exhibit 4.2

Offense Levels, Base Fines, Culpability Scores, and Possible Total Fines under the U.S. Sentencing Commission Guidelines for Organizations

Offense Level	Base Fine	Culpability Scores					
		0.05	0.5	1.0	2.0	3.0	4.0
6 or less	$ 5,000	$ 250	$ 2,500	$ 5,000	$ 10,000	$ 15,000	$ 20,000
7	7,500	375	3,750	7,500	15,000	22,500	30,000
8	10,000	500	5,000	10,000	20,000	30,000	40,000
9	15,000	750	7,500	15,000	30,000	45,000	60,000
10	20,000	1,000	10,000	20,000	40,000	60,000	80,000
11	30,000	1,500	15,000	30,000	60,000	90,000	120,000
12	40,000	2,000	20,000	40,000	80,000	120,000	160,000
13	60,000	3,000	30,000	60,000	120,000	180,000	240,000
14	85,000	4,250	42,500	85,000	170,000	255,000	340,000
15	125,000	6,250	62,500	125,000	250,000	375,000	500,000
16	175,000	8,750	87,500	175,000	350,000	525,000	700,000
17	250,000	12,500	125,000	250,000	500,000	750,000	1,000,000
18	350,000	17,500	175,000	350,000	700,000	1,050,000	1,400,000
19	500,000	25,000	250,000	500,000	1,000,000	1,500,000	2,000,000
20	650,000	32,500	325,000	650,000	1,300,000	1,950,000	2,600,000
21	910,000	45,500	455,000	910,000	1,820,000	2,730,000	3,640,000
22	1,200,000	60,000	600,000	1,200,000	2,400,000	3,600,000	4,800,000
23	1,600,000	80,000	800,000	1,600,000	3,200,000	4,800,000	6,400,000
24	2,100,000	105,000	1,050,000	2,100,000	4,200,000	6,300,000	8,400,000
25	2,800,000	140,000	1,400,000	2,800,000	5,600,000	8,400,000	11,200,000
26	3,700,000	185,000	1,850,000	3,700,000	7,400,000	11,100,000	14,800,000
27	4,800,000	240,000	2,400,000	4,800,000	9,600,000	14,400,000	19,200,000
28	6,300,000	315,000	3,150,000	6,300,000	12,600,000	18,900,000	25,200,000
29	8,100,000	405,000	4,050,000	8,100,000	16,200,000	24,300,000	32,400,000
30	10,500,000	525,000	5,250,000	10,500,000	21,000,000	31,500,000	42,000,000
31	13,500,000	675,000	6,750,000	13,500,000	27,000,000	40,500,000	54,000,000
32	17,500,000	875,000	8,750,000	17,500,000	35,000,000	52,500,000	70,000,000
33	22,000,000	1,100,000	11,000,000	22,000,000	44,000,000	66,000,000	88,000,000
34	28,500,000	1,425,000	14,250,000	28,500,000	57,000,000	85,500,000	114,000,000
35	36,000,000	1,800,000	18,000,000	36,000,000	72,000,000	108,000,000	144,000,000
36	45,500,000	2,275,000	22,750,000	45,500,000	91,000,000	136,500,000	182,000,000
37	57,500,000	2,875,000	28,750,000	57,500,000	115,000,000	172,500,000	230,000,000
38 or more	72,500,000	3,625,000	36,250,000	72,500,000	145,000,000	217,500,000	290,000,000

Source: "Chapter Eight—Part C—Fines," 2007 Federal Sentencing Guidelines, available online at http://www.ussc.gov/2007guid/tabconchapt8.htm [accessed 15 July 2008].

started an effective compliance program (discussed below) to encourage ethical behavior *before* the illegal activity occurs.[17] The method used to determine a company's punishment illustrates the importance of establishing a compliance program, as illustrated in Exhibit 4.2.

The first step is to compute the *base fine* by determining what *level of offense* has occurred. The level of the offense (i.e., its seriousness) varies depending on the kind of crime, the loss incurred by the victims, and how much planning went into the crime. For example, simple fraud is a level 6 offense (there are 38 levels in all). But if the victims of that fraud lost more than $5 million, that level 6 offense becomes a level 22 offense. Moreover, anything beyond minimal

planning to commit the fraud results in an increase of two levels to a level 24 offense. How much difference would this make to the company? As Exhibit 4.2 shows, crimes at or below level 6 incur a base fine of $5,000, whereas the base fine for level 24 is $2.1 million. So the difference is $2.095 million! The base fine for level 38, the top-level offense, is a hefty $72.5 million.

After assessing a *base fine*, the judge computes a culpability score, which is a way of assigning blame to the company. The culpability score can range from a minimum of 0.05 to a maximum of 4.0. The greater the corporate responsibility in conducting, encouraging, or sanctioning illegal or unethical activity, the higher the culpability score. A company that already has a compliance program and voluntarily reports the offense to authorities will incur a culpability score of 0.05. By contrast, a company whose management secretly plans, approves, and participates in illegal or unethical activity will receive the maximum score of 4.0.

The culpability score is critical because the total fine is computed by multiplying the base fine by the culpability score. Going back to our level 24 fraud offense, the left point of the upper arrow in Exhibit 4.2 shows that a company with a compliance program that turns itself in will be fined only $105,000 ($2,100,000 × 0.05). In contrast, a company that secretly planned, approved, and participated in illegal activity will be fined $8.4 million ($2,100,000 × 4.0), as shown by the right point of the upper arrow. The difference is even greater for level 38 offenses. As shown by the left point of the bottom arrow, a company with a compliance program and a 0.05 culpability score is fined only $3.625 million, whereas a company with the maximum 4.0 culpability score is fined a whopping $290 million, as indicated by the right point of the bottom arrow. These differences clearly show the importance of having a compliance program in place. Over the last decade, 1,494 companies have been charged under the U.S. Sentencing Commission Guidelines. Seventy-six percent of those charged were fined, with the average fine exceeding $2 million. Company fines are on average twenty times larger now than before the guidelines were implemented in 1991.[18]

Fortunately for companies that want to avoid paying these stiff fines, the U.S. Sentencing Commission Guidelines clearly spell out the seven necessary components of an effective compliance program to aid companies in their efforts to set up appropriate compliance programs.[19] Exhibit 4.3 lists those components. Caremark International, a managed-care service provider in Delaware, pleaded guilty to criminal charges related to its physician contracts and improper patient referrals. When it was then sued by shareholders for negligence and poor management, the Delaware court dismissed the case, ruling that the company's ethics compliance program, built on the components described in Exhibit 4.3, was a good-faith attempt to monitor employees and that the company did not knowingly allow illegal and unethical behavior to occur. The court went on to rule that a compliance program based on the U.S. Sentencing Commission Guidelines was enough to shield the company from liability.[20]

Exhibit 4.3

Compliance Program Steps from the U.S. Sentencing Commission Guidelines for Organizations

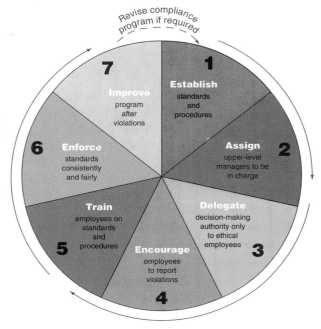

Source: D. R. Dalton, M. B. Metzger, and J. W. Hill, "The 'New' U.S. Sentencing Commission Guidelines: A Wake-up Call for Corporate America," *Academy of Management Executive* 8 (1994): 7–16.

How Do You Make Ethical Decisions?

On a cold morning in the midst of a winter storm, schools were closed, and most people had decided to stay home from work. Nevertheless, Richard Addessi had already showered, shaved, and dressed for the office. He kissed his wife Joan goodbye, but before he could get to his car, he fell dead on the garage floor of a sudden heart attack. Addessi was 4 months short of his 30-year anniversary with the company. Having begun work at IBM at the age of 18, he was just 48 years old.[21]

You're the vice president in charge of benefits at IBM. Given that he was only 4 months short of being eligible for full retirement benefits, do you award those benefits to Richard Addessi's wife and daughters? If the answer is yes, they will receive his full retirement benefits of $1,800 a month and free lifetime medical coverage. If you say no, his widow and two daughters will receive only $340 a month. They will also have to pay $473 a month to continue their current medical coverage. As the VP in charge of benefits at IBM, what would be the ethical thing for you to do?

 After reading the next two sections, you should be able to

3   describe what influences ethical decision making.

4   explain what practical steps managers can take to improve ethical decision making.

3 Influences on Ethical Decision Making

Although some ethical issues are easily solved, many do not have clearly right or wrong answers. And, even though the answers are rarely clear, managers do need to have a clear sense of *how* to arrive at an answer in order to manage this ethical ambiguity well.

The ethical answers that managers choose depend on 3.1 the ethical intensity of the decision, 3.2 the moral development of the manager, and 3.3 the ethical principles used to solve the problem.

3.1 Ethical Intensity of the Decision

Managers don't treat all ethical decisions the same.

Ethical intensity the degree of concern people have about an ethical issue

Magnitude of consequences the total harm or benefit derived from an ethical decision

Social consensus agreement on whether behavior is bad or good

Probability of effect the chance that something will happen and then harm others

The IBM manager who has to decide whether to deny or extend full benefits to Joan Addessi and her children is going to treat that decision much more seriously than the decision of how to deal with an assistant who has been taking computer paper home for personal use. These decisions differ in their **ethical intensity,** or the degree of concern people have about an ethical issue. When addressing an issue of high ethical intensity, managers are more aware of the impact their decision will have on others. They are more likely to view the decision as an ethical or moral decision rather than as an economic decision. They are also more likely to worry about doing the right thing.

Six factors must be taken into account when determining the ethical intensity of an action, as shown in Exhibit 4.4. **Magnitude of consequences** is the total harm or benefit derived from an ethical decision. The more people who are harmed or the greater the harm to those people, the larger the magnitude of consequences. **Social consensus** is agreement on whether behavior is bad or good. **Probability of effect** is the chance that something will happen and then result in harm to others. If we combine these factors, we can see the effect they can have on ethical intensity. For example, if there is *clear agreement* (social consensus) that a managerial

Exhibit 4.4

Six Factors That Contribute to Ethical Intensity

Magnitude of consequences
Social consensus
Probability of effect
Temporal immediacy
Proximity of effect
Concentration of effect

Source: T. M. Jones, "Ethical Decision Making by Individuals in Organizations: An Issue-Contingent Model," *Academy of Management Review* 16 (1991): 366–395R. Reprinted by permission.

Exhibit 4.5
Kohlberg's Stages of Moral Development

Stage 1 Punishment and Obedience	Stage 2 Instrumental Exchange	Stage 3 Good Boy, Nice Girl	Stage 4 Law and Order	Stage 5 Social Contract	Stage 6 Universal Principle
Preconventional		Conventional		Postconventional	
Self-Interest		Societal Expectations		Internalized Principles	

Source: W. Davidson III and D. Worrell, "Influencing Managers to Change Unpopular Corporate Behavior through Boycotts and Divestitures," *Business & Society* 34 (1995): 171–196.

3.2 Moral Development

A friend of yours has given you the latest version of Microsoft Office. She stuffed the software disks in your backpack with a note saying that you should install it on your computer and get it back to her in a couple of days. You're tempted. No one would find out. Even if someone does, Microsoft probably isn't going to come after you. Microsoft goes after the big fish—companies that illegally copy and distribute software to their workers and pirates that illegally sell cheap unauthorized copies. What would you do?[23]

decision or action is *certain* (probability of effect) to have *large negative consequences* (magnitude of consequences) in some way, then people will be highly concerned about that managerial decision or action, and ethical intensity will be high. Although Addessi's family will be profoundly affected by IBM's decision, they are one family, and the magnitude of consequences and the probability of effect for others will be quite low if the benefits are denied.

Temporal immediacy is the time between an act and the consequences the act produces. Temporal immediacy is stronger if a manager has to lay off workers next week as opposed to 3 months from now. **Proximity of effect** is the social, psychological, cultural, or physical distance of a decision maker from those affected by his or her decisions. Thus, proximity of effect is greater for the manager who works with employees who are to be laid off than it is for the higher-ups who ordered the layoffs. If the person responsible for the decision were Addessi's direct supervisor, who had known him and his family through his tenure at the company, the ethical intensity would be higher than it would be for an executive who had never met him. Finally, whereas the magnitude of consequences is the total effect across all people, **concentration of effect** is how much an act affects the average person. Temporarily laying off 100 employees for 10 months without pay has a greater concentration of effect than temporarily laying off 1,000 employees for 1 month.

Which of these six factors has the most impact on ethical intensity? Studies indicate that managers are much more likely to view decisions as ethical when the magnitude of consequences (total harm) is high and there is a social consensus (agreement) that a behavior or action is bad.[22]

In part, according to psychologist Lawrence Kohlberg, your decision will be based on your level of moral development. Kohlberg identified three phases of moral development with two stages in each phase (see Exhibit 4.5).[24] At the **preconventional level of moral development,** people decide based on selfish reasons. For example, if you are in Stage 1, the punishment and obedience stage, your primary concern will be to avoid trouble for yourself. So you won't copy the software because you are afraid of being caught and punished. Yet, in Stage 2, the instrumental exchange stage, you worry less about punishment and more about doing things that directly advance your wants and needs. So you copy the software.

People at the **conventional level of moral development** make decisions that conform to societal expectations. In other words, they look to others for guidance on ethical issues. In Stage 3, the good boy, nice girl stage, you normally do what the other "good boys" and "nice girls" are doing. If everyone else is illegally copying software, you will, too. But if they aren't, you won't either. In the law and order stage, Stage 4, you again look for external guidance

Temporal immediacy the time between an act and the consequences the act produces

Proximity of effect the social, psychological, cultural, or physical distance between a decision maker and those affected by his or her decisions

Concentration of effect the total harm or benefit that an act produces on the average person

Preconventional level of moral development the first level of moral development in which people make decisions based on selfish reasons

Conventional level of moral development the second level of moral development in which people make decisions that conform to societal expectations

© Martin Diebel/IfStop/Getty Images

Most people in the workplace need leadership when it comes to ethical decision making.

with the law (Stage 4) or what others believe is best for society (Stage 5). For example, those with socialist or communist beliefs might choose to copy the software because they believe goods and services should be owned by society rather than by individuals and corporations.

Kohlberg believed that people would progress sequentially from earlier to later stages as they became more educated and mature. But only 20 percent of adults ever reach the postconventional stage of moral development in which internal principles guide their decisions. Most adults are in the conventional stage of moral development and look to others for guidance on ethical issues. This means that most people in the workplace need leadership when it comes to ethical decision making.[25]

3.3 Principles of Ethical Decision Making

Beyond an issue's ethical intensity and a manager's level of moral maturity, the particular ethical principles that managers use will also affect how they solve ethical dilemmas. Unfortunately, there is no one ideal principle to use in making ethical business decisions. According to professor LaRue Hosmer, a number of different ethical principles can be used to make business decisions: long-term self-interest, personal virtue, religious injunctions, government requirements, utilitarian benefits, individual rights, and distributive justice.[26] All of these ethical principles encourage managers and employees to take others' interests into account when making ethical decisions. At the same time, however, these principles can lead to very different ethical actions, as we can see by using these principles to decide whether to award full benefits to Joan Addessi and her children.

According to the **principle of long-term self-interest,** you should never take any action that is not in your or your organization's long-term self-interest. Although this sounds as if the principle promotes selfishness, it doesn't. What we do to maximize our long-term interests (save more, exercise every day, watch what we eat) is often very different from what we do to maximize short-term interests (max out our credit cards, be couch potatoes, eat whatever we want). At any given time, IBM has nearly 1,000 employees who are just months away from retirement. Because of the costs involved, it serves IBM's long-term interest to pay full benefits only after employees have put in their 30 years.

The **principle of personal virtue** holds that you should never do anything that is not honest, open, and truthful and that you would not be glad to see reported

but do whatever the *law* permits; so you won't copy the software.

People at the **postconventional level of moral development** use internalized ethical principles to solve ethical dilemmas. In Stage 5, the social contract stage, you will refuse to copy the software because, as a whole, society is better off when the rights of others—in this case, the rights of software authors and manufacturers—are not violated. In Stage 6, the universal principle stage, you might or might not copy the software, depending on your principles of right and wrong. Moreover, you will stick to your principles even if your decision conflicts

Postconventional level of moral development the third level of moral development in which people make decisions based on internalized principles

Principle of long-term self-interest an ethical principle that holds that you should never take any action that is not in your or your organization's long-term self-interest

Principle of personal virtue an ethical principle that holds that you should never do anything that is not honest, open, and truthful and that you would not be glad to see reported in the newspapers or on TV

Drugs and Scientific Credibility

Merck, one of the largest U.S. pharmaceutical companies, came under fire from members of the medical community in 2008. The *Journal of the American Medical Association* accused the company of paying academic authors to publish ghostwritten stories about its now-withdrawn painkiller, Vioxx, and selectively reporting information about how the drug may have been linked with the deaths of Alzheimer's patients. Academic studies offer valuable information about drugs but can also be a powerful marketing tool. Ethical standards in carrying out and publishing drug studies are critical in maintaining scientific credibility. Merck defended its procedures as normative, but its questionable actions put the company's virtue at risk and could undermine its long-term credibility. Using a defensive strategy, Merck promised to cease the practice of ghostwriting.

Source: R. Winslow and A. Johnson, "Merck's Publishing Ethics Are Questioned by Studies," *The Wall Street Journal*, 16 April 2008, B4. J. Goldstein, "In Latest Vioxx Settlement, Merck Swears Off Ghostwriting," *The Wall Street Journal*, 20 May 2008, available online at http://blogs.wsj.com/health/2008/05/20/in-latest-vioxx-settlement-merck-swears-off-ghostwriting/trackback/ [accessed 17 July 2008].

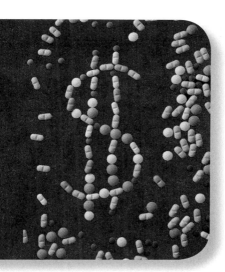

in the newspapers or on TV. Using the principle of personal virtue, IBM might have quietly awarded Joan Addessi her husband's full benefits, avoiding the potential for negative media coverage.

The **principle of religious injunctions** holds that you should never take an action that is unkind or that harms a sense of community, such as the positive feelings that come from working together to accomplish a commonly accepted goal. Using this principle, IBM would be concerned foremost with compassion and kindness and would award full benefits to Joan Addessi.

According to the **principle of government requirements,** the law represents the minimal moral standards of society, and so you should never take any action that violates the law. Using this principle, IBM would deny full benefits to Joan Addessi because her husband did not work for the company for 30 years.

The **principle of utilitarian benefits** states that you should never take an action that does not result in greater good for society. In short, you should do whatever creates the greatest good for the greatest number. At first, this principle seems to suggest that IBM should award full benefits to Joan Addessi. If IBM did this with any regularity, however, the costs would be enormous, profits would shrink, and IBM would have to cut its stock dividend, harming countless shareholders, many of whom rely on their dividends for retirement income. In this case, the principle does not lead to a clear choice.

The **principle of individual rights** holds that you should never take an action that infringes on others' agreed-upon rights. Using this principle, IBM would deny Joan Addessi full benefits. If it followed the rules specified in its pension plan and granted her due process, meaning the right to appeal the decision, then IBM would not be violating her rights. In fact, it could

be argued that providing full benefits to Joan Addessi would violate the rights of employees who had to wait 30 years to receive full benefits.

Finally, under the **principle of distributive justice,** you should never take any action that harms the least fortunate among us in some way. This principle is designed to protect the poor, the uneducated, and the unemployed. Although Joan Addessi could probably find a job, it's unlikely that after 20 years as a stay-at-home mom, she could easily find one that would support her and her daughters in the manner to which they were accustomed. Using the principle of distributive justice, IBM would award her full benefits.

As mentioned at the beginning of this chapter, one of the practical aspects of ethical decisions is that no matter *what* you decide, someone or some group will be unhappy. This corollary is also true: No matter *how* you decide, someone or some group will be unhappy. Some will argue that you should have used a different principle or weighed concerns differently. Conse-

Principle of religious injunctions an ethical principle that holds that you should never take any action that is not kind and that does not build a sense of community

Principle of government requirements an ethical principle that holds that you should never take any action that violates the law, for the law represents the minimal moral standard

Principle of utilitarian benefits an ethical principle that holds that you should never take any action that does not result in greater good for society

Principle of individual rights an ethical principle that holds that you should never take any action that infringes on others' agreed-upon rights

Principle of distributive justice an ethical principle that holds that you should never take any action that harms the least fortunate among us: the poor, the uneducated, the unemployed

quently, although all of these ethical principles encourage managers to balance others' needs against their own, they can also lead to very different ethical actions. So even when managers strive to be ethical, there are often no clear answers when it comes to doing the right thing.

So, what did IBM decide to do? Since Richard Addessi had not completed 30 full years with the company, IBM officials felt they had no choice but to give Joan Addessi and her two daughters the smaller, partial retirement benefits. Do you think IBM's decision was ethical? It's likely many of you don't. You may wonder how the company could be so heartless as to deny Richard Addessi's family the full benefits to which you believe they were entitled. Yet others might argue that IBM did the ethical thing by strictly following the rules laid out in its pension benefit plan. Indeed, an IBM spokesperson stated that making exceptions would violate the federal Employee Retirement Income Security Act of 1974. After all, being fair means applying the rules to everyone.

4 Practical Steps to Ethical Decision Making

*Managers can encourage more ethical decision making in their organizations by **4.1 carefully selecting and hiring ethical employees, 4.2 establishing a specific code of ethics, 4.3 training employees to make ethical decisions,** and **4.4 creating an ethical climate.***

4.1 Selecting and Hiring Ethical Employees

As an employer, you can increase your chances of hiring an honest person by giving job applicants integrity tests. **Overt integrity tests** estimate job applicants' honesty by directly asking them what they think or feel about theft or about punishment of unethical behaviors.[27] For example, an employer might ask an applicant, "Don't most people steal from their companies?" Surprisingly, unethical people will usually answer "yes" to such questions, because they believe that the world is basically dishonest and that dishonest behavior is normal.[28]

Personality-based integrity tests indirectly estimate job applicants' honesty by measuring psychological traits such as dependability and consci-

Corporate Responsibility

Johnson & Johnson knows the value of a strong code of ethics. The company has a credo that outlines four main responsibilities: to doctors, nurses, patients, mothers, and all others who use its products; to employees; to the communities where J & J operates and those where it does not; and to its stockholders. That credo undergirds everything the company produces, from Tylenol to prescription medications to baby shampoo.

Source: "Our Credo," Johnson & Johnson, available online at http://www.jnj.com/connect/about-jnj/jnj-credo, [accessed 13 November 2008].

© Susan Trigg/iStockphoto.com

entiousness. For example, prison inmates serving time for white-collar crimes (counterfeiting, embezzlement, and fraud) scored much lower than a comparison group of middle-level managers on scales measuring reliability, dependability, honesty, conscientiousness, and abiding by rules.[29] These results show that companies can selectively hire and promote people who will be more ethical.[30]

4.2 Codes of Ethics

Today, almost all large corporations have similar ethics codes in place. Still, two things must happen if those codes are to encourage ethical decision making and behavior.[31] First, a company must communicate its code inside and outside the company. Johnson & Johnson's credo is an example of a well-communicated code of ethics. With the click of a computer mouse, anyone inside or outside the company can obtain detailed information about the company's specific ethical business practices.

Second, in addition to having an ethics code with general guidelines like "do unto others as you would have others do unto you," management must also develop practical ethical standards and procedures specific to the company's line of business. Nortel has produced a brochure, available to employees and the public on the company website, which lays out the specifics of how employees are expected to act. For example, it helps employees gauge whether an action creates a conflict of interest by laying out specific criteria. A conflict of interest "prevents you from effectively and efficiently performing your regular duties, causes you to compete against the Company, influences your judgment when acting on behalf of Nortel in a way that could hurt the Company, or causes you to misuse Company resources."[32] Specific codes of ethics such as this make it much easier for employees to decide what to do when they want to do the right thing.

4.3 Ethics Training

In addition to establishing ethical standards for the company, managers must sponsor and be involved in ethics and compliance training in order to create an ethical company culture.[33] The first objective of ethics training is to develop employees' awareness of ethics.[34] This means helping employees recognize which issues are ethical issues and then avoid rationalizing unethical behavior by thinking, "This isn't really illegal or immoral" or "No one will ever find out." Several companies have created board games to improve awareness of ethical issues.[35] At Weyerhauser, when employees pushed for more specific guidance on ethics, the ethics department added a series of multiple-choice questions to the ethics scenarios that it used in its training programs. Each question has four answers from which to choose, two of which are typically good choices.[36] Specific company-related questions and scenarios make it easier for managers and employees to recognize and be aware of ethical issues and situations.

The second objective for ethics training programs is to achieve credibility with employees. Some companies have hurt the credibility of their ethics programs by having outside instructors and consultants conduct the classes.[37] Employees often complain that outside instructors and consultants are teaching theory that has nothing to do with their jobs and the practical dilemmas they actually face on a daily basis. This is why Lockheed Martin, a defense and aerospace company, frequently has its top managers teach ethics classes. For instance, Manny Zuleuta, a senior vice president of shared services, led seven employees through a DVD-based scenario in which they viewed a worker complaining to his boss's manager that his boss yells at him all of the time. Later, the boss apologizes. But then, according to the employee, the boss retaliates against him by giving him bad assignments. Ethics training becomes even more credible when top managers teach the initial ethics classes to their subordinates, who in turn teach their subordinates.[38] Michael Hoffman, executive director for the Center for Business Ethics at Bentley College, says that having managers teach ethics courses greatly reinforces the seriousness with which employees treat ethics in the workplace.[39] Unfortunately, though, 25 percent of large companies don't require top managers to attend, much less teach, ethics classes.[40]

The third objective of ethics training is to teach employees a practical model of ethical decision making. A basic model should help them think about the consequences their choices will have on others and consider how they will choose between different solutions. Exhibit 4.6 presents a basic model of ethical decision making.

4.4 Ethical Climate

Organizational culture is key to fostering ethical decision making. The 2007 National Business Ethics Survey

Exhibit 4.6

A Basic Model of Ethical Decision Making

1. **Identify the problem.** What makes it an ethical problem? Think in terms of rights, obligations, fairness, relationships, and integrity. How would you define the problem if you stood on the other side of the fence?

2. **Identify the constituents.** Who has been hurt? Who could be hurt? Who could be helped? Are they willing players, or are they victims? Can you negotiate with them?

3. **Diagnose the situation.** How did it happen in the first place? What could have prevented it? Is it going to get worse or better? Can the damage now be undone?

4. **Analyze your options.** Imagine the range of possibilities. Limit yourself to the two or three most manageable. What are the likely outcomes of each? What are the likely costs? Look to the company mission statement or code of ethics for guidance.

5. **Make your choice.** What is your intention in making this decision? How does it compare with the probable results? Can you discuss the problem with the affected parties before you act? Could you disclose without qualm your decision to your boss, the CEO, the board of directors, your family, or society as a whole?

6. **Act.** Do what you have to do. Don't be afraid to admit errors. Be as bold in confronting a problem as you were in causing it.

Source: L. A. Berger, "Train All Employees to Solve Ethical Dilemmas," *Best's Review—Life-Health Insurance Edition* 95 (1995): 70–80.

Whistleblowing

Many federal and state laws protect the rights of whistleblowers. Resources to support potential whistleblowers include the National Whistleblower Center website (http://whistleblowers.org) which offers FAQs, a wealth of information on relevant law, a blog, and attorney referrals. The Sarbanes-Oxley Act of 2002 made it a serious crime for publicly owned companies to retaliate in any way against corporate whistleblowers. Managers who punish whistleblowers can be imprisoned for up to 10 years. To make it easier to report violations, many companies like Boeing have established anonymous hotlines to encourage the reporting of unethical and illegal behavior. Still, the 2007 National Business Ethics Survey reports that 36 percent of individuals who witness such behavior do not report it due to fear of retaliation. Although support mechanisms are in place, strong ethical climates are needed to support their use.

Source: "Sarbanes Oxley Implementation Central," available online at http://thecaq.aicpa.org/Resources/Sarbanes+Oxley/ [accessed 17 July 2008]; "2007 National Business Ethics Survey," available online at http://www.ethics.org [accessed 17 July 2008].

AMAZINGLY, THOUGH, NOT ALL COMPANIES FIRE ETHICS VIOLATORS.

reported that only 24 percent of employees who work at companies with a strong ethical climate (where core beliefs are widely shared and strongly held) have observed others engaging in unethical behavior, whereas 98 percent of those who work in organizations with a weak ethical climate (where core beliefs are not widely shared or strongly held) have observed others engaging in unethical behavior. In a strong ethical climate, employees are also more likely to report violations because they expect that management wants them to and won't retaliate against them for doing so.[41] We learned in Chapter 3 that leadership is an important factor in creating an organizational culture. So, it's no surprise that in study after study, when researchers ask, "What is the most important influence on your ethical behavior at work?" the answer comes back, "My manager." The first step in establishing an ethical climate is for managers, especially top managers, to act ethically themselves.

A second step in establishing an ethical climate is for top management to be active in and committed to the company ethics program.[42] Business writer Dayton Fandray says, "You can have ethics offices and officers and training programs and reporting systems, but if the CEO doesn't seem to care, it's all just a sham. It's not surprising to find that the companies that really do care about ethics make a point of including senior management in all of their ethics and compliance programs."[43]

A third step is to put in place a reporting system that encourages managers and employees to report potential ethics violations. **Whistleblowing,** that is, reporting others' ethics violations, is a difficult step for most people to take.[44] Potential whistleblowers often fear that they, and not the ethics violators, will be punished.[45] This is exactly what happened to Sandy Baratta, who used to be a vice president at Oracle, a maker of database software used by most large companies. Baratta was fired, she alleges, for complaining about Oracle's treatment of women and its unethical business practices. Under California's whistleblower protection laws, a jury awarded her $2.6 million in damages.[46]

The factor that does the most to discourage whistleblowers from reporting problems, however, is lack of company action on their complaints.[47] Thus, the final step in developing an ethical climate is for management to fairly and consistently punish those who violate the company's code of ethics. Amazingly, though, not all companies fire ethics violators. In fact, 8 percent of surveyed companies admit that they would promote top performers even if they violated ethical standards.[48]

Whistleblowing reporting others' ethics violations to management or legal authorities

What Is Social Responsibility?

Social responsibility is a business' obligation to pursue policies, make decisions, and take actions that benefit society.[49] Unfortunately, because there are strong disagreements over to whom and for what in society organizations are responsible, it can be difficult for managers to know what is or will be perceived as socially responsible corporate behavior. In a recent McKinsey & Co. study of 1,144 top executives from around the world, 79 percent predicted that at least some responsibility for dealing with future social and political issues would fall on corporations, but only 3 percent said they do a good job of dealing with these issues.[50]

After reading the next four sections, you should be able to

5   explain to whom organizations are socially responsible.

6   explain for what organizations are socially responsible.

7   explain how organizations can choose to respond to societal demands for social responsibility.

8   explain whether social responsibility hurts or helps an organization's economic performance.

5 To Whom Are Organizations Socially Responsible?

There are two perspectives concerning whom organizations are socially responsible to: the shareholder model and the stakeholder model. According to the late Nobel Prize–winning economist Milton Friedman, the only social responsibility that organizations have is to satisfy their owners, that is, company shareholders. This view—called the **shareholder model**—holds that the only social responsibility that businesses have is to maximize profits. By maximizing profit, the firm maximizes shareholder wealth and satisfaction. More specifically, as profits rise, the company stock owned by shareholders generally increases in value.

Friedman argued that it is socially irresponsible for companies to divert time, money, and attention from maximizing profits to social causes and charitable organizations. The first problem, he believed, is that organizations cannot act effectively as moral agents for all company shareholders. Although shareholders are likely to agree on investment issues concerning a company, it's highly unlikely that they have common views on what social causes a company should or should not support. Rather than act as moral agents, Friedman argued, companies should maximize profits for shareholders. Shareholders can then use their time and increased wealth to contribute to the social causes, charities, or institutions they want rather than those that companies want.

The second major problem, Friedman said, is that the time, money, and attention diverted to social causes undermine market efficiency.[51] In competitive markets, companies compete for raw materials, talented workers, customers, and investment funds. A company that spends money on social causes will have less money to purchase quality materials or to hire talented workers who can produce a valuable product at a good price. If customers find the company's product less desirable, its sales and profits will fall. If profits fall, the company's stock price will decline, and the company will have difficulty attracting investment funds that could be used to fund long-term growth. In the end, Friedman argues, diverting the firm's money, time, and resources to social causes hurts customers, suppliers, employees, and shareholders. Russell Roberts, an economist at George Mason University, agrees, saying, "Doesn't it make more sense to have companies do what they do best, make good products at fair prices, and then let consumers use the savings for the charity of their choice?"[52]

By contrast, under the **stakeholder model**, management's most important responsibility is not just maximizing profits, but the firm's long-term survival, which is achieved by satisfying not just shareholders, but the interests of multiple corporate stakeholders.[53] **Stakeholders** are persons or groups who are interested in and affected by the organization's actions.[54] They are called "stakeholders" because they have a stake in what those actions are.

Social responsibility
a business's obligation to pursue policies, make decisions, and take actions that benefit society

Shareholder model a view of social responsibility that holds that an organization's overriding goal should be to maximize profit for the benefit of shareholders

Stakeholder model a theory of corporate responsibility that holds that management's most important responsibility, long-term survival, is achieved by satisfying the interests of multiple corporate stakeholders

Stakeholders persons or groups with a "stake" or legitimate interest in a company's actions

Consequently, stakeholder groups may try to influence the firm to act in their own interests. Exhibit 4.7 shows the various stakeholder groups that the organization must satisfy to ensure its long-term survival.

Being responsible to multiple stakeholders raises two basic questions. First, how does a company identify its stakeholders? Second, how does a company balance the needs of different stakeholders? Distinguishing between primary and secondary stakeholders can help answer these questions.[55]

Some stakeholders are more important to the firm's survival than others. **Primary stakeholders** are groups on which the organization depends for its long-term survival. They include shareholders, employees, customers, suppliers, governments, and local communities. When managers are struggling to balance the needs of different stakeholders, the stakeholder model suggests that the needs of primary stakeholders take precedence over the needs of secondary stakeholders. But among primary stakeholders, are some more important than others? In practice, yes, as CEOs typically give somewhat higher priority to shareholders, employees, and customers than to suppliers, governments, and local communities.[56] Addressing the concerns of primary stakeholders is important because if a stakeholder group becomes dissatisfied and terminates its relationship with the company, the company could be seriously harmed or go out of business.

Secondary stakeholders, such as the media and special interest groups, can influence or be influenced by a company. Unlike the primary stakeholders, however, they do not engage in regular transactions with the company and are not critical to its long-term survival. Nevertheless, secondary stakeholders are still important because they can affect public perceptions and opinions about a company's socially responsible behavior. For instance, after hundreds of protests by animal-rights activists, including groups such as the People for the Ethical Treatment of Animals (PETA), Smithfield Foods, the nation's largest pork producer, announced that it would phase out small "gestation crates" in which it confined pregnant female pigs at its company-owned farms. In this case, a secondary stakeholder was able to mobilize public opinion and convince Smithfield's primary stakeholders and large customers, such as McDonald's and Wal-Mart, to exert pressure on the company to discontinue the practice.[57]

Primary stakeholder any group on which an organization relies for its long-term survival

Secondary stakeholder any group that can influence or be influenced by a company and can affect public perceptions about its socially responsible behavior

PRIMARY STAKEHOLDERS:

SECONDARY STAKEHOLDERS:

Exhibit 4.7
Stakeholder Model of Corporate Social Responsibility

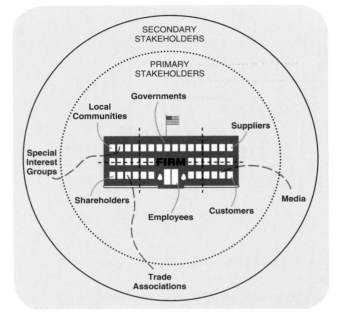

Source: Republished with permission of Academy of Management, P.O. Box 3020, Briar Cliff Manor, NY, 10510-8020. "The Stakeholder Theory of the Corporation: Concepts, Evidence and Implications" (Figure), T. Donaldson and L. E. Preston, *Academy of Management Review* 20 (1995). Reproduced by permission of the publisher via Copyright Clearance Center, Inc.

So, to whom are organizations socially responsible? Many commentators, especially economists and financial analysts, continue to argue that organizations are responsible only to shareholders. Increasingly, however, top managers have come to believe that they and their companies must be socially responsible to their stakeholders. Today, surveys show that as many as 80 percent of top-level managers believe that it is unethical to focus just on shareholders. Twenty-nine states have changed their laws to allow company boards of directors to consider the needs of employees, creditors, suppliers, customers, and local communities as well as those of shareholders.[58] Although there is not complete agreement, a majority of opinion makers would argue that companies must be socially responsible to their stakeholders.

6 For What Are Organizations Socially Responsible?

If organizations are to be socially responsible to stakeholders, what are they to be socially responsible *for*? Well, companies can best benefit their stakeholders by fulfilling their economic, legal, ethical, and discretionary responsibilities. Economic and legal responsibilities play a larger part in a company's social responsibility than do ethical and discretionary responsibilities. However, the relative importance of these various responsibilities depends on society's expectations of corporate social responsibility at a particular point in time.[59] A century ago, society expected businesses to meet their economic and legal responsibilities and little else. Today, when society judges whether businesses are socially responsible, ethical and discretionary responsibilities are considerably more important than they used to be.

Historically, **economic responsibility,** or the expectation that a company will make a profit by producing a product or service valued by society, has been a business' most basic social responsibility. Organizations that don't meet their financial and economic expectations come under tremendous pressure. For example, company boards are very, very quick these days to fire CEOs. CEOs are three times more likely to be fired today than two decades ago. Typically, all it takes is two or three bad quarters in a row. William Rollnick, who became acting chairman of Mattel after the company fired its previous CEO, says, "There's zero forgiveness. You screw up and you're dead."[60] On an annual basis, roughly 4% of CEOs of large companies are fired each year.[61] Nearly one-third of all CEOs, however, are eventually fired because of their inability to successfully change their companies.[62]

Legal responsibility is a company's social responsibility to obey society's laws and regulations as it tries to meet its economic responsibilities. For instance, companies award stock options so that managers and employees are rewarded when the company does well. Stock options give you the right to purchase shares of stock at a set price. Let's say that on June 1st, the company awards you the right (or option) to buy 100 shares of stock, which, on that day, sells for $10 a share. If the stock price falls below $10, the options are worthless. But, if the stock price rises to $15 a share, you can exercise your options by paying the company $1,000 (100 shares at $10 a share), and then sell those 100 shares at $15 per share (the current price) for $1,500 and make $500. But if your options had been dated to, say, January 1st when the stock was selling for $5, you'd make $1,000 instead of $500. It would be unethical and illegal, however, to backdate your options to when the stock sold for a lower price. But, that's exactly what the president and COO did at Monster Worldwide (which runs Monster.com). By improperly backdating his options, he earned an additional $24 million.[63] At Monster, however, backdating was condoned by the CEO,

who routinely backdated options for members of the management team.[64]

Ethical responsibility is a company's social responsibility not to violate accepted principles of right and wrong when conducting business. Cyrus Hassankola has been "going out of business" for nearly two decades. Swiss-educated, but from Iran, he entered the Oriental rug business in Zurich. Because there were so many shops, he advertised that his was "going out of business." The store stayed open several more months and made a lot of money. He then opened and closed 4 more rug stores after running highly profitable "going out of business" sales. After moving to the United States, Hassankola replicated this strategy in five states, until, weary of moving around, he opened a store in Dallas and officially named it "Going Out of Business," with the hope that it would pull in customers on a regular basis. It's not illegal in Texas to name your store "Going Out of Business," but you are required to get a license for "going out of business" sales. The larger issue, however, is that most people would agree it's the wrong thing to do. David Beasley, of Dallas's Better Business Bureau, says, "I understand the desire to stay in business. But you can't do it by going out of business."[65] So, Hassankola's store is now the "Cyrus Rug Gallery," which has a "Liquidation Sale" banner out front. Because different stakeholders may disagree about what is or is not ethical, meeting ethical responsibilities is more difficult than meeting economic or legal responsibilities.

Discretionary responsibilities pertain to the social roles that businesses play in society beyond their economic, legal, and ethical responsibilities. For example, dozens of companies support the fight against hunger at The Hunger Site (http://www.thehungersite.com). Each time someone clicks on the "donate free food" button (only one click per day per visitor), sponsors of The Hunger Site donate money to pay for food to be sent to Bosnia, Indonesia, Mozambique, or wherever people suffer from hunger. Thanks to the corporate sponsors and the clicks of 59 million annual visitors, nearly 8 million cups of food are distributed each year.[66]

Economic responsibility the expectation that a company will make a profit by producing a valued product or service

Legal responsibility a company's social responsibility to obey society's laws and regulations

Ethical responsibility a company's social resonsibility not to violate accepted principles of right and wrong when conducting business

Discretionary responsibility the expectation that a company will voluntarily serve a social role beyond its economic, legal, and ethical responsibilities

Discretionary responsibilities such as this one are voluntary. Companies are not considered unethical if they don't perform them. Today, however, corporate stakeholders expect companies to do much more than in the past to meet their discretionary responsibilities.

7 Responses to Demands for Social Responsibility

Social responsiveness refers to a company's strategy for responding to stakeholders' expectations concerning economic, legal, ethical, or discretionary responsibility. A social responsibility problem exists whenever company actions do not meet stakeholders' expectations. One model of social responsiveness identifies four strategies for responding to social responsibility problems: reactive, defensive, accommodative, and proactive. These strategies differ in the extent to which the company is willing to act to meet or exceed stakeholders' expectations.

A company using a **reactive strategy** will do less than stakeholders expect. It may deny responsibility for a problem or fight any suggestions that it should solve a problem. By contrast, a company using a **defensive strategy** will admit responsibility for a problem but would do the least required to meet stakeholders' expectations. Second Chance Body Armor makes bulletproof vests for police officers. According to company founder Richard Davis, tests indicated that the protective material in its vests deteriorated quickly under high temperatures and humidity, conditions under which the vests are typically used. As a result, Davis concluded that even vests that were only 2 years old were potentially unsafe. Nevertheless, he couldn't convince the company's executive committee to recall the vests (an accommodative strategy). Davis says he told the committee that it had three choices: recall the vests and stop selling them, do nothing and wait "until a customer is injured or killed," or wait until the problem becomes public and "be forced to make excuses as to why we didn't recognize and correct the problem."[67] After two vests were pierced by bullets, which killed one police officer and wounded another, Second Chance announced that it would fix or replace 130,000 potentially defective vests. Although the company finally admitted responsibility for the problem, management decided to do only the minimum toward meeting stakeholders' expectations (fix a defective product). Second Chance, therefore, used a defensive strategy.

A company using an **accommodative strategy** will accept responsibility for a problem and take a progressive approach by doing all that could be expected to solve the problem. Unilever, one of the world's largest consumer product companies, annually buys 1.5 million tons of palm oil to be used in margarine, ice cream, soap, and shampoo. Using protests and viral videos to get the message out, Greenpeace claimed that Unilever was responsible for destroying forests in Indonesia and Malaysia to make way for palm oil plantations.[68] Unilever accepted responsibility for the problem, stating, ". . . following a public challenge from Greenpeace, we formalized our commitment to draw all our palm oil from certified sustainable sources by 2015. We also agreed to support a moratorium on any further deforestation in South-East Asia."[69] Unilever also formed a coalition of 50 businesses and nonprofits to influence palm oil growers and began working with Greenpeace to promote change in the industry.

Finally, a company using a **proactive strategy** will anticipate responsibility for a problem before it occurs, do more than expected to address the problem, and lead its industry in its approach. Honda Motors announced that it would include side-curtain air bags (that drop from the roof and protect pas-

© Pixland/Jupiterimages

Exhibit 4.8

Social Responsiveness Strategies

Reactive	Defensive	Accommodative	Proactive
Fight all the way	Do only what is required	Be progressive	Lead the industry

Withdrawal	Public Relations Approach	Legal Approach	Bargaining	Problem Solving

DO NOTHING ←——————————————————————→ DO MUCH

Source: A. B. Carroll, "A Three-Dimensional Conceptual Model of Corporate Performance," *Academy of Management Review* 4 (1979): 497–505. Reproduced by permission.

sengers' heads) and front-side air bags (that come out of the door to protect against side-impact collisions) as standard equipment on all of its cars. Although more expensive car brands, such as Lexus and Volvo, already included these safety features, Honda was the first to make them standard on all models. Charlie Baker, Honda's vice president for U.S. research and development, said, "We are convinced this is the right direction and will save lives."[70] Exhibit 4.8 summarizes the four social responsiveness strategies.

8 Social Responsibility and Economic Performance

One question that managers often ask is, "Does it pay to be socially responsible?" In previous editions of this textbook, the answer was "no," as early research indicated that there was no inherent relationship between social responsibility and economic performance.[71] Recent research, however, leads to different conclusions. There is no tradeoff between social responsibility and economic performance. [72] And, there is a small, positive relationship between social responsibility and economic performance that strengthens with corporate reputation.[73] Let's explore what each of these results means.

First, there is no tradeoff between being socially responsible and economic performance.[74] Being socially responsible usually won't make a business less profitable. What this suggests is that the costs of being socially responsible—and those costs can be high, especially early on—can be offset by a better product or an improved corporate reputation, which results in stronger sales or higher profit margins. For example, Unilever replaced its laundry detergent All with All Small and Mighty, a con-

centrated formula that reduces the amount needed to wash a load of clothes by two-thirds. Bringing All Small and Mighty onto the market required Unilever to change its packaging (new bottle molds had to be created), its advertising, and its distribution methods. Unilever incurred significant upfront costs to be more socially responsible with All Small and Mighty detergent, but in the long run, customers will be getting a more efficiently packaged product and retailers will be able to fit more bottles on their shelves.

Second, it usually does pay to be socially responsible, and that relationship becomes stronger particularly when a company or its products have a strong reputation for social responsibility.[75] For example, GE, long one of the most admired and profitable corporations in the world, was one of the first and largest Fortune 500 companies to make a strategic commitment to providing environmentally friendly products and service. CEO Jeffrey Immelt wants GE to "develop and drive the technologies of the future that will protect and clean our environment."[76] GE calls its strategy "ecomagination," which it says is "helping to solve the world's biggest environmental challenges while driving profitable growth for GE."[77] And, in just 5 years, GE has increased the number of ecomagination products and services from 17 to 80, with annual sales of more than $17 billion and annual revenue growth increasing by double digits.[78]

Finally, even if there is generally a small positive relationship between social responsibility and economic performance, which becomes stronger when a company or its products have a positive reputation for social responsibility, and even if there is no tradeoff between social responsibility and economic performance, there is no guarantee that socially responsible companies will be profitable. Simply put, socially responsible companies experience the same ups and downs in economic performance that traditional businesses do. Despite its outstanding reputation as a socially responsible company, Ben & Jerry's Ice Cream consistently had financial troubles after going public (selling shares of stock to the public) 15 years ago. In fact, the financial problems became so severe that the founders, Ben Cohen and Jerry Greenfield, sold the company to British-based Unilever.[79] Being socially responsible may be the right thing to do and is usually associated with increased profits, but it doesn't guarantee business success.

8 >>

Communication

After reading this chapter, you should be able to do the following:

1. Describe the interpersonal communication process and the role of listening in the process.

2. Describe the five communication skills of effective supervisors.

3. Explain five communication barriers and the gateways through them.

4. Distinguish between defensive and nondefensive communication.

5. Explain the impact of nonverbal communication.

> *Interpersonal communication is central to health and well-being, both at home and on the job.*

LEARNING OUTCOME 1

Interpersonal Communication

Communication evokes a shared or common meaning in another person. **Interpersonal communication** occurs between two or more people in an organization. It is central to health and well-being, both at home and on the job. Reading, listening, managing and interpreting information, and serving clients are among the interpersonal communication skills identified by the Department of Labor as necessary for success in the workplace.[1] In Chapter 7, we noted that interpersonal communication is the key to unlocking social support for preventive stress management.[2] It is also important in building and sustaining human relationships at work. Recent advances in information technology and data management cannot replace interpersonal communication. Figure 8.1 illustrates the key elements of interpersonal communication: the communicator, the receiver, the perceptual screens, and the message.

An Interpersonal Communication Model

The **communicator** is the person sending the message. The **receiver** is the person accepting the message. **Perceptual screens** are the windows through which we interact. The communicator's and the receiver's respective perceptual screens influence the quality, accuracy, and clarity of the message. They can allow the message to transmit smoothly, or they can cause static and distortion. Perceptual screens are built upon the sender's and receiver's individual attributes, such as age, gender, values, beliefs, past experiences, cultural influences, and individual needs. The degree to which these screens are open significantly influences both sent and received messages.

communication
The evoking of a shared or common meaning in another person.

interpersonal communication
Communication between two or more people in an organization.

communicator
The person sending a message.

receiver
The person accepting a message.

perceptual screen
A window through which one interacts with others. It influences the quality, accuracy, and clarity of the communication.

6 Explain positive, healthy communication.
7 Identify communication technologies and how they affect the communication process.

©Andreas Laubscher/iStockphoto.com

121

FIGURE 8.1 A Basic Interpersonal Communication Model

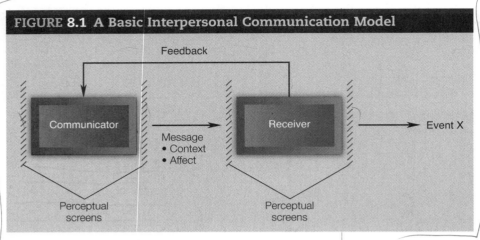

The **message** contains the thoughts and feelings that the communicator intends to evoke in the receiver. The message has two primary components. The thought or conceptual component of the message (its content) is contained in the words, ideas, symbols, and concepts chosen to relay the message. The feeling or emotional component of the message (its affect) is contained in the intensity, demeanor, and gestures of the communicator. The emotional component of the message adds overtones of joy, anger, fear, or pain to the conceptual component. This addition often enriches and clarifies the message.

Feedback may or may not be activated in communication. It occurs when the receiver provides the communicator with a response to the message. More broadly, feedback occurs when information is fed back to the sender that completes two-way communication.

The **language** of the message is important. Language is a broad term denoting the words, their pronunciations, and the methods of combining them used and understood by a group of people. Culture and situation dictate the specific language utilized in a message.

Data are the uninterpreted, unanalyzed elements of a message. **Information** is data with meaning to the person who interprets or analyzes them. Messages are conveyed through a medium, such as a telephone or face-to-face discussion. Messages differ in **richness**, the ability of a medium to convey meaning to a receiver.[3] Table 8.1 compares different media with regard to data capacity and richness. Attributes of communication media affect how influence-seeking behavior is generated and perceived in organizations.[4]

Reflective Listening

Even though it isn't explicitly noted in the communication model, good listening is paramount to effective communication. **Reflective listening** is the skill of carefully listening to a message and immediately repeating it back to the speaker. This technique helps the communicator clarify the intended message and correct inaccuracies or misunderstandings. Reflective listening emphasizes the role of the receiver or audience in interpersonal communication. Managers use this technique to understand other people and help them solve problems at work.[5] Reflective listening enables the listener to comprehend the communicator's meaning, reduce perceptual distortions, and overcome interpersonal barriers that lead to communication failures. Especially useful in problem solving, reflective listening can be learned in a short time. Given its positive effects on behavior and emotion in the corporate environment, reflective listening is a valuable skill to possess.[6]

Reflective listening can be characterized as personal, feeling oriented, and responsive.[7] First, it emphasizes the personal elements of the communication process. The reflective listener demonstrates empathy and concern for the communicator as a person, not an object. Second,

---

message

The thoughts and feelings that the communicator is attempting to evoke in the receiver.

feedback

Information fed back that completes two-way communication.

language

The words, their pronunciations, and the methods of combining them used and understood by a group of people.

data

Uninterpreted and unanalyzed facts.

information

Data that have been interpreted, analyzed, and have meaning to some user.

richness

The ability of a medium to convey meaning to a receiver.

reflective listening

Carefully listening to a message and immediately repeating it back to the speaker.

TABLE 8.1 Data Capacity and Richness of Various Media

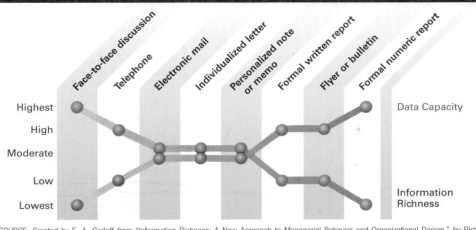

SOURCE: Created by E. A. Gerloff from "Information Richness: A New Approach to Managerial Behavior and Organizational Design," by Richard L. Daft and R. H. Lengel in *Research in Organizational Behavior* 6 (1984): 191–233. Reprinted by Jai Press Inc.

reflective listening emphasizes the feelings communicated in the message—the receiver must pay special attention to the feeling component as she repeats the message. Third, reflective listening emphasizes a rational and considerate response. Receivers should distinguish their own feelings and thoughts from those of the speaker. The conversation's focus must remain at all times on the ideas and emotions of the speaker in order for the receiver to effectively respond to them. A good reflective listener does not lead the speaker according to his own thoughts and feelings.

Reflective listening necessitates four levels of verbal response: affirming contact, paraphrasing expressed thoughts and feelings, clarifying implicit thoughts and feelings, and reflecting core feelings not fully expressed. Nonverbal behaviors are also important in reflective listening. Silence and eye contact are responses that enhance reflective listening.

Each of these responses will be illustrated through an example: the interaction between a software engineer, who has just discovered a major problem in a large information system she is building for a difficult customer, and her supervisor.

Affirming Contact The receiver affirms contact with the communicator by making periodic statements such as "I see," "Okay," and "Yes, I understand." The purpose of an affirmation response is to communicate attentiveness, not necessarily agreement. In the case of the software engineer, the supervisor might make affirming statements during appropriate pauses as the engineer talks through the problem. Affirming contact is especially reassuring to a speaker in the early stages of expression, especially when there may be some associated anxiety or discomfort.

As the problem is more fully explored and expressed, it is increasingly important for the receiver to employ other reflective responses.

Paraphrasing the Expressed After an appropriate length of time, the receiver might paraphrase the expressed thoughts and feelings of the speaker. Paraphrasing is useful because it reflects back to the speaker his or her thoughts and feelings as the receiver heard them. This verbal response enables the receiver to build greater empathy, openness, and acceptance into the relationship while ensuring the accuracy of the communication process.

In the case of the software engineer, the supervisor may find paraphrasing the engineer's message particularly useful for both of them in developing a clearer understanding of the system problem. He might say, "I can tell that you're very upset about this problem. Even though you're not quite sure how it happened, it sounds like you have a few good leads." It is difficult to solve a problem until it is clearly understood.

Clarifying the Implicit People often communicate implicit thoughts and feelings about a problem in addition to their explicitly expressed message. Implicit ideas and emotions are not clearly or fully expressed. The receiver may or may not assume that the implicit is within the awareness of the speaker. For example, the software engineer may be anxious about how to approach the difficult customer with the system problem. This may be implicit in her discussion with her supervisor because of a previous discussion about this customer. If her feelings of anxiety are not expressed, the supervisor may want to clarify them. He might say, "You seem particularly stressed . . . were you worried about the client's reaction?" This would help the engineer shift the focus of her attention from the main problem, which is in the software, to the important issue of discussing the matter with the customer.

Reflecting Core Feelings Next, the receiver should look beyond the speaker's explicit and implicit messages. Core feelings are the speaker's deepest and

[*The purpose of an affirmation response is to communicate attentiveness, not necessarily agreement.*]

most important emotions, beliefs, and values. If the software engineer had not been aware of any anxiety in her relationship with the difficult customer, her supervisor's ability to sense the tension and bring it to the engineer's awareness would exemplify the reflection of core feelings.

The receiver runs a risk of overreaching if a secure, empathetic relationship with the speaker has not already been established or if strongly repressed feelings are reflected back. Even if the receiver is correct, the speaker may not want those feelings brought to her awareness. Therefore, it is important to exercise caution and care in reflecting core feelings to a speaker.

Silence Long periods of silence may cause discomfort or embarrassment, but silence can help both speaker and listener in reflective listening. From the speaker's perspective, silence may be useful in moments of thought or confusion about how to express difficult ideas or feelings. The software engineer may need some patient silence from her supervisor as she thinks through what to say next. Listeners can use brief periods of silence to sort their own thoughts and feelings from those of the speaker. In the case of the software engineer's supervisor, any personal feelings toward the difficult customer should not intrude on the engineer's immediate problem. Silence provides time to identify and isolate the listener's personal responses and exclude them from the dialogue.

Eye Contact Eye contact is a nonverbal behavior that may promote openness in communication between two people. During a dialogue, the absence of appropriate eye contact tends to close communication. The presence of inappropriate eye contact can also hinder a relationship. Cultural and individual differences influence what constitutes appropriate and inappropriate eye contact. For example, direct eye contact initiated by women and children is discouraged in India. Too much direct eye contact, regardless of the individual or culture, can have an intimidating effect.

Moderate direct eye contact communicates openness and affirmation without causing either speaker or listener to feel intimidated. Periodic aversion of the eyes allows for a sense of privacy and control, even in intense interpersonal communication. The software engineer and the supervisor make eye contact throughout their discussion, though each looks away periodically to ease the tension of intimacy.

One-Way versus Two-Way Communication Reflective listening encourages two-way communication. **Two-way communication** is an interactive form of communication in which there is an exchange of thoughts, feelings, or both, and through which shared meaning often occurs. Problem solving and decision making are often examples of two-way communication. **One-way communication** occurs when a person sends a message to another person and no feedback, questions, or interaction follow. Giving instructions and giving directions are examples of one-way communication.

One-way communication tends to be efficient, although how efficient it is depends on the amount and complexity of information communicated and the medium chosen. Even though it is faster than two-way communication, one-way communication is often less accurate. This is especially true for complex tasks that require clarification for completion. When time and accuracy are both important to the successful completion of a task and two-way communication is not an option (such as in combat or emergency situations), extensive training prior to execution enhances accuracy and efficiency.[8] Firefighters and military combat personnel engage extensively in such training to minimize the need for communication during

Two-way communication involves exchange.

©Digital Vision/Getty Images

two-way communication
An interactive form of communication in which there is an exchange of thoughts, feelings, or both.

one-way communication
Communication in which a person sends a message to another person and no feedback, questions, or interaction follow.

emergencies. These highly trained professionals rely on abbreviated one-way communication as a shorthand for more complex information. However, this communication only works within the range of situations for which the professionals are specifically trained.

It is difficult to draw generalizations about individual preference for one-way or two-way communication. Communicators with a stronger need for feedback or who are comfortable with conflict or confusing questions may find two-way communication more satisfying. By contrast, receivers who believe that a message is straightforward may be satisfied with one-way communication and be impatient with lengthy two-way communication.

LEARNING OUTCOME 2

Communication Skills for Effective Managers

Interpersonal communication is a critical foundation for effective performance and individual well-being in organizations. Power is intertwined in the language of communication between managers and their employees.[9] This power dynamic is especially critical when leaders are articulating vision and attempting to achieve buy-in from employees.[10] One large study of managers in a variety of industries found that those with the most effective work units engaged in routine communication with their employees, whereas the managers with the highest promotion rates engaged in networking activities with superiors.[11] A study of banking managers found that higher performing managers are better and less apprehensive communicators than lower performing managers.[12] Oral communication and managerial cooperation are important contextual performance skills that have positive effects on the psychosocial quality of the work environment.[13]

Research on manager–employee communication identifies five communication skills that distinguish good supervisors from bad ones.[14] A good supervisor is an expressive speaker, an empathetic listener, a persuasive leader, a sensitive person, and an informative manager. Some supervisors are effective without possessing each of these skills, and some organizations value one or two skills over the others. Because dyadic relationships are at the core of much organization-based communication, possessing all five skills makes a supervisor that much more effective in communicating to her employees.[15]

Expressiveness

Effective supervisors express their thoughts, ideas, and feelings openly and aren't afraid to voice opinions in meetings. They tend toward extroversion. Supervisors who are not talkative or who tend toward introversion may at times leave their employees wondering what they're thinking about certain issues. Supervisors who speak out

[The Inspiring Unspoken]

Set against the backdrop of a recession marked by massive layoffs, bankruptcies, and other economic difficulties, President Barack Obama's inaugural address was seen as an opportunity to set a clear path forward. While the language of the speech was important, so was Obama's choice of nonverbal communication—up to 93 percent of the emotional meaning of a message comes through nonverbal cues. In order to strengthen his message, Obama employed eye contact and an active tone of voice. Instead of limiting eye contact to temporary glances at particular segments of the audience, he swept his gaze continually over the massive crowd, scanning from extreme left to extreme right. This communicated his awareness of the enormity of the audience, beyond those present to the millions watching on television and the Internet. Obama's dynamic use of vocal tone in the address proved to be his most emotionally evocative deployment of nonverbal communication. An early tone of confidence afforded an air of command and imparted strong meaning to Obama's words. A sobering, forceful tone conveyed the gravity of subjects such as economic hardship and sacrifice. The address was concluded in an optimistic tone that communicated a compelling vision of a brighter future. Nonverbal behaviors such as eye contact and tone were insurmountably important to the success of Obama's address, and they continue to strengthen his messages as his presidency continues.

SOURCE: W.A. Gentry, "Nonverbal Obama: Aside From His Words," *Business Week Online*, 21 January 2009: 4.

©Jaxon Reed/Reuters/Landov

let the people they work with know where they stand, what they believe, and how they feel.

Empathy and Sensitivity

In addition to being expressive speakers, good supervisors are willing, empathetic, reflective listeners. Empathetic listeners are able to hear the emotional dimensions of the messages people send them, as well as the content of the ideas and issues. Good supervisors are approachable and willing to listen to suggestions and complaints. In a recent study of physicians, those with higher perceptions of control were more open in their communication, and patients found them more empathetic.[16]

Good supervisors are also sensitive to the feelings, self-images, and psychological defenses of their employees. They know how and when to communicate with employees to maximize psychological health. For example, employees' accomplishments, honors, and achievements should be announced in public, while criticism should be delivered in private. The best supervisors are sensitive to the self-esteem of others.

Persuasion

All supervisors must exercise power and influence in organizations if they want to ensure high performance and achieve positive results. Effective supervisors tend to be persuasive leaders, distinguished by their use of persuasive language to influence others. They are not deceitful or autocratic—they encourage results earnestly instead of manipulating others.

Sometimes, emergencies and high-risk situations necessitate the abandonment of sensitive and subtle persuasion. In cases such as a fire at an oil rig or a life-threatening trauma in an emergency room, a supervisor must be direct and assertive.

Informative

Finally, good supervisors keep their employees well informed by appropriately and selectively disseminating information. Failing to effectively filter information may lead to either information overload or a lack of sufficient information for task accomplishment. Good supervisors give advance notice of organizational changes and explain the rationale for organizational policies.

A person may become a good supervisor even in the absence of one of these communication skills. For example, a manager with special talents in planning, organizing, or decision making may compensate for a shortcoming in expressiveness or sensitivity. No matter their perceived skill level or effectiveness, when supervisors and employees engage in open communication and forward planning, they have a greater number of agreements about the employee's performance and behavior.[17]

LEARNING OUTCOME 3

Barriers and Gateways to Communication

Barriers to communication are factors that distort, disrupt, or even halt successful communication. They may be temporary and easily resolved or long-lasting and deeply rooted. Roughly 20 percent of communication problems can be prevented or solved by communication policy guidelines.[18] Gateways to communication are the openings that break down communication barriers. Awareness and recognition are the first steps in opening the gateways. Obvious barriers to communication in the workplace are physical separation (employees in different geographic locations or buildings) and status differences (related to the organizational hierarchy). Not so obvious are the barriers caused by gender differences, cultural diversity, and language.

Gender Differences

Communication barriers can be attributed in part to differences in conversational styles.[19] When individuals of different economic backgrounds converse, the receiver's understanding may not be the same as the speaker's meaning. In a similar vein, men and women tend to have different conversational styles. For example, women often prefer to converse face to face, whereas men are comfortable conversing while sitting side by side, concentrating on a focal point in front of them. Hence, conversational differences may result in a barrier of communication between men and women. Male–female conversation is really cross-cultural communication. In a work context, one study found that female employees sent less information to their supervisors and experienced less information overload than did male employees.[20]

The "What about You?" list on the Chapter Review Card gives you an opportunity to evaluate your own listening skills.

---

barriers to communication
Factors that distort, disrupt, or even halt successful communication.

gateways to communication
Openings that break down communication barriers.

An important gateway through the gender barrier is the development of an awareness and appreciation of gender-specific differences in conversational style. These differences can enrich organizational communication and empower professional relationships.[21] A second gateway is to actively seek clarification of the person's meaning rather than freely interpreting meaning from one's own frame of reference.

Cultural Diversity

Culturally influenced values and patterns of behavior can be very confusing barriers to communication. Significant differences in work-related values exist among people in the United States, Germany, the United Kingdom, Japan, and other nations.[22] These differences in value impact motivation, leadership, and teamwork in work organizations.[23] Habitual patterns of interaction can obstruct communication in any given culture. For example, the German culture places greater value on authority and hierarchical differences than does the United States. It is therefore more difficult for German workers to engage in open communication with their supervisors than it is for U.S. workers.[24]

When a person from one culture views people from another culture through the lens of a stereotype, she discounts the individual differences that exist within that foreign culture. For example, a stereotype of

Culture provides the context for consensually derived metaphors that facilitate understanding.

Americans common throughout Asia is that they are aggressive and arrogant, and thus insensitive and unapproachable. Stereotypes of Asians common throughout America are that they are studious, subservient, and assimilative. Individuals who depend on the accuracy of cultural stereotypes may unknowingly create barriers in communicating with people from other cultures.

One gateway through the barrier of diversity is increasing cultural awareness and sensitivity. Further, companies can provide seminars for expatriate managers as part of their training for overseas assignments. Bernard Isautier, president and CEO of Petro Kazakstan, believes that understanding and communication are two keys to harmonious workplace diversity, an essential ingredient for success in international markets.[25] A second gateway is developing or acquiring a guide for understanding and interacting with members of other cultures. One approach to initiating diversity training is to describe a nation by way of a suitable metaphor.[26] For example, Irish pubs, the Spanish bullfight, and American football are consensually derived metaphors for culturally specific conversational styles that can enable those outside the culture to understand members within.

[The FAME Method]

After it encountered employee trepidation during a difficult period of reorganization, drug manufacturer AstraZeneca resolved to teach its leadership teams how to properly engage apprehensive workers. The company developed a method of leadership communication called FAME: Focus, Articulate, Model, and Engage.

- First, leaders develop a clear *focus* for what they want employees to think, feel and do in the midst of change.
- Second, leaders *articulate* that vision using words that employees can remember and repeat.
- Third, leaders *model* the behavior for employees, using their own communicatory strengths.
- Fourth, leaders *engage* employees, demonstrating to them how they fit into the bigger picture.

AstraZeneca found that the FAME method enables leaders to ease employee anxiety while developing their own styles of effective communication. Leadership communication is a learned skill that can make supervisors more self-aware and confident in their interactions with employees. This improves performance, morale, and business relationships across the board.

SOURCE: D. Walters and D. Norton, "Leadership Communication—The AstraZeneca Way," *Strategic Communication Management* 12 (Dec 2007/Jan 2008): 16–19.

DEALING WITH DEFENSIVE PEOPLE

Catherine Crier gained extensive experience in defensive communication while serving as a trial lawyer and judge. She carried this knowledge over into a new career as a news anchor for CNN, ABC, Fox News, and Court TV. Her four basic rules of engagement are to:

1. define the situation,
2. clarify the person's position,
3. acknowledge the person's feelings, and
4. bring the focus back to the facts.

Language

Although English is the international language of aviation, it is not the international language of business. Growing numbers of business men and women are bilingual or multilingual, but even subtle distinctions in dialects within the same language can be barriers. For example, the word *chemist* means a molecular scientist in the United States and a drugstore worker in Great Britain. Language barriers are created across disciplines and professional boundaries by technical terminology. Acronyms and professional jargon may be very useful tools of communication to those on the inside of a discipline; such language can convey precise meaning between professionals. However, acronyms and technical terminology may only serve to confuse and derail any attempt at clear understanding by those unfamiliar with the profession. When doing business, it's best to use simple, direct, declarative language. One should speak in brief sentences and employ terms or words already used by one's audience. As much as possible, one should speak in the language of the listener. Above all else, one should not use jargon or technical language except with those who clearly understand it.

defensive communication
Messages that are aggressive, malevolent, passive, or withdrawn.

nondefensive communication
Messages that are assertive, direct, and powerful.

LEARNING OUTCOME 4

Defensive and Nondefensive Communication

In the workplace, defensive language creates barriers between people, whereas nondefensive communication helps to open and deepen relationships.[27] Defensive communication includes aggressive, malevolent messages as well as passive, withdrawn messages. Nondefensive communication is assertive, direct, and powerful. Though it can be misinterpreted as aggressiveness, assertiveness is indeed nondefensive. Though corporations are increasingly engaged in situations that call for nondefensive language (such as courtroom battles and media exchanges), these are particularly fertile for defensive communication.

Defensive communication leads to a wide range of problems, including injured feelings, communication barriers, alienation in working relationships, destructive and retaliatory behaviors, nonproductive efforts, and problem-solving failures. When such problems arise in organizations, everyone is prone to blame everyone else for what is not working.[28] Defensive reactions such as counterattack and sheepish withdrawal derail communication. These responses tend to lend heat, not light, to the process of communication. Defensive communication often evokes more defensive communication.

Nondefensive communication, in contrast, provides a positive and productive basis for asserting and defending oneself against aggression without further damaging the communication process. An assertive, nondefensive style restores order, balance, and effectiveness in working relationships. Discussion of nondefensive communication and defense communication follow.

Defensive Communication at Work

The two basic patterns of defensiveness are dominant defensiveness and subordinate defensiveness. Subordinate defensiveness is characterized by passive or submissive behavior. The psychological attitude of the subordinately defensive person is "You are right, and I am wrong." People with low self-esteem may be prone to this form of defensive behavior, as may people at lower organizational levels. Individuals who are subordinately defensive do not adequately assert their thoughts and feelings. Their input is likely to be lost, even if it is critical to organizational performance.[29] Passive-aggressive behavior is a form of defensive-

©Andersen Ross/Blend Images/Getty Images

[The Finger]

Junior officers in a regional banking organization nicknamed the bank chairman "The Finger." When giving orders or admonishing someone, he would point his index finger in a domineering, intimidating, emphatic manner that caused defensiveness on the part of the recipient.

©Reza Estakhrian/Stone/Getty Images

ness that begins as subordinate defensiveness and ends up as dominant defensiveness. It is behavior that appears very passive, though it actually masks underlying aggression and hostility.

In contrast, dominant defensiveness is characterized by overtly aggressive and domineering behavior. It is offensive in nature, sometimes culminating in verbal or physical harassment. The psychological attitude of the dominantly defensive person is "I am right, and you are wrong." People who are egotistical or overcompensating for low self-esteem may exhibit this pattern of behavior, as may people in higher-level positions within the organizational hierarchy.

Defensive Tactics

Defensive tactics are subversive actions that employ defensive communication. Unfortunately, these tactics are common in many work organizations. Until defensiveness and defensive tactics are recognized for what they are at an organizational level, it is difficult to address them or respond to them in nondefensive ways. In many cases, defensive tactics raise ethical dilemmas for victims and their supervisors. At what point does simple defensiveness become unethical behavior? Consider the following defensive tactics.

Power plays are tactics used to control and manipulate others. Restricting the choices of employees, enforcing either/or conditions, intentionally ignoring or insulting others, bullying, and displaying overt aggression are all power plays. The underlying dynamic in power plays is that of domination and control. The aggressor attempts to gain the upper hand in the relationship by making the victim feel inferior and thus vulnerable to control.

Labeling is often used to portray another person as abnormal or deficient. Medical and legal labels are often used out of context for this purpose. The words "paranoid," "retarded," and "insane" have specific, clinical meanings that are discarded in defensive labeling. Similar to labeling is publicly raising doubts about a person's abilities, values, sexual orientation, or other personal aspects. This tactic

breeds confusion and uncertainty, but tends to lack the specificity and clarity of labeling.

Disseminating misleading information, a form of deception, is the selective presentation of information intentionally designed to leave an inaccurate impression in the listener's mind. This obfuscated information can be used to scapegoat or pass the buck, which shifts responsibility for an error or problem to the wrong person. If information cannot be altered, defensive individuals may simply blame others for their own wrongdoing.

Finally, hostile jokes are a passive-aggressive defensive tactic. Because a jocular framing is used to mask aggressive and even overtly mean sentiments, hostile jokes often go uncited. They should not be confused with good humor, which is both therapeutic and nondefensive. Jokes created at the expense of others are destructive to self-esteem and workplace communication.

Nondefensive Communication

Nondefensive communication is a healthy alternative to defensive communication in working relationships. An individual who consistently communicates nondefensively may be characterized as centered, assertive, controlled, informative, realistic, and honest. Nondefensive communication is powerful because the speaker exhibits self-control and self-possession without rejecting the listener. It should be self-affirming without being self-aggrandizing—a sometimes difficult balance to maintain.

Converting defensive patterns of communication to nondefensive ones builds relationships at work. Behaviors that build relationships simultaneously reduce adverse responses, such as blame and anger, when negative events occur at work.[30]

To strengthen nondefensive patterns, the subordinately defensive person must learn to be more assertive. One way to do this is, instead of asking for permission to do something, to report what one intends to do and invite confirmation. Another way is to stop using self-deprecating phrases such as "I'm just following orders." One should drop the *just* and convert the message into a self-assertive, declarative statement.

To strengthen nondefensive patterns, the dominantly defensive person must learn to be less aggressive. This may be especially difficult because it requires overcoming the sense of certitude. Those who are working to overcome dominant defensiveness should be particularly sensitive to feedback from others about their behavior. To change this behavior, one should stop giving and denying permission. Instead, one should give others free rein (except in situations where permission is essential to clearance or the security of the task). Alternatively, instead of becoming inappropriately angry, one should provide information about the adverse consequences of a particular course of action.

Nonverbal Communication

Defensive and nondefensive communication focus on the language used in delivering a message. However, most of a message's meaning (an estimated 65 to 90 percent) is conveyed through nonverbal communication.[31] Nonverbal communication includes all elements of communication, such as gestures and the use of space, that do not involve words or language.[32] The four basic types of nonverbal communication that managers need to understand are proxemics, kinesics, facial and eye behavior, and paralanguage. Managers also need to understand that nonverbal communication is influenced by both psychological and physiological processes.[33]

The interpretation of nonverbal communication is specific to the context of the interaction and the actors. That is, the particular meaning of any nonverbal cue relies on its sender, receiver, and the environment in which the cue occurs. For example, some federal and state judges attempt to curb nonverbal communication in the courtroom. Though it may mean nothing outside of the courtroom, some nonverbal behavior may unfairly influence jurors' decisions if displayed during a trial. Beyond the contextual element, nonverbal behavior is also culturally bound. (Recall from Chapter 2 the difference in meaning the "okay" hand gesture has in different countries.)

Proxemics

The study of an individual's perception and use of space, including territorial space, is called proxemics.[34] Territorial space refers to bands of concentric space radiating outward from the body. These bands are commonly known as comfort zones. Figure 8.2 illustrates the four zones of territorial space common to U.S. culture.

Territorial space varies greatly around the world. Both the sizes of comfort zones and their acceptable modes of interaction are culturally defined. People often become uncomfortable when operating in territorial spaces different from those with which they are familiar.

According to leading proxemics researcher Edward Hall, Americans working in the Middle East tend to back away to a comfortable distance when conversing with Arabs. Because Arabs' comfortable conversation distance is closer than that of Americans, Arabs sometimes perceive Americans as cold and aloof. One Arab wondered, "What's the matter? Does he find me somehow offensive?"[35] The circumference of personal space tends to be larger in cultures with cool climates, such as the United States, Great Britain, and northern Europe, and smaller in cultures with warm climates, such as southern Europe, the Caribbean, India, and South America.[36]

Our relationships shape our use of territorial space. For example, we hold hands with or put an arm around significant others to pull them into intimate space. Conversely, we can use territorial space to shape our interactions. A 4-foot-wide desk pushes business interactions into the social distance zone. Not comfortable with that definition of space, one SBC manager met with her seven first-line supervisors around her 4-foot desk. Being elbow to elbow placed the supervisors in one another's intimate space. They appeared to act more like friends and frequently talked about their children, favorite television shows, and other personal concerns. When the manager

---

nonverbal communication

All elements of communication that do not involve words or language.

proxemics

The study of an individual's perception and use of space.

territorial space

Bands of concentric space radiating outward from the body.

FIGURE 8.2 Zones of Territorial Space in U.S. Culture

12 feet — 4 feet — 1½ feet — a — b — c — d →

©iStockphoto.com

Zone a, **intimate space:** spouses, significant others, family members, and others with whom one has an intimate relationship
Zone b, **personal distance:** friends
Zone c, **social distance:** business associates and acquaintances
Zone d, **public distance:** strangers

Competitive stands require face-to-face seating.

©Photos.com/Jupiterimages

moved the staff meetings to a larger room and thus relocated the supervisors into each others' social distance zones, the personal exchanges ceased, and they acted more like business associates again.

Seating dynamics, another aspect of proxemics, is the art of seating people in certain positions according to their purpose in communication. Figure 8.3 depicts some common seating dynamics. To encourage cooperation, one should seat the adjoining party beside oneself, facing the same direction. To facilitate direct and open communication, one should seat the other party across a corner of one's desk or in another place where he will be at right angles. This allows for more honest disclosure. To take a competitive stand with someone, one must position the person directly across from oneself. Suppose a manager holds a meeting around a conference table, and two of the attendees are disrupting the meeting by chatting loudly. Where should they be seated? If the manager places the two disruptive attendees on either side of herself, the argument should be stifled (unless one is so bold as to lean in front of the manager to keep chatting).

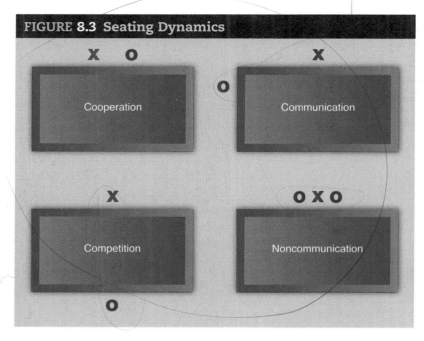

FIGURE 8.3 Seating Dynamics

X O — Cooperation

X · O — Communication

X / O — Competition

O X O — Noncommunication

Kinesics

Kinesics is the study of body movement and posture.[37] Like proxemics, kinesics is bound to culture. With this in mind, we can interpret some common U.S. gestures. Rubbing one's hands together and inhaling sharply indicate anticipation. Stress is indicated by balled fists, clenched teeth, hand wringing, and rubbing the temples. Nervousness may be indicated by drumming fingers, pacing, or jingling coins in one's pocket. Kinesics also includes insulting gestures like giving someone "the finger."

Facial and Eye Behavior

The face is a rich source of nonverbal communication. Facial expression and eye behavior are used to communicate an emotional state, reveal behavioral intentions, cue the receiver, and may even give unintended clues to emotions the sender is trying to hide.[38] Unintended facial movements can undermine the illusion of truthfulness, especially in stressful situations.[39]

Culture, environment, and specific actors must be taken into consideration when interpreting smiles, frowns, raised eyebrows, and other expressions. One study of Japanese and U.S. students illustrated the point. The students were shown a stress-inducing film, and their facial expressions were videotaped. When alone, the students had almost identical expressions. When in the presence of others, however, the Japanese students masked their facial expressions of unpleasant feelings much better than the American students did.[40]

As mentioned earlier, eye contact can enhance reflective listening. Along with smiling, eye contact is an easy way to express honesty and positive emotion.[41] However, eye contact must be understood in a cultural context. A direct gaze indicates dedication, truthfulness, and forthrightness in the United States. This may not be true in other cultures. For example, Barbara Walters was uncomfortable interviewing Libyan head of state Muammar al-Gaddafi because he refused to look directly at her. However, in Libya it is a serious offense for a man to look directly at a woman.[42] In many Asian cultures it is considered polite to bow in deference to a superior rather than to look in the supervisor's eyes.

Paralanguage

Paralanguage consists of variations in speech, such as pitch, loudness, tempo, tone, duration,

kinesics
The study of body movement and posture.

Fast Fact

Crossing one's arms has been shown to increase persistence, which in turn leads to better performance. Two studies used anagrams to demonstrate this relationship. Participants who crossed their arms when presented with an unsolvable anagram persisted longer in trying to decode the impossible. In another study with solvable anagrams, participants who crossed their arms were not only more persistent—their performance was also better (they solved the anagram more frequently). So if you think body posture and position don't inform subjective experience and influence behavior, you might want to reconsider.

SOURCE: R. Friedman and A. J. Elliott, "The Effect of Arm Crossing on Persistence and Performance," *European Journal of Social Psychology* 38 (2008): 449–461.

communicative disease
Loneliness and social isolation resulting from the absence of heartfelt communication in relationships.

laughing, and crying.[43] People make assumptions about the communicator by deciphering paralanguage cues. A female's high-pitched, breathy voice may lead coworkers to stereotype her as a "dumb blonde." Rapid, loud speech may be taken as a sign of nervousness or anger. Interruptions such as "mmm" and "okay" may be used to speed up the speaker so that the receiver can get in a few words. Clucking of the tongue and the "tsk-tsk" sound are used to shame someone. All these cues relate to how something is said.

LEARNING OUTCOME **6**

Positive, Healthy Communication

The absence of heartfelt communication in relationships leads to loneliness and social isolation. This condition has been labeled communicative disease by James Lynch.[44] Communicative disease has adverse effects on the heart and cardiovascular system, and can ultimately lead to premature death. According to Lynch, the only cure for communicative disease is to reengage in thoughtful, heartwarming conversation with friends and loved ones. Though feelings may be more important to the communication process than cognition, a stable balance between the two is integral. This balance between head and heart is achieved when a person displays positive emotional competence and can maintain a healthy internal conversation between his thoughts and emotions.

Positive, healthy communication is an important aspect of working together in both the interpersonal and intrapersonal settings.[45] Working together occurs when individuals cooperate in order to reach a shared goal. Healthy communication based on trust and truthfulness is a pillar of working together. Honest competition within the workplace is consistent with the concept of working together. Sincere, well-managed competition can bring out the best in all those involved.

Healthy communication is at the core of personal integrity and managerial success. This is evident in the most successful executives, as well as in the executive branch of the U.S. government.[46] President Ronald Reagan was nicknamed "the great communicator" for his ability to connect with the American people. He affected strong ethical character, personal integrity, and simplicity in his communication. Reagan exemplified Lynch's concept of heartfelt communication, as his language in speeches and interviews seemed to stem from core values and heartfelt aspirations. Communication from the heart is communication anchored in personal integrity and ethical character.

Personal integrity is a product of emotional competence and a stable balance of head and heart, as mentioned earlier. Psychologist Karol Wasylyshyn has shown that one method of developing personal integrity is to coach an executive in developing her capacity to talk through challenging issues, both personally and professionally.[47] James Campbell Quick and Marilyn Macik-Frey developed a similar coaching program that works to cultivate executives' inner selves through deep, interpersonal communication.[48] This executive coaching model relies on what Lynch might call a "healing dialogue" between executive and coach. In addition to improving interpersonal communication between executives and employees, this model can enhance positive, healthy communication in a wider range of human relationships.

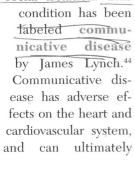

Ronald Reagan, The Great Communicator.

Communicating through New Technologies

Nonverbal behaviors can be important in establishing trust in working relationships, but modern technologies may challenge our ability to maintain that trust. Managers in today's business world have access to more communication tools than ever before. These technologies have surprisingly little impact on work culture, but they do influence behavior and effective communication. Information technology can encourage or discourage moral dialogue, and these types of conversations are central to addressing ethical issues at work.[49]

Written Communication

Even though many organizations are working toward paperless offices and paperless interfaces with their customers, written communication is far from dead—there are many types of written communication still necessary to business. Manuals and reports are generally the longest forms of written communication found in the office. Policy manuals are important in organizations because they establish guidelines for decision making and codes of conduct. Operations and procedures manuals explain how to perform various tasks and resolve problems that may occur at work. Reports, such as annual company finance reports, may summarize the results of a committee's or department's work or provide information on progress toward certain objectives.

Letters and memorandums (memos) are briefer than manuals and reports and are more frequently used in larger organizations. Letters are used to communicate formally with individuals and businesses outside the organization. They vary substantially in length and topic. Memos are also used for formal, internal communication within an organization. They are sometimes used as historical records of specific events or occurrences that individuals within the organization can later refer back to.

The shortest kind of written communication is the form, which may be used to collect information from constituencies inside or outside the organization.

HOT Trend: Tweeting for Turnout

More and more, companies are turning to social networking sites like Facebook and Twitter to track customer perceptions of products. On Facebook, companies can establish and monitor pages for specific products, marketing campaigns, public faces, or the companies themselves. On Twitter, companies can link to images and external websites in 140-character micro-blog posts. The direct line of communication facilitated by online corporate networking instills a sense of empowerment in customers. They can send messages and join product discussions on Facebook and follow up-to-the-minute news on Twitter. For companies, this online interaction translates to invaluable and cost-effective market research and advertising. Internally, social networking sites can be used to communicate efficiently and effectively. Employees can use Facebook to plan meetings and events, and to network with potential clients. Each of the 429 employees of the online retailer Zappo's, including CEO Tony Hsieh, use Twitter accounts to follow breaking company news and keep in contact with each other and the outside world.

SOURCE: R. Donkin, "Irrational resistance to innovation," *Human Resources* (August 2008): 20.

©Robert Llewellyn/Imagestate RM/Photolibrary / © iStockphoto.com

Communication Technologies

Computer-mediated communication influences virtually all behavior in the work environment. E-mail, voice mail, instant messaging, and facsimile (fax) machines have been common in the business world for more than a decade. Recently, large information databases have become relatively commonplace. These databases provide a tremendous amount of information at the push of a button. An example of an information database is the electronic card catalog system used in university libraries throughout the world. These systems, sometimes linked with each other to form massive networks of data, store information about books' and journals' contents, distributions, and availability.

But the newest technology to impact the work environment is the smartphone, which is nearly as ubiquitous at work as standard cell phones are in our personal lives. Smartphones combine the capabilities of advanced cell phones with PC-like applications and connectivity.

Examples include the Apple iPhone, the Palm Pre, and RIM's BlackBerry Storm. The smartphone's introduction was particularly transformative for sales jobs involving travel. While they are widely used, not all reactions to smartphones are positive. For example, one oil producer did not want his daily commute disturbed by outside interference—he used driving as a time for thought and relaxation. Some estimates suggest that using a phone while driving is as risky as driving while under the influence of alcohol. For this reason, some states have outlawed talking and texting while driving a motor vehicle.

How Do Communication Technologies Affect Behavior?

Information communication technology (ICT) is an extensive category of new developments in interpersonal communication that allow fast, even immediate, access to information. E-mail, teleconferencing, and Wi-Fi are all classified as ICT. It can facilitate the instant exchange of information in minutes or seconds across geographic boundaries and time zones. With adequate ICT implementation, schedules and office hours become irrelevant. That is, considerations of time and distance that once beleaguered international and intranational business become far less important in the exchange. Given its impact on the way business is done, ICT has a significant influence on people's behavior.

Computer-mediated communication is impersonal in nature. Instant messaging, e-mail, and other forms of online communication can depreciate the richness of personal interaction. Studies show that using these technologies may increase one's likelihood to flame—to make rude, needlessly argumentative or obscene comments.[50] Employees' interpersonal skills such as tact and graciousness subside online, and managers tend to be more blunt when using electronic media. People who normally participate in discussions quietly and politely may become more intimate, impolite, or uninhibited when they communicate using computer conferencing or electronic mail.[51]

Another effect of computer-mediated communication is that the nonverbal cues we rely on to decipher a message are absent. Gesturing, touching, facial expressions, and eye contact are not possible, so

information communication technology (ICT)

An extensive category of new developments in interpersonal communication that allow fast, even immediate, access to information.

the emotional aspect of the message is difficult to discern. Clues to power such as organizational position and departmental membership may not be available, so the social context of the exchange is often altered.

Communication via technology also changes group dynamic by equalizing participation. As a result, charismatic or higher status members may lose some power.[52] Studies of group decision making have shown that computer-mediated groups took longer to reach consensus than face-to-face groups. In addition, they were less cooperative, more uninhibited, and there was less influence from any one dominant person. Another study found that ICTs, especially e-mail and e-meetings, reduce tension caused by intercultural communication.[53] Groups that communicate via computer seem to experience a breakdown of social and organizational barriers.

The potential for overload is particularly great when individuals are first introduced to new communication technologies. Both the sheer volume of information available and its speed of delivery are staggering. An individual can easily become overwhelmed by information and must learn to be selective about its access.

While modern ICT may make work easier and increase employees' productivity, it can also prove precarious for managers. In the wake of mobile e-mail, instant messaging and texting, managers are more accessible to coworkers, subordinates, and the boss today than they've ever been. Work can no longer be compartmentalized between the hours of 8:00 and 5:00.

Further, many new technologies encourage polyphasic activity, or multi-tasking (that is, doing more than one thing at a time). Managers can simultaneously make phone calls, send instant messages, and work on memos. Polyphasic activity has its advantages in terms of getting more done—but only up to a point. Paying attention to more than one thing at a time splits a person's attention and may reduce effectiveness at individual tasks. Focusing on multiple tasks can become a destructive habit, making it psychologically difficult for a person to let go of work.

Finally, new technologies may make people less patient with face-to-face communication. The speed of electronic media may lead to expectations of acceleration in all forms of communication. However, if they spend too much time communicating online, individuals may come to miss social interaction with others, and may find their social needs unmet. Communicating via computer often means the end of small talk. In the name of speed, amenity is sacrificed for efficiency.

Chapter 5: Leadership Mind and Heart

Your Leadership Challenge

After reading this chapter, you should be able to:

- Recognize how mental models guide your behavior and relationships.

- Engage in independent thinking by staying mentally alert, thinking critically, and being mindful rather than mindless.

- Break out of categorized thinking patterns and open your mind to new ideas and multiple perspectives.

- Begin to apply systems thinking and personal mastery to your activities at school or work.

- Exercise emotional intelligence, including being self-aware, managing your emotions, motivating yourself, displaying empathy, and managing relationships.

- Apply the difference between motivating others based on fear and motivating others based on love.

Chapter Outline

As Lieutenant Colonel Howard Olson surveys the crowd before him, he knows that most of the people in the room outrank him. Still, Olson opens his talk with the following statement: "Each and every one of you has something that makes you a jerk. . . . Some of you have more than one. I know. I've talked to you."

The lecture is part of what the United States Army informally calls "charm school," a week-long course held annually for the select few who are promoted to brigadier general. Everyone knows about the Army's skill at getting new recruits in boot camp to think and act in a new way, but few people have seen firsthand the training it uses to get high-ranking officers to make a mental and emotional leap. At charm school, new generals are advised to get in touch with their inner jerk and work on overcoming that aspect of their personality.

Other recurring themes during the training include avoiding even the appearance of ethical violations, leading with moral courage, and overcoming arrogance, the "first deadly sin of the general officer." Lieutenant General John Keane, a long-time infantry commander, reminds officers that they must "lead from the front: You've got to put yourself in harm's way. . . . You must feel the horror they feel, the loneliness and despair. . . ." It's a reminder that the great officers are those who genuinely care about their soldiers.[1]

There's no equivalent training in corporate America, but the lessons taught at the Army's charm school are also being taken to heart at many of today's business organizations, where leaders are learning to build work relationships based on trust, humility, caring, and respect.

People cannot be separated from their emotions, and it is through emotion that leaders generate a commitment to shared vision and mission, values and culture, and caring for the work and each other. Noted leadership author and scholar Warren Bennis has said that "there's no difference between being a really effective leader and becoming a fully integrated person."[2] This chapter and the next examine current thinking about the importance of leaders becoming fully integrated people by exploring the full capacities of their minds and spirits. By doing so, they help others reach their full potential and contribute fully to the organization. We first define what we mean by leader capacity. Then we expand on some of the ideas introduced in the previous chapter to consider how the capacity to shift our thinking and feeling can help leaders alter their behavior, influence others, and be more effective. We discuss the concept of mental models, and look at how qualities such as independent thinking, an open mind, and systems thinking are important for leaders. Then we take a closer look at human emotion as illustrated in the concept of emotional intelligence and the emotions of love versus fear in leader–follower relationships. The next chapter will turn to spirit as reflected in moral leadership and courage.

Leader Capacity versus Competence

Traditionally, effective leadership, like good management, has been thought of as competence in a set of skills; once these specific skills are acquired, all one has to do to succeed is put them into action. However, as we all know from personal experience, working effectively with other people requires much more than practicing specific, rational skills; it often means drawing on subtle aspects of ourselves—our thoughts, beliefs, or feelings—and appealing to those aspects in others. Anyone who has participated on an athletic team knows how powerfully thoughts and emotions can affect performance. Some players are not as highly skilled from a technical standpoint but put forth amazing performances by playing with heart. Players who can help others draw on these positive emotions and thoughts often emerge as team leaders.

In organizations, just like on the playing field, skills competence is important, but it is not enough. Although leaders have to attend to organizational issues such as production schedules, structure, finances, costs, profits, and so forth, they also tend to human issues, particularly in times of uncertainty and rapid change. Current issues that require leaders to use more than rational skills include how to give people a sense of meaning and purpose when major changes occur almost daily; how to make employees feel valued and respected in an age of massive layoffs and job uncertainty; and how to keep morale and motivation high in the face of corporate bankruptcies and dissolutions, ethical scandals, and economic crises.

Capacity
the potential each of us has to do more and be more than we are now

In this chapter, rather than discussing *competence*, we explore a person's *capacity* for mind and heart. Whereas competence is limited and quantifiable, capacity is unlimited and defined by the potential for expansion and growth.[3] **Capacity** means the potential each of us has to be more than we are now. The U.S. Army's leadership expression "Be, Know, Do," puts *Be* first because who a leader is as a person—his or her character, values, spirit, and moral center—colors everything else.

Developing leadership capacity goes beyond learning the skills for organizing, planning, or controlling others. It also involves something deeper and more subtle than the leadership traits and styles we discussed in

Chapters 2 and 3. Living, working, and leading based on our capacity means using our whole selves, including intellectual, emotional, and spiritual abilities and understandings. A broad literature has emphasized that being a whole person means operating from mind, heart, spirit, and body.[4] Although we can't "learn" capacity the way we learn a set of skills, we can expand and develop leadership capacity. Just as the physical capacity of our lungs is increased through regular aerobic exercise, the capacities of the mind, heart, and spirit can be expanded through conscious development and regular use. In the previous chapter, we introduced some ideas about how individuals think, make decisions, and solve problems based on values, attitudes, and patterns of thinking. This chapter builds on some of those ideas to provide a broader view of the leadership capacities of mind and heart.

Mental Models

A mental model can be thought of as an internal picture that affects a leader's actions and relationships with others. **Mental models** are theories people hold about specific systems in the world and their expected behavior.[5] A system means any set of elements that interact to form a whole and produce a specified outcome. An organization is a system, as is a football team, a sorority pledge drive, a marriage, the registration system at a university, or the claims process at an insurance company.

Leaders have many mental models that tend to govern how they interpret experiences and how they act in response to people and situations. For example, one mental model about what makes an effective team is that members share a sense of team ownership and feel that they have authority and responsibility for team actions and outcomes.[6] A leader with this mental model would likely push power, authority, and decision making down to the team level and strive to build norms that create a strong group identity and trust among members. However, a leader with a mental model that every group needs a strong leader to take control and make the decisions is less likely to encourage norms that lead to effective teamwork. Exhibit 5.1 shows the mental model that Google's top leaders use to keep the company on the cutting edge as its core business of search matures. At Google, risk-taking, a little craziness, and making mistakes is encouraged for the sake of innovation. Too much structure and control is considered death to the company.[7]

Leaders at Google, as well as other organizations, strive to create mental models that are aligned with organizational

Mental models
theories people hold about specific systems in the world and their expected behavior

Action Memo

As a leader, you can become aware of your mental models and how they affect your thinking and behavior. You can learn to regard your assumptions as temporary ideas and strive to expand your mindset.

Exhibit 5.1 Google Leaders' Mental Model

- Stay uncomfortable
- Let failure coexist with triumph
- Use a little less "management" than you need
- Defy convention
- Move fast and figure things out as you go

Source: Based on Adam Lashinsky, "Chaos by Design," *Fortune* (October 2, 2006). pp. 86–98.

needs, goals, and values. However, personal values, attitudes, beliefs, biases, and prejudices can all affect one's mental model. A leader's assumptions play an important role in shaping his or her mental model, but leaders can examine their assumptions and shift mental models when needed to keep their organizations healthy.[8]

Assumptions

In the previous chapter, we discussed two very different sets of attitudes and assumptions that leaders may have about subordinates, called Theory X and Theory Y, and how these assumptions affect leader behavior. A leader's assumptions naturally are part of his or her mental model. Someone who assumes that people can't be trusted will act very differently in a situation than someone who has the assumption that people are basically trustworthy. Leaders have assumptions about events, situations, and circumstances as well as about people. Assumptions can be dangerous because people tend to accept them as "truth." For example, the author of a recent book about the U.S. involvement in Iraq suggests that the original decision to go to war was based on a set of faulty assumptions (such as that Iraq possessed weapons of mass destruction). Bush administration leaders were so sure their assumptions were right that they looked for intelligence to support their views and ignored any counsel of military leaders and intelligence professionals that contradicted those beliefs.[9]

U.S. auto manufacturers provide an example from the business world. Leaders at these companies for too long assumed that their way of doing business, which kept the companies profitable for decades, would continue to be successful even as the environment changed dramatically. At General Motors, Rick Wagoner was asked by the Obama administration to resign as chairman and CEO because the government's auto task force believed a new set of assumptions was needed at the flailing company.

IN THE LEAD

General Motors

Everyone agrees that Rick Wagoner loved General Motors and genuinely believed he was doing what was right for the company. "He came to work every morning with the devotion of a priest," said one GM executive. The problem was, Wagoner approached the job of CEO with a set of flawed assumptions based on working for GM since 1977, when it was still the auto-manufacturing king.

GM was already in trouble when Wagoner took over. Indeed, the company had been losing market share since the 1960s and had been in "perpetual turnaround" since the 1980s. One problem at GM is that the corporate culture emphasized conformity and consistency, and leaders, including Wagoner, had a tough time breaking out of that mindset. During his nine years as CEO—even as thousands of people were laid off, market share tanked, and the stock price fell from $70 to less than $4—Wagoner maintained a belief in the basic strength and solidity of the company's business model. He couldn't accept, for instance, that in a changed environment, GM was spreading itself way too thin with too many car and truck models. Considering the multitude of GM's brands, each requiring expensive technical and marketing support, Wagoner decided to cut only one brand, Oldsmobile, from the lineup. He resisted a 2006 drive to forge a partnership with Nissan/Renault because he believed GM could and should stand on its own. Similarly, he never took any drastic measures to change the company's costly labor and benefits structure. In other words, Wagoner ran the company pretty much the way it had been run in the 1970s and 1980s. Only shortly before he was asked to step down in 2009 did Wagoner acknowledge the need for a new approach to doing business.

It remains to be seen whether new CEO Fritz Henderson, also a GM insider, has the right mental model needed to save the company. However, Henderson and Ed Whitacre Jr., who took over as chairman after GM emerged from Chapter 11 bankruptcy, say they are committed to making radical changes. In connection with a government-led restructuring, the two have significantly thinned the bloated management ranks, asking hundreds of executives to step down, replaced more than half the board with new members who aren't mired in the old way of thinking and doing things, appointed an executive specifically in charge of leading the overhaul of GM's corporate culture, and formed a small cross-functional leadership team to speed up decision making.[10]

Everyone who cares about the U.S. auto industry is hoping new leaders can bring more realistic assumptions to the challenge of reinventing GM. Whitacre, a highly skilled leader who took Southwestern Bell from the smallest regional Bell company to the largest and renamed it AT&T, has made it clear that he won't tolerate the "seemingly endless patience" the old board had with Rick Wagoner. He says the board will evaluate Henderson and his management team on a daily basis to see if they have the right mental model to lead GM over the long term. "He's there to make a success of GM, or he'll die trying," said a former colleague of Whitacre.[11]

As the example of General Motors illustrates, it is important for leaders to regard their assumptions as temporary ideas rather than fixed truths. The more aware a leader is of his or her assumptions, the more the leader understands how assumptions guide behavior and decisions. In addition, the leader can question whether long-held assumptions fit the reality of the current situation. Questioning assumptions can help leaders understand and shift their mental models.

Changing Mental Models

The mindset of the top leader has always played a key role in organizational success. A Harvard University study ranking the top 100 business leaders of the twentieth century found that they all shared what the researchers refer to as "contextual intelligence," the ability to sense the social, political, technological, and economic context of the times and adopt a mental model that helped their organizations best respond.[12] In a world of rapid and discontinuous change, the greatest factor determining the success of leaders and organizations may be the ability to change one's mental model.[13]

For business leaders, the uncertainty and volatility of today's environment is hard to ignore. As one reflection, consider the free fall in the stock market in 2008 and early 2009. Stock analysts' research reports began using the word *decremental* to describe the widespread decline in corporate profitability and loss of earning power.[14] Words from a 2006 *Fortune* article by Geoff Colvin seem even more fitting for today's environment: "The forecast for most companies is continued chaos with a chance of disaster."[15] Coping with this volatility requires a tremendous shift in mental models for most leaders. Yet many leaders become prisoners of their own assumptions and mindsets. They find themselves simply going along with the traditional way of doing things—whether it be running a manufacturing company such as General Motors, managing a foundation, handling insurance claims, selling cosmetics, or coaching a basketball team—without even realizing they are making decisions and acting within the limited frame of their own mental model.[16]

A study by Stephan Lewandowsky, a psychology professor at the University of Western Australia, Crawley, demonstrates the tremendous power mental models can have on our thinking. Researchers showed more than 860 people in Australia, Germany, and the United States a list of events associated with the United States–led invasion of Iraq. Some were true, some were originally reported as fact by the media but later retracted, and some were completely invented for the study. After interpreting the results, researchers determined that people tended to believe the "facts" that fit with their mindset about the Iraqi war, even if those facts were clearly not true. People who accepted as valid the official U.S. justification for the war continued to believe reports that cast the United States in a good light and the Iraqi forces in a bad light, even if they knew the reports had been retracted. Those who were suspicious of U.S. motives easily discounted the misinformation. Lewandowsky says supporters of the war held fast to believing what they originally heard, even though they knew it had been retracted, "because it fits with their mental model, which people seek to retain whatever it takes." This is an important point: People tend to believe what they want to believe because doing otherwise "would leave their world view a shambles."[17]

Despite the mental discomfort and sense of disorientation it might cause, leaders must allow their mental models to be challenged and even demolished.[18] Becoming aware of assumptions and understanding how they influence emotions and actions is the first step toward being able to shift mental models and see the world in a new way. Leaders can break free from outdated mental models. They can recognize that what worked yesterday may not work today. Following conventional wisdom about how to do things may be the surest route to failure. Effective leaders learn to continually question their own beliefs, assumptions, and perceptions in order to see things in unconventional ways and meet the challenge of the future head on.[19] Leaders also encourage others to question the status quo and look for new ideas. Getting others to shift their mental models is perhaps even more difficult than changing one's own, but leaders can use a variety of techniques to bring about a shift in thinking, as described in the Leader's Bookshelf.

Developing a Leader's Mind

How do leaders make the shift to a new mental model? The leader's mind can be developed beyond the non-leader's in four critical areas: independent thinking, open-mindedness, systems thinking, and personal mastery. Taken together, these four disciplines provide a foundation that can help leaders examine their mental models and overcome blind spots that may limit their leadership effectiveness and the success of their organizations.

Independent Thinking

Independent thinking means questioning assumptions and interpreting data and events according to one's own beliefs, ideas, and thinking, not according to pre-established rules, routines, or categories defined by others. People who think independently are willing to stand apart, to have opinions, to say what they think, and to determine a course of action based on what they personally believe rather than on what other people think or say. Good leadership isn't about following the rules of others, but standing up for what you believe is best for the organization.

To think independently means staying mentally alert and thinking critically. Independent thinking is one part of what is called leader mindfulness.[20]

Independent thinking
questioning assumptions and interpreting data and events according to one's own beliefs, ideas, and thinking, rather than pre-established rules or categories defined by others

Leader's Bookshelf

Changing Minds: The Art and Science of Changing Our Own and Other People's Minds
by Howard Gardner

After about the age of 10, psychologist Howard Gardner asserts, people tend to retreat to old ideas rather than open up to new possibilities. "I'm not stating on small matters it's difficult to change people's minds," Gardner writes. "But on fundamental ideas of how the world works, about what your enterprise is about, about what your life goals are, about what it takes to survive—it's on these topics that it's very difficult . . . ."

Why? Because, over time, as people gain more formal and informal knowledge, patterns of thought become engraved in our minds, making it tough to shift to fresh ways of thinking. Yet lasting change in mindset is achievable, Gardner believes, if leaders use specific mind-changing tools.

GETTING OTHERS TO SEE THINGS DIFFERENTLY

Based on decades of extensive psychological research and observation, Gardner details seven "levers of change" that can be used to shift people's mindsets. He advises leaders to "think of them as arrows in a quiver" that can be used in different combinations for different circumstances. Here are some of Gardner's lessons:

- *Take your time, and approach change from many vantage points.* To shift people's way of thinking, leaders get the message out many different times in many different ways, using a variety of approaches and symbols. Gardner calls this *representational redescription*, which means finding diverse ways to get the same desired mind change across to people. "Give your message in more than one way, arranging things so the [listener] has a different experience." For example, simply talking about something in a different setting, such as over coffee or a drink after work, can sometimes be effective because the usual assumptions and resistances may be diminished.

- *Don't rely on reason alone.* Using a rational approach complemented by research and statistical data can shore up your argument. But effective leaders know they have to touch people's emotions as well, which Gardner calls *resonance*. Using stories, imagery, and real-world events can be a highly effective way to bring about change. Gardner uses the example of former British Prime Minister Margaret Thatcher. Thatcher effectively shifted the mindset of her constituency toward the idea that Britain could reemerge as a leading global power because her message resonated with people.

As the daughter of a poor grocer, Thatcher worked her way through school and raised a family before she entered politics.

- *Don't underestimate how powerful resistances can be.* As head of Monsanto, Robert Shapiro strongly believed in the benefits of genetically altered foods, and he assumed that the rest of the world would gladly embrace them. He was wrong, and his company suffered greatly because of his failure to understand and effectively address the resistances he encountered. Gardner identifies several specific types of barriers and advises leaders to arm themselves as if for battle when trying to change minds.

LASTING CHANGE IS VOLUNTARY CHANGE

Some people tend to think secrecy and manipulation is the quickest way to bring about change, and Gardner admits that in the short run, deception is effective. However, he emphasizes that change doesn't stick unless people change voluntarily. Manipulation backfires. Leaders who want to effect lasting changes in mindset wage their change campaigns openly and ethically.

Changing Minds, by Howard Gardner, is published by Harvard Business School Press.

Mindfulness can be defined as continuously reevaluating previously learned ways of doing things in the context of evolving information and shifting circumstances. Mindfulness involves independent thinking, and it requires leader curiosity and learning. Mindful leaders are open minded and stimulate the thinking of others through their curiosity and questions. Mindfulness is the opposite of *mindlessness*, which means blindly accepting rules and labels created by others. Mindless people let others do the thinking for them, but mindful leaders are always looking for new ideas and approaches.

Mindfulness
the process of continuously reevaluating previously learned ways of doing things in the context of evolving information and shifting circumstances

In the world of organizations, circumstances are constantly changing. What worked in one situation may not work the next time. In these conditions, mental laziness and accepting others' answers can hurt the organization and all its members. Leaders apply critical thinking to explore a situation, problem, or question from multiple perspectives and integrate all the available information into a possible solution. When leaders think critically, they question all assumptions, vigorously seek divergent opinions, and try to give balanced consideration to all alternatives.[21]

Leaders at today's best-performing organizations deliberately seek board members who can think independently and are willing to challenge senior management or other board members. Consider the board member at Medtronic who stood his ground against the CEO and 11 other members concerning an acquisition. The board approved the acquisition, but then-CEO Bill George was so persuaded by the dissenter's concerns that he reconvened the board by conference call. After hearing the dissenting board member's cogent argument that the deal would take Medtronic into an area it knew nothing about and divert attention from its core business, the board reconsidered and decided against the deal.[22]

Thinking independently and critically is hard work, and most of us can easily relax into temporary mindlessness, accepting black-and-white answers and relying on standard ways of doing things. Companies that have gotten into trouble in recent years often had executives and board members who failed to question enough or to challenge the status quo. For example, bank directors have been faulted for the deepening financial troubles at some of the Federal Home Loan Banks, a group of 12 regional cooperative banks created by Congress in 1932 to support the housing market. Analysts at Federal Financial Analytics, a research firm in Washington, D.C., say directors mindlessly went along with bank executives' decisions to buy large amounts of private-label mortgage securities packaged by Wall Street, rather than asking tough questions about the risks involved.[23]

Action Memo

Evaluate your skill in three dimensions of mindfulness, including intellectual stimulation, by completing the exercise in Leader's Self-Insight 5.1

Good leaders also encourage followers to be mindful rather than mindless. Bernard Bass, who has studied charismatic and transformational leadership, talks about the value of *intellectual stimulation*—arousing followers' thoughts and imaginations as well as stimulating their ability to identify and solve problems creatively.[24] People admire leaders who awaken their curiosity, challenge them to think and learn, and encourage openness to new, inspiring ideas and alternatives.

Open-Mindedness

One approach to independent thinking is to break out of the mental boxes, the categorized thinking patterns we have been conditioned to accept as correct. Leaders have to "keep their mental muscle loose."[25]

The power of the conditioning that guides our thinking and behavior is illustrated by what has been called the *Pike Syndrome*. In an experiment, a northern pike is placed in one half of a large glass-divided aquarium, with numerous minnows placed in the other half. The hungry pike makes repeated attempts to get the minnows, but succeeds only in battering itself against the glass, finally learning that trying to reach the minnows is futile. The glass divider is then removed, but the pike makes no attempt to attack the minnows because it has been

Think back to how you behaved toward others at work or in a group when you were in a formal or informal leadership position. Please respond to the following items based on how frequently you did each behavior. Indicate whether each item is Mostly False or Mostly True for you.

	Mostly False	Mostly True
1. Enjoyed hearing new ideas.	_____	_____
2. Challenged someone to think about an old problem in a new way.	_____	_____
3. Tried to integrate conversation points at a higher level.	_____	_____
4. Felt appreciation for the viewpoints of others.	_____	_____
5. Would ask someone about the assumptions underlying his or her suggestions.	_____	_____
6. Came to my own conclusion despite what others thought.	_____	_____
7. Was open about myself to others.	_____	_____
8. Encouraged others to express opposing ideas and arguments.	_____	_____
9. Fought for my own ideas.	_____	_____
10. Asked "dumb" questions.	_____	_____
11. Offered insightful comments on the meaning of data or issues.	_____	_____
12. Asked questions to prompt others to think more about an issue.	_____	_____
13. Expressed a controversial opinion.	_____	_____
14. Encouraged opposite points of view.	_____	_____
15. Suggested ways of improving my and others' ways of doing things.	_____	_____

Scoring and Interpretation

Give yourself one point for each Mostly True checked for items 1–8 and 10–15. Give yourself one point for checking Mostly False for item 9. A total score of 12 or higher would be considered a high level of overall mindfulness. There are three subscale scores that represent three dimensions of leader mindfulness. For the dimension of open or beginner's mind, sum your responses to questions 1, 4, 7, 9, and 14. For the dimension of independent thinking, sum your scores for questions 3, 6, 11, 13, and 15. For the dimension of intellectual stimulation, sum your scores for questions 2, 5, 8, 10, and 12.

My scores are:
Open or Beginner's Mind: _____
Independent Thinking: _____
Intellectual Stimulation: _____

These scores represent three aspects of leader mindfulness—what is called open mind or beginner's mind, independent thinking, and intellectual stimulation.

A score of 4.0 or higher on any of these dimensions is considered high because many people do not practice mindfulness in their leadership or group work. A score of 3 is about average, and 2 or less would be below average. Compare your three subscale scores to understand the way you use mindfulness. Analyze the specific questions for which you did not get credit to see more deeply into your pattern of mindfulness strengths or weaknesses. Open mind, independent thinking, and intellectual stimulation are valuable qualities to develop for effective leadership.

Sources: The questions above are based on ideas from R. L. Daft and R. M. Lengel, *Fusion Leadership*, Chapter 4 (San Francisco: Berrett-Koehler, 2000); B. Bass and B. Avolio, *Multifactor Leadership Questionnaire*, 2nd ed. (Menlo Park, CA: Mind Garden, Inc.); and P. M. Podsakoff, S. B. MacKenzie, R. H. Moorman, and R. Fetter, "Transformational Leader Behaviors and Their Effects on Followers' Trust in Leader, Satisfaction, and Organizational Citizenship Behaviors," *Leadership Quarterly* 1, no. 2 (1990), pp. 107–42.

conditioned to believe that reaching them is impossible. When people assume they have complete knowledge of a situation because of past experiences, they exhibit the Pike Syndrome, a trained incapacity that comes from rigid commitment to what was true in the past and an inability to consider alternatives and different perspectives.[26]

Leaders have to forget many of their conditioned ideas to be open to new ones. This openness—putting aside preconceptions and suspending beliefs and opinions—can be referred to as "beginner's mind." Whereas the expert's mind rejects new ideas based on past experience and knowledge, the beginner's

Consider This!
An Empty Sort of Mind

Reflecting on How Winnie the Pooh Found Eeyore's Missing Tail:

"An Empty sort of mind is valuable for finding pearls and tails and things because it can see what's in front of it. An Overstuffed mind is unable to. While the clear mind listens to a bird singing, the Stuffed-Full-of-Knowledge-and-Cleverness mind wonders what *kind* of bird is singing. The more Stuffed Up it is, the less it can hear through its own ears and see through its own eyes. Knowledge and Cleverness tend to concern themselves with the wrong sorts of things, and a mind confused by Knowledge, Cleverness, and Abstract Ideas tends to go chasing off after things that don't matter, or that don't even exist, instead of seeing, appreciating, and making use of what is right in front of it."

Source: Benjamin Hoff, *The Tao of Pooh* (New York: E. P. Dutton, 1982), pp. 146–147.

© majaiva

mind reflects the openness and innocence of a young child just learning about the world. The value of a beginner's mind is captured in the story told in this chapter's *Consider This*.

One leader who illustrates the importance of keeping an open mind is Lisa Drakeman, who went from teaching religion at Princeton to being CEO of a biotechnology company. Drakeman found that being a business leader meant she needed to think and act in a new way. She had to learn how to delegate and how to get employees to share their ideas and opinions rather than acting as a teacher with all the answers. One of the most important lessons she learned? "Don't be afraid to look stupid by asking basic questions," Drakeman says.[27]

Action Memo

As a leader, you can train yourself to think independently. You can be curious, keep an open mind, and look at a problem or situation from multiple perspectives before reaching your conclusions.

Effective leaders strive to keep open minds and cultivate an organizational environment that encourages curiosity and learning. They understand the limitations of past experience and reach out for diverse perspectives. Rather than seeing any questioning of their ideas as a threat, these leaders encourage everyone throughout the organization to openly debate assumptions, confront paradoxes, question perceptions, and express feelings.[28]

Leaders can use a variety of approaches to help themselves and others keep an open mind. At McKinsey & Co., worldwide managing director Rajat Gupta reads poetry at the end of the partners' regular meetings. Poetry and literature, he says, "help us recognize that we face tough questions and that we seldom have perfect answers."[29]

Systems Thinking

Systems thinking
the ability to see the synergy of the whole rather than just the separate elements of a system and to learn to reinforce or change whole system patterns

Systems thinking means the ability to see the synergy of the whole rather than just the separate elements of a system and to learn to reinforce or change whole system patterns.[30] Many people have been trained to solve problems by breaking a complex system, such as an organization, into discrete parts and working to make each part perform as well as possible. However, the success of each piece does not add up to the success of the whole. In fact, sometimes changing one part to make it better actually makes the whole system function less effectively. Consider that, in recent years, new drugs have been a lifesaver for people living with HIV, but the drop in mortality rates has led to a reduction in perceived risk and therefore more incidences of risky behavior. After years of decline, HIV infection rates began rising again, indicating that the system of HIV treatment is not well understood. As another example, a small city embarked on a road-building program to solve traffic congestion without whole-systems thinking. With new roads available, more people began moving to the suburbs. The solution actually increased traffic congestion, delays, and pollution by enabling suburban sprawl.[31]

It is the *relationship* among the parts that form a whole system—whether it be a community, an automobile, a nonprofit agency, a human being, or a business organization—that matters. Systems thinking enables leaders to look for patterns of movement over time and focus on the qualities of rhythm, flow, direction, shape, and networks of relationships that accomplish the performance of the whole. Systems thinking is a mental discipline and framework for seeing patterns and interrelationships.

It is important to see organizational systems as a whole because of their complexity. Complexity can overwhelm leaders, undermining confidence. When leaders can see the structures that underlie complex situations, they can facilitate improvement. But it requires a focus on the big picture. Leaders can develop what David McCamus, former chairman and CEO of Xerox Canada, calls "peripheral vision"—the ability to view the organization through a wide-angle lens, rather than a telephoto lens—so that they perceive how their decisions and actions affect the whole.[32]

An important element of systems thinking is to discern circles of causality. Peter Senge, author of *The Fifth Discipline*, argues that reality is made up of circles rather than straight lines. For example, Exhibit 5.2 shows circles of influence for producing new products. In the circle on the left, a high-tech firm grows rapidly by pumping out new products quickly. New products increase revenues, which enable the further increase of the R&D budget to add more new products.

Exhibit 5.2 Two Circles of Causality in an Organization

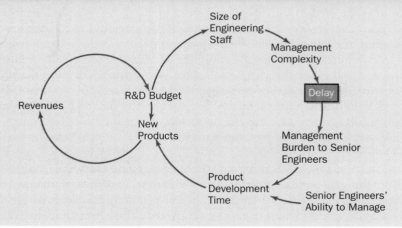

Source: From *The Fifth Discipline: The Art and Practice of the Learning Organization* by Peter M. Senge, p. 97. Copyright © 1990 by Peter M. Senge. Used by permission of Doubleday, a division of Bantam Doubleday Dell Publishing Group, Inc.

But another circle of causality is being influenced as well. As the R&D budget grows, the engineering and research staff increases. The burgeoning technical staff becomes increasingly hard to manage. The management burden falls on senior engineers, who provide less of their time for developing new products, which slows product development time. The slowing of product development time has a negative impact on new products, the very thing that created organizational success. Maintaining product development time in the face of increasing management complexity depends upon senior engineers' management ability. Thus, understanding the circle of causality enables leaders to allocate resources to the training and development of engineering leadership as well as directly to new products. Without an understanding of the system, top leaders would fail to understand why increasing R&D budgets can actually increase product development time and reduce the number of new products coming to market.

The other element of systems thinking is learning to influence the system with reinforcing feedback as an engine for growth or decline. In the example of new products, after managers see how the system works, they can allocate revenues to speed new products to market, either by hiring more engineers, or by training senior engineers in management and leadership skills. They can guide the system when they understand it conceptually. Without this kind of understanding, managers will hit blockages in the form of seeming limits to growth and resistance to change because the large complex system will appear impossible to manage. Systems thinking is a significant solution.

Personal Mastery

Another concept introduced by Senge is *personal mastery,* a term he uses to describe the discipline of personal growth and learning, of mastering yourself in a way that facilitates your leadership and achieves desired results.[33]

Personal mastery embodies three qualities—personal vision, facing reality, and holding creative tension. First, leaders engaged in personal mastery know and clarify what is important to them. They focus on the end result, the vision or dream that motivates them and their organization. They have a clear vision of a desired future, and their purpose is to achieve that future. One element of personal mastery, then, is the discipline of continually focusing and defining what one wants as the desired future and vision.

Second, facing reality means a commitment to the truth. Leaders are relentless in uncovering the mental models that limit and deceive them and are willing to challenge assumptions and ways of doing things. These leaders are committed to the truth, and will break through denial of reality in themselves and others. Their quest for truth leads to a deeper awareness of themselves and of the larger systems and events within which they operate. Commitment to the truth enables them to deal with reality, which increases the opportunity to achieve desired results.

Third, often there is a large gap between one's vision and the current situation. The gap between the desired future and today's reality, say between the dream of starting a business and the reality of having no capital, can be discouraging. But the gap is the source of creative energy. Acknowledging and living with the disparity between the truth and the vision, and facing it squarely, is the source of resolve and creativity to move forward. The effective leader resolves the tension by letting the vision pull reality toward it, in other words, by reorganizing current activities to work toward the vision. The leader works in a way that moves things toward the vision. The less effective way is to let reality pull

Personal mastery
the discipline of personal growth and learning and of mastering yourself; it embodies personal visions, facing reality, and holding creative tension

the vision downward toward it. This means lowering the vision, such as walking away from a problem or settling for less than desired. Settling for less releases the tension, but it also engenders mediocrity. Leaders with personal mastery learn to accept both the dream and the reality simultaneously, and to close the gap by moving toward the dream.

All five elements of mind are interrelated. Independent thinking and open-mindedness improve systems thinking and enable personal mastery, helping leaders shift and expand their mental models. Since they are all interdependent, leaders working to improve even one element of their mental approach can move forward in a significant way toward mastering their minds and becoming more effective.

Emotional Intelligence—Leading with Heart and Mind

Psychologists and other researchers, as well as people in all walks of life, have long recognized the importance of cognitive intelligence, or IQ, in determining a person's success and effectiveness. In general, research shows that leaders score higher than most people on tests of cognitive ability, such as IQ tests, and that cognitive ability is positively associated with effective leadership.[34] Increasingly, leaders and researchers are recognizing the critical importance of emotional intelligence, or EQ, as well. Some have suggested that emotion, more than cognitive ability, drives our thinking and decision making, as well as our interpersonal relationships.[35] **Emotional intelligence** refers to a person's abilities to perceive, identify, understand, and successfully manage emotions in self and others. Being emotionally intelligent means being able to effectively manage ourselves and our relationships.[36]

Emotional understanding and skills impact our success and happiness in our work as well as our personal lives. Leaders can harness and direct the power of emotions to improve follower satisfaction, morale, and motivation, as well as to enhance overall organizational effectiveness. The U.S. Air Force started using EQ to select recruiters after learning that the best recruiters scored higher in EQ competencies. Leaders who score high in EQ are typically more effective and rated as more effective by peers and subordinates.[37] Moreover, in a study of entrepreneurs, researchers at Rensselaer Polytechnic Institute found that those who are more expressive of their own emotions and more in tune with the emotions of others make more money, as illustrated in Exhibit 5.3.

Emotional intelligence
a person's abilities to perceive, identify, understand, and successfully manage emotions in self and others

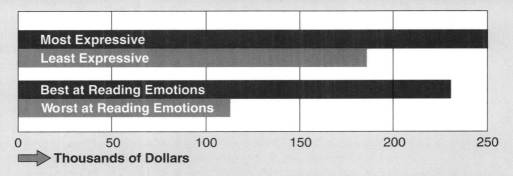

Exhibit 5.3 Emotional Intelligence and Earning Power

Most Expressive
Least Expressive
Best at Reading Emotions
Worst at Reading Emotions

0   50   100   150   200   250
➡ Thousands of Dollars

Entrepreneurs who scored in the top 10 percent in these two categories earn more money than those in the bottom 10 percent.

Source: Rensselaer Polytechnic Institute, Lally School of Management and Technology, as reported in *BusinessWeek Frontier* (February 5, 2001), p. F4.

Some leaders act as if people leave their emotions at home when they come to work, but we all know this isn't true. Indeed, a key component of leadership is being emotionally connected to others and understanding how emotions affect working relationships and performance.

What Are Emotions?

There are hundreds of emotions and more subtleties of emotion than there are words to explain them. One important ability for leaders is to understand the range of emotions people have and how these emotions may manifest themselves. Many researchers accept eight categories or "families" of emotions, as illustrated in Exhibit 5.4.[38] These categories do not resolve every question about how to categorize emotions, and scientific debate continues. The argument for there being a set of core emotions is based partly on the discovery that specific facial expressions for four of them (fear, anger, sadness, and enjoyment) are universally recognized. People in cultures around the world have been found to recognize these same basic emotions when shown photographs of facial expressions. The primary emotions and some of their variations follow.

- *Anger:* fury, outrage, resentment, exasperation, indignation, animosity, annoyance, irritability, hostility, violence
- *Sadness:* grief, sorrow, gloom, melancholy, self-pity, loneliness, dejection, despair, depression
- *Fear:* anxiety, apprehension, nervousness, concern, consternation, wariness, edginess, dread, fright, terror, panic
- *Enjoyment:* happiness, joy, relief, contentment, delight, amusement, pride, sensual pleasure, thrill, rapture, gratification, satisfaction, euphoria
- *Love:* acceptance, respect, friendliness, trust, kindness, affinity, devotion, adoration, infatuation
- *Surprise:* shock, astonishment, amazement, wonder
- *Disgust:* contempt, disdain, scorn, abhorrence, aversion, distaste, revulsion
- *Shame:* guilt, embarrassment, chagrin, remorse, humiliation, regret, mortification, contrition

Exhibit 5.4 Eight Families of Emotions

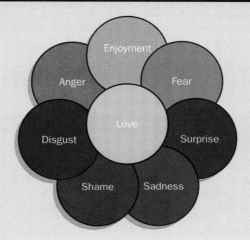

Leaders who are attuned to their own feelings and the feelings of others can use their understanding to enhance the organization. For example, studies of happiness in the workplace find that employee happiness can play a major role in organizational success. And a *Gallup Management Journal* survey emphasizes that leaders, especially frontline supervisors, have a lot to do with whether employees have positive or negative feelings about their work lives.[39]

The Components of Emotional Intelligence

The competencies and abilities of emotional intelligence are grouped into four fundamental categories, as illustrated in Exhibit 5.5.[40] It is important to remember that emotional intelligence can be learned and developed. Anyone can strengthen his or her abilities in these four categories.

Self-awareness might be considered the basis of all the other competencies. It includes the ability to recognize and understand your own emotions and how they affect your life and work. People who are in touch with their emotions are better able to guide their own lives. Leaders with a high level of self-awareness learn to trust their "gut feelings" and realize that these feelings can provide useful information about difficult decisions. Answers are not always clear as to whether to propose a major deal, let an employee go, reorganize a business, or revise job responsibilities. When the answers are not available from external sources, leaders have to rely on their own feelings. This component also includes the ability to accurately assess your own strengths and limitations, along with a healthy sense of self-confidence.

Self-management, the second key component, includes the ability to control disruptive, unproductive, or harmful emotions and desires. An interesting experiment from the 1960s sheds some light on the power of self-management. A group of four-year-olds and five-year-olds were offered a marshmallow, which the researcher placed in front of each child on the desk. Then, the children were told that if they could wait a few minutes while the researcher ran an errand, they would be given two marshmallows. Some children were unable to resist the temptation of a marshmallow "right now" and ate theirs immediately. Others employed all sorts

Self-awareness
the ability to recognize and understand your own emotions and how they affect your life and work

Self-management
the ability to control disruptive or harmful emotions

Exhibit 5.5 The Components of Emotional Intelligence

	SELF	OTHERS
AWARENESS	**Self-Awareness** • Emotional self-awareness • Accurate self-assessment • Self-confidence	**Social Awareness** • Empathy • Organizational awareness • Service orientation
BEHAVIOR	**Self-Management** • Emotional self-control • Trustworthiness • Conscientiousness • Adaptability • Optimism • Achievement-orientation • Initiative	**Relationship Management** • Development of others • Inspirational leadership • Influence • Communication • Change catalyst • Conflict management • Bond building • Teamwork and collaboration

Source: Adapted from Richard E. Boyatzis and Daniel Goleman, *The Emotional Competence Inventory—University Edition* (Boston, MA: The Hay Group, 2001).

of techniques, from singing or talking to themselves to hiding under the desk, to resist their impulses and earn the reward of two marshmallows instead of one. Researchers then followed the children over a period of 20 years and found some interesting results. As young men and women, the ones who had resisted the desire to eat the marshmallow revealed a much higher ability to handle stress and embrace difficult challenges. They also were more self-confident, trustworthy, dependable, and tenacious in pursuing goals.[41] The children who developed techniques for self-management early in life carried these with them into adulthood.

It is never too late for people to learn how to manage their emotions and impulses. Leaders learn to balance their own emotions so that worry, desire, anxiety, fear, or anger do not get in the way, thus enabling them to think clearly and be more effective. Managing emotions does not mean suppressing or denying them but understanding them and using that understanding to deal with situations productively.[42]

Other characteristics in this category include *trustworthiness*, which means consistently displaying honesty and integrity, *conscientiousness*, which means managing and honoring your responsibilities, and *adaptability*, which refers to the ability to adjust to changing situations and overcome obstacles. Showing initiative to seize opportunities and achieve high internal standards is also a part of self-management. Leaders skilled at self-management remain hopeful and optimistic despite obstacles, setbacks, or even outright failures. Martin Seligman, a professor of psychology at the University of Pennsylvania, once advised the MetLife insurance company to hire a special group of job applicants who tested high on optimism but failed the normal sales aptitude test. Compared to salespeople who passed the regular aptitude test but scored high on pessimism, the "optimistic" group made 21 percent more sales in their first year and 57 percent more in the second.[43]

Social awareness relates to one's ability to understand others. Socially aware leaders practice **empathy**, which means being able to put yourself in other people's shoes, sense their emotions, and understand their perspective. These leaders understand that effective leadership sometimes means pushing people beyond their comfort zone, and they are sensitive to the fear or frustration this can engender in followers. They learn to engage in "professional intimacy," which means they can display compassion and concern for others without becoming so wrapped up in others' emotions that it clouds their judgment.[44] Socially aware leaders are also capable of understanding divergent points of view and interacting effectively with many different types of people and emotions. The related characteristic of *organizational awareness* refers to the ability to navigate the currents of organizational life, build networks, and effectively use political behavior to accomplish positive results. This component also includes a *service orientation*, which refers to the ability to recognize and serve the needs of employees, customers, or clients.

Relationship management refers to the ability to connect with others and build positive relationships. Leaders with high emotional intelligence treat others with compassion, sensitivity, and kindness.[45] This aspect of EQ encompasses developing others, inspiring others with a powerful vision, learning to listen and communicate clearly and convincingly, and using emotional understanding to influence others in positive ways. Leaders use their understanding of emotions to inspire change and lead people toward something better, to build teamwork and collaboration, and to resolve conflicts that inevitably arise. These leaders cultivate and maintain a web of relationships both within and outside the organization.

Social awareness
one's ability to understand and empathize with others

Empathy
being able to put yourself in someone else's shoes

Relationship management
the ability to connect with others and build positive relationships

For example, Jim McNerney has reinvigorated Boeing by using his relationship management abilities. McNerney is known as a good listener, a motivator, and a team-builder who inspires people with his vision and his integrity. He spent much of his first six months as CEO talking with employees around the company to understand Boeing's strengths and challenges and emphasize the need for cooperation and teamwork.[46]

Taken together, the four components shown in Exhibit 5.5 build a strong base of emotional intelligence that leaders can use to more effectively guide teams and organizations. One research project suggests that all effective leadership styles arise from different components of emotional intelligence.[47] The best leaders combine styles or vary their styles, depending on the situation or problem at hand, by using all of the components. By being sensitive to their own and others' emotions, these leaders can recognize what effect they are having on followers and seamlessly adjust their approach to create a positive result. Consider how Mike Krzyzewski, coach of the Duke University Blue Devils, uses emotional intelligence to bring out the best in his players.

Action Memo

As a leader, you can empathize with others, treat people with compassion and sensitivity, build teamwork, and learn to listen, interpret emotions, and resolve interpersonal conflicts.

IN THE LEAD

Mike Krzyzewski, Duke University Blue Devils

Mike Krzyzewski doesn't think of himself as a basketball coach. He considers himself a leader who just happens to coach basketball. And for Krzyzewski, almost everything in leadership depends on one element: personal relationships.

Although he's a tough man with tough standards, Krzyzewski has been accused of "coaching like a girl" because of his interactive, emotionally charged style. When the legendary coach of Duke University's Blue Devils recruits a player, for example, he tells him, "We're developing a relationship here, and if you're not interested, tell me sooner rather than later." The emphasis on relationships comes partly from Krzyzewski's years playing, and later coaching, at the U.S. Military Academy at West Point, which he calls the greatest leadership school in the world because it teaches officers how to bond soldiers together. As a coach, Krzyzewski emphasizes teamwork rather than individual performers, fosters a family feeling among players, and says he coaches "by feel." That is, he gets to know his players as individuals and learns how they can best interact to succeed. He builds such strong positive relationships among players that they communicate constantly and effortlessly on the court, sometimes without saying a word.

Leading a basketball team, Krzyzewski believes, is just like leading a business, a military unit, a school, a volunteer group, or anything else: "You gotta get through all their layers and get right into their hearts."[48]

Mike Krzyzewski has created the kind of workplace that many of today's organizations need—one in which leaders are more interactive than "command-and-control," where leadership and decision making is spread across all levels, and where individual goals are met through teamwork and collaboration. In an environment where relationships with employees and customers are becoming more important than technology and material resources, interest in developing leaders' emotional intelligence continues to grow. All leaders have to pay attention to the emotional climate in their organization. Recent events

Action Memo

Evaluate your level of emotional intelligence by completing the questionnaire in Leader's Self-Insight 5.2.

For each of the following items, rate how well you display the behavior described. Before responding, try to think of actual situations in which you have had the opportunity to use the behavior. Indicate whether each item below is Mostly False or Mostly True for you.

	Mostly False	Mostly True
1. Associate different internal physiological cues with different emotions.	_____	_____
2. Relax when under pressure in situations.	_____	_____
3. Know the impact that your behavior has on others.	_____	_____
4. Initiate successful resolution of conflict with others.	_____	_____
5. Know when you are becoming angry.	_____	_____
6. Recognize when others are distressed.	_____	_____
7. Build consensus with others.	_____	_____
8. Produce motivation when doing uninteresting work.	_____	_____
9. Help others manage their emotions.	_____	_____
10. Make others feel good.	_____	_____
11. Identify when you experience mood shifts.	_____	_____
12. Stay calm when you are the target of anger from others.	_____	_____
13. Know when you become defensive.	_____	_____
14. Follow your words with actions.	_____	_____
15. Engage in intimate conversations with others.	_____	_____
16. Accurately reflect people's feelings back to them.	_____	_____

Scoring and Interpretation

Sum your Mostly True responses to the 16 questions to obtain your overall emotional intelligence score. Your score for self-awareness is the total of questions 1, 5, 11, and 13. Your score for self-management is the total of questions 2, 8, 12, and 14. Your score for social awareness is the sum of questions 3, 6, 9, and 15. Your score for relationship management is the sum of questions 4, 7, 10, and 16. This questionnaire provides some indication of your emotional intelligence. If you received a total score of 14 or more, you are certainly considered a person with high emotional intelligence. A score from 10 to 13 means you have a good platform of emotional intelligence from which to develop your leadership capability. A score of 7 to 9 would be moderate emotional intelligence. A score below 7 indicates that you realize that you are probably below average in emotional intelligence.

For each of the four components of emotional intelligence—self-awareness, self-management, social awareness, and relationship management—a score of 4 is considered high, whereas a score of 2 or fewer would be considered low. Review the discussion in this chapter about the four components of emotional intelligence and think about what you might do to develop those areas where you scored low. Compare your scores to those of other students. What can you do to improve your scores?

Source: Adapted from Hendrie Weisinger, *Emotional Intelligence at Work* (San Francisco: Jossey-Bass, 1998), pp. 214–215.

marble: © Kirill Matkov   sunset: © Marco Regalia

and challenges have thrust emotions to the forefront for both individuals and organizations.

The Emotionally Competent Leader

In discussing Abraham Lincoln's leadership, noted historian Doris Kearns Goodwin attributes the 16th U.S. President's almost magical touch not to charisma or political astuteness, but to emotional intelligence.[49] How is emotional intelligence related to effective leadership? A high level of self-awareness and an ability to manage one's own emotions enable a leader to display self-confidence, earn respect and trust, and consider the needs of others. Emotionally competent leaders are more resilient, more adaptable to ever-changing circumstances, more willing to step outside their comfort zone, and more open to the opinions and ideas of others.[50]

Emotional intelligence is also important for leaders because the emotional state of the leader impacts the entire team, department, or organization. Most of us recognize that we can "catch" emotions from others. If we're around someone who is smiling and enthusiastic, the positive emotions rub off on us. Conversely, someone in a bad mood can bring us down. At Mesa Airlines, CEO Jonathan Ornstein's former administrative assistant says she was in charge of tracking the unpredictable and frequently short-tempered leader's moods and warning other executives when they needed to stay away. "Sometimes he would come into the office in a bad mood . . . and it would set the tone for the whole office," she says.[51] This *emotional contagion*[52] means that leaders who are able to maintain balance and keep themselves motivated can serve as positive role models to help motivate and inspire those around them. The energy level of the entire organization increases when leaders are optimistic and hopeful rather than angry or depressed. The ability to empathize with others and to manage interpersonal relationships also contributes to motivation and inspiration because it helps leaders create feelings of unity and team spirit.

Action Memo

As a leader, you can develop emotional intelligence and act as a positive role model by being optimistic and enthusiastic.

Perhaps most importantly, emotional intelligence enables leaders to recognize and respect followers as whole human beings with feelings, opinions, and ideas of their own. They can use their emotional intelligence to help followers grow and develop, see and enhance their self-image and feelings of self-worth, and help meet their needs and achieve their personal goals.

In one study, two-thirds of the difference between average and top performing leaders was found to be due to emotional competence, with only one-third due to technical skills.[53] There are many training programs for developing one's emotional intelligence, but people can also take some simple steps on their own. Here are a few ideas that have been suggested as ways to enhance emotional intelligence:[54]

- *Take responsibility for your life.* Some people are always looking for someone to blame when things go wrong. Taking responsibility means assuming ownership for the situations and the condition of your own life, which provides a foundation for emotional intelligence. It is natural to want to blame someone or something else for problems, but taking responsibility gives you power and control over your own emotions and engenders respect from others.
- *Take a course in public speaking.* Many people have a fear of public speaking, so this is a good way to practice self-management, such as learning to control nervousness and self-consciousness. In addition, being a good public speaker means understanding the audience. The best speakers make it more about the audience and less about themselves. Thus, practicing public speaking can help you learn to empathize with others and take their needs and interests into account.
- *Practice meditation or yoga.* The disciplines of meditation and yoga promote mindfulness, as described earlier, and enable the individual to attain a state of relaxed awareness. Meditation and yoga can help you learn to manage your emotions so that stress, depression, and negative thoughts and feelings don't cloud your judgment and control your actions.

The Emotional Intelligence of Teams

Much of the work in today's organizations, even at top management levels, is done in teams rather than by individuals. Although most studies of emotional intelligence have focused on individuals, research is beginning to emerge concerning how emotional intelligence relates to teams. For example, one study found that untrained teams made up of members with high emotional intelligence performed as well as trained teams made up of members who rated low on emotional intelligence.[55] The high emotional intelligence of the untrained team members enabled them to assess and adapt to the requirements of teamwork and the tasks at hand.

Moreover, research has suggested that emotional intelligence can be developed as a *team* competency and not just an individual competency.[56] That is, teams themselves—not just their individual members—can become emotionally intelligent. Leaders build the emotional intelligence of teams by creating norms that support emotional development and influence emotions in constructive ways. Emotionally intelligent team norms are those that (1) create a strong group identity, (2) build trust among members, and (3) instill a belief among members that they can be effective and succeed as a team.

Leaders "tune in" to the team's emotional state and look for unhealthy or unproductive norms that inhibit cooperation and team harmony.[57] Building the emotional intelligence of the team means exploring unhealthy norms, deliberately bringing emotions to the surface, and understanding how they affect the team's work. Raising these issues can be uncomfortable, and a leader needs both courage and individual emotional intelligence to guide a team through the process. Only by getting emotions into the open can the team build new norms and move to a higher level of group satisfaction and performance. Leaders continue to build emotional intelligence by encouraging and enabling the team to explore and use emotion in its everyday work.

Leading with Love versus Leading with Fear

Traditionally, leadership has been based on inspiring fear in employees. An unspoken notion among many senior-level executives is that fear is a good thing and benefits the organization.[58] Indeed, fear can be a powerful motivator, but many of today's leaders are learning that an environment that reflects care and respect for people is much more effective than one in which people are fearful. When organizational success depended primarily on people mindlessly following orders, leading with fear often met the organization's needs. Today, though, success in most organizations depends on the knowledge, mindpower, commitment, and enthusiasm of everyone in the organization. A fear-based organization loses its best people, and the knowledge they take with them, to other firms. In addition, even if people stay with the organization, they typically don't perform up to their real capabilities. There is evidence that people who experience positive emotions at work perform better.[59]

Action Memo

To learn about your own motivations concerning love versus fear, complete the exercise in Leader's Self-Insight 5.3.

One major drawback of leading with fear is that it creates avoidance behavior, because no one wants to make a mistake, and this inhibits growth and change. Leaders can learn to bind people together for a shared purpose through more positive forces such as caring and compassion, listening, and connecting to others on a personal level. The emotion that attracts people to take risks, learn, grow, and move the organization forward comes from love, not fear. Douglas Conant, CEO of Campbell Soup, profiled in Chapter 2, says true leaders get employees to "fall in love with your company's agenda" by engaging with them personally and treating them with respect.[60]

The following items describe reasons why you work. *Answer the questions twice,* the first time for doing work (or homework) that is not your favorite, and the second time for doing a hobby or sports activity that you enjoy. *Consider each item thoughtfully and respond according to your inner motivation and experience.* Indicate whether each item below is Mostly False or Mostly True for you.

	Mostly False	Mostly True
1. I feel it is important to perform well so I don't look bad.	_____	_____
2. I have to force myself to complete the task.	_____	_____
3. I don't want to have a poor outcome or get a poor grade.	_____	_____
4. I don't want to embarrass myself or do less well than others.	_____	_____
5. The experience leaves me feeling relieved that it is over.	_____	_____
6. My attention is absorbed entirely in what I am doing.	_____	_____
7. I really enjoy the experience.	_____	_____
8. Time seems to pass more quickly than normal.	_____	_____
9. I am completely focused on the task at hand.	_____	_____
10. The experience leaves me feeling great.	_____	_____

Scoring and Interpretation

These items reflect motivation shaped by either love or fear. Your "fear of failure" score is the number of Mostly True answers for questions 1–5. Your "love of task" score is the number of Mostly True answers for questions 6–10. A score of 4 or 5 would be considered high for either love or fear, and a score of 0–2 would be considered low. You would probably score more points for "love of task" for your hobby or sports activity than for homework.

Some people are motivated by high internal standards and fear of not meeting those standards. This may be called fear of failure, which often spurs people to great accomplishment. Love of task provides a great intrinsic pleasure but won't always lead to high achievement. Love of task is related to the idea of "flow" wherein people become fully engaged and derive great satisfaction from their activity. Would love or fear influence your choice to become a leader or how you try to motivate others? Discuss with other students the relative importance of love or fear motivation in your lives.

Love in the workplace means genuinely caring for others and sharing one's knowledge, understanding, and compassion to enable others to grow and succeed.

Showing respect and trust not only enables people to perform better, but it also allows them to feel emotionally connected with their work so that their lives are richer and more balanced. Leaders can rely on negative emotions such as fear to fuel productive work, but by doing so they may slowly destroy people's spirits, which ultimately is bad for employees and the organization.[61]

Fear in Organizations

The workplace can hold many kinds of fear, including fear of failure, fear of change, fear of personal loss, and fear of the boss. All of these fears can prevent people from doing their best, from taking risks, and from challenging and changing the status quo. Fear gets in the way of people feeling good about their work, themselves, and the organization. It creates an atmosphere in which people feel powerless, so that their confidence, commitment, enthusiasm, imagination, and motivation are diminished.[62]

Action Memo

As a leader, you can choose to lead with love, not with fear. You can show respect and trust toward followers and help people learn, grow, and contribute their best to achieve the organization's vision.

Aspects of Fear A particularly damaging aspect of fear in the workplace is that it can weaken trust and communication. Employees feel threatened by repercussions if they speak up about work-related concerns. A survey of employees in 22 organizations around the country found that 70 percent of them "bit their tongues" at work because they feared repercussions. Twenty-seven percent reported that they feared losing their credibility or reputation if they spoke up. Other fears reported were lack of career advancement, possible damage to the relationship with their supervisor, demotion or losing their job, and being embarrassed or humiliated in front of others.[63] When people are afraid to speak up, important issues are suppressed and problems hidden. Employees are afraid to talk about a wide range of issues, but by far the largest category of "undiscussables" is the behavior of executives, particularly their interpersonal and relationship skills. When leaders inspire fear, they destroy the opportunity for feedback, blinding them to reality and denying them the chance to correct damaging decisions and behaviors.

Relationship with Leaders Leaders control the fear level in the organization. Exhibit 5.6 outlines some indicators of love-based versus fear-based leadership in organizations. Organizations driven by love are marked by openness and authenticity, a respect for diverse viewpoints, and emphasis on positive interpersonal relationships. Organizations driven by fear, on the other hand, are characterized by cautiousness and secrecy, blaming others, excessive control, and emotional distance among people. The relationship between an employee and his or her direct supervisor is the primary factor determining the level of fear experienced at work. Unfortunately, the legacy of fear and mistrust associated with traditional hierarchies in which bosses gave orders and employees jumped to obey "or else" still colors life in many organizations. Leaders can create a new environment that enables people to feel safe speaking their minds. Leaders can act from love rather than fear to free employees and the organization from the chains of the past.

Bringing Love to Work

Organizations have traditionally rewarded people for strong qualities such as rational thinking, ambition, and competitiveness. These qualities are important,

Exhibit 5.6 Indicators of Love versus Fear in Organizations

Fear-Driven Indicators	Love-Driven Indicators
Caution and secrecy	Openness and authenticity, even when it's difficult
Blaming and attacking	Understanding diverse viewpoints
Excessive control	Expecting others to do great things
Sidelines criticalness	Involvement and discernment
Coming unglued	Keeping perspective
Aloofness and distance	Interpersonal connection
Resistance hidden	Resistance out in open, explored
Separate and competing interests	Alignment and common ground sought

Source: Daniel Holden, "Team Development: A Search for Elegance," *Industrial Management* (September–October 2007), pp. 20–25.

but their overemphasis has left many organizational leaders out of touch with their softer, caring, creative capabilities, unable to make emotional connections with others and afraid to risk showing any sign of weakness. In other words, many leaders act from their own fear, which creates fear in others. A leader's fear can manifest itself in arrogance, selfishness, deception, unfairness, and disrespect for others.[64]

Leaders can develop their capacity for the positive emotions of love and caring. When Walt Bettinger, CEO of Charles Schwab, was in college, he learned a lesson he tries to apply every day. The professor handed each student a blank sheet of paper and gave them one final exam question: *What's the name of the lady who cleans this building?* The students had spent four hours a night twice a week in the building for 10 weeks, encountering the cleaning lady several times a night as they went to get a soft drink or use the restroom. Bettinger says: "I didn't know Dottie's name—her name was Dottie—but I've tried to know every Dottie since."[65]

Most of us have experienced the power of love at some time in our lives. There are many different kinds of love—for example, the love of a mother for her child, romantic love, brotherly love, or the love of country, as well as the love some people feel for certain sports, hobbies, or recreational pursuits. Despite its power, the "L" word is often looked upon with suspicion in the business world.[66] However, there are a number of aspects of love that are directly relevant to work relationships and organizational performance.

Love as motivation is the force within that enables people to feel alive, connected, energized, and "in love" with life and work. Western cultures place great emphasis on the mind and the rational approach. However, it is the heart rather than the mind that powers people forward. Recall a time when you wanted to do something with all your heart, and how your energy and motivation flowed freely. Also recall a time when your head said you had to do a task, but your heart was not in it. Motivation is reduced, perhaps to the point of procrastination. There's a growing interest in helping people feel a genuine passion for their work.[67] People who are engaged rather than alienated from their work are typically more satisfied, productive, and successful.

Love as feelings involves attraction, fascination, and caring for people, work, or other things. This is what people most often think of as love, particularly in relation to romantic love between two people. However, love as feelings is also relevant in work situations. Feelings of compassion and caring for others are a manifestation of love, as are forgiveness, sincerity, respect, and loyalty, all of which are important for healthy working relationships. One personal feeling is a sense of *bliss,* best articulated for the general public by Joseph Campbell in his PBS television series and companion book with Bill Moyers, *The Power of Myth.*[68] Finding your bliss means doing things that make you light up inside, things you do for the joy of doing rather than for material rewards. Most of us experience moments of this bliss when we become so absorbed in enjoyable work activities that we lose track of time. This type of feeling and caring about work is a major source of charisma. Everyone becomes more charismatic to others when they pursue an activity they truly care about.

Love as action means more than feelings; it is translated into behavior. Stephen Covey points out that in all the great literature, love is a verb rather than a noun.[69] Love is something you do, the sacrifices you make and the giving of yourself to others. The following poignant example from the Iraq war illustrates this aspect of love.

IN THE LEAD

Cpl. Jason Dunham, United States Marine Corps; Petty Officer Michael Monsoor, United States Navy; Sgt. Rafael Peralta, United States Marine Corps; Sgt. James Witkowski, Army Reserve; Spc. Ross McGinnis, United States Army

When asked why his friend Ross McGinnis threw himself on an enemy grenade that was thrown into their Humvee, U.S. Army Staff Sgt. Ian Newland simply said, "He loved us." McGinnis was killed; the other soldiers, though wounded, survived.

During the Iraq war, at least four other U.S. soldiers—Jason Dunham and Rafael Peralta of the U.S. Marines; Michael Monsoor, a Navy EOD Technician; and Army Reserve Sgt. James Witkowski—died because they used their own bodies to shield their comrades from grenades. "What a decision that is," said Frank Farley, a professor who studies bravery. "I can't think of anything more profound in human nature."

Soldiers who survive when a comrade makes the ultimate sacrifice to save them typically struggle with feelings of guilt, depression, and anxiety and need strong counseling to cope with what has happened. However, another result is that most of them feel they need to live their lives in a way that will honor their fallen comrade. "I try not to live my life in vain for what he's done," said Newland about McGinnis's death. A Navy lieutenant with the SEALs said something similar about Peralta when he indicated that "everything pretty much revolves around what he did."[70]

These soldiers were heroic, but Ross McGinnis's father Tom McGinnis said he didn't want his son depicted as larger-than-life. "He wasn't exceptional. He was just like you and me. He made a split-second decision. He did what he thought was right."[71] Tom McGinnis's statement is a reminder that we all have the opportunity to act out of love and compassion rather than fear and indifference.

Most of us are never called upon to sacrifice our lives for others, but in all groups and organizations feelings of compassion, respect, and loyalty are translated into action, such as acts of friendliness, teamwork, cooperation, listening, understanding, and serving others above oneself. Sentiments emerge as action.

Why Followers Respond to Love

Most people yearn for more than a paycheck from their jobs. Leaders who lead with love have extraordinary influence because they meet five unspoken employee needs:

Hear and understand me.
Even if you disagree with me, please don't make me wrong.
Acknowledge the greatness within me.
Remember to look for my loving intentions.
Tell me the truth with compassion.[72]

When leaders address these subtle emotional needs directly, people typically respond by loving their work and becoming emotionally engaged in solving problems and serving customers. Enthusiasm for work and the organization increases. People want to believe that their leaders genuinely care. From the followers' point of view, love versus fear has different motivational potential.

● **Fear-based motivation:** I need a job to pay for my basic needs (fulfilling lower needs of the body). You give me a job, and I will give you just enough to keep my job.

Fear-based motivation motivation based on fear of losing a job

- **Love-based motivation**: If the job and the leader make me feel valued as a person and provide a sense of meaning and contribution to the community at large (fulfilling higher needs of heart, mind, and body), then I will give you all I have to offer.[73]

Many examples throughout this book illustrate what happens when positive emotion is used. One management consultant went so far as to advise that finding creative ways to love could solve every imaginable leadership problem.[74] Rational thinking and technical skills are important, but leading with love builds trust, stimulates creativity, inspires commitment, and unleashes boundless energy.

Love-based motivation
motivation based on feeling valued in the job

Leadership Essentials

- Leaders use emotional as well as intellectual capabilities and understandings to guide organizations through a turbulent environment and help people feel energized, motivated, and cared for in the face of rapid change, uncertainty, and job insecurity. Leaders can expand the capacities of their minds and hearts through conscious development and practice.

- Leaders should be aware of how their mental models affect their thinking and may cause "blind spots" that limit understanding. Becoming aware of assumptions is a first step toward shifting one's mental model and being able to see the world in new and different ways. Four key issues important to expanding and developing a leader's mind are independent thinking, open-mindedness, systems thinking, and personal mastery.

- Leaders should also understand the importance of emotional intelligence. Four basic components of emotional intelligence are self-awareness, self-management, social awareness, and relationship management. Emotionally intelligent leaders can have a positive impact on organizations by helping employees grow, learn, and develop; creating a sense of purpose and meaning; instilling unity and team spirit; and basing relationships on trust and respect, which allows employees to take risks and fully contribute to the organization. Most work in organizations is done in teams, and emotional intelligence applies to teams as well as to individuals. Leaders develop a team's emotional intelligence by creating norms that foster a strong group identity, building trust among members, and instilling a belief among members that they can be effective and succeed as a team.

- Traditional organizations have relied on fear as a motivator. Although fear does motivate people, it prevents people from feeling good about their work and often causes avoidance behavior. Fear can reduce trust and communication so that important problems and issues are hidden or suppressed. Leaders can choose to lead with love instead of fear. Love can be thought of as a motivational force that enables people to feel alive, connected, and energized; as feelings of liking, caring, and bliss; and as actions of helping, listening, and cooperating. Each of these aspects of love has relevance for organizational relationships. People respond to love because it meets unspoken needs for respect and affirmation. Rational thinking is important to leadership, but it takes love to build trust, creativity, and enthusiasm.

Discussion Questions

1. How do you feel about developing the emotional qualities of yourself and other people in the organization as a way to be an effective leader? Discuss.

2. Do you agree that people have a capacity for developing their minds and hearts beyond their current level of competency? Can you give an example? Discuss.

3. Why is it so hard for people to change their assumptions? What are some specific reasons why leaders need to be aware of their mental models?

4. Discuss the similarities and differences between mental models and open-mindedness.

5. What is the concept of personal mastery? How important is it to a leader?

6. Which of the four elements of emotional intelligence do you consider most essential to an effective leader? Why?

7. Consider fear and love as potential motivators. Which is the best source of motivation for college students? For members of a new product development team? For top executives at a media conglomerate? Why?

8. Have you ever experienced love and/or fear from leaders at work? How did you respond? Is it possible that leaders might carry love too far and create negative rather than positive results? Discuss.

9. Do you think it is appropriate for a leader to spend time developing a team's emotional intelligence? Why or why not?

10. Think about the class for which you are reading this text as a system. How might making changes without whole-systems thinking cause problems for students?

Leadership at Work

MENTORS

Think of a time when someone reached out to you as a mentor or coach. This might have been a time when you were having some difficulty, and the person who reached out would have done so out of concern for you rather than for their own self interest.

Below, briefly describe the situation, who the mentor was, and what the mentor did for you.

_____

_____

_____

Mentoring comes from the heart, is a generous act, and is usually deeply appreciated by the recipient. How does it feel to recall the situation in which a mentor assisted you?

_____

_____

_____

Share your experience with one or more students. What are the common characteristics that mentors possess based on your combined experiences?

_____

_____

_____

In Class: A discussion of experiences with mentors is excellent for small groups. The instructor can ask each group to identify the common characteristics that their mentors displayed, and each group's conclusions can be written on the board. From these lists of mentor characteristics, common themes associated with mentors can be defined. The instructor can ask the class the following key questions: What are the key characteristics of mentors? Based on the key mentor characteristics, is effective mentoring based more on a person's heart or mind? Will you (the student) reach out as a mentor to others in life, and how will you do it? What factors might prevent you from doing so?

Leadership Development: Cases for Analysis

THE NEW BOSS

Sam Nolan clicked the mouse for one more round of solitaire on the computer in his den. He'd been at it for more than an hour, and his wife had long ago given up trying to persuade him to join her for a movie or a rare Saturday night on the town. The mind-numbing game seemed to be all that calmed Sam down enough to stop agonizing about work and how his job seemed to get worse every day.

Nolan was chief information officer at Century Medical, a large medical products company based in Connecticut. He had joined the company four years ago, and since that time Century had made great progress integrating technology into its systems and processes. Nolan had already led projects to design and build two highly successful systems for Century. One was a benefits-administration system for the company's human resources department. The other was a complex Web-based purchasing system that streamlined the process of purchasing supplies and capital goods. Although the system had been up and running for only a few months, modest projections were that it would save Century nearly $2 million annually. The new Web-based system dramatically cut the time needed for processing requests and placing orders. Purchasing managers now had more time to work collaboratively with key stakeholders to identify and select the best suppliers and negotiate better deals.

Nolan thought wearily of all the hours he had put in developing trust with people throughout the company and showing them how technology could not only save time and money but also support team-based work, encourage open information sharing, and give people more control over their own jobs. He smiled briefly as he recalled one long-term HR employee, 61-year-old Ethel Moore. She had been terrified when Nolan first began showing her the company's intranet, but she was now one of his biggest supporters. In fact, it had been Ethel who had first approached him with an idea about a Web-based job posting system. The two had pulled together a team and developed an idea for linking Century managers, internal recruiters, and job applicants using artificial intelligence software on top of an integrated Web-based system. When Nolan had presented the idea to his boss, executive vice president Sandra Ivey, she had enthusiastically endorsed it. Within a few weeks the team had authorization to proceed with the project.

But everything began to change when Ivey resigned her position 6 months later to take a plum job in New York. Ivey's successor, Tom Carr, seemed to have little interest in the project. During their first meeting, Carr had openly referred to the project as a waste of time and money. He immediately disapproved several new features suggested by the company's internal recruiters, even though the project team argued that the features could double internal hiring and save millions in training costs. "Just stick to the original plan and get it done. All this stuff needs to be handled on a personal basis anyway," Carr countered. "You can't learn more from a computer than you can talking to real people—and as for internal recruiting, it shouldn't be so hard to talk to people if they're already working right here in the company." Carr seemed to have no understanding of how and why technology was being used. He became irritated when Ethel Moore referred to the system as "Web-based." He boasted that he had never visited Century's intranet site and suggested that "this Internet obsession" would blow over in a few years anyway. Even Ethel's enthusiasm couldn't get through to him. "Technology is for those people in the IS department. My job is people, and yours should be, too," Carr shouted. Near the end of the meeting, Carr even jokingly suggested that the project team should just buy a couple of good filing cabinets and save everyone some time and money.

Nolan sighed and leaned back in his chair. The whole project had begun to feel like a joke. The vibrant and innovative human resources department his team had imagined now seemed like nothing more than a pipe dream. But despite his frustration, a new thought entered Nolan's mind: "Is Carr just stubborn and narrow-minded or does he have a point that HR is a people business that doesn't need a high-tech job posting system?"

Sources: Based on Carol Hildebrand, "New Boss Blues," *CIO Enterprise,* Section 2 (November 15, 1998), pp. 53–58; and Megan Santosus, "Advanced Micro Devices' Web-Based Purchasing System," *CIO,* Section 1 (May 15, 1998), p. 84. A version of this case originally appeared in Richard L. Daft, *Organization Theory and Design,* 7th ed. (Cincinnati, OH: South-Western, 2001), pp. 270–271.

QUESTIONS

1. Describe the two different mental models represented in this story.
2. What are some of the assumptions that shape the mindset of Sam Nolan? Of Tom Carr?
3. Do you think it is possible for Carr to shift to a new mental model? If you were Sam Nolan, what would you do?

THE USS *FLORIDA*

The atmosphere in a Trident nuclear submarine is generally calm and quiet. Even pipe joints are cushioned to prevent noise that might tip off a pursuer. The Trident ranks among the world's most dangerous weapons—swift, silent, armed with 24 long-range missiles carrying 192 nuclear warheads. Trident crews are the cream of the Navy crop, and even the sailors who fix the plumbing exhibit a white-collar decorum. The culture aboard ship is a low-key, collegial one in which sailors learn to speak softly and share close quarters with an ever-changing roster of shipmates. Being subject to strict security restrictions enhances a sense of elitism and pride. To move up and take charge of a Trident submarine is an extraordinary feat in the Navy—fewer than half the officers qualified for such commands ever get them. When Michael Alfonso took charge of the USS *Florida,* the crew welcomed his arrival. They knew he was one of them—a career Navy man who joined up as a teenager and moved up through the ranks. Past shipmates remembered him as basically a loner, who could be brusque but generally pleasant enough. Neighbors on shore found Alfonso to be an unfailingly polite man who kept mostly to himself.

The crew's delight in their new captain was short-lived. Commander Alfonso moved swiftly to assume command, admonishing his sailors that he would push them hard. He wasn't joking—soon after the *Florida* slipped into deep waters to begin a postoverhaul shakedown cruise, the new captain loudly and publicly reprimanded those whose performance he considered lacking. Chief Petty Officer Donald MacArthur, chief of the navigation division, was only one of those who suffered Alfonso's anger personally. During training exercises, MacArthur was having trouble keeping the boat at periscope depth because of rough seas. Alfonso announced loudly, "You're disqualified." He then precipitously relieved him of his diving duty until he could be recertified by extra practice. Word of the incident spread quickly. Crew members, accustomed to the Navy's adage of "praise in public, penalize in private," were shocked. It didn't take long for this type of behavior to have an impact on the crew, according to Petty Officer Aaron Carmody: "People didn't tell him when something was wrong. You're not supposed to be afraid of your captain, to tell him stuff. But nobody wanted to."

The captain's outbursts weren't always connected with job performance. He bawled out the supply officer, the executive officer, and the chief of the boat because the soda dispenser he used to pour himself a glass of Coke one day contained Mr. Pibb instead. He exploded when he arrived unexpectedly at a late-night meal and found the fork at his place setting missing. Soon, a newsletter titled *The Underground* was being circulated by the boat's plumbers, who used sophomoric humor to spread the word about the captain's outbursts over such petty matters. By the time the sub reached Hawaii for its "Tactical Readiness Evaluation," an intense week-long series of inspections by staff officers, the crew was almost completely alienated. Although the ship tested well, inspectors sent word to Rear Admiral Paul Sullivan that something seemed to be wrong on board, with severely strained relations between captain and crew. On the Trident's last evening of patrol, much of the crew celebrated with a film night—they chose *The Caine Mutiny* and *Crimson Tide,* both movies about Navy skippers who face mutinies and are relieved of command at sea. When Humphrey Bogart, playing the captain of the fictional USS *Caine,* exploded over a missing quart of strawberries, someone shouted, "Hey, sound familiar?"

When they reached home port, the sailors slumped ashore. "Physically and mentally, we were just beat into the ground," recalls one. Concerned about reports that the crew seemed "despondent," Admiral Sullivan launched an informal inquiry that eventually led him to relieve Alfonso of his command. It was the first-ever firing of a Trident submarine commander. "He had the chance of a lifetime to experience the magic of command, and he squandered it," Sullivan said. "Fear and intimidation lead to certain ruin." Alfonso himself seemed dumbfounded by Admiral Sullivan's actions, pointing out that the USS *Florida* under his command posted "the best-ever grades assigned for certifications and inspections for a postoverhaul Trident submarine."

Source: Based on Thomas E. Ricks, "A Skipper's Chance to Run a Trident Sub Hits Stormy Waters," *The Wall Street Journal* (November 20, 1997), pp. A1, A6.

QUESTIONS

1. Analyze Alfonso's impact on the crew in terms of love versus fear. What might account for the fact that he behaved so strongly as captain of the USS *Florida*?

2. Which do you think a leader should be more concerned about aboard a nuclear submarine—high certification grades or high-quality interpersonal relationships? Do you agree with Admiral Sullivan's decision to fire Alfonso? Discuss.

3. Discuss Commander Alfonso's level of emotional intelligence in terms of the four components listed in the chapter. What advice would you give him?

References

1   Thomas E. Ricks, "Charmed Forces: Army's 'Baby Generals' Take a Crash Course in Sensitivity Training," *The Wall Street Journal* (January 19, 1998), p. A1.

2   Warren Bennis, quoted in Tricia Bisoux, "What Makes Great Leaders," *BizEd* (September–October 2005), pp. 40–45.

3   Robert B. French, "The Teacher as Container of Anxiety: Psychoanalysis and the Role of Teacher," *Journal of Management Education* 21, no. 4 (November 1997), pp. 483–495.

4   This basic idea is found in a number of sources, among them: Jack Hawley, *Reawakening the Spirit in Work* (San Francisco: Berrett-Koehler, 1993); Aristotle, *The Nicomachean Ethics,* trans. by the Brothers of the English Dominican Province, rev. by Daniel J. Sullivan (Chicago: Encyclopedia Britannica, 1952); Alasdair MacIntyre, *After Virtue: A Study in Moral Theory* (Notre Dame, IN: University of Notre Dame Press, 1984); and Stephen Covey, *The Seven Habits of Highly Effective People: Powerful Lessons in Personal Change* (New York: Fireside Books/Simon & Schuster, 1990).

5   Vanessa Urch Druskat and Anthony T. Pescosolido, "The Content of Effective Teamwork Mental Models in Self-Managing Teams: Ownership, Learning, and Heedful Interrelating," *Human Relations* 55, no. 3 (2002), pp. 283–314; and Peter M. Senge, *The Fifth Discipline: The Art and Practice of the Learning Organization* (New York: Doubleday, 1990).

6   Druskat and Pescosolido, "The Content of Effective Teamwork Mental Models."

7   Adam Lashinsky, "Chaos by Design," *Fortune* (October 2, 2006), pp. 86–98.

8   The following discussion is based partly on Robert C. Benfari, *Understanding and Changing Your Management Style* (San Francisco: Jossey-Bass, 1999), pp. 66–93.

9   George Packer, *The Assassins' Gate: America in Iraq* (New York: Farrar, Straus & Giroux, 2005).

10 Micheline Maynard, "The Steady Optimist Who Oversaw G. M.'s Decline," *The New York Times* (March 30, 2009), http://www.nytimes.com/2009/03/30/business/30wagoner.html?emc=etal (accessed March 31, 2009); Bill Vlasic, "Abrupt Transition for G.M. with Wagoner's Dismissal," *International Herald Tribune* (April 2, 2009), p. 19; John D. Stoll, "Shake-Up at GM: Wagoner, with Knack for Survival, Hits Dead End," *The Wall Street Journal Asia* (March 31, 2009), p. 15; Alex Taylor III, "GM and Me," *Fortune* (December 8, 2008), pp. 92–100; Bill Vlasic, "A G. M. Vow to Get Leaner Now Includes Its Top Ranks," *The New York Times* (July 11, 2009), p. B1; and Jeremy Smerd, "Outsider Thinking for GM HR," *Workforce Management* (August 17, 2009), p. 1.

11 Vlasic, "Abrupt Transition for G.M."; Bill Vlasic, "G. M. Chairman Vows to Defend Market Share," *The New York Times* (August 5, 2009), p. B1; and David Hendricks, "Whitacre Pitches 1st GM Ad As If He Had Written It," *San Antonio Express-News* (September 19, 2009), p. C1.

12 Anthony J. Mayo and Nitin Nohria, *In Their Time: The Greatest Business Leaders of the 20th Century* (Boston: Harvard Business School Press, 2005).

13 Geoffrey Colvin, "The Most Valuable Quality in a Manager," *Fortune* (December 29, 1997), pp. 279–280; and Marlene Piturro, "Mindshift," *Management Review* (May 1999), pp. 46–51.

14 Jeff D. Opdyke, "Decremental? Fitting Word for Ugly Times," *The Wall Street Journal* (March 2, 2009), p. C1.

15 Geoffrey Colvin, "Managing in Chaos," *Fortune* (October 2, 2006), pp. 76–82.

16 Gary Hamel, "Why . . . It's Better to Question Answers Than to Answer Questions," *Across the Board* (November–December 2000), pp. 42–46; and Jane C. Linder and Susan Cantrell, "It's All in the Mind (set)," *Across the Board* (May–June 2002), pp. 39–42.

17 Reported in Sharon Begley, "People Believe a 'Fact' That Fits Their Views, Even If It's Clearly False" (Science Journal column), *The Wall Street Journal* (February 4, 2005), p. A8.

18 Anil K. Gupta and Vijay Govindarajan, "Cultivating a Global Mindset," *Academy of Management Executive* 16, no. 1 (2002), pp. 116–126.

19 Hamel, "Why . . . It's Better to Question Answers Than to Answer Questions"; and Colvin, "Managing in Chaos."

20 Daniel Levinthal and Claus Rerup, "Crossing an Apparent Chasm: Bridging Mindful and Less-Mindful Perspectives on Organizational Learning," *Organization Science* 17, no. 4 (August 2006), pp. 502–513; and Ellen Langer and John Sviokla, "An Evaluation of Charisma from the Mindfulness Perspective," unpublished manuscript, Harvard University. Part of this discussion is also drawn from Richard L. Daft and Robert H. Lengel, *Fusion Leadership: Unlocking the Subtle Forces That Change People and Organizations* (San Francisco: Berrett-Koehler, 1998).

21 T. K. Das, "Educating Tomorrow's Managers: The Role of Critical Thinking," *The International Journal of Organizational Analysis* 2, no. 4 (October 1994), pp. 333–360.

22 Carol Hymowitz, "Building a Board That's Independent, Strong, and Effective" (In the Lead column), *The Wall Street Journal* (November 19, 2002), p. B1.

23 James R. Hagerty, "Directors Are Faulted at Home Loan Banks," *The Wall Street Journal* (May 23–24, 2009), p. A3.

24 Bernard M. Bass, *Leadership and Performance Beyond Expectations* (New York: The Free Press, 1985); and B. M. Bass, *New Paradigm Leadership: An Inquiry into Transformational Leadership* (Alexandria, VA: U.S. Army Research Institute for the Behavioral and Social Sciences, 1996).

25 Leslie Wexner, quoted in Rebecca Quick, "A Makeover That Began at the Top," *The Wall Street Journal* (May 25, 2000), pp. B1, B4.

26 The Pike Syndrome has been discussed in multiple sources.

27 Jeanne Whalen, "Theory & Practice: Chance Turns a Teacher into a CEO—Religion Lecturer Leaves Academic Path and Learns to Run a Biotech Start-Up," *The Wall Street Journal* (October 17, 2005), p. B4.

28 Chris Argyris, *Flawed Advice and the Management Trap* (New York: Oxford University Press, 2000); and Eileen C. Shapiro, "Managing in the Cappuccino Economy" (review of *Flawed Advice*), *Harvard Business Review* (March–April 2000), pp. 177–183.

29 Rajat Gupta, quoted in *Fast Company* (September 1999), p. 120.

30 This section is based on Peter M. Senge, *The Fifth Discipline: The Art and Practice of the Learning Organization* (New York: Doubleday, 1990); John D. Sterman, "Systems Dynamics Modeling: Tools for Learning in a Complex World," *California Management Review* 43, no. 4 (Summer, 2001), pp. 8–25; and Ron Zemke, "Systems Thinking," *Training* (February 2001), pp. 40–46.

31 These examples are cited in Sterman, "Systems Dynamics Modeling."

32 Peter M. Senge, Charlotte Roberts, Richard B. Ross, Bryan J. Smith, and Art Kleiner, *The Fifth Discipline Fieldbook* (New York: Currency/Doubleday, 1994), p. 87.

33 Senge, *The Fifth Discipline*.

34 Timothy A. Judge, Amy E. Colbert, and Remus Ilies, "Intelligence and Leadership: A Quantitative Review and Test of Theoretical Propositions," *Journal of Applied Psychology* (June 2004), pp. 542–552.

35 Daniel Goleman, *Emotional Intelligence: Why It Can Matter More Than IQ* (New York: Bantam Books, 1995); John D. Mayer and David Caruso, "The Effective Leader: Understanding and Applying Emotional Intelligence," *Ivey Business Journal* (November–December 2002); Pamela Kruger, "A Leader's Journey," *Fast Company* (June 1999), pp. 116–129; and Hendrie Weisinger, *Emotional Intelligence at Work* (San Francisco: Jossey-Bass, 1998).

36 Based on Goleman, *Emotional Intelligence*; Goleman, "Leadership That Gets Results," *Harvard Business Review* (March–April 2000), pp. 79–90; J. D. Mayer, D. R. Caruso, and P. Salovey, "Emotional Intelligence Meets Traditional Standards for an Intelligence," *Intelligence* 27, no. 4 (1999), pp. 266–298; Neal M. Ashkanasy and Catherine S. Daus, "Emotion in the Workplace: The New Challenge for Managers," *Academy of Management Executive* 16, no.1 (2002), pp. 76–86; and Weisinger, *Emotional Intelligence at Work*.

37 Studies reported in Stephen Xavier, "Are You at the Top of Your Game? Checklist for Effective Leaders," *Journal of Business Strategy* 26, no. 3 (2005), pp. 35–42.

38 This section is based largely on Goleman, *Emotional Intelligence: Why It Can Matter More Than IQ*, pp. 289–290.

39 Jerry Krueger and Emily Killham, "At Work, Feeling Good Matters," *Gallup Management Journal* (December 8, 2005).

40 Goleman, "Leadership That Gets Results"; and Richard E. Boyatzis and Daniel Goleman, *The Emotional Competence Inventory—University Edition* (Boston, MA: The Hay Group, 2001).

41 Dave Marcum, Steve Smith, and Mahan Khalsa, "The Marshmallow Conundrum," *Across the Board* (March–April 2004), pp. 26–30.

42 Weisinger, *Emotional Intelligence at Work*.

43 Alan Farnham, "Are You Smart Enough to Keep Your Job?" *Fortune* (January 15, 1996), pp. 34–47.

44 Peter J. Frost, "Handling the Hurt: A Critical Skill for Leaders," *Ivey Management Journal* (January–February 2004).

45 Rolf W. Habbel, "The Human[e] Factor: Nurturing a Leadership Culture," *Strategy & Business* 26 (First Quarter 2002), pp. 83–89.

46 Marilyn Adams, "Straightened Up and Flying Right," *USA Today* (February 26, 2007), http://www.usatoday.com (accessed February 26, 2007); and Diane Brady, "Being Mean Is So Last Millennium," *BusinessWeek* (January 15, 2007), p. 61.

47 Research study results reported in Goleman, "Leadership That Gets Results."

48 Michael Sokolove, "Follow Me," *The New York Times Magazine* (February 2006), p. 96.

49 Diane Coutu, "Leadership Lessons from Abraham Lincoln," *Harvard Business Review* (April 2009), pp. 43–47.

50 Xavier, "Are You at the Top of Your Game?"

51 Jeff Bailey, "Outsize Personality Tries to Create a Regional Airline to Match," *The New York Times* (January 19, 2007), p. C1.

52 E. Hatfield, J. T. Cacioppo, and R. L. Rapson, *Emotional Contagion* (New York: Cambridge University Press, 1994).

53 Study by Daniel Goleman, co-chairman of The Consortium for Research on Emotional Intelligence in Organizations, reported in Diann Daniel, "Soft Skills for CIOs and Aspiring CIOs: Four Ways to Boost Your Emotional Intelligence," *CIO* (June 25, 2007), http://www.cio.com (accessed October 18, 2007).

54 Daniel, "Soft Skills for CIOs."

55 P. J. Jordan, N. M. Ashkanasy, C. E. J. Härtel, and G. S. Hooper, "Workgroup Emotional Intelligence: Scale Development and Relationship to Team Process Effectiveness and Goal Focus," *Human Resource Management Review* 12, no. 2 (Summer 2002), pp. 195–214.

56 This discussion is based on Vanessa Urch Druskat and Steven B. Wolf, "Building the Emotional Intelligence of Groups," *Harvard Business Review* (March 2001), pp. 81–90.

57 Daniel Goleman, Richard Boyatzis, and Annie McKee, "The Emotional Reality of Teams," *Journal of Organizational Excellence* (Spring 2002), pp. 55–65.

58 This discussion is based in part on Kathleen D. Ryan and Daniel K. Oestreich, *Driving Fear out of the Workplace: How to Overcome the Invisible Barriers to Quality, Productivity, and Innovation* (San Francisco: Jossey-Bass, 1991); and Scott A. Snook, "Love and Fear and the Modern Boss," *Harvard Business Review* (January 2008), pp. 16–17.

59 S. Lyubomirsky, L. King, and E. Diener, "The Benefits of Frequent Positive Affect: Does Happiness Lead to Success?" *Psychological Bulletin* 131, no. 6 (2005), pp. 803–855; R. Cropanzano and T. A. Wright, "When a 'Happy' Worker Is Really a 'Productive' Worker: A Review and Further Refinement of the Happy-Productive Worker Theory," *Consulting Psychology Journal: Practice and Research* 53, no. 3 (2001), pp. 182–199; and S. G. Barsade and D. E. Gibson, "Why Does Affect Matter in Organizations?" *Academy of Management Perspectives* 21, no. 1 (2007), pp. 36–59.

60 Carol Hymowitz, "Business Is Personal, So Managers Need to Harness Emotions" (In the Lead column), *The Wall Street Journal* (November 13, 2006), p. B1.

61 David E. Dorsey, "Escape from the Red Zone," *Fast Company* (April/May 1997), pp. 116–127.

62 This section is based on Ryan and Oestreich, *Driving Fear out of the Workplace;* and Therese R. Welter, "Reducing Employee Fear: Get Workers and Managers to Speak Their Minds," *Small Business Report* (April 1991), pp. 15–18.

63 Ryan and Oestreich, *Driving Fear out of the Workplace,* p. 43.

64 Donald G. Zauderer, "Integrity: An Essential Executive Quality," *Business Forum* (Fall 1992), pp. 12–16.

65 Kristy J. O'Hara, "Role Player," *Smart Business Akron/Canton* (March 2009), p. 14.

66 Hawley, *Reawakening the Spirit at Work*, p. 55; and Rodney Ferris, "How Organizational Love Can Improve Leadership," *Organizational Dynamics* 16, no. 4 (Spring 1988), pp. 40–52.

67 Barbara Moses, "It's All About Passion," *Across the Board* (May–June 2001), pp. 55–58.

68 Joseph Campbell with Bill Moyers, *The Power of Myth* (New York: Doubleday, 1988).

69 Covey, *The Seven Habits of Highly Effective People,* p. 80.

70 Gregg Zoroya, "Coping After a Hero Dies Saving You in Iraq," *USA Today* (September 20, 2007), p. A1; "Marine to Receive Medal of Honor for Iraq Heroism," http://www.cnn.com/2006/US/11/10/medal.honor (accessed April 8, 2009); and "Army Sgt. James Witkowski," *Military Times: Honor the Fallen,* http://www.militarycity.com/valor/1220880.html (accessed April 8, 2009).

71 Zoroya, "Coping After a Hero Dies Saving You."

72 Hyler Bracey, Jack Rosenblum, Aubrey Sanford, and Roy Trueblood, *Managing from the Heart* (New York: Dell Publishing, 1993), p. 192.

73 Madan Birla with Cecilia Miller Marshall, *Balanced Life and Leadership Excellence* (Memphis, TN: The Balance Group, 1997), pp. 76–77.

74 Ferris, "How Organizational Love Can Improve Leadership."

11 >>

Power and Political Behavior

LEARNING OUTCOMES

After reading this chapter, you should be able to do the following:

1 Describe the concept of power.

2 Identify forms and sources of power in organizations.

3 Describe the role of ethics in using power.

4 Identify symbols of power and powerlessness in organizations.

5 Define *organizational politics* and understand the role of political skill and major influence tactics.

"Individuals have many forms of power to use in their work settings."

6 Identify ways to manage political behavior in organizations.

© ComstockImages/Jupiterimages

The Concept of Power

Power is the ability to influence another person. As an exchange relationship, it occurs in transactions between an agent and a target. The agent is the person using the power, and the target is the recipient of the attempt to use power.[1]

Because power is an ability, individuals can learn to use it effectively. **Influence** is the process of affecting the thoughts, behavior, and feelings of another person. **Authority** is the right to influence another person.[2] It is important to understand the subtle differences among these terms. For instance, a manager may have authority but no power. She may have the right, by virtue of her position as boss, to tell someone what to do. But she may not have the skill or ability to influence other people.

In a relationship between the agent and the target, there are many influence attempts that the target considers legitimate. Working forty hours per week, greeting customers, solving problems, and collecting bills are actions that, when requested by the manager, are considered legitimate by a customer service representative. Requests such as these fall within the employee's **zone of indifference**—the range in which attempts to influence the employee are perceived as legitimate and are acted on without a great deal of thought.[3] The employee accepts that the manager has the authority to request such behaviors and complies with the requests. Some requests, however, fall outside the zone of indifference, so the manager must work to enlarge the employee's zone of indifference. Enlarging the zone is accomplished with power (an ability) rather than with authority (a right).

Suppose the manager asks the employee to purchase a birthday gift for the manager's wife or to overcharge a customer for a

power
The ability to influence another person.

influence
The process of affecting the thoughts, behavior, and feelings of another person.

authority
The right to influence another person.

zone of indifference
The range in which attempts to influence a person will be perceived as legitimate and will be acted on without a great deal of thought.

service call. The employee may think that the manager has no right to ask these things. These requests fall outside the zone of indifference. They're viewed as extraordinary, and the manager has to operate from outside the authority base to induce the employee to fulfill them. In some cases, no power base is enough to induce the employee to comply, especially if the employee considers the behaviors requested by the manager to be unethical.

LEARNING OUTCOME 2

Forms and Sources of Power in Organizations

Individuals have many forms of power to use in their work settings. Some of them are interpersonal—used in interactions with others. One of the earliest and most influential theories of power comes from John French and Bertram Raven, who tried to determine the sources of power managers use to influence other people.

Interpersonal Forms of Power

French and Raven identified five forms of interpersonal power that managers use. They are reward, coercive, legitimate, referent, and expert power.[4]

Reward power is power based on an agent's ability to control rewards that a target wants. For example, managers control the rewards of salary increases, bonuses, and promotions. Reward power can lead to better performance, but only as long as the employee sees a clear and strong link between performance and rewards. To use reward power effectively, then, the manager should be explicit about the behavior being rewarded and should make the connection clear between the behavior and the reward.

Coercive power is power that is based on an agent's ability to cause the target to have an unpleasant experience. To coerce someone into doing something means to force the person to do it, often with threats of

Politics Can BackFIRE

Failure to understand power and politics can be costly in terms of image. Public outrage erupted in late 2008 as financial institutions that had been aided by governmental grants and loans paid billions of dollars in bonuses to employees. That year, Goldman Sachs Group CEO Lloyd Blankfein was awarded a pay package totaling $42.9 million, part of which was subsidized by the company's receipt of $10 billion in loans from the U.S. government. In 2009, Blankfein expressed remorse for such bonuses, calling the outrage "understandable and appropriate." Politically charged behavior can achieve desired results, but it can also backfire if trust is breached.

SOURCE: D. Wagner, "Goldman CEO Says Pay Backlash Is 'Appropriate'," Associated Press (September 9, 2009), http://www.google.com/hostednews/ap/article/ALeqM5ivLNgQLm244XwzdWKuwqilXWgnawD9AK1lH00.

© Erlendur Berg/SuperStock

punishment. Managers using coercive power may verbally abuse employees or withhold support from them.

Legitimate power, which is similar to authority, is power that is based on position and mutual agreement. The agent and target agree that the agent has the right to influence the target. It doesn't matter that a manager thinks he has the right to influence his employees. For legitimate power to be effective, the employees must also believe the manager has the right to tell them what to do. In Native American societies, the chieftain has legitimate power; tribe members believe in his right to influence the decisions in their lives.

Referent power is an elusive power that is based on interpersonal attraction. The agent has referent power over the target because the target identifies with or wants to be like the agent. Charismatic individuals are often thought to have referent power. Interestingly, the agent need not be superior to the target in any way. People who use referent power well are most often individualistic and respected by the target.

Expert power is the power that exists when an agent has specialized knowledge or skills that the target needs. For expert power to work, three conditions must be in place. First, the target must trust that the expertise given is accurate. Second, the knowledge involved must be relevant and useful to the target. Third, the target's perception of the agent as an expert is crucial. Using easy-to-

reward power
Power based on an agent's ability to control rewards that a target wants.

coercive power
Power that is based on an agent's ability to cause an unpleasant experience for a target.

legitimate power
Power that is based on position and mutual agreement; agent and target agree that the agent has the right to influence the target.

referent power
An elusive power that is based on interpersonal attraction.

expert power
The power that exists when an agent has specialized knowledge or skills that the target needs.

> ## *Which type of interpersonal power is most effective? Some of the results are surprising.*

understand language signals the target that the expert has an appreciation for real-world concerns and increases the target's trust in the expert.[5]

Which type of interpersonal power is most effective? Research has focused on this question since French and Raven introduced their five forms of power. Some of the results are surprising. Reward power and coercive power have similar effects.[6] Both lead to compliance. That is, employees will do what the manager asks them to, at least temporarily, if the manager offers a reward or threatens them with punishment. Reliance on these sources of power is dangerous, however, because it may require the manager to be physically present and watchful in order to apply rewards or punishment when the behavior occurs. Constant surveillance creates an uncomfortable situation for managers and employees and eventually results in a dependency relationship. Employees will not work unless the manager is present.

Legitimate power also leads to compliance. When told "Do this because I'm your boss," most employees will comply. However, the use of legitimate power has not been linked to organizational effectiveness or to employee satisfaction.[7] In organizations where managers rely heavily on legitimate power, organizational goals are not necessarily met.

Referent power is linked with organizational effectiveness. It is the most dangerous power, however, because it can be too extensive and intensive in altering the behavior of others. Charismatic leaders need an accompanying sense of responsibility for others. Christopher Reeve's referent power made him a powerful spokesperson for research on spinal injuries and stem cell research.

Expert power has been called the power of the future.[8] Of the five forms of power, it has the strongest relationship with performance and satisfaction. It is through expert power that vital skills, abilities, and knowledge are passed on within the organization. Employees internalize what they observe and learn from managers they perceive to be experts.

The results on the effectiveness of these five forms of power pose a challenge in organizations. The least effective power bases—legitimate, reward, and coercive—are the ones most likely to be used by managers.[9] Managers inherit these power bases as part of the position when they take a supervisory job. In contrast, the most effective power bases—referent and expert—are ones that must be developed and strengthened through interpersonal rela-

tionships with employees. Marissa Mayer, vice president of search products and user experience at Google, is well respected and liked by her colleagues. She is described as someone with a lot of technical knowledge, and she is comfortable in social environments. This represents her expert power and referent power—she has an advanced degree in computer science from Stanford University and is known for her ability to connect with people. At 33 years old, she has had a very successful career at Google and is one of the most powerful female executives in the country.[10] Expert power and social networks help CEOs influence their top management teams in ways that are profitable for the firm.

Intergroup Sources of Power

Groups or teams within an organization can also use power from several sources. One source of intergroup power is control of *critical resources*.[11] When one group controls an important resource that another group desires, the first group holds power. Controlling resources needed by another group allows the power-holding group to influence the actions of the less powerful group. This process can continue in an upward spiral. Groups seen as powerful tend to be given more resources from top management.[12]

Groups also have power to the extent that they control **strategic contingencies**—activities that other groups depend on in order to complete their tasks.[13] The dean's office, for example, may control the number of faculty positions to be filled in each department of a college. The departmental hiring plans are thus contingent on approval from the dean's office. In this case, the dean's office controls the strategic contingency of faculty hiring, and thus has power.

Three factors can give a group control over a strategic contingency.[14] One is the *ability to cope with uncertainty*. If a group can help another group deal with uncertainty, it has power. One organizational group that has gained power in recent years is the legal department. Faced with increasing government regulations and fears of litigation, many other departments seek guidance from the legal department.

Another factor that can give a group control power is a *high degree of centrality* within the organization. If a group's functioning is important to the organization's success, it has high centrality. The sales force in a computer firm, for

> **strategic contingencies**
> Activities that other groups depend on in order to complete their tasks.

example, has power because of its immediate effect on the firm's operations and because other groups (accounting and servicing groups, for example) depend on its activities.

The third factor that can give a group power is *nonsubstitutability*—the extent to which a group performs a function that is indispensable to an organization. A team of computer specialists may be powerful because of its expertise with a system. It may have specialized experience that another team cannot provide.

The strategic contingencies model thus shows that groups hold power over other groups when they can reduce uncertainty, when their functioning is central to the organization's success, and when the group's activities are difficult to re-

information power

Access to and control over important information.

place.[15] The key to all three of these factors, as you can see, is dependency. When one group controls something that another group needs, it creates a dependent relationship—and gives one group power over the other.

Using Power Ethically

Managers can work at developing all five forms of power for future use. The key to using them well is to use them ethically, as Table 11.1 shows. Coercive power, for example, requires careful administration if it is to be used in an ethical manner. Employees should be informed of the rules in advance, and any punishment should be used consistently, uniformly, and privately. The key to using all five types of interpersonal power ethically is to be sensitive to employees' concerns and to communicate well.

To French and Raven's five power sources we can add a source that is very important in today's organizations. **Information power** is access to and control over important information. Consider, for example, the CEO's administrative assistant. He or she has information about the CEO's schedule that people need if they are going to get in to see the CEO. Central to the idea of information power is the person's position in the communication networks in the organization, both formal and informal. Also important is the idea of framing, which is the "spin" that managers put on information. Managers not only pass information on to subordinates, they interpret this information and influence the subordinates' perceptions of it. Information power occurs not only in the downward direction; it may also flow upward from subordinates to managers. In manufacturing plants, database operators often control information about plant metrics and shipping performance that is vital to managerial decision making. Information power can also flow laterally. Salespeople convey information from the outside environment (their customers) that is essential for marketing efforts.

Determining whether a power-related behavior is ethical is complex. Another way to look at the ethics surrounding the

TABLE 11.1 Guidelines for the Ethical Use of Power

FORM OF POWER	GUIDELINES FOR USE
Reward Power	Verify compliance. Make feasible, reasonable requests. Make only ethical requests. Offer rewards desired by subordinates. Offer only credible rewards.
Coercive power	Inform subordinates of rules and penalties. Warn before punishing. Administer punishment consistently and uniformly. Understand the situation before acting. Maintain credibility. Fit punishment to the infraction. Punish in private.
Legitimate power	Be cordial and polite. Be confident. Be clear and follow up to verify understanding. Make sure request is appropriate. Explain reasons for request. Follow proper channels. Exercise power consistently. Enforce compliance. Be sensitive to subordinates' concerns.
Referent power	Treat subordinates fairly. Defend subordinates' interests. Be sensitive to subordinates' needs and feelings. Select subordinates similar to oneself. Engage in role modeling.
Expert power	Maintain credibility. Act confident and decisive. Keep informed. Recognize employee concerns. Avoid threatening subordinates' self-esteem.

SOURCE: *Leadership in Organizations* by Gary A. Yukl. Copyright © 1981. Reprinted by permission of Pearson Education, Inc., Upper Saddle River, N.J.

>>
> Does the behavior produce a good outcome for people both inside and outside the organization?
> Does the behavior respect the rights of all parties?
> Does the behavior treat all parties equitably and fairly?

use of power is to ask three questions that show the criteria for examining power-related behaviors:[16]

1 *Does the behavior produce a good outcome for people both inside and outside the organization?* This question represents the criterion of *utilitarian outcomes.* The behavior should result in the greatest good for the greatest number of people. If the power-related behavior serves only the individual's self-interest and fails to help the organization reach its goals, it is considered unethical. A salesperson might be tempted to deeply discount a product in order to make a sale that would win a contest. Doing so would be in her self-interest but would not benefit the organization.

2 *Does the behavior respect the rights of all parties?* This question emphasizes the criterion of *individual rights.* Free speech, privacy, and due process are individual rights that are to be respected, and power-related behaviors that violate these rights are considered unethical.

3 *Does the behavior treat all parties equitably and fairly?* This question represents the criterion of *distributive justice.* Power-related behavior that treats one party arbitrarily or benefits one party at the expense of another is unethical. Granting a day of vacation to one employee in a busy week in which coworkers must struggle to cover for him might be considered unethical.

To be considered ethical, power-related behavior must meet all three criteria. If the behavior fails to meet the criteria, then alternative actions should be considered. Unfortunately, most power-related behaviors are not easy to analyze. Conflicts may exist among the criteria; for example, a behavior may maximize the greatest good for the greatest number of people but may not treat all parties equitably. Individual rights may need to be sacrificed for the good of the organization. A CEO may need to be removed from power for the organization to be saved. Still, these criteria can be used on a case-by-case basis to sort through the complex ethical issues surrounding the use of power. The ethical use of power is one of the hottest topics in the current business arena, due to the abuse of power by top executives, such as Bernie Madoff, who allegedly ran a $50 billion Ponzi scheme that financially ruined people and businesses around the world.

Positive versus Negative Power

We turn now to a theory of power that takes a strong stand on the "right" versus "wrong" kind of power to use in organizations. David McClelland has spent a great deal of his career studying the need for power and the ways managers use power. As was discussed in Chapter 5, he believes that there are two distinct faces of power, one negative and one positive.[17] The negative face of power is **personal power**—power used for personal gain. Managers who use personal power are commonly described as "power hungry." Former Illinois Governor Rod Blagojevich allegedly used his power as an elected official to try to sell President Obama's

personal power
Power used for personal gain.

[**Volkswagen: Perks and Prostitutes Scandal**]

German automotive company Volkswagen was rocked recently by a string of scandals involving both executives and labor union leaders. Former head of human resources Peter Hartz was found guilty of attempting to buy support from Klaus Volkert, head of the company's employee works council, for plans to cut costs and restructure the company. Volkert had demanded, and received, $2.5 million in bonuses and $786,000 for luxury vacations, clothes, jewelry, and bogus consulting fees. Other labor union leaders were bribed with shopping sprees for spouses, holiday visits with prostitutes, and cash bonuses. Although Volkswagen has removed some of the offenders from power, the close ties between labor and executives that gave rise to the scandal exist to this day.

SOURCE: M. Landler, "Sentence in Volkswagen Scandal," *New York Times,* February 23, 2008. Accessed online at http://www.nytimes.com/2008/02/23/business/worldbusiness/23volkswagen.htm; "Hit by an Earthquake: How Scandals Have Led to a Crisis in German Corporate Governance," Knoweldge @ Wharton. Accessed at http://knowledge.wharton.upenn.edu/printer_friendly.cfm?articleid=1695.

© iStockphoto.com

Senate seat in exchange for money, ambassadorships, and even a salary for his wife. People who approach relationships with an exchange orientation often use personal power to ensure that they get at least their fair share—and often more—in the relationship. They are most interested in their own needs and interests. One way to encourage ethical behavior in organizations is to encourage principled dissent. This refers to valid criticism that can benefit the organization rather than mere complaints about working conditions. Much like whistle-blowers who can serve as checks on powerful people within the organization, dissenters can pinpoint wrong-doings, encourage employee voice in key issues and create a climate conducive to ethical use of power.[18]

Individuals who rely on personal power at its extreme might be considered Machiavellian—willing to do whatever it takes to get one's own way. Niccolo Machiavelli was an Italian statesman during the sixteenth century who wrote *The Prince*, a guide for acquiring and using power.[19] Among his methods for using power was manipulating others, believing that it was better to be feared than loved. Machiavellians (or high Machs) are willing to manipulate others for personal gain, and are unconcerned with others' opinions or welfare.

The positive face of power is social power—power used to create motivation or to accomplish group goals. McClelland clearly favors the use of social power by managers. People who approach relationships with a communal orientation focus on the needs and interests of others. They rely on social power.[20] McClelland has found that managers who use power successfully have four power-oriented characteristics:

1. *Belief in the authority system.* They believe that the institution is important and that its authority system is valid. They are comfortable influencing and being influenced. The source of their power is the authority system of which they are a part.

2. *Preference for work and discipline.* They like their work and are very orderly. They have a basic value preference for the Protestant work ethic, believing that work is good for a person over and beyond its income-producing value.

3. *Altruism.* They publicly put the company and its needs before their own needs. They are able to do this because they see their own well-being as integrally tied to the corporate well-being.

4. *Belief in justice.* They believe justice is to be sought above all else. People should receive that to which they are entitled and that which they earn.

McClelland takes a definite stand on the proper use of power by managers. When power is used for the good of the group, rather than for individual gain, it is positive.

LEARNING OUTCOME 4

Symbols of Power

Organization charts show who has authority, but they do not reveal much about who has power. We'll now look at two very different ideas about the symbols of power. The first one comes from Rosabeth Moss Kanter. It is a scholarly approach to determining who has power and who feels powerless. The second is a semiserious look at the tangible symbols of power by Michael Korda.

Kanter's Symbols of Power

Kanter provides several characteristics of powerful people in organizations:[21]

1. *Ability to intercede for someone in trouble.* An individual who can pull someone out of a jam has power.

2. *Ability to get placements for favored employees.* Getting a key promotion for an employee is a sign of power.

3. *Exceeding budget limitations.* A manager who can go above budget limits without being reprimanded has power.

4. *Procuring above-average raises for employees.* One faculty member reported that her department head distributed 10 percent raises to the most productive

social power
Power used to create motivation or to accomplish group goals.

What can you do when you recognize that employees are feeling powerless?

The key to overcoming powerlessness is to share power and delegate decision-making authority to employees.

© Don Carstens/Brand X Pictures/Jupiterimages

faculty members although the budget allowed for only 4 percent increases. "I don't know how he did it; he must have pull," she said.

5. *Getting items on the agenda at meetings.* If a manager can raise issues for action at meetings, it's a sign of power.

6. *Access to early information.* Having information before anyone else does is a signal that a manager is plugged into key sources.

7. *Having top managers seek out their opinion.* When top managers have a problem, they may ask for advice from lower-level managers. The managers they turn to have power.

A theme that runs through Kanter's list is doing things for others—for people in trouble, for employees, for bosses. There is an active, other-directed element in her symbols of power.

You can use Kanter's symbols of power to identify powerful people in organizations. They can be particularly useful in finding a mentor who can effectively use power.

Kanter's Symbols of Powerlessness

Kanter also wrote about symptoms of powerlessness—a lack of power—in managers at different levels of the organization. First-line supervisors, for example, often display three symptoms of powerlessness: overly close supervision, inflexible adherence to the rules, and a tendency to do the job themselves rather than training their employees to do it. Staff professionals such as accountants and lawyers display different symptoms of powerlessness. When they feel powerless, they tend to resist change and try to protect their turf. Top executives can also feel powerless. They show symptoms such as focusing on budget cutting, punishing others, and using dictatorial, top-down communication. Acting in certain ways can lead employees to believe that a manager is powerless. By making external attributions (blaming others or circumstances) for negative events, a manager looks as if he or she has no power.[22]

Korda's Symbols of Power

Michael Korda takes a different look at symbols of power in organizations.[23] He discusses three unusual symbols: office furnishings, time power, and standing by.

Furniture is not just physically useful; it also conveys a message about power. Locked file cabinets are signs that the manager has important and confidential information in the office. A rectangular (rather than round) conference table enables the most important person to sit at the head of the table. The size of one's desk may convey the amount of power. Most executives prefer large, expensive desks.

Time power means using clocks and watches as power symbols. Korda says that the biggest compliment a busy executive can pay a visitor is to remove his watch and place it face down on the desk, thereby communicating "my time is yours." He also notes that the less powerful the executive, the more intricate the watch. Moreover, managers who are really secure in their power wear no watch at all, since they believe nothing important can happen without them. A full calendar is also proof of power. Personal planners are left open on the desk to display busy schedules.

Standing by is a game in which people are obliged to keep their cell phones, pagers, etc. with them at all times so executives can reach them. The idea is that the more you can impose your schedule on other people, the more power you have. In fact, Korda defines *power* as follows: There are more people who inconvenience themselves on your behalf than there are people on whose behalf you would inconvenience yourself. Closely tied to this is the ability to make others perform simple tasks for you, such as getting your coffee or fetching the mail.

While Kanter's symbols focus on the ability to help others, Korda's symbols focus on status—a person's relative standing in a group based on prestige and having other people defer to him or her.[24] By identifying powerful people and learning from their modeled behavior, you can learn the keys to power use in the organization.

Political Behavior in Organizations

Like power, the term *politics in organizations* may conjure up a few negative images. However, organizational politics is not necessarily negative; it is the use of power and influence in organizations. Because organizations are arenas in which people have competing interests, effective managers must reconcile competing interests. Organizational politics are central to managing. As people try to acquire power and expand their power base, they use various tactics and strategies. Some are sanctioned (acceptable to the organization); others are not. Political behavior refers to actions not officially sanctioned by an organization that are taken to influence others in order to meet one's personal goals.[25] Sometimes personal goals are aligned

powerlessness
A lack of power.

organizational politics
The use of power and influence in organizations.

political behavior
Actions not officially sanctioned by an organization that are taken to influence others in order to meet one's personal goals.

[Trying to influence your employees? Consider the relationship.]

Managers have several options in regard to influence, but success may depend on more than which particular tactic is chosen. Recent research indicates that the ways employees view their relationships with their leaders impact the efficacy of the influence tactic. When leaders use ingratiation and employees feel they have good relationships with their supervisors, employees are less likely to resist change. When employees judge their relationships with supervisors to be poor, they are more likely to resist change when ingratiation is used. This holds true when leaders employ punishment or tactics that attempt to establish credibility. These findings indicate that before leaders determine how they should influence their followers, they need to consider the relationship. When the relationship is perceived as low quality by the employee, ingratiation, punishment, and legitimating tactics may result in increased resistance.

SOURCE: S. A. Furst and D. M. Cable "Employee Resistance to Change: Managerial Influence Tactics and Leader-Member Exchange." *Journal of Applied Psychology*, 93 (2008): 453–462.

with team or organizational goals, and they can be achieved in support of others' interests. But other times personal goals and the interests of others collide, and individuals pursue politics at the expense of others' interests.[26]

Politics is a controversial topic among managers. Some managers take a favorable view of political behavior; others see it as detrimental to the organization. Some workers who perceive their workplace as highly political actually find the use of political tactics more satisfying and report greater job satisfaction when they engage in political behavior. Some people may therefore thrive in political environments, while others may find office politics distasteful and stressful.[27]

Most people are also amazingly good at recognizing political behavior at all levels of the firm. Employees are not only keenly aware of political behavior at their level but can also spot political behavior at both their supervisor's level and the topmost levels of the organization.[28]

Many organizational conditions encourage political activity. Among them are unclear goals, autocratic decision making, ambiguous lines of authority, scarce resources, and uncertainty.[29] Even supposedly objective activities may involve politics. One such activity is the performance appraisal process. A study of sixty executives who had extensive experience in employee evaluation indicated that political considerations were nearly always part of the performance appraisal process.[30]

The effects of political behavior in organizations can be quite negative when the political behavior is strategically undertaken to maximize self-interest. If people within the organization are competitively pursuing selfish ends, they're unlikely to be attentive to the concerns of others. The workplace can seem less helpful, more threatening, and more unpredictable. People focus on their own concerns rather than on organizational goals. This represents the negative face of power described earlier by David McClelland as personal power. If employees view the organization's political climate as extreme, they experience more anxiety, tension, fatigue, and burnout. They are also dissatisfied with their jobs and are more likely to leave.[31]

However, not all political behavior is destructive. Though positive political behavior still involves self-interest, when it is aligned with organizational goals, the self-interest is perceived positively by employees. Political behavior is also viewed positively when it is seen as the only means by which to accomplish something. Job satisfaction and one's satisfaction with coworkers and supervisors is affected by any kind of political behavior.[32]

Influence Tactics

Influence is the process of affecting the thoughts, behavior, or feelings of another person. That other person could be the boss (upward influence), an employee (downward influence), or a coworker (lateral influence). There are eight basic types of influence tactics. They are listed and described in Table 11.2.[33]

Research has shown that the four tactics used most frequently are consultation, rational persuasion, inspirational appeals, and ingratiation. Upward appeals and coalition tactics are used moderately. Exchange tactics are used least often.

Influence tactics are used for impression management, which was described in Chapter 3. In impression management, individuals use influence tactics to control others' impressions of them. One way in which people engage in impression management is through image building. Another way is to use impression management to get support for important initiatives or projects.

Ingratiation is an example of one tactic often used for impression management. Ingratiation can take many forms, including flattery, opinion conformity, and sub-

© iStockphoto.com

TABLE 11.2 Influence Tactics Used in Organizations

TACTICS	DESCRIPTION	EXAMPLES
Pressure	The person uses demands, threats, or intimidation to convince you to comply with a request or to support a proposal.	If you don't do this, you're fired. You have until 5:00 to change your mind, or I'm going without you.
Upward appeals	The person seeks to persuade you that the request is approved by higher management or appeals to higher management for assistance in gaining your compliance with the request.	I'm reporting you to my boss. My boss supports this idea.
Exchange	The person makes an explicit or implicit promise that you will receive rewards or tangible benefits if you comply with a request or support a proposal or reminds you of a prior favor to be reciprocated.	You owe me a favor. I'll take you to lunch if you'll support me on this.
Coalition	The person seeks the aid of others to persuade you to do something or uses the support of others as an argument for you to agree also.	All the other supervisors agree with me. I'll ask you in front of the whole committee.
Ingratiation	The person seeks to get you in a good mood or to think favorably of him or her before asking you to do something.	Only you can do this job right. I can always count on you, so I have another request.
Rational persuasion	The person uses logical arguments and factual evidence to persuade you that a proposal or request is viable and likely to result in the attainment of task objectives.	This new procedure will save us $150,000 in overhead. It makes sense to hire John; he has the most experience.
Inspirational appeals	The person makes an emotional request or proposal that arouses enthusiasm by appealing to your values and ideals or by increasing your confidence that you can do it.	Being environmentally conscious is the right thing. Getting that account will be tough, but I know you can do it.
Consultation	The person seeks your participation in making a decision or planning how to implement a proposed policy, strategy, or change.	This new attendance plan is controversial. How can we make it more acceptable? What do you think we can do to make our workers less fearful of the new robots on the production line?

SOURCE: First two columns from G. Yukl and C. M. Falbe, "Influence Tactics and Objectives in Upward, Downward, and Lateral Influence Attempts," *Journal of Applied Psychology* 75 (1990): 132–140. Copyright © 1990 by the American Psychological Association. Reprinted with permission.

servient behavior.[34] Exchange is another influence tactic that may be used for impression management. Offering to do favors for someone in an effort to create a favorable impression is an exchange tactic.

Which influence tactics are most effective? It depends on the target of the influence attempt and the objective. Individuals use different tactics for different purposes, and they use different tactics for different people. Influence attempts with subordinates, for example, usually involve assigning tasks or changing behavior. With peers, the objective is often to request help. With superiors, influence attempts are often made to request approval, resources, political support, or personal benefits. Rational persuasion and coalition tactics are used most often to get support from peers and superiors to change company policy. Consultation and inspirational appeals are particularly effective for gaining support and resources for a new project.[35] Overall, the most

effective tactic in terms of achieving objectives is rational persuasion. Pressure is the least effective tactic.

Influence tactics are often used on bosses in order to get the boss to evaluate the employee more favorably or to give the employee a promotion. Two tactics—rational persuasion and ingratiation—appear to work effectively in this way. Employees who use these tactics receive higher performance evaluations than other employees who don't use rational persuasion and ingratiation.[36] When supervisors believe an employee's motive for doing favors for the boss is simply to be a good citizen, they are likely to reward that employee. However, when the motive is seen as brownnosing (ingratiation), supervisors respond negatively.[37] And, as it becomes more obvious that the employee has something to gain by impressing the boss, the likelihood that ingratiation will succeed decreases. So, how does one use ingratiation effectively?

Results from a study conducted among supervisors and subordinates of a large state agency indicate that subordinates with higher scores on political skill used ingratiation regularly and received higher performance ratings, whereas individuals with lower scores on political skill who used ingratiation frequently received lower performance ratings.[38] Additionally, another research study demonstrated that supervisors rated subordinate ingratiation behavior as less manipulative if the subordinate was highly politically skilled.[39] These results indicate that political skill might be one factor that enables people to use ingratiation effectively.

Still, a well-disguised ingratiation is hard to resist. Attempts that are not obvious usually succeed in increasing the target's liking for the ingratiator.[40] Most people have trouble remaining neutral when someone flatters them or agrees with them. However, witnesses to the ingratiation are more likely to question the motive behind the flattery or agreement. Observers are more skeptical than the recipients of the ingratiation.

There is evidence that men and women view politics and influence attempts differently. Men tend to view political behavior more favorably than do women. When both men and women witness political behavior, they view it more positively if the agent is of their gender and the target is of the opposite gender.[41] Women executives often view politics with distaste and expect to be recognized and promoted only on the merit of their work. A lack of awareness of organizational politics is a barrier that holds women back in terms of moving into senior executive ranks.[42] Women may have fewer opportunities to develop political skills be-

cause of a lack of mentors and role models and because they are often excluded from informal networks.[43]

Different cultures prefer different influence tactics at work. One study found that American managers dealing with a tardy employee tended to rely on pressure tactics such as "If you don't start reporting on time for work, I will have no choice but to start docking your pay." In contrast, Japanese managers relied on influence tactics that either appealed to the employee's sense of duty ("It is your duty as a responsible employee of this company to begin work on time.") or emphasized a consultative approach ("Is there anything I can do to help you overcome the problems that are preventing you from coming to work on time?").[44]

Influence can also stem from the way a person's personality fits into his or her work environment. A recent study found that extraverts have more influence in team-oriented work environments, whereas conscientious employees have more influence in environments where individuals work alone on technical tasks.[45]

It is important to note that influence tactics do have some positive effects. When investors form coalitions and put pressure on firms to increase their research and development efforts, it works.[46] However, some influence tactics, including pressure, coalition building, and exchange, can have strong ethical implications. There is a fine line between being an impression manager and being seen as a manipulator.

How can a manager use influence tactics well? First, a manager can develop and maintain open lines of communication in all directions: horizontally, vertically and laterally. Then, the manager can treat the targets of influence attempts—whether managers, employees, or peers—with basic respect. Finally, the manager can understand that influence relationships are reciprocal—they are two-way relationships. As long as the influence attempts are directed toward organizational goals, the process of influence can be advantageous to all involved.

Political Skill

Researchers at Florida State University have generated an impressive body of research on political skill.[47] Political skill is a distinct interpersonal attribute that is important for managerial success. Researchers suggest that that political skill should be considered in hiring and promotion decisions. They found that leader's political skills have a positive effect on team performance, trust for the leader, and support for the leader.[48] Furthermore, political skill buffers the negative effects of stressors such as role conflict in work settings. This set of research findings points to the importance of developing political skill for managerial success.[49]

© InspirestocK/Jupiterimages

[*There is a fine line between being an impression manager and being seen as a manipulator.*]

So what exactly is **political skill**? It is the ability to get things done through positive interpersonal relationships outside the formal organization. Politically skilled individuals have the ability to accurately understand others and use this knowledge to influence others in order to meet personal or organizational goals. Political skill is made up of four key dimensions; social astuteness, interpersonal influence, networking ability, and sincerity. Social astuteness refers to accurate perception and evaluation of social situations. Socially astute individuals manage social situations in ways that present them in the most favorable light.

Interpersonal influence refers to a subtle and influential personal style that is effective in getting things done. Individuals with interpersonal influence are very flexible in adapting their behavior to differing targets of influence or differing contexts in order to achieve one's goals. Networking ability is an individual's capacity to develop and retain diverse and extensive social networks. People who have networking ability are effective in building successful alliances and coalitions, thus making them skilled at negotiation and conflict resolution. Sincerity refers to an individual's ability to portray forthrightness and authenticity in all of their dealings. Individuals who can appear sincere inspire more confidence and trust, thus making them very successful in influencing other people.[50]

These four dimensions of political skill can each be learned. Several organizations now offer training to help develop their employees' political skill. Political skill is important at all levels of the organization. The most potent cause of failure among top executives is lack of social effectiveness.[51] High self-monitors and politically savvy individuals score higher on an index of political skill, as do individuals who are emotionally intelligent.

Military settings are particularly demanding in their need for leaders who can adapt to changing situations and maintain a good reputation. In such an environment, politically skilled leaders are seen as more sincere in their motives, can more readily perceive and adapt to work events, and thus build a strong positive reputation among followers. In fact, political skill can be acquired through a social learning process and by having a strong mentor. Such a mentor then serves as a role model and helps the protégé navigate organizational politics and helps him/her learn the informal sources of power and politics in the organization.[52] Individuals who have political skill have been shown to be more likely to engage in OCBs, have more total promotions, have higher perceived career success, and greater life satisfaction.[53, 54]

> **"What about You?" on the Chapter 11 Review Card helps you assess your political skill.**

LEARNING OUTCOME 6

Managing Political Behavior in Organizations

Politics cannot and should not be eliminated from organizations. Managers can, however, take a proactive stance and manage the political behavior that inevitably occurs.[55]

The first step in managing political behavior is to recognize it. Some behaviors to watch for include networking, finding key players to support initiatives, making friends with powerful people, bending the rules, and self-promoting. Lesser-used tactics include misinformation, spreading rumors, and blackmailing.[56]

To diffuse these behaviors, open communication is an important tool. Uncertainty tends to increase political behavior, and communication that reduces uncertainty is important. One way to open communication is to clarify the sanctioned and nonsanctioned political behaviors in the organization. For example, managers may want to encourage social power as opposed to personal power.[57]

Another key is to clarify expectations regarding performance. This can be accomplished through the use of clear, quantifiable goals and through the establishment of a clear connection between goal accomplishment and rewards.[58]

Participative management is yet another key. Often, people engage in political behavior when they feel excluded from decision-making processes in the organization. By including them, managers will encourage positive input and eliminate behind-the-scenes maneuvering.

Encouraging cooperation among work groups is another strategy for managing political behavior. Managers can instill a unity of purpose among work teams by rewarding cooperative behavior and by implementing activities that emphasize the integration of team efforts toward common goals.[59]

Managing scarce resources well is also important. An obvious solution to the problem of scarce resources is to increase the resource pool, but few managers have this luxury. Clarifying the resource allocation process and making the connection between performance and resources explicit can help discourage dysfunctional political behavior.

Providing a supportive organizational climate is another way to manage political behavior effectively. A supportive climate allows employees to discuss controversial issues promptly

political skill
The ability to get things done through favorable interpersonal relationships outside of formally prescribed organizational mechanisms.

TABLE 11.3 Managing Your Relationship with Your Boss

Make Sure You Understand Your Boss and Her Context, Including:
Her goals and objectives.
The pressures on her.
Her strengths, weaknesses, and blind spots.
Her preferred work style.

Assess Yourself and Your Needs, Including:
Your own strengths and weaknesses.
Your personal style.
Your predisposition toward dependence on authority figures.

Develop and Maintain a Relationship that:
Fits both your needs and styles.
Is characterized by mutual expectations.
Keeps your boss informed.
Is based on dependability and honesty.
Selectively uses your boss's time and resources.

SOURCE: Reprinted by permission of *Harvard Business Review*. From "Managing Your Boss," by J. J. Gabarro and J. P. Kotter, (May–June 1993): p. 155. Copyright © 1993 by the Harvard Business School Publishing Corporation; all rights reserved.

and openly. This prevents the issue from festering and potentially causing friction among employees.[60]

Managing political behavior at work is important. The perception of dysfunctional political behavior can lead to dissatisfaction.[61] When employees perceive that there are dominant interest groups or cliques at work, they are less satisfied with pay and promotions. When they believe that the organization's reward practices are influenced by who you know rather than how well you perform, they are less satisfied.[62] In addition, when employees believe that their coworkers are exhibiting increased political behavior, they are less satisfied with their coworkers. Open communication, clear expectations about performance and rewards, participative decision-making practices, work group cooperation, effective management of scarce resources, and a supportive organizational climate can help managers prevent the negative consequences of political behavior.

Managing Up: Managing the Boss

One of the least discussed aspects of power and politics is the relationship between you and your boss. This is a crucial relationship, because your boss is your most important link with the rest of the organization.[63] The employee–boss relationship is one of mutual dependence; you depend on your boss to give you performance feedback, provide resources, and supply critical information. Your

boss depends on you for performance, information, and support. Because it's a mutual relationship, you should take an active role in managing it. Too often, the management of this relationship is left to the boss; but if the relationship doesn't meet the employee's needs, chances are the employee hasn't taken the responsibility to manage it proactively.

Table 11.3 shows the basic steps to take in managing your relationship with your boss. The first step is to try to understand as much as you can about your boss. What are the person's goals and objectives? What kind of pressures does the person face in the job? Many individuals naively expect the boss to be perfect and are disappointed when they find that this is not the case. What are the boss's strengths, weaknesses, and blind spots? Because this is an emotionally charged relationship, it is difficult to be objective; but this is a critical step in forging an effective working relationship. What is the boss's preferred work style? Does the person prefer everything in writing or hate detail? Does the boss prefer that you make appointments or is dropping in acceptable? The point is to gather as much information about your boss as you can and to try to put yourself in that person's shoes.

The second step in managing this important relationship is to assess yourself and your own needs much in the same way you analyzed your boss's. What are your strengths, weaknesses, and blind spots? What is your work style? How do you normally relate to authority figures? Some of us have tendencies toward counterdependence; that is, we rebel against the boss as an authority and view the boss as a hindrance to our performance. Or, in contrast, we might take an overdependent stance, passively accepting the employee–boss relationship and treating the boss as an all-wise, protective parent. What is your

Ways to Keep the Boss Informed

- Give the boss a weekly to-do list as a reminder of the progress toward goals.
- When you read something pertaining to your work, clip it out for the boss. Most busy executives appreciate being given materials they don't have time to find for themselves.
- Give the boss interim reports, and let the boss know if the work schedule is slipping.
- Don't wait until it's too late to take action.

© Laurence Mouton/PhotoAlto/Jupiterimages

tendency? Knowing how you react to authority figures can help you understand your interactions with your boss.

Once you have done a careful self-analysis and tried to understand your boss, the next step is to work to develop an effective relationship. Both parties' needs and styles must be accommodated. A fundraiser for a large volunteer organization related a story about a new boss, describing him as cold, aloof, unorganized, and inept. She made repeated attempts to meet with him and clarify expectations, and his usual reply was that he didn't have the time. Frustrated, she almost looked for a new job. "I just can't reach him!" was her refrain. Then she stepped back to consider her boss's and her own styles. Being an intuitive-feeling type of person, she prefers constant feedback and reinforcement from others. Her boss, an intuitive-thinker, works comfortably without feedback from others and has a tendency to fail to praise or reward others. She sat down with him and cautiously discussed the differences in their needs. This discussion became the basis for working out a comfortable relationship. "I still don't like him, but I understand him better," she said.

Another aspect of managing the relationship involves working out mutual expectations. One key activity is to develop a plan for work objectives and have the boss agree to it.[64] It is important to do things right, but it is also important to do the right things. Neither party to the relationship is a mind reader, so clarifying the goals is a crucial step. Keeping the boss informed is also a priority. No one likes to be caught off guard.

The employee–boss relationship must be based on dependability and honesty. This means giving and receiving positive and negative feedback. Most of us are reluctant to give any feedback to the boss, but positive feedback is welcomed at the top. Negative feedback, while tougher to initiate, can clear the air. If given in a problem-solving format, it can even bring about a closer relationship.[65]

Finally, remember that your boss is on the same team you are. The golden rule is to make your boss look good, because you expect the boss to do the same for you.

Sharing Power: Empowerment

As modern organizations grow flatter, eliminating layers of management, empowerment becomes more and more important. Jay Conger defines empowerment as "creating conditions for heightened motivation through the development of a strong sense of personal self-efficacy."[66] This means sharing power in such a way that individuals learn to believe in their ability to do the job. The driving idea of empowerment is that the individuals closest to the work and to the customers should make the decisions and that this makes the best use of employees' skills and talents. You can empower yourself by developing your sense of self-efficacy.

Four dimensions comprise the essence of empowerment: meaning, competence, self-determination, and impact.[67] *Meaning* is a fit between the work role and the employee's values and beliefs. It is the engine of empowerment through which employees become energized about their jobs. If employees' hearts are not in their work, they cannot feel empowered. *Competence* is the belief that one has the ability to do the job well. Without competence, employees will feel inadequate and lack a sense of empowerment. *Self-determination* is having control over the way one does his or her work. Employees who feel they're just following orders from the boss cannot feel empowered. *Impact* is the belief that one's job makes a difference within the organization. Without

[Kiva: Empowering Entrepreneurs]

With a click of the mouse, anyone can become a microfinance lender to an entrepreneur in Peru or another developing nation. In microfinance, an individual in a developed country makes a microloan to an individual or small business in a country where such resources can go a long way in growing and selling vegetables, making bricks, or raising goats. Kiva, a non-profit organization founded by Matt and Jessica Flannery in 2005, facilitates these transactions through a website that blends microfinance and social networking. On the site, various microfinance institutions post profiles of qualified entrepreneurs for lenders to browse. Each profile includes a picture of the entrepreneur, a description of the business, and a plan for effective use of the loan. The lender receives updates on how the entrepreneur is doing and when she expects to pay the loan back.

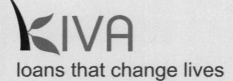

Lenders have the option to relend the money, donate it to Kiva's operations, or keep it. Kiva's loans are managed by microfinance institutions with plenty of experience—the default rate is less than 1%, and 98% of the loans are paid back in full. Kiva expects to loan $1 billion within 10 years. Bill Clinton and Oprah Winfrey are lenders, as are 495,000 other individuals. The number of entrepreneurs who have been empowered through Kiva exceeds 105,000. One could say that Kiva allows anyone to empower someone—a powerful idea.

SOURCE: www.kiva.org; "When Small Loans Make a Big Difference," Forbes.com, June 3, 2008. Accessed at http://www.forbes.com/2008/06/03/kiva-microfinance-uganda-ent-fin-cx_0603whartonkiva.html.

empowerment
Sharing power in such a way that individuals learn to believe in their ability to do the job.

a sense of contributing to a goal, employees cannot feel empowered.

Employees need to experience all four of the empowerment dimensions in order to feel truly empowered. Only then will organizations reap the hoped-for rewards from empowerment efforts: employees with increased organizational commitment, better job performance, and reduced job stress.[68]

Empowerment is easy to advocate but difficult to put into practice. Conger offers some guidelines on how leaders can empower others.

First, managers should express confidence in employees and set high performance expectations. Positive expectations can go a long way toward enabling good performance, as the Pygmalion effect shows (Chapter 3).

Second, managers should create opportunities for employees to participate in decision making. This means participation in the forms of both voice and choice. Employees should not just be asked to contribute their opinions about any issue; they should also have a vote in the decision that is made. One method for increasing participation is using self-managed teams, which, as discussed in Chapter 9, are the ultimate in empowered teams because they take on decisions and activities that traditionally belong to managers.

Third, managers should remove bureaucratic constraints that stifle autonomy. Often, companies have antiquated rules and policies that prevent employees from managing themselves. An example is a collection agency, where a manager's signature was once required to approve long-term payment arrangements for delinquent customers. Collectors, who spoke directly with customers, were the best judges of whether the payment arrangements were workable, and having to consult a manager made them feel closely supervised and powerless. The rule was dropped, and collections increased.

Fourth, managers should set inspirational or meaningful goals. When individuals feel they "own" a goal, they are more willing to take personal responsibility for it.

Empowerment is a matter of degree. Jobs can be thought of in two dimensions: job content and job context. Job content consists of the tasks and procedures necessary for doing a particular job. Job context is broader. It is the reason the organization needs the job and includes the way the job fits into the organization's mission, goals, and objectives. These two dimensions are depicted in Figure 11.1, the employee empowerment grid.

Both axes of the grid contain the major steps in the decision-making process. As shown on the horizontal axis, decision-making authority over job content increases in

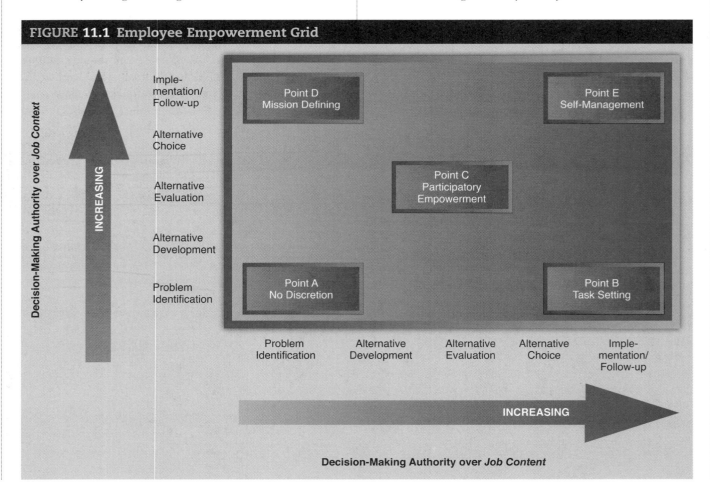

FIGURE 11.1 Employee Empowerment Grid

terms of greater involvement in the decision-making process. Similarly, the vertical axis shows that authority over job context increases with greater involvement in that decision-making process. Combining job content and job context authority in this way produces five points that vary in terms of the degree of empowerment.[69]

No Discretion (point A) represents the traditional, assembly-line job—highly routine and repetitive with no decision-making power. Recall from Chapter 7 that if these jobs have a demanding pace and if workers have no discretion, distress will result.

Task Setting (point B) is the essence of most empowerment programs in organizations today. In this case, the worker is empowered to make decisions about the best way to get the job done but has no decision responsibility for the job context.

Participatory Empowerment (point C) represents a situation that is typical of autonomous work groups that have some decision-making power over both job content and job context. Their involvement is in identifying problems, developing alternatives, and evaluating alternatives, but the actual choice of alternatives is often beyond their power. Participatory empowerment can lead to job satisfaction and productivity.

Mission Defining (point D) is an unusual case of empowerment and is seldom seen. Here, employees have power over job context but not job content. An example would be a unionized team that is asked to decide whether their jobs could be better done by an outside vendor. Deciding to outsource would dramatically affect the mission of the company, but would not affect job content, which is specified in the union contract. Assuring these employees of continued employment regardless of their decision would be necessary for this case of empowerment.

Self-Management (point E) represents total decision-making control over both job content and job context. It is the ultimate expression of trust. One example is TXI Chaparral Steel (part of Texas Industries), where employees redesign their own jobs to add value to the organization.

Empowerment should begin with job content and proceed to job context. Because the workforce is so diverse, managers should recognize that some employees are more ready for empowerment than others. Managers must diagnose situations and determine the degree of empowerment to extend to employees. Recently, the management of change in organizations was identified as another area wherein empowerment can have a strong effect. Empowered employees are more likely to participate in and facilitate change processes in organizations as they feel more committed to the organizations' success.[70]

The empowerment process also carries with it a risk of failure. When you delegate responsibility and authority, you must be prepared to allow employees to fail; and failure is not something most managers tolerate well. At Merck, some say CEO Ray Gilmartin empowered scientists too much and that their failures cost Merck its profitability and reputation as one of *Fortune*'s Most Admired Companies. One example of this empowerment involved a diabetes drug that early research showed caused tumors in mice. Scientists argued that in spite of early studies showing the drug wasn't viable, research should continue, and it did . . . until the drug was finally axed, costing the company considerably in terms of time and money.[71]

BY THE NUMBERS

5 types of interpersonal power

$10 billion Goldman Sachs' loan from the U.S. government

1515 year *The Prince* was published

105,000 number of entrepreneurs empowered by Kiva

8 influence tactice used in organizations

$786,000 Klaus Volkert's allowance for luxury vacations, clothes, jewelry, and bogus consulting fees

©Courtesy of Chapel House Photography

13 >>

Conflict and Negotiation

LEARNING OUTCOMES

After reading this chapter, you should be able to do the following:

1 Describe the nature of conflicts in organizations.

2 Explain the role structural and personal factors play in causing conflict in organizations.

3 Discuss the nature of group conflict in organizations.

4 Describe the factors that influence conflict between individuals in organizations.

The Nature of Conflicts in Organizations

All of us have experienced conflict of various types, yet we probably fail to recognize the variety of conflicts that occur in organizations. *Conflict* is defined as any situation in which incompatible goals, attitudes, emotions, or behaviors lead to disagreement or opposition between two or more parties.[1]

Today's organizations may face greater potential for conflict than ever before in history. The marketplace, with its increasing competition and globalization, magnifies differences among people in terms of personality, values, attitudes, perceptions, languages, cultures, and national backgrounds.[2] With the increasing diversity of the workforce comes the potential for incompatibility and conflict.

Importance of Conflict Management Skills for the Manager

Estimates show that managers spend about 21 percent of their time, or one day every week, dealing with conflict.[3] As such, conflict management skills are a major predictor of managerial success.[4] A critical indicator of a manager's ability to manage conflict is his or her emotional intelligence (EI), which is the power to control one's emotions and perceive emotions in others, adapt to change, and manage adversity. (Conflict management skills may be more a reflection of EI than of IQ.) People who lack emotional intelligence, especially empathy or the ability to see life from another person's perspective, are more likely to be causes of conflict than managers of conflict.[5]

Functional versus Dysfunctional Conflict

Not all conflict is bad. In fact, some types of conflict encourage new solutions to problems and enhance creativity in the organization. In these cases, managers will want to encourage the conflicts. Thus, the key to conflict management is to stimulate functional conflict and prevent or resolve dysfunctional conflict. The difficulty, however, is distinguishing between dysfunctional and functional conflicts. The consequences of conflict can be positive or negative, as shown in Table 13.1.

5 Describe effective and ineffective techniques for managing conflict.

6 Identify five styles of conflict management.

©Russell Stewart/iStockphoto.com

TABLE 13.1 Consequences of Conflict

POSITIVE CONSEQUENCES	NEGATIVE CONSEQUENCES
• Leads to new ideas • Stimulates creativity • Motivates change • Promotes organizational vitality • Helps individuals and groups establish identities • Serves as a safety valve to indicate problems	• Diverts energy from work • Threatens psychological well-being • Wastes resources • Creates a negative climate • Breaks down group cohesion • Can increase hostility and aggressive behaviors

Functional conflict is a healthy, constructive disagreement between two or more people. Functional conflict can produce new ideas, learning, and growth among individuals. When individuals engage in constructive conflict, they develop a better awareness of themselves and others. In addition, functional conflict can improve working relationships; when two parties work through their disagreements, they feel they have accomplished something together. By releasing tensions and solving problems in working together, morale is improved.[6] Functional conflict can lead to innovation and positive change for the organization.[7] Because it tends to encourage creativity among individuals, this positive form of conflict can translate into increased productivity.[8] A key to recognizing functional conflict is that it is often cognitive in origin; that is, it arises from someone challenging old policies or thinking of new ways to approach problems. One occasion when managers should work to stimulate conflict is when they suspect their group is suffering from groupthink.[9]

Dysfunctional conflict is an unhealthy, destructive disagreement between two or more people. Its danger is that it takes the focus away from the work to be done and places it on the conflict itself and the parties involved. Excessive conflict drains energy that could be used more productively. A key to recognizing a dysfunctional conflict is that its origin is often emotional or behavioral. Disagreements that involve personalized anger and resentment directed at specific individuals rather than specific ideas are dysfunctional.[10] Individuals involved in dysfunctional conflict tend to act before thinking, and they often rely on threats, deception, and verbal abuse to communicate. Dysfunctional conflict can often lead to aggressive acts or retaliation, which can be directed at supervisors, peers, subordinates, or even service providers.[11] In dysfunctional conflict, losses to both parties may exceed any potential gain from the conflict.

Diagnosing Conflict

Diagnosing conflict as good or bad is not easy. The manager must look at the issue, the context of the conflict, and the parties involved. Once the manager has diagnosed the type of conflict, he or she can either work to resolve it (if it is dysfunctional) or to stimulate it (if it is functional).

It is easy to make mistakes in diagnosing conflicts. Sometimes task conflict, which is functional, can be misattributed as being personal, and dysfunctional conflict can follow. Developing trust within the work group can keep this misattribution from occurring.[12] A study of group effectiveness found that decision-making groups made up of friends were able to engage more openly in disagreement than groups made up of strangers, allowing the friends' groups to make more effective decisions. When group members (friends) felt comfortable and trusting enough to express conflicting opinions, optimal performance resulted. But decision-making groups made up of friends and strangers exhibited both high levels of conflict *and* low levels of performance, suggesting that open disagreement in these groups was not helpful. This finding should serve as a cautionary tale for managers trying to apply one country's management style and techniques in another cultural setting.[13]

functional conflict

A healthy, constructive disagreement between two or more people.

dysfunctional conflict

An unhealthy, destructive disagreement between two or more people.

 The following questions can be used to diagnose the nature of the conflict a manager faces:

> Are the parties approaching the conflict from a hostile standpoint?
> Is the outcome likely to be a negative one for the organization?
> Do the potential losses of the parties exceed any potential gains?
> Is energy being diverted from goal accomplishment?

If the majority of the answers to these questions is yes, then the conflict is probably dysfunctional.

FIGURE 13.1 Causes of Conflict in Organizations

Structural Factors
- Specialization
- Interdependence
- Common resources
- Goal differences
- Authority relationships
- Status inconsistencies
- Jurisdictional ambiguities

Conflict

Personal Factors
- Skills and abilities
- Personalities
- Perceptions
- Values and ethics
- Emotions
- Communication barriers
- Cultural differences

©Polka Dot Images/Jupiterimages

Causes of Conflict in Organizations

Conflict is pervasive in organizations. To manage it effectively, managers should understand the many sources of conflict. They can be classified into two broad categories: structural factors, which stem from the nature of the organization and the way in which work is organized, and personal factors, which arise from differences among individuals. Figure 13.1 summarizes the causes of conflict within each category.

Structural Factors

The causes of conflict related to the organization's structure include specialization, interdependence, common resources, goal differences, authority relationships, status inconsistencies, and jurisdictional ambiguities.

Specialization When jobs are highly specialized, employees become experts at certain tasks. For example, one software company has one specialist for databases, one for statistical packages, and another for expert systems. Highly specialized jobs can lead to conflict, because people have little awareness of the tasks that others perform.

A classic conflict of specialization may occur between salespeople and engineers. Engineers are technical specialists responsible for product design and quality. Salespeople are marketing experts and liaisons with customers. Salespeople are often accused of making delivery promises to customers that engineers cannot keep because the sales force lacks the technical knowledge necessary to develop realistic delivery deadlines.

Interdependence Work that is interdependent requires groups or individuals to depend on one another to accomplish goals.[14]

Depending on other people to get work done is fine when the process works smoothly. When there is a problem, however, it becomes very easy to blame the other party, and conflict escalates. In a garment manufacturing plant, for example, when the fabric cutters get behind in their work, the workers who sew the garments are delayed as well. Considerable frustration may result when the workers at the sewing machines feel their efforts are being blocked by the cutters' slow pace and their pay is affected because they are paid piece-rate.

Common Resources Any time multiple parties must share resources, there is potential for conflict.[15] This potential is enhanced when the shared resources become scarce. For example, managers often share secretarial support. Not uncommonly, one secretary supports ten or more managers, each of whom believes his or her work is most important. This puts pressure on the secretary and leads to potential conflicts in prioritizing and scheduling work.

©Image Source Pink/Jupiterimages

> *Individuals do not leave their personalities at the doorstep when they enter the workplace.*

4 Goal Differences When work groups have different goals, these goals may be incompatible. For example, in one cable television company, the salesperson's goal was to sell as many new installations as possible. This created problems for the service department, because its goal was timely installations. With increasing sales, the service department's workload became backed up, and orders were delayed. Often these types of conflicts occur because individuals do not have knowledge of another department's objectives.

5 Authority Relationships A traditional boss–employee relationship is hierarchical in nature, with a boss who is superior to the employee. For many employees, such a relationship is not a comfortable one, because another individual has the right to tell them what to do. Some people resent authority more than others, and obviously this creates conflicts. In addition, some bosses are more autocratic than others; this compounds the potential for conflict in the relationship. As organizations move toward the team approach and empowerment, there should be less potential for conflict from authority relationships.

6 Status Inconsistencies Some organizations have a strong status difference between management and nonmanagement workers. Managers may enjoy privileges—such as flexible schedules, reserved parking spaces, and longer lunch hours—that are not available to nonmanagement employees. This may result in resentment and conflict.

7 Jurisdictional Ambiguities Have you ever telephoned a company with a problem and had your call transferred through several different people and departments? This situation illustrates jurisdictional ambiguity—that is, unclear lines of responsibility within an organization.[16] The classic situation here involves the hardware/software dilemma. You call the company that made your computer, and they inform you that the problem is caused by the software. You call the software division, and they tell you it's the hardware . . . .

II Personal Factors

jurisdictional ambiguity

The presence of unclear lines of responsibility within an organization.

Not all conflicts arise out of structural factors in the organization. Some conflicts arise out of differences among individuals.

The causes of conflict that arise from individual differences include skills and abilities, personalities, perceptions, values and ethics, emotions, communication barriers, and cultural differences.

1 Skills and Abilities Diversity in skills and abilities may be positive for the organization, but it also holds potential for conflict, especially when jobs are interdependent. Experienced, competent workers may find it difficult to work alongside new and unskilled recruits. Workers can become resentful when their new boss, fresh from college, knows a lot about managing people but is unfamiliar with the technology with which they are working.

2 Personalities Individuals do not leave their personalities at the doorstep when they enter the workplace. Personality conflicts are realities in organizations. It is as naïve to expect that you will like all of your coworkers, as it is to expect that they all like you.

One personality trait that many people find difficult to deal with is abrasiveness.[17] An abrasive person ignores the interpersonal aspects of work and the feelings of colleagues. Abrasive individuals are often achievement oriented and hardworking, but their perfectionist, critical style often leaves others feeling unimportant. The working style of abrasive individuals causes stress and strain for those around them.[18]

3 Perceptions Differences in perception can also lead to conflict. For example, managers and workers may not have a shared perception of what motivates people. In this case, the reward system can create conflicts if managers provide what they think employees want rather than what employees really want.

4 Values and Ethics Differences in values and ethics can be sources of disagreement. Older workers, for example, value company loyalty and probably would not take a sick day when they were not really ill. Younger workers, valuing mobility, like the concept of "mental health days," or calling in sick to get away from work. This may not be true for all workers, but it illustrates that differences in values can lead to conflict.

Most people have their own sets of values and ethics. The extent to which they apply these ethics in the workplace varies. Some people have strong desires for approval from others and will work to meet others' ethical standards. Some people are relatively unconcerned about approval from others and strongly apply their own ethical standards. Still others operate seemingly without regard to ethics or values.[19] When conflicts about values or ethics do arise, heated disagreement is common because of the personal nature of the differences.

Emotions Conflict by its nature is an emotional interaction, and the emotions of the parties involved in conflict play a pivotal role in how they perceive the negotiation and respond to one another.[20] In fact, emotions are now considered critical elements of any negotiation and must be included in any examination of the process and how it unfolds.[21]

One important research finding has been that emotion can play a problematic role in negotiations. In particular, when negotiators begin to act based on emotions rather than on cognitions, they become much more likely to reach an impasse.[22]

Communication Barriers Communication barriers such as physical separation and language can create distortions in messages, and these can lead to conflict. Another communication barrier is value judgment, in which a listener assigns a worth to a message before it is received. For example, suppose a team member is a chronic complainer. When this individual enters the manager's office, the manager is likely to devalue the message before it is even delivered. Conflict can then emerge.

Cultural Differences Although cultural differences are assets in organizations, sometimes they can be sources of conflict. Often, these conflicts stem from a lack of understanding of another culture. In one MBA class, for example, Indian students were horrified when American students challenged the professor. Meanwhile, the American students thought the students from India were too passive. Subsequent discussions revealed that professors in India expected to be treated deferentially and with great respect. While students might challenge an idea vigorously, they would rarely challenge the professor. Diversity training that emphasizes education on cultural differences can make great strides in preventing misunderstandings.

©Rim Light/PhotoLink/Photodisc/Getty Images

Forms of Group Conflict in Organizations

Conflict in an organization can take on any of several different forms that can mainly be sorted into two core groups: conflicts that occur at the group level and conflicts that occur at the individual level. Conflicts at each level can be further classified as either *inter* or *intra*. It is important to note that the prefix *inter* means "between," whereas the prefix *intra* means "within." Conflict at the group level can occur between organizations (interorganizational), between groups (intergroup), or within a group (intragroup).

Interorganizational Conflict

Conflict that occurs between two or more organizations is called interorganizational conflict. Competition can heighten interorganizational conflict. Corporate takeovers, mergers, and acquisitions can also produce interorganizational conflict. What about the interorganizational conflict between Major League Baseball's players' union and ownership, which is sometimes characterized as a battle between millionaires and multimillionaires (not sure which is which)? The players regularly go on strike to extract more of the profits from the owners, while the owners cry that they are not making a dime.

Intergroup Conflict

When conflict occurs between groups or teams, it is known as intergroup conflict. Conflict between groups can have positive effects within each group, such as increased group cohesiveness, increased focus on tasks, and increased loyalty to the group. There are, however, negative consequences as well. Groups in conflict tend to develop an "us against them" mentality whereby each sees the other team as the enemy, becomes more hostile, and decreases its communication with the other group. Groups are

interorganizational conflict
Conflict that occurs between two or more organizations.

intergroup conflict
Conflict that occurs between groups or teams in an organization.

even more competitive and less cooperative than individuals. The inevitable outcome is that one group gains and the other group loses.[23]

Competition between groups must be managed carefully so that it does not escalate into dysfunctional conflict. Research has shown that when groups compete for a goal that only one group can achieve, negative consequences like territoriality, aggression, and prejudice toward the other group can result.[24] Managers should encourage and reward cooperative behaviors across groups. Some effective ways of doing this include modifying performance appraisals to include assessing intergroup behavior and using an external supervisor's evaluation of intergroup behavior. Group members will be more likely to help other groups when they know that the other group's supervisor will be evaluating their behavior and that they will be rewarded for cooperation.[25] In addition, managers should encourage social interactions across groups so that trust can be developed. Trust allows individuals to exchange ideas and resources with members of other groups and results in innovation when members of different groups cooperate.[26]

Intragroup Conflict

Conflict that occurs within groups or teams is called **intragroup conflict**. Some conflict within a group is functional. It can help the group avoid groupthink, as we discussed in Chapter 10.

Even the newest teams, virtual teams, are not immune to conflict. The nuances and subtleties of face-to-face communication are often lacking in these teams, and misunderstandings can result. To avoid dysfunctional conflicts, virtual teams should make sure their tasks fit their methods of interacting. Complex strategic decisions may require face-to-face meetings rather than e-mails or threaded discussions. Face-to-face and telephone interactions early on can eliminate later conflicts and allow virtual teams to move on to use electronic communication because trust has been developed.[27]

LEARNING OUTCOME 4

Individual Conflict in Organizations

As with groups, conflict can occur between individuals or within a single individual.

GENERATION CLASH

>> An emerging challenge in conflict management is the intergenerational conflict brought about by the diversity in age in the U.S. workforce. Some sources of intergenerational conflict are

> employee benefit packages being designed to appeal more to one age group than another, or

> older employees fearing that younger new hires may take over their jobs.

Organizations should design flexible employee benefit systems that have a broader appeal to a diverse age group and encourage social interaction to reduce these perceived threats and create trust.[28]

Types of Intrapersonal Conflict

When conflict occurs within an individual, it is called **intrapersonal conflict**. There are several types of intrapersonal conflict, including interrole, intrarole, and person–role conflicts. A role is a set of expectations placed on an individual by others.[29] The person occupying the focal role is the role incumbent, and the individuals who place expectations on the person are role senders. Figure 13.2 depicts a set of role relationships.

Interrole conflict occurs when a person experiences conflict among the multiple roles in his or her life. One interrole conflict that many employees experience is work/home conflict, in which their role as worker clashes with their role as spouse or parent.[30] Work/home conflict can arise from time constraints, strain, and having responsibilities for people in the workplace and at home.[31] Work/home conflict has become even more common with the rise of work-at-home professionals and telecommuting, as the home becomes the office and the boundary between work and family life is blurred.[32] Recently, organizations are leveraging their use of information technology to gain a competitive edge. This has translated into ambitious and highly involved employees using office communications (e.g., voice mail, e-mail, and so on) even after hours. Such after-hours communication usage is associated with increased work-life conflict as reported by the employee and a significant other.[33]

Intrarole conflict is conflict within a single role. It often arises when a person receives conflicting messages from role senders about how to perform a certain role. Suppose a manager receives counsel from her department head that she needs to socialize less with the nonmanagement employees. She is also told by her project manager

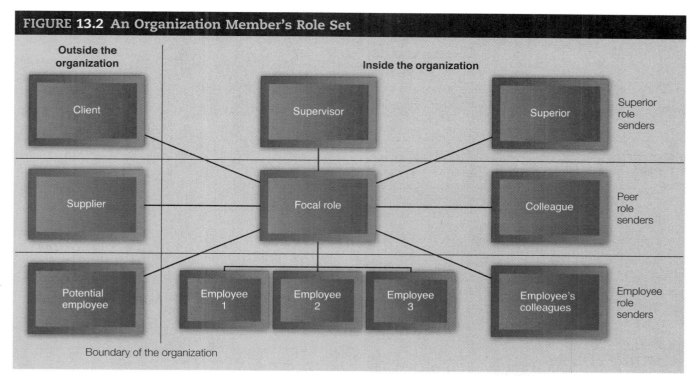

FIGURE 13.2 An Organization Member's Role Set

Outside the organization

Inside the organization

Client

Supervisor

Superior — Superior role senders

Supplier

Focal role

Colleague — Peer role senders

Potential employee

Employee 1

Employee 2

Employee 3

Employee's colleagues — Employee role senders

Boundary of the organization

that she needs to be a better team member, and that she can accomplish this by socializing more with the other nonmanagement team members. This situation is one of intrarole conflict.

Person–role conflict occurs when an individual in a particular role is expected to perform behaviors that clash with her personal values.[34] Salespeople, for example, may be required to offer the most expensive item in the sales line first to the customer, even when it is apparent that the customer does not want or cannot afford it. A computer salesman may be required to offer a large, elaborate system to a student he knows is on a tight budget. This may conflict with the salesman's values, and he may experience person–role conflict.

Intrapersonal conflicts can have positive consequences. Often, professional responsibilities clash with deeply held values. A budget shortfall may force you to lay off a loyal, hardworking employee. Your daughter may have a piano recital on the same day your largest client is scheduled to be in town visiting the office. In such conflicts, we often have to choose between right and right; that is, there's no correct response. These may be thought of as *defining moments* that challenge individuals to choose between two or more things in which they believe.[35] Character is formed in defining moments because they cause individuals to shape their identities. They help people crystallize their values and serve as opportunities for personal growth.

Managing Intrapersonal Conflict

Intrapersonal conflict can be managed with careful self-analysis and diagnosis of the situation. Three actions in particular can help prevent or resolve intrapersonal conflicts.

First, when seeking a new job, you should find out as much as possible about the values of the organization.[36] Many person–role conflicts center around differences between the organization's values and the individual's values. Research has shown that when there is a good fit between the values of the individual and the organization, the individual is more satisfied and committed and is less likely to leave the organization.[37]

person–role conflict

Conflict that occurs when an individual in a particular role is expected to perform behaviors that clash with his or her personal values.

©Stock4B-RF/Getty Images

Second, to manage intrarole or interrole conflicts, role analysis is a good tool.[38] In role analysis, the individual asks the various role senders what they expect of him or her. The outcomes are clearer work roles and the reduction of conflict and ambiguity.[39] Role analysis is a simple tool that clarifies the expectations of both parties in a relationship and reduces the potential for conflict within a role or between roles.

Third, political skills can help buffer the negative effects of stress that stem from role conflicts. Effective politicians can negotiate role expectations when conflicts occur. All these forms of conflict can be managed. An understanding of the many forms is a first step.

Managing Interpersonal Conflict

Conflict that occurs between two or more individuals, or **interpersonal conflict**, can arise from many individual differences, including personalities, attitudes, values, perceptions. To manage interpersonal conflict, it is helpful to understand power networks in organizations, and defense mechanisms exhibited by individuals when they are in conflict situations.

Power Networks According to Mastenbroek, individuals in organizations are organized in three basic types of power networks.[40] Based on these power relationships, certain kinds of conflict tend to emerge. Figure 13.3 illustrates three basic kinds of power relationships in organizations.

The first relationship is equal versus equal, in which there is a horizontal balance of power among the parties. An example of this type of relation-

FIGURE 13.3 Power Relationships in Organizations

Types of power relationships	Behavioral tendencies and problems	Interventions
1) Equal vs. equal	Suboptimization • Tendency to compete with one another • Covert fighting for positions • Constant friction in border areas	• Defining demarcation lines • Improving coordination procedures • Integrating units • Teaching negotiating skills • Clarifying common interest • Activating central authority
2) High vs. low	Control versus autonomy • Resistance to change • Motivation problems	• Bureaucratizing power through rules • Using a different style of leadership • Structural and cultural interventions
3) High vs. middle vs. low	Role conflict, role ambiguity, stress • Concessions, double-talk, and use of sanctions and rewards to strengthen the position	• Improving communication • Clarifying tasks • Horizontalization, vertical task expansion • Teaching power strategies

SOURCE: W. F. G. Mastenbroek, *Conflict Management and Organization Development*, 1987. Copyright John Wiley & Sons Limited. Reproduced with permission.

ship would be a conflict between individuals from two different project teams. The behavioral tendency is toward suboptimization; that is, the focus is on a win–lose approach to problems, and each party tries to maximize its power at the expense of the other party. Conflict within this type of network can lead to depression, low self-esteem, and other distress symptoms. Interventions such as improving coordination between the parties and working toward common interests can help manage these conflicts.

The second power network is high versus low, or a powerful versus a less powerful relationship. Conflicts that emerge here take the basic form of the powerful individuals trying to control others, with the less powerful people trying to become more autonomous. Conflict in this network can lead to job dissatisfaction, low organizational commitment, and turnover.[41] Organizations typically respond to these conflicts by tightening the rules. However, the more successful ways of managing these

[Quick Tips for Managing Intrapersonal Conflict]

1. Apply for jobs at companies that have values that match your own.
2. Use role analysis.
3. Develop political skills.

interpersonal conflict

Conflict that occurs between two or more individuals.

> ## Most people do not react well to negative feedback.

conflicts are to try a different style of leadership, such as a coaching and counseling style, or to change the structure to a more decentralized one.

The third power network is high versus middle versus low. This power network illustrates the classic conflicts felt by middle managers. Two particular conflicts are evident for middle managers: role conflict, in which conflicting expectations are placed on the manager from bosses and employees, and role ambiguity, in which the expectations of the boss are unclear. Improved communication among all parties can reduce role conflict and ambiguity. In addition, middle managers can benefit from training in positive ways to influence others.

Knowing the typical kinds of conflicts that arise in various kinds of relationships can help a manager diagnose conflicts and devise appropriate ways to manage them.

Defense Mechanisms When individuals are involved in conflict with another human being, frustration often results.[42] Conflicts can often arise within the context of a performance appraisal session. Most people do not react well to negative feedback, as was illustrated in a classic study.[43] In this study, when employees were given criticism about their work, more than 50 percent of their responses were defensive.

When individuals are frustrated, as they often are in interpersonal conflict, they respond by exhibiting defense mechanisms.[44] Defense mechanisms are common reactions to the frustration that accompanies conflict.

Aggressive mechanisms, such as fixation, displacement, and negativism, are aimed at attacking the source of the conflict. In fixation, an individual fixates on the conflict, or keeps up a dysfunctional behavior that obviously will not solve the conflict. An example of fixation occurred in a university, where a faculty member became embroiled in a battle with the dean because the faculty member felt he had not received a large enough salary increase. He persisted in writing angry letters to the dean, whose hands were tied because of a low budget allocation to the college. **Displacement** means directing anger toward someone who is not the source of the conflict. For example, a manager may respond harshly to an employee after a telephone confrontation with an angry customer. Another aggressive defense mechanism is **negativism**, an aggressive mechanism in which a person responds with pessimism to any attempt at solving a problem. Negativism is illustrated by a manager who, when appointed to a committee on which she did not want to serve, made negative comments throughout the meeting.

Compromise mechanisms, such as compensation, identification, and rationalization, are used by individuals to make the best of a conflict situation. **Compensation** is a compromise mechanism in which an individual attempts to make up for a negative situation by devoting himself or herself to another pursuit with increased vigor. Compensation can be seen when a person makes up for a bad relationship at home by spending more time at the office. **Identification** is a compromise mechanism whereby an individual patterns his or her behavior after another's. One supervisor at a construction firm, not wanting to acknowledge consciously that she was not likely to be promoted, mimicked the behavior of her boss, even going so far as to buy a car just like the boss's. **Rationalization** is trying to justify one's behavior by constructing bogus reasons for it. Employees may rationalize unethical behavior like padding their expense accounts because "everyone else does it."

Withdrawal mechanisms are exhibited when frustrated individuals try to flee from a conflict using either physical or psychological means. Flight, conversion, and fantasy are examples of withdrawal mechanisms. Physically escaping a conflict is **flight**. An employee taking a day off after a blowup with the boss is an example. **Withdrawal** may take the form of emotionally leaving a conflict, such as exhibiting an "I don't care anymore" attitude. **Conversion** is a process whereby emotional conflicts become expressed in physical symptoms. Most of us have experienced the conversion reaction of a headache following an emotional exchange with another person. **Fantasy** is a withdrawal

fixation
An aggressive mechanism in which an individual keeps up a dysfunctional behavior that obviously will not solve the conflict.

displacement
An aggressive mechanism in which an individual directs his or her anger toward someone who is not the source of the conflict.

negativism
An aggressive mechanism in which a person responds with pessimism to any attempt at solving a problem.

compensation
A compromise mechanism in which an individual attempts to make up for a negative situation by devoting himself or herself to another pursuit with increased vigor.

identification
A compromise mechanism whereby an individual patterns his or her behavior after another's.

rationalization
A compromise mechanism characterized by trying to justify one's behavior by constructing bogus reasons for it.

flight/withdrawal
A withdrawal mechanism that entails physically escaping (flight) or psychologically escaping (withdrawal) a conflict.

conversion
A withdrawal mechanism in which emotional conflicts are expressed in physical symptoms.

fantasy
A withdrawal mechanism that provides an escape from a conflict through daydreaming.

mechanism that provides an escape from a conflict through daydreaming. In the Internet age, fantasy as an escape mechanism has found new meaning. A study conducted by International Data Corporation (IDC) showed that 30 to 40 percent of all Internet surfing at work is nonwork-related and that more than 70 percent of companies have had sex sites accessed from their networks, suggesting that employees' minds aren't always focused on their jobs.[45]

When employees exhibit withdrawal mechanisms, they often fake it by pretending to agree with their bosses or coworkers in order to avoid facing an immediate conflict. Many employees fake it because the firm informally rewards agreement and punishes dissent. The long-term consequence of withdrawal and faking it is emotional distress for the employee.[46]

Knowledge of these defense mechanisms can be extremely beneficial to a manager. By understanding the ways in which people typically react to interpersonal conflict, managers can be prepared for employees' reactions and help them uncover their feelings about a conflict.

LEARNING OUTCOME 5

Conflict Management Strategies and Techniques

The overall approach (or strategy) you use in a conflict is important in determining whether the conflict will have a positive or negative outcome.

These overall strategies are competitive versus cooperative strategies. Table 13.2 depicts the two strategies and four different conflict scenarios. The competitive strategy is founded on assumptions of win–lose and entails dishonest communication, mistrust, and a rigid position from both parties.[47] The cooperative strategy is founded on different assumptions: the potential for win–win outcomes, honest communication, trust, openness to risk and vulnerability, and the notion that the whole may be greater than the sum of the parts.

To illustrate the importance of the overall strategy, consider the case of two groups competing for scarce resources. Suppose budget cuts have to be made at an insurance company. The claims manager argues that the sales training staff should be cut, because agents are fully trained. The sales training manager argues that claims personnel should be cut, because the company is processing fewer claims. This could turn into a dysfunctional brawl, with both sides refusing to give ground. This would constitute a win–lose, lose–win, or lose–lose scenario. Personnel cuts could be made in only one department, or in both departments. In all three cases, the organization winds up in a losing position with the competitive approach.

TABLE 13.2 Win–Lose versus Win–Win Strategies

STRATEGY	DEPARTMENT A	DEPARTMENT B	ORGANIZATION
Competitive	Lose	Lose	Lose
	Lose	Win	Lose
	Win	Lose	Lose
Cooperative	Win–	Win–	Win

Even in such intense conflicts as those over scarce resources, a win–win strategy can lead to an overall win for the organization. In fact, conflicts over scarce resources can be productive if the parties have cooperative goals—a strategy that seeks a winning solution for both parties. To achieve a win–win outcome, the conflict must be approached with open-minded discussion of opposing views. Through open-minded discussion, both parties integrate views and create new solutions that facilitate productivity and strengthen their relationship; the result is feelings of unity rather than separation.[48]

In the example of the conflict between the claims manager and sales training manager, open-minded discussion might reveal that there are ways to achieve budget cuts without cutting personnel. Sales support might surrender part of its travel budget, and claims might cut out overtime. This represents a win–win situation for the company. The budget has been reduced, and relationships between the two departments have been preserved. Both parties have given up something (note the "win–" in Table 13.2), but the conflict has been resolved with a positive outcome.

You can see the importance of the broad strategy used to approach a conflict. We now move from broad strategies to more specific techniques.

Ineffective Techniques

There are many specific techniques for dealing with conflict. Before turning to techniques that work, it should be recognized that some actions commonly taken in organizations to deal with conflict are not effective.[49]

Nonaction is doing nothing in hopes that the conflict will disappear. Generally, this is not a good technique, because most conflicts do not go away, and the individuals involved in the conflict react with frustration.

Secrecy, attempting to hide a conflict or an issue that has the potential to create conflict, only creates suspicion. An example is an organizational policy of pay secrecy. In some organizations, discussion of salary is grounds for dismissal. When this is the case, employees suspect that the company has something to hide.

Administrative orbiting is delaying action on a conflict by buying time, usually by telling the individuals involved that the problem is being worked on or that the boss is still thinking about the issue. Like nonaction, this technique leads to frustration and resentment.

Due process nonaction is a procedure set up to address conflicts that is so costly, time consuming, or personally risky that no one will use it. Some companies' sexual harassment policies are examples of this technique. To file a sexual harassment complaint, detailed paperwork is required, the accuser must go through appropriate channels, and the accuser risks being branded a troublemaker. Thus, the company has a procedure for handling complaints (due process), but no one uses it (nonaction).

Character assassination is an attempt to label or discredit an opponent. Character assassination can backfire and make the individual who uses it appear dishonest and cruel. It often leads to name-calling and accusations by both parties, who both end up losers in the eyes of those who witness the conflict.

Effective Techniques

Fortunately, there are effective conflict management techniques. These include appealing to superordinate goals, expanding resources, changing personnel, changing structure, and confronting and negotiating.

Superordinate Goals An organizational goal that is more important to both parties in a conflict than their individual or group goals is a **superordinate goal**.[50] Superordinate goals cannot be achieved by an individual or by one group alone. The achievement of these goals requires cooperation by both parties.

One effective technique for resolving conflict is to appeal to a superordinate goal—in effect, to focus the parties on a larger issue on which they both agree. This helps them realize their similarities rather than their differences.

nonaction
Doing nothing in hopes that a conflict will disappear.

secrecy
Attempting to hide a conflict or an issue that has the potential to create conflict.

administrative orbiting
Delaying action on a conflict by buying time.

due process nonaction
A procedure set up to address conflicts that is so costly, time consuming, or personally risky that no one will use it.

character assassination
An attempt to label or discredit an opponent.

superordinate goal
An organizational goal that is more important to both parties in a conflict than their individual or group goals.

©Corbis/Jupiterimages

In the conflict between service representatives and cable television installers that was discussed earlier, appealing to a superordinate goal would be an effective technique for resolving the conflict. Both departments can agree that superior customer service is a goal worthy of pursuit and that this goal cannot be achieved unless cables are installed properly and in a timely manner, and customer complaints are handled effectively. Quality service requires that both departments cooperate to achieve the goal.

Expanding Resources One conflict resolution technique is so simple that it may be overlooked. If the conflict's source is common or scarce resources, providing more resources may be a solution. Of course, managers working with tight budgets may not have the luxury of obtaining additional resources. Nevertheless, it is a technique to be considered. In the example earlier in this chapter, one solution to the conflict among managers over secretarial support would be to hire more secretaries.

Changing Personnel In some cases, long-running severe conflict may be traced to a specific individual. For example, managers with lower levels of emotional intelligence have been demonstrated to have more negative work attitudes, to exhibit less altruistic behavior, and to produce more negative work outcomes. A chronically disgruntled manager who exhibits low EI may not only frustrate his employees but also impede his department's performance. In such cases, transferring or firing an individual may be the best solution, but only after due process.[51]

Changing Structure Another way to resolve a conflict is to change the structure of the organization. One way of accomplishing this is to create an integrator role. An integrator is a liaison between groups with very different interests. In severe conflicts, it may be best that the integrator be a neutral third party.[52] Creating the integrator role is a way of opening dialogue between groups that have difficulty communicating.

Using cross-functional teams is another way of changing the organization's structure to manage conflict. In the old methods of designing new products in organizations, many departments had to contribute, and delays resulted from difficulties in coordinating the activities of the various departments. Using a cross-functional team made up of members from different departments improves coordination and reduces delays by allowing many activities to be performed at the same time rather than sequentially.[53] The team approach allows members from different departments to work together and reduces the potential for conflict. However, recent research

also suggests that such functional diversity can lead to slower informational processing in teams due to differences in members' perceptions of what might be required to achieve group goals. When putting together cross-functional teams, organizations should emphasize superordinate goals and train team members on resolving conflict. One such training technique could involve educating individual members in other functional areas so that everyone on the team can have a shared language.[54] In teamwork, it is helpful to break up a big task so that it becomes a collection of smaller, less complex tasks, and to have smaller teams work on the smaller tasks. This helps to reduce conflict, and organizations can potentially improve the performance of the overall team by improving the outcomes in each subteam.[55]

Confronting and Negotiating Some conflicts require confrontation and negotiation between the parties. Both of these strategies require skill on the part of the negotiator and careful planning before engaging in negotiations. The process of negotiating involves an open discussion of problem solutions, and the outcome often is an exchange in which both parties work toward a mutually beneficial solution.

Negotiation is a joint process of finding a mutually acceptable solution to a complex conflict. There are two major negotiating approaches: distributive bargaining and integrative negotiation.[56] **Distributive bargaining** is an approach in which the goals of one party are in direct conflict with the goals of the other party. Resources are limited, and each party wants to maximize its share of the resources (get its piece of the pie). It is a competitive or win–lose approach to negotiations. Sometimes distributive bargaining causes negotiators to focus so much on their differences that they ignore their common ground. In these cases, distributive

WHEN TO NEGOTIATE

>> Negotiating is a useful strategy under the following conditions:

> There are two or more parties. Negotiation is primarily an interpersonal or intergroup process.

> There is a conflict of interest between the parties such that what one party wants is not what the other party wants.

> The parties are willing to negotiate because each believes it can use its influence to obtain a better outcome than by simply taking the side of the other party.

> The parties prefer to work together rather than to fight openly, give in, break off contact, or take the dispute to a higher authority.

distributive bargaining

A negotiation approach in which the goals of the parties are in conflict, and each party seeks to maximize its resources.

> *Men may choke when they're expected to fulfill the stereotype of being strong negotiators, fearing that they might not be able to live up to it.*

bargaining can become counterproductive. The reality is, however, that some situations are distributive in nature, particularly when the parties are interdependent. If a negotiator wants to maximize the value of a single deal and is not worried about maintaining a good relationship with the other party, distributive bargaining may be an option.

In contrast, **integrative negotiation** is a negotiation approach in which the parties' goals are not seen as mutually exclusive, but the focus is on both sides achieving their objectives. Integrative negotiation focuses on the merits of the issues and is a win–win approach. (How can we make the pie bigger?) For integrative negotiation to be successful, certain preconditions must be present. These include having a common goal, faith in one's own problem-solving abilities, a belief in the validity of the other party's position, motivation to work together, mutual trust, and clear communication.[57]

Cultural differences in negotiation must be acknowledged. Japanese negotiators, for example, when working with American negotiators, tend to see their power as coming from their role (buyer versus seller). Americans, in contrast, view their power as their ability to walk away from the negotiations.[58] Neither culture understands the other very well, and the negotiations can resemble a dance in which one person is waltzing while the other is doing a samba. The collectivism–individualism dimension (discussed in Chapter 2) has a great bearing on negotiations. Americans, with their individualism, negotiate from a position of self-interest; Japanese focus on the good of the group. Cross-cultural negotiations can be more effective if you learn as much about other cultures as possible.

Gender may also play a role in negotiation. There appears to be no evidence that men are better negotiators than women or vice versa. The differences lie in how negotiators are treated. Women are blatantly discriminated against in terms of the offers made to them in negotiations.[59] Gender stereotypes also affect the negotiating process. Women may be seen as accommodating, conciliatory, and emotional (negatives in negotiations) and men may be seen as assertive, powerful, and convincing (positive for negotiations) in accordance with traditional stereotypes. Sometimes, when women feel they're being stereotyped, they exhibit stereotype reactance, which is a tendency to display behavior inconsistent with (or opposite of) the stereotype. This means they become more assertive and convincing. Alternatively, men may choke when they're expected to fulfill the stereotype, fearing that they might not be able to live up to it.

LEARNING OUTCOME **6**

Conflict Management Styles

Managers have at their disposal a variety of conflict management styles: avoiding, accommodating, competing, compromising, and collaborating. One way of classifying styles of conflict management is to examine the styles' assertiveness (the extent to which you want your goals met) and cooperativeness (the extent to which you want to see the other party's concerns met).[60] Figure 13.4 graphs the five conflict management styles using these two dimensions. Table 13.3 on page 219 lists appropriate situations for using each conflict management style.

Avoiding

Avoiding is a style low on both assertiveness and cooperativeness. Avoiding is a deliberate decision to take no action on a conflict or to stay out of a

HOT *Trend: Boss-napping*

Top executives in France should watch their backs. Given that the public believes more and more that the only way their needs will be heard is through boss-napping (a play on the word *kidnapping*), incidences of executives being held hostage by workers demanding concessions are becoming more frequent. At the 3M factory at Orleans, employees demanding severance packages for laid-off workers and guarantees of security for the remaining employees held the company's industrial director hostage for more than 24 hours until a deal was reached. Sony's CEO and human resources director were held while unions bartered better terms for dismissed workers. Eventually the boss-nappers got €13 million added to their redundancy package. Boss-napping may be an illegal tactic, but it certainly seems to be effective.

SOURCES: T. McNicoll, "Sure, Kidnap the Man," *Newsweek* (April 25, 2009). http://www.newsweek.com/id/195092; A. Sage, "Angry French Workers Turn to Bossnapping to Solve Their Problems," *TimesOnline* (April 4, 2009). http://www.timesonline.co.uk/tol/news/world/europe/article6031822.ece.

---

integrative negotiation

A negotiation approach in which the parties' goals are not seen as mutually exclusive, but the focus is on both sides achieving their objectives.

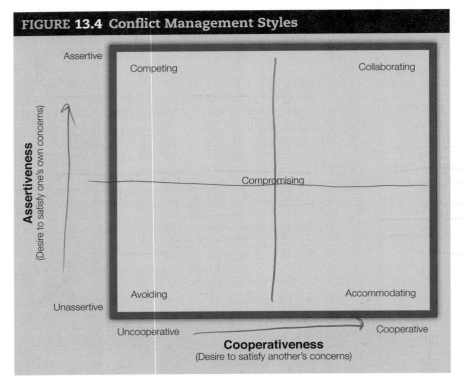

FIGURE 13.4 Conflict Management Styles

Assertiveness (Desire to satisfy one's own concerns)

Assertive

Competing

Collaborating

Compromising

Avoiding

Accommodating

Unassertive

Uncooperative

Cooperative

Cooperativeness (Desire to satisfy another's concerns)

SOURCE: K. W. Thomas, "Conflict and Conflict Management," in M. D. Dunnette, *Handbook of Industrial and Organizational Psychology* (Chicago: Rand McNally, 1976), 900. Used with permission of M. D. Dunnette.

conflict situation. In recent times, Airbus, a European manufacturer of aircraft, has faced massive intraorganizational conflict stemming from major expansions that included French, German, Spanish, and British subsidiaries within the same parent company. Power struggles among executives combined with massive changes in organizational structure are believed to have led to this type of conflict. Airbus seems to be adopting the avoidance strategy in an effort to let these conflicts subside on their own.[61] Some relationship conflicts, such as those involving political norms and personal tastes, may distract team members from their tasks and avoiding may be an appropriate strategy.[62] When the parties are angry and need time to cool down, it may be best to use avoidance. There is a potential danger in using an avoiding style too often, however. Research shows that overuse of this style results in negative evaluations from others in the workplace.[63]

Accommodating

A style in which you are concerned that the other party's goals be met but relatively unconcerned with getting your own way is called accommodating. It is cooperative but unassertive. Appropriate situations for accommodating include times when you find you are wrong, when you want to let the other party have his or her way so that that individual will owe you similar treatment later, or when the relationship is important. Overreliance on accommodating has its dangers. Managers who constantly defer to others may find that others lose respect for them. In addition, accommodating

managers may become frustrated because their own needs are never met, and they may lose self-esteem.[64] Research has also shown that individuals will over-estimate the importance of the relationship and accommodate at the expense of actual outcomes. Research has shown that two females involved in conflict or negotiation overuse accommodation more than two males involved in similar situations.[65]

Competing

Competing is a style that is very assertive and uncooperative. You want to satisfy your own interests and are willing to do so at the other party's expense. In an emergency or in situations where you know you are right, it may be appropriate to put your foot down. For example, environmentalists forced Shell Oil Company (part of Royal Dutch/Shell Group) to scrap its plans to build a refinery in Delaware after a bitter "To Hell with Shell" campaign.[66] Relying solely on competing strategies is dangerous, though. Managers who do so may become reluctant to admit when they are wrong and may find themselves surrounded by people who are afraid to disagree with them. In team settings, it has been noted earlier that task conflict and relationship conflict could occur together although task conflict is seen as functional whereas relationship conflict is seen as dysfunctional for the team. In a recent study, dyads of participants were exposed to task-based conflict. One of the two members of the dyads was trained on using either the competing conflict handling style or the collaborative style. Results indicated that the competing style led to the most relationship conflict, whereas the collaborative style led to the least relationship conflict.[67]

Compromising

The compromising style is intermediate in both assertiveness and cooperativeness, because each party must give up something to reach a solution to the conflict. Compromises are often made in the final hours of union–management negotiations, when time is of the essence. Compromise may be an effective backup style when efforts toward collaboration are not successful.[68]

It is important to recognize that compromises are not optimal solutions. Compromise

©Jody Dole/Stone/Getty Images

TABLE 13.3 Uses of Five Styles of Conflict Management

CONFLICT-HANDLING STYLE	APPROPRIATE SITUATION
Competing	1. When quick, decisive action is vital (e.g., emergencies). 2. On important issues where unpopular actions need implementing (e.g., cost cutting, enforcing unpopular rules, discipline). 3. On issues vital to company welfare when you know you are right. 4. Against people who take advantage of noncompetitive behavior.
Collaborating	1. To find an integrative solution when both sets of concerns are too important to be compromised. 2. When your objective is to learn. 3. To merge insights from people with different perspectives. 4. To gain commitment by incorporating concerns into a consensus. 5. To work through feelings that have interfered with a relationship.
Compromising	1. When goals are important but not worth the effort or potential disruption of more assertive modes. 2. When opponents with equal power are committed to mutually exclusive goals. 3. To achieve temporary settlements to complex issues. 4. To arrive at expedient solutions under time pressure. 5. As a backup when collaboration or competition is unsuccessful.
Avoiding	1. When an issue is trivial or more important issues are pressing. 2. When you perceive no chance of satisfying your concerns. 3. When potential disruption outweighs the benefits of resolution. 4. To let people cool down and regain perspective. 5. When gathering information supersedes immediate decision. 6. When others can resolve the conflict more effectively. 7. When issues seem tangential or symptomatic of other issues.
Accommodating	1. When you find you are wrong—to allow a better position to be heard, to learn, and to show your reasonableness. 2. When issues are more important to others than to yourself—to satisfy others and maintain cooperation. 3. To build social credits for later issues. 4. To minimize loss when you are outmatched and losing. 5. When harmony and stability are especially important. 6. To allow employees to develop by learning from mistakes.

SOURCE: K. W. Thomas, "Toward Multidimensional Values in Teaching: The Example of Conflict Behaviors," *Academy of Management Review* 2 (1977): 309–325. Reproduced by permission of the publisher via Copyright Clearance Center, Inc.

means partially surrendering one's position for the sake of coming to terms. Often, when people compromise, they inflate their demands to begin with. The solutions reached may only be temporary, and often compromises do nothing to improve relationships between the parties in the conflict.

Collaborating

A win–win style that is high on both assertiveness and cooperativeness is known as collaborating. Working toward it involves an open and thorough discussion of the conflict and arriving at a solution that is satisfactory to both parties. Situations where collaboration may be effective include times when both parties need to be committed to a final solution or when a combination of different perspectives can be formed into a solution. Long term, it leads to improved relationships and effective performance.[69] Teams

that use collaboration effectively view conflict as a mutual problem that needs common consideration to achieve resolution. Understanding this, team members have confidence that other members will work toward mutually beneficial solutions and ultimately generate diverse ideas to facilitate team performance.[70]

Research on the five styles of conflict management indicates that although most managers favor a certain style, they have the capacity to change styles as the situation demands.[71] A study of project managers found that managers who used a combination of competing and avoiding styles were seen as ineffective by the engineers who worked on their project teams.[72] In another study of conflicts between R&D project managers and technical staff, competing and avoiding styles resulted in more frequent conflict and lower performance, whereas the collaborating style resulted in less frequent conflict and better performance.[73]

9B09M001

ETHICS OF OFFSHORING: NOVO NORDISK AND CLINICAL TRIALS IN EMERGING ECONOMIES

On a warm day in early spring 2008, the telephone is ringing in the office of Anders Dejgaard, chief medical officer of Novo Nordisk, a leading developer and manufacturer of insulin and related products. A business journalist of the Danish national newspaper *Berlingske Tidende* is on the line and asking for an interview. Dejgaard knows her from several conversations relating to business practices in the pharmaceutical industry.

The journalist is investigating the offshoring of clinical trials by Danish companies. A report recently published in the Netherlands alleges that multinational pharmaceutical companies routinely conduct trials in developing countries under allegedly unethical conditions. Also, the Danish National Committee on Biomedical Research Ethics has expressed concerns because Danish pharmaceutical companies are not obtaining ethical reviews in Denmark for such trials despite the offer from this committee. Thus, she wants to discuss Novo Nordisk's position on these issues.

Dejgaard reflects on how to react. Several articles on ethical aspects related to medical research in the Third World had appeared in the Danish press in recent months, creating an atmosphere of suspicion towards the industry.[1] Should he meet with the journalist and if so, what should he tell her? Or should he rather focus on his forthcoming business trip to new production facilities and send Novo Nordisk's press officer to meet the journalist? In his mind flashes the possibility of derogatory headlines in the tabloid press. As a company emphasizing corporate responsibility, the interaction with the media presents both opportunities and risks to Novo Nordisk.

---

[1] See in particular B. Alfter, "De fattige er verdens nye forsøgskaniner. Krav om kontrol med medicinalindustrien," Information, Feb. 26, 2008, pp. 4-5, and B. Lambeck and S.G. Jensen, "Halvdelen af al medicin afprøves i den tredje verden," Politiken, Oct. 6, 2007.

NOVO NORDISK[2]

Novo Nordisk A/S had been created in 1989 through a merger between two Danish companies, Novo Industri A/S and Nordisk Gentofte A/S. Both had been established in the 1920s as manufacturers of insulin, a crucial medication for diabetes. Over decades of fierce competition, they had become leading providers of insulin and related pharmaceutical products. Novo Industri had been pursuing an internationally oriented strategy from the outset, and by 1936 was supplying insulin to 40 countries. A significant step in the internationalization of the company was a major push into the U.S. market in 1979. At the time, Food and Drug Administration (FDA) regulations required Novo Industri to replicate its clinical studies in the United States to obtain the approval of the marketing of their new products. In 1989, the two companies merged and in 2000 the merged company spun off the enzyme business "Novozymes."

In 2008, Novo Nordisk presents itself as a focused company within the healthcare industry and a world leader in diabetes care. It claims the broadest and most innovative diabetes product portfolio in the industry, including the most advanced insulin delivery systems. In addition, Novo Nordisk holds leading positions in areas such as haemostasis management, growth hormone therapy and hormone replacement therapy. Sales reached DKr41.8 billion (about US$8 billion) in 2007, of which DKr30.5 billion were in diabetes care and DKr11.4 billion were in biopharmaceuticals.

Innovation is considered pivotal to the success of Novo Nordisk, as it was to its predecessor companies. Continuous innovations allow the development of more refined, and thus more effective, insulin preparations, and new delivery systems, such as Novopen®, that facilitate the administration of the treatment, including self-administration by patients. In 2008, about 18 per cent of employees are working within research and development.

In 2008, Novo Nordisk holds market shares for insulin of about 56 per cent in Europe, 41 per cent in North America and 73 per cent in Japan and employs about 26,000 people, of whom 12,689 are located in Denmark, 3,411 in the rest of Europe, 3,940 in North America and the remainder in Asia Pacific and the rest of the world. Production facilities are located in six countries and products are marketed in 179 countries.

The shares of Novo Industri were first listed on the Copenhagen Stock Exchange in 1974 and on the London Stock Exchange in 1981 as the first Scandinavian company to be listed in London. In 2008, Novo Nordisk's B shares are listed on the stock exchanges in both Copenhagen and London, while its American depositary receipts (ADRs) are listed on the New York Stock Exchange.

Novo Nordisk emphasizes corporate social responsibility as part of its image, pursing a triple bottom line approach: environmental and social responsibility along with economic viability. This commitment is demonstrated through its values and its environmental and social responsibility policies that are reported on its website (see Appendix 1).

Critical milestones in Novo Nordisk's ambition to be recognized as a leader of corporate sustainability include the publication in 1994 of its Environmental Report. It was the first company in Denmark and one of the first in the world to do so. This was followed in 1999 by the first annual Social Report. In 2001, Novo Nordisk established the World Diabetes Foundation, a charity aiming to improve diabetes care in developing countries, where diabetes is becoming an epidemic as it had in Europe and North America a few decades earlier.

---

[2] *This section draws on the company website, www.novonordisk.com, and an undated (circa 2002) document, "Novo Nordisk History," available via this website.*

In recognition of its sustainability engagement, Novo Nordisk had been included in the Dow Jones Global Sustainability Indices, where it was ranked as "best in class" in the healthcare category in 2007. At home, Novo Nordisk is frequently ranked as having the most highly regarded corporate image by Danish magazines *Berlingske Nyhedmagasin*, *Børsen* and *Ingeniøren*.

New Medications: Development and Approval

Novo Nordisk, like other pharmaceutical and medical companies, heavily invests in the development of new medications offering more effective, safe and user-friendly treatments. New product development involves the creation of new drugs or modifications in their use, for instance their dosage and the form of administration.

To bring new drugs or medical devices to market, they must be approved by the relevant authorities — the FDA in the United States and European Medicines Agency (EMEA) in the European Union. The approval of drugs and medical devices requires proof of their efficacy and their safety. Efficacy refers to scientific evidence that the drug improves patients' conditions as claimed by the manufacturer. Safety refers to the absence of substantive negative side-effects. Thus, to obtain approval, pharmaceutical companies have to provide scientific evidence that the drug improves the conditions of patients and is free of disproportional side-effects.

This evidence has to be based on, among other data, clinical trials in which the drug has been tested on actual patients. The clinical trials are normally conducted in four stages. Phase 1 involves a small number of healthy volunteers and serves to assess the kinetic properties and tolerability of the drug. Phase 2 is performed on larger groups of patients to assess how well the drug works and to establish the doses that give the desired effect and to continue its safety assessment. Phase 3 trials often involve thousands of patients and aims to provide a definitive assessment of how effective and safe the drug is. All data generated in the three phases form an essential part of submissions to the regulatory authorities (FDA, EMEA and their counterparts in other countries) for drug approval. With this approval, the drug can then be marketed for the approved indications. Further trials, in phase 4, may be required to obtain permission to extend the labelling of a drug to new indications (e.g. a different disease) or specific groups, such as children or pregnant women.

Phase 3 and 4 trials require a large number of patients with the specific disease that the drug is to improve. A typical approval process conducted by Novo Nordisk might require six to eight different phase 3 trials with different patient groups or combinations of the drug component, each involving about 400 to 800 patients. Such trials are often conducted as multinational studies involving up to 15 countries. With increasing requirements for patient exposure for approval and increasing numbers of drugs being tested, the recruitment of patients is often a major challenge. Typically, trials are conducted at multiple hospitals that all must follow the same trial protocol to ensure the consistency of data and compliance with existing "good clinical practice" (GCP) guidelines. Multi-site trials also facilitate the recruitment of patients with diverse backgrounds, for instance different ethnicities and diets, while helping to demonstrate their universal properties. Doctors and nurses but not patients are normally paid for this work and hospitals often find it attractive to participate in trials that allow access to new medications and front line research. Clinical trials, especially phase 3, are a major cost factor in the development of new medications and they often take many years to conduct (on average eight years).

In the early 2000s, major pharmaceutical industries increasingly moved parts of their trials, especially phases 3 and 4, to countries outside their traditional areas of operations, especially to Eastern Europe, South America, India and China. Hospitals in these areas provide access to qualified medical staff and larger numbers of patients with the specific conditions, while potentially being able to administer a trial at lower costs. Moreover, the efficacy of drugs may also vary across contexts, for instance due to genetic, dietary, climatic or other environmental conditions. In such cases, multi-site trials help to establish the efficacy of medications across contexts. Some countries, such as Japan, India and China, in fact require that trials are at least in part conducted locally to approve a new medication in the respective countries. However, the conduct of clinical trials in these areas also raises a range of ethical issues.

Ethical Issues in Medical Research[3]

Ethical issues in the pharmaceutical industry have received considerable media attention over several decades, as the industry has failed to live up to the expectations of some interest groups. In particular, clinical trials raise a number of widely recognized issues. Medical professionals, and with them many NGOs and media, focus on the medical ethics grounded in the Hippocratic oath that commits doctors to treat each patient to the best of their abilities, never to cause intentional harm and to maintain patient confidentiality. Scientists and approval authorities have been concerned about the scientific rigor of the tests to provide solid evidence of the effects of a new drug, and thus to protect potential future users of the drug. At the same time, pharmaceutical companies have to operate with limited financial resources and to satisfy shareholders and thus cannot spend more resources than expected future revenues would justify. Accordingly, the industry has been accused of performing trials in developing countries with lower attention to ethical principles — "ethical bribing," with patients acting as guinea pigs that do not understand and/or care about the risk involved but just want to get free medication and with investigators not meeting the competence requirements, etc. Allegedly, all this just serves to generate documentation for compounds that are to be sold only in developed countries.

Medical (Hippocratic) ethics concern primarily the individual patients that are participating in any experiment. The relationship between the doctor and the subject participating in a trial is thus governed by the doctor's responsibility to care for his or her patient. Past incidences where this principle had been violated continue to affect popular perceptions of medical research. Most infamously, the Tuskegee syphilis study left 400 impoverished and unwitting African-American men in Macon County, Alabama, untreated to study how they developed the disease — an experiment initiated in 1932 and terminated only in the 1970s.

To prevent such scandals, professional medical organizations have developed guidelines and principles of ethics to guide their research, notably the Helsinki Declaration of the World Medical Association (see Appendix 2). These widely accepted ethical principles aim to protect subjects, e.g., patients, participating in such research. These include:

- Voluntary informed consent: Each patient has to agree voluntarily to participate in the research based on being fully informed about the purposes of the study and potential risks for the individual. Sponsors and local site investigators thus normally write an "informed consent" document that informs potential subjects of the true risks and potential benefits, which is signed by each patient or their legal guardian before any trial procedure.

---

[3] This section draws in particular on E.J. Emanuel, D. Wendler and C. Grady, "What makes clinical research ethical?" Journal of the American Medical Association, 283:20, 2000, pp. 2701-2711, and Michael A. Santoro and Thomas M. Gorrie, Ethics and the Pharmaceutical Industry, Cambridge University Press, 2005.

- Respect of patients: The privacy of the subject should be protected and they should be free to withdraw from the experiment at any time without reasoning. The doctor's professional responsibility to the patient should take precedence over any other considerations.
- Independent review: Any medical and pharmacological research has to be assessed on its scientific merits and ethicality by an independent review board (IRB) that is independent from those involved in or sponsoring the research.

Scientific ethics are concerned about the validity of the results of the scientific inquiry and thus the methodological rigour of the study. Thus, a study has to use valid measurements and statistical techniques and samples that are unbiased and sufficiently large that they can generate trustworthy and valid results.

Such scientific rigour is important to anyone who may in the future use an approved drug or medical device. Awareness of the need for rigorous tests prior to launching new medications had been triggered by various scandals of the 1960s, notably the Thalidomide scandal involving a pain killer used by women to ease sleep problems and pregnancy sickness. Due to side-effects of this medication, thousands of children worldwide were born with incomplete arms or legs, before the drug was withdrawn. In consequence to this and other scandals, the licensing and approval procedures for drugs have been tightened to ensure that only drugs with scientifically proven efficacy and safety are marketed.

Ethical businesses have to balance activities done in the interest of the wider society with their pursuit of profits. The late Nobel prize-winning economist Milton Friedman famously declared that the primary social responsibility of business is to make profits.[4] Under efficient markets, which he firmly believed in, this would generate the most mutually beneficial outcome. Thus, he argued, firms ought to give precedence to shareholders over any other interest groups.

Others argue that firms should engage in corporate social responsibility because it can be expected to benefit their bottom line in the long run, for instance through reputation effects. Yet others argue that firms have an intrinsic, normative responsibility to use their influence to do good for society and to aspire to the highest moral standards, independent of the profit motive. However, even so, their financial resources will be limited. Like organizations in the governmental or non-profit sector, businesses have to make critical decisions about how best to use their scarce resources.

Ethics of Placebo Experiments[5]

Particular concerns have arisen for placebo trials, that is, trials where a control group of patients receives a treatment without any active ingredient for the disease. The purpose of placebo trials is, normally, to provide evidence of product efficacy by showing statistically significant improvements of the conditions of patients receiving the active treatment, compared to those receiving a placebo treatment.

Placebo trials are especially important for diseases that are affected by the so-called placebo effect, that is, patients' conditions improving because of the positive effect of receiving a form of treatment rather than the specific medication. This has been shown to be quite substantive, for instance, for schizophrenia and

---

[4] M. Friedman, "The social responsibility of business is to increase profits," *The New York Times Magazine*, September 13, 1970; reprinted in K.E. Meyer, *Multinational Enterprises and Host Economies*, Elgar, Cheltenham, 2009.
[5] This section draws on contemporary discussions in the medical literature, in particular E.J. Emanuel and F.G. Miller, "The ethics of placebo-controlled trials e- A middle ground," *New England Journal of Medicine*, 345:12, 2001, pp. 915-919, and R. Temple and S.S. Ellenberg, "Placebo-controlled trials and active-controlled trials in the evaluation of new treatments," *Annals of Internal Medicine*, 133:6, 2000, pp. 455-463.

other psychiatric conditions. Both American and European authorities thus often require placebo trials as prerequisite for the approval of new medications.

Alternatives to placebo trials include the use of active controls, in which the control groups receive a previously marketed medication with known properties. Yet these types of trials are often not sufficient to provide the required rigorous evidence regarding the efficacy of the medication.[6] Placebo trials may create risks for patients in the placebo group, in particular when patients are denied a treatment that is known to improve their condition. The Helsinki Declaration therefore requires avoiding placebo experiments unless very special reasons require them or no alternative treatment of the illness is available (see Appendix 2, item 29). Ethics review boards have become very restrictive in permitting placebo trials. There have been arguments from some groups that one reason for the pharmaceutical industry to place studies in developing countries is the possibility of performing placebo trials that otherwise can be difficult to get approval for in developed countries.

Novo Nordisk generally avoids placebo trials. Usually, they are used only in phase 1 trials in healthy volunteers when new drug candidates are being developed. These trials are normally located near its main research centres in Europe and rarely in non-Western countries.

Media Spotlights

In February 2008, a report from the Dutch NGO SOMO raised public awareness of placebo trials conducted by major pharmaceutical companies in developing countries.[7] The report was critical of trials that had been submitted to the FDA and the EMEA for drug approval. Its primary concern was that key information about ethical aspects of these clinical trials was not available to it as an external observer and it found incidences where patients suffered serious harm after receiving a placebo in a trial.

The report focused on three case studies of clinical trials for recently approved drugs conducted in Eastern Europe and Asia, based on publicly available information. It concluded that

> trial subjects in these countries are more vulnerable and their rights are less secured than in high income countries. Conditions such as poverty, illiteracy, poor health systems and inadequate research ethics committees result in international ethical standards not being met. Current EU legislation requires that results from unethical clinical trials . . . not be accepted for marketing authorization. With three case studies on recently approved drugs in the EU (Abilify, Olmetec, and Seroquel), SOMO demonstrates that this principle is being violated. European authorities devote little to no attention to the ethical aspects of the clinical trials submitted, and they accept unethical trials as well as trials of poor quality.[8]

---

[6] *An active-control trial infers efficacy from non-significant differences of performance compared to the active-control drug. Such non-significance, however, can be caused by a number of other influences. Moreover, this test is problematic if the active-control drug is subject to large placebo effects varying with study designs. On the merits and concerns of active-control trials, see e.g., Temple and Ellenberg, "Placebo-controlled trials and active-controlled trials in the evaluation of new treatments," 2000, and B.T. Walsh, S.N. Seidman, R. Sysko and M. Gould, "Placebo response in studies of major depression: Variable, substantial and growing," Journal of the American Medical Association, 287:14, 2002, pp. 1840-1847.*
[7] *I. Schipper and F. Weyzing, "Ethics for Drug Testing in Low and Middle Income Countries: Considerations for European Market Authorisation," Stichting Onderzoek Multinationale Ondernemingen (SOMO), 2008, http://somo.nl/publications-en/Publication_2472, accessed October 2008.*
[8] *Ibid, abstract on the cover page.*

In its conclusions, the report alleges that local regulation and the enforcement of ethical principles are less strict, partly because local independent review boards are less qualified and partly because they are less keen on restricting what is potentially a revenue earner. The authors thus advocate global harmonization of ethical criteria along the principles currently used by ethics committees in Europe: " . . . there must be no discrepancy between the ethical criteria used to approve research protocols in Western Europe and in low and middle income economies to avoid the creation of 'easy countries.'" [9]

The media picked up, in particular, the case of a schizophrenic patient committing suicide while participating in a trial of the anti-schizophrenia medicine Seroquel by Astra-Zeneca. Moreover, media reported that 10 per cent of recipients in the placebo group had to be hospitalized because of worsening conditions. Careful reading of the original report suggests that 8.3 per cent (p. 64) of a group of 87 patients (p. 62) were affected, which adds to seven persons. No assessment of the likelihood of such incidents under alternative medication available at the time had been included in the report.

Concerns have also been raised by the Danish National Committee on Biomedical Research Ethics.[10] In particular, the committee criticizes the industry for not accepting the committee's offer to provide independent ethical reviews before submitting to local ethics committees as a service to the industry. The chairperson for the committee, Johannes Gaub, chief medical officer at Odense Hospital, told the media:

> Like production companies locate their factories in low wage areas, the medical industry is outsourcing its scientific experiments in the same way. The costs of conducting medical trials in developing countries are only a fraction of what they are in the West because of the low wages . . . In the USA it costs about DKr 150,000 to move one patient through a trial. In Denmark, it costs DKr 80,000. I don't really know the price in developing countries, but it is a fraction of that.

Gaub also rejects the concern of the industry that hospitals in Denmark would not be able to conduct trials of the necessary scale, given the growing requirements worldwide to provide clinical trial data for approvals around the world:

> We have considerable spare capacity in Denmark. Despite the high costs we have a well-functioning health system. We have data about patients because of our national identity number system, and there are many clinical researchers in the hospitals who would be happy to participate in the trials of new medications . . . It is actually worrying that we do not receive more applications in Denmark. We need clinical research to maintain the high level of health science that we so far have had in the country.[11]

Danish politicians also joined the debate. In a statement to the health committee of the national parliament, the minister for health emphasized that E.U. regulation for the approval of new medicines requires that trials conducted outside the European Union have been implemented in accordance with the European Union's own rules as well as with ethical principles such as the Helsinki Declaration. The minister thus concluded:

---

[9] I. Schipper and F. Weyzing, "Ethics for Drug Testing in Low and Middle Income Countries: Considerations for European Market Authorisation," 2008, p. 68.
[10] For further information on the Danish National Committee on Biomedical Research Ethics, see www.cvk.im.dk/cvk/site.aspx?p=119.
[11] Both citations are from B. Erhardtsen, "Medicinalindustrien dropper frivillig etisk blåstempling," Berlingske Tidende, April 5, 2008, Inland section, pp. 6-7 (case author's translation).

I find no reason to take initiatives to constrain research projects by the Danish medical industry outside the EU. In this context, I consider it important to emphasize that all clinical trials that shall be used as a basis for applications for approval of marketing of a medication in the EU must comply with the EU's laws on good clinical practice and the ethical principles regarding medical research with human subjects.[12]

Also, other politicians joined the debate. For example, Member of Parliament Birgitte Josefsen (V)[13] urged Danish pharmaceutical companies to hold the ethical flag high: "The medical industry ought to be very careful about whom they use as test persons. That should be people who have resources to say 'no'. A poor Indian mother with three children is not the right one to become a test person." [14]

Novo Nordisk's Position on Clinical Trials

Anders Dejgaard is pondering the complexity of the ethical issues. As corporate sustainability features highly on Novo Nordisk's agenda, the ethically appropriate handling of clinical trials is important to the company. It conducts clinical trials globally to test the safety and efficacy of new drug candidates in order to obtain global marketing authorization. These trials always follow a common protocol and thus the same standards at all trials sites. Trials sites are selected based on a variety of criteria, including the quality of regulatory authorities, ethical review processes and medical practices. Moreover, drugs have to be tested on the types of patients who will later become users of the drug and trial subjects should have access to the drugs after the process has been completed. In addition, Novo Nordisk will only conduct trials in countries where it has affiliates with the necessary competence to arrange and monitor the trials. In 2008, these criteria were met in about 65 countries worldwide.

Novo Nordisk has adapted the global guidelines and recommendations by all the professional bodies and publishes its policies on clinical trials on its website (see Appendix 3). This includes enhanced global exposure of investigated products through its own website as well as websites sponsored by the FDA (see Appendix 3). Novo Nordisk conducts research in therapies that require global trials and the inclusion of different ethnic populations. The company also anticipates a need to increase the number of clinical trials due to an expanding pipeline and more extensive global and local regulatory requirements. Its ethical principles and standard operating procedures, which apply globally, are designed to ensure due respect for the safety, rights, integrity, dignity, confidentiality and well-being of all human beings participating in Novo Nordisk-sponsored trials. Novo Nordisk is auditing 10 per cent of all trials, while at the same time the American and European authorities, FDA and EMEA, are making random checks of about one per cent of Novo Nordisk's clinical trials. These random checks have never identified ethical problems in clinical trials in developing countries. Since trials are normally conducted in multiple countries, the same standards are applied everywhere, for both ethical and scientific reasons (consistency of results).

At the same time, Dejgaard is irritated about the request for an additional ethics approval by the Danish National Committee on Biomedical Research Ethics. He estimates that it would add three months to the preparation of each new trial. In his own experience, the ethical reviews in those locations he worked in are as rigorous as in Western countries and he does not recognize an added benefit, as the Danish committee

---

[12] *J.K. Nielsen, Besvarlse af spørgsmal nr. 20 (alm. del) som Folketingets Sundhedsudvalg har stillet til indenrigs - og sundhedsministeren (Written reply to a question in the health committee of the Danish parliament), January 9, 2008. (Archives of the Danish government: Indenrigs or Sundhedministeriet, Lægemiddelkontoret, J.nr. 2007-13009-599, Sagsbeh: nhj) (case author's translation).*
[13] *(V) refers to Venstre, one of the parties of the minority government at the time.*
[14] *Berlingske Tidende website, www.berlingske.dk/article/20080403/danmark/704030057, April 3, 2008, accessed October 2008 (case author's translation).*

would be no better in assessing a trial than a local ethics committee. On the contrary, he finds the suggestion more appropriate for a colonial empire. Moreover, specific local issues, such as ethnic or religious minorities, would be better understood by local committees.

Yet various issues come to mind. Is Novo Nordisk doing its research and development in an appropriate manner or are there issues that could be done better in view of Novo Nordisk's triple bottom line commitments? Are Novo Nordisk's standard operating procedures being properly implemented in all developing countries that participate in the programs and how is such compliance to be monitored? How should Novo Nordisk manage its simultaneous relationships with various regulatory authorities, independent review boards at various sites and with the Danish National Committee on Biomedical Research Ethics?

Most pressing is the decision on how to handle the journalist. Should he meet her in person, send a public relations person or not meet at all and reply in writing, citing the corporate website? If he is to meet her, what should be the key messages that he should get across and how should he prepare himself for any questions she might raise during the meeting?

Klaus Meyer (www.klausmeyer.co.uk) is a professor of strategy and international business at the School of Management, University of Bath, Bath, U.K.

Appendix 1

CORPORATE SUSTAINABILITY AT NOVO NORDISK (EXTRACTS)

At Novo Nordisk, we refer to corporate sustainability as companies' ability to sustain and develop their business in the long-term perspective, in harmony with society. This implies a more inclusive view of business and its role; one in which engagements with stakeholders are not just used to legitimise corporate decisions, but rather the foundation for how it conducts and grows its business. It is about innovation, opportunity and planning for the long term.

The Triple Bottom is the principle behind our way of doing business. The company's Articles of Association state that it 'strives to conduct its activities in a financially, environmentally and socially responsible way.' This is a commitment to sustainable development and balanced growth, and it has been built into corporate governance structures, management tools and methods of assessing and rewarding individuals' performance…

The stakeholder dimension: Novo Nordisk needs to stay attuned to emerging trends and 'hot issues' on the global agenda in order to respond and to contribute to the debate. Stakeholder engagement is an integrated part of our business philosophy. We have long-standing engagements with stakeholders that are vital for building trust and understanding of a variety of issues. By involving stakeholders in the decision-making processes, decisions are better founded and solutions more likely to succeed. Stakeholders are defined as any individual or group that may affect or be affected by a company's activities.

Translating commitment to action: Corporate sustainability has made a meaningful difference to our business, and we believe it is a driver of our business success. This is best illustrated in three examples:

Business ethics: Surveys indicate that ethical behaviour in business is today the number one driver of reputation for pharmaceutical companies. Any company that is not perceived by the public as behaving in an ethical manner is likely to lose business, and it takes a long time to regain trust. While the Novo Nordisk Way of Management is a strong guide to our behaviour, we decided we needed more detailed guidance in the area of business ethics. In 2005 we therefore framed a new business ethics policy, in line with universally accepted high standards, backed by a set of procedures. Since then we have trained managers and employees, held workshops and offered e-learning on the new policy.

Climate change: We need to act to put a brake to human-induced climate change. While the implications of climate change pose major business risks, there are also opportunities. We have partnered with the WWF [World Wildlife Fund] in the Climate Savers programme and set an ambitious target to achieve a 10% reduction in our company's CO_2 emissions by 2014, compared with 2004 emission levels. This will occur through optimised production, energy savings, and greater use of renewable energy supplies.

The diabetes pandemic: Today, diabetes is recognised as a pandemic. Novo Nordisk responds to this major societal challenge by working in partnerships with many others to rally the attention of policy-makers and influencers to change diabetes. We have made a promise of **Changing Diabetes®** and have framed **a strategy for inclusive access to diabetes care**. We established the **World Diabetes Foundation**, and have made several initiatives to advocate for change and build evidence of diabetes developments. **The National Changing Diabetes® programme** and **DAWN** are examples of education and awareness programmes implemented by Novo Nordisk affiliates in their respective countries. Our **Changing Diabetes® Bus** that promotes Novo Nordisk's global Changing Diabetes® activities had reached 86,000 people by the end of 2007 during its world tour. Its primary goal is to support the **UN Resolution on diabetes**, which was passed in December 2006.

Source: www.novonordisk.com, accessed November 2008.

Appendix 2

HELSINKI DECLARATION OF THE WORLD MEDICAL ASSOCIATION
(EXCERPTS)

10. It is the duty of the physician in medical research to protect the life, health, privacy, and dignity of the human subject.

13. The design and performance of each experimental procedure involving human subjects should be clearly formulated in an experimental protocol. This protocol should be submitted for consideration, comment, guidance, and where appropriate, approval to a specially appointed ethical review committee, which must be independent of the investigator, the sponsor or any other kind of undue influence. This independent committee should be in conformity with the laws and regulations of the country in which the research experiment is performed. The committee has the right to monitor ongoing trials. The researcher has the obligation to provide monitoring information to the committee, especially any serious adverse events. The researcher should also submit to the committee, for review, information regarding funding, sponsors, institutional affiliations, other potential conflicts of interest and incentives for subjects.

14. The research protocol should always contain a statement of the ethical considerations involved and should indicate that there is compliance with the principles enunciated in this Declaration.

15. Medical research involving human subjects should be conducted only by scientifically qualified persons and under the supervision of a clinically competent medical person. The responsibility for the human subject must always rest with a medically qualified person and never rest on the subject of the research, even though the subject has given consent.

16. Every medical research project involving human subjects should be preceded by careful assessment of predictable risks and burdens in comparison with foreseeable benefits to the subject or to others. This does not preclude the participation of healthy volunteers in medical research. The design of all studies should be publicly available.

17. Physicians should abstain from engaging in research projects involving human subjects unless they are confident that the risks involved have been adequately assessed and can be satisfactorily managed. Physicians should cease any investigation if the risks are found to outweigh the potential benefits or if there is conclusive proof of positive and beneficial results.

18. Medical research involving human subjects should only be conducted if the importance of the objective outweighs the inherent risks and burdens to the subject. This is especially important when the human subjects are healthy volunteers.

19. Medical research is only justified if there is a reasonable likelihood that the populations in which the research is carried out stand to benefit from the results of the research.

20. The subjects must be volunteers and informed participants in the research project.

21. The right of research subjects to safeguard their integrity must always be respected. Every precaution should be taken to respect the privacy of the subject, the confidentiality of the patient's information and to minimize the impact of the study on the subject's physical and mental integrity and on the personality of the subject.

Appendix 2 (continued)

22. In any research on human beings, each potential subject must be adequately informed of the aims, methods, sources of funding, any possible conflicts of interest, institutional affiliations of the researcher, the anticipated benefits and potential risks of the study and the discomfort it may entail. The subject should be informed of the right to abstain from participation in the study or to withdraw consent to participate at any time without reprisal. After ensuring that the subject has understood the information, the physician should then obtain the subject's freely-given informed consent, preferably in writing. If the consent cannot be obtained in writing, the non-written consent must be formally documented and witnessed.

23. When obtaining informed consent for the research project the physician should be particularly cautious if the subject is in a dependent relationship with the physician or may consent under duress. In that case the informed consent should be obtained by a well-informed physician who is not engaged in the investigation and who is completely independent of this relationship.

29. The benefits, risks, burdens and effectiveness of a new method should be tested against those of the best current prophylactic, diagnostic, and therapeutic methods. This does not exclude the use of placebo, or no treatment, in studies where no proven prophylactic, diagnostic or therapeutic method exists.

Note of clarification on paragraph 29 of the WMA Declaration of Helsinki
The WMA hereby reaffirms its position that extreme care must be taken in making use of a placebo-controlled trial and that in general this methodology should only be used in the absence of existing proven therapy. However, a placebo-controlled trial may be ethically acceptable, even if proven therapy is available, under the following circumstances:

- Where for compelling and scientifically sound methodological reasons its use is necessary to determine the efficacy or safety of a prophylactic, diagnostic or therapeutic method; or
- Where a prophylactic, diagnostic or therapeutic method is being investigated for a minor condition and the patients who receive placebo will not be subject to any additional risk of serious or irreversible harm.

All other provisions of the Declaration of Helsinki must be adhered to, especially the need for appropriate ethical and scientific review.

30. At the conclusion of the study, every patient entered into the study should be assured of access to the best proven prophylactic, diagnostic and therapeutic methods identified by the study.

Note of clarification on paragraph 30 of the WMA Declaration of Helsinki
The WMA hereby reaffirms its position that it is necessary during the study planning process to identify post-trial access by study participants to prophylactic, diagnostic and therapeutic procedures identified as beneficial in the study or access to other appropriate care. Post-trial access arrangements or other care must be described in the study protocol so the ethical review committee may consider such arrangements during its review.

Source: www.wma.net/e/policy/b3.htm, accessed October 2008.

Appendix 3

CLINICAL TRIALS: NOVO NORDISK'S POSITION

- Clinical trials sponsored by Novo Nordisk will always be conducted according to the Helsinki Declaration, which describes human rights for patients participating in clinical trials, and similar international ethical guidelines such as the Nuremberg code, the Belmont report and CIOMMS, and the International Conference of Harmonisation (ICH) guidelines for current good clinical practice (cGCP).
- The above guidelines and regulations are the foundation for our clinical Standard Operating Procedures (SOPs) including the SOP on the 'principles of clinical trials'. These standards are laid out to ensure the safety, rights, integrity, confidentiality and well-being of persons involved in Novo Nordisk trials globally.
- Novo Nordisk will apply the same procedures wherever we sponsor clinical trials. This means that all subjects enrolled in Novo Nordisk trials are protected by the same rights, high ethical standards and regulations irrespective of location of the study.
- The interest and well-being of the trial subject should always prevail over the interest of science, society and commerce.
- Novo Nordisk will not conduct clinical trials for drug development in countries where we do not intend to market the investigational drug. In any country where we do undertake clinical trials we will ensure that a proper internal organisation and a proper regulated external environment exist.
- Clinical trials should only be done if they can be scientifically and medically justified, and all Novo Nordisk-sponsored trials should be based on sound scientific methodology described in a clear and detailed protocol. Placebo will only be used as comparator when scientifically and ethically justified.
- No trial activity in Novo Nordisk-sponsored trials will start before approval is obtained from external local ethics committees and health authorities.
- We will always ensure that investigators involved in Novo Nordisk clinical trials are skilled in the therapeutic area and are trained in GCP. No procedure involving a person undergoing clinical trial activities will take place before the appropriate freely given informed consent is obtained based on proper information on potential risk of participation in the trial. A patient can at any time withdraw from a clinical trial without giving any reason. In cases where trial subjects are incompetent, physically or mentally incapable of giving consent, or if the person is a minor, Novo Nordisk will follow local regulations for obtaining consent.
- Products used in Novo Nordisk-sponsored clinical trials will be manufactured and controlled according to international and local regulations and laws. Novo Nordisk will conduct frequent site monitoring to ensure that the study is executed according to the study protocol, and that data used in statistical analysis and reporting reflects the data obtained from the involved patients during the trial. Safety information from any Novo Nordisk trial will be monitored on a continuous basis and appropriate actions will be taken if risks of the investigational product outweigh the potential benefits.
- Patients participating in Novo Nordisk-sponsored clinical trials will always be offered best available and proven treatment after study termination. The treatment will be offered at the discretion of the responsible physician. If study medication is not marketed the responsible physician can apply for medication on a named patient basis. Post-study medication will be described in the protocol and informed consent.
- Novo Nordisk will ensure proper indemnification of trial subjects in case a trial product or procedures in a Novo Nordisk-sponsored trial cause bodily harm to a trial subject.
- Novo Nordisk strives to have all clinical trial results published according to accepted international guidelines, and we will always ensure transparency of our studies by publishing protocol synopses on the external website: **www.clinicaltrials.gov**. Study results from trials involving marketed drugs can be accessed via **www.clinicalstudyresults.org**. Furthermore, Novo Nordisk has its own online repository for clinical trials activities: novonordisk-trials.com. Novo Nordisk is collating all information about bioethics in the R&D area on **www.novonordisk.com/R&D/bioethics**.

Source: www.novonordisk.com, accessed November 2008.

JOHANNES VAN DEN BOSCH SENDS AN EMAIL

Professor Joe DiStefano prepared this mini-case as a basis for class discussion rather than to illustrate either effective or ineffective handling of a business situation.

The mini-case reports events as they occurred. The email exchanges in both cases are reported verbatim, except for the names, which have been changed. Professor DiStefano acknowledges with thanks the cooperation of "Johannes van den Bosch" in providing this information and his generous permission to use the material for executive development.

After having had several email exchanges with his Mexican counterpart over several weeks without getting the expected actions and results, Johannes van den Bosch was getting a tongue-lashing from his British MNC client, who was furious at the lack of progress. Van den Bosch, in the Rotterdam office of BigFiveFirm, and his colleague in the Mexico City office, Pablo Menendez, were both seasoned veterans, and van den Bosch couldn't understand the lack of responsiveness.

A week earlier, the client, Malcolm Smythe-Jones, had visited his office to express his mounting frustration. But this morning he had called with a stream of verbal abuse. His patience was exhausted.

Feeling angry himself, van den Bosch composed a strongly worded message to Menendez, and then decided to cool off. A half hour later, he edited it to "stick to the facts" while still communicating the appropriate level of urgency. As he clicked to send the message, he hoped that it would finally provoke some action to assuage his client with the reports he had been waiting for.

He reread the email, and as he saved it to the mounting record in Smythe-Jones's file, he thought, "I'm going to be happy when this project is over for another year!"

Message for Pablo Menendez

Subject: *IAS 1998 Financial statements*

Author: *Johannes van den Bosch (Rotterdam)*

Date: *10/12/99 1:51 p.m.*

Dear Pablo,

This morning I had a conversation with Mr. Smythe-Jones (CF0) and Mr. Parker (Controller) re the finalization of certain 1998 financial statements. Mr. Smythe-Jones was not in a very good mood.

He told me that he was very unpleased by the fact that the 1998 IAS financial statements of the Mexican subsidiary still has not been finalized. At the moment he holds us responsible for this process. Although he recognizes that local management is responsible for such financial statements, he blames us for not being responsive on this matter and inform him about the process adequately. I believe he also recognizes that we have been instructed by Mr. Whyte (CEO) not to do any handholding, but that should not keep us from monitoring the process and inform him about the progress.

He asked me to provide him tomorrow with an update on the status of the IAS report and other reports pending.

Therefore I would like to get the following information from you today:

- What has to be done to finalize the Mexican subsidiary's IAS financials;

- Who has to do it (local management, B&FF Mexico, client headquarters, B&FF Rotterdam,

- A timetable when things have to be done in order to finalize within a couple of weeks or sooner;

- A brief overview why it takes so long to prepare and audit the IAS f/s

- Are there any other reports for 1998 pending (local gaap, tax), if so the above is also applicable for those reports.

As of today I would like to receive an update of the status every week. If any major problems arise during the finalization process I would like to be informed immediately. The next status update is due January 12, 2000.

Mr. Smythe-Jones also indicated that in the future all reports (US GAAP, local GAAP and IAS) should be normally finalized within 60 days after the balance sheet date. He will hold local auditors responsible for monitoring this process.

Best regards and best wishes for 2000.

Johannes

JOHANNES VAN DEN BOSCH RECEIVES A REPLY

Professor Joe DiStefano prepared this mini-case as a basis for class discussion rather than to illustrate either effective or ineffective handling of a business situation.

The mini-case reports events as they occurred. The email exchanges in both cases are reported verbatim, except for the names, which have been changed. Professor DiStefano acknowledges with thanks the cooperation of "Johannes van den Bosch" in providing this information and his generous permission to use the material for executive development.

A little more than an hour later, with his own patience again wearing thin, Johannes van den Bosch watched with relief as Pablo Menendez's name popped into his Inbox messages. His smile quickly turned to disbelief, and then horror, as he read the response from Mexico City. Not only was the client's need still unmet, but now he had another problem! Stung by the apparent anger from Menendez, and totally puzzled as to the cause, he reread the email to make sure he had not misunderstood the message.

------*Original Message*------

From:	*Menendez, Pablo (Mexico City)*
Sent:	*Wednesday December 10, 23:11*
To:	*van den Bosch, Johannes (Rotterdam)*
Subject:	*RE: IAS 1998 financial statements*
Importance:	*High*

Dear Johannes,

I am not surprised of the outcome of your meeting with Mr. Smythe-Jones (CFO). However, I cannot answer your request until I heard from local management. As it was agreed on the last meeting, we were precluded from doing any work without first getting approval from management at the headquarters and we were instructed by local management from not doing anything until they finalized what was required from us. It appears to me to be a Catch 22 game! I believe we (your Firm and ours) should not fall in the game of passing the ball to someone else before getting a clear understanding of what is going on. We have had several meetings with local management where the issue has been raised and were responded that other priorities were established by the headquarters (on my end I thought they tell you everything they have been instructed of locally, unfortunately it does not seem to be the case). In my opinion it looks very easy that you accept from management at the headquarters to hold us accountable from something we are not responsible of, and this does not mean I do not understand the pressure you are receiving from your end. However, we are not the enemy. I am not sending copy of this message to our client because I believe that internal issues have to be primarily dealt of internally without involving our clients in the internal politics. The last is what myself truly believe.

Could you tell me how can you accept a deadline from our Firm without first having involved local management? Don't you think they are the first to be involved local management? Don't you think they are the first to be involved on this? I may be wrong but if we are in an international Firm I think we should understand the other side and not just blame someone else of our client's problems. .

I really do not want to be rude, but you do not let me any option.

Despite the differences we have had, it has been a pleasure working with you.

Best regards and seasons greeting.

Pablo Menendez

Worried that he had somehow offended Menendez, van den Bosch printed off a copy of the email which he had sent the day before, and asked the two partners on either side of his office for their reaction to the message. The audit and tax specialists, one Dutch and the other Belgian, had nearly identical replies. "It seems to me that you got the point across clearly, Johannes," they said. "You laid out the facts and proposed actions to solve the problem. Why do you ask?" they queried. When he showed them the letter, they too were puzzled. "Smythe-Jones will no doubt be the next person to send me a message!" he thought. As a frown reflected his increasingly grim mood, van den Bosch wondered what he should do now.

Harvard Business Review

www.hbr.org

Should Evan try to persuade the board to hang on to Rob, or should he back an ouster for the innovative but abrasive CEO?

Four commentators offer expert advice.

The CEO Who Couldn't Keep His Foot out of His Mouth

by Lisa Burrell

Reprint R0612A

Four years into the job, a top executive has revitalized his company's financial performance. But his verbal gaffes threaten to ruin staff morale, alienate customers, and drag down the firm's share price. Is it time for him to go?

HBR CASE STUDY

The CEO Who Couldn't Keep His Foot out of His Mouth

by Lisa Burrell

"Here's where the one-year-olds hang out," said Evan Breyer, the chairman and founder of Growing Places, ushering the small tour group into the Infant 2 room. He couldn't remember the last time he'd helped with a tour at the child care company's flagship facility. Probably not since he'd opened it seven years ago. This was a special case, though—he needed to be on hand to meet some important guests. Besides, he always got a kick out of seeing the children.

Judy Snow, the vice president of corporate affairs, led everyone inside. Four kids decked out in big, sloppy art shirts, elbow deep in shaving cream, were seated along the outer curve of a cashew-shaped table. They smeared and slapped at the mess in front of them.

"That's one of our sensory stations," Judy said. "As you can see, it's a hit."

The other three children in the room were digging through a large toy chest and stockpiling choice pieces of loot. Elmo dolls of all sizes

figured heavily in the mix. Judy gestured toward a shelf holding tubs of Cheerios, raisins, and Goldfish crackers, joking to the tour group, "Anyone want a snack?"

In response to this apparently general invitation, a little girl dropped the maracas she'd been clutching and toddled over to the food. The teacher closest to the bins dipped into the raisins with a Dixie cup and said, "Okay, Ada, but just a few."

Judy chuckled and continued with her spiel about activities that develop fine motor skills. After they finished up in Infant 2, Evan thought, they should peek in on the babies—a sweet note to end the tour on—before meeting up with Rob Miranda, the CEO, for lunch.

Evan had asked Judy to arrange this walkabout to woo a potential sponsor for a new program. The board of Growing Places wanted the company to provide scholarships for kids whose families demonstrated financial need, and a cor-

---

HBR's cases, which are fictional, present common managerial dilemmas and offer concrete solutions from experts.

porate sponsor seemed like the perfect way to pay for the scholarships. Of the companies considered, the most promising turned out to be Thrivand, a maker of infant formulas, cereals, and beginners' foods. The board hoped to offer scholarships at a number of the company's day care facilities to start with and then, if the sponsor was pleased with the good press, extend the program to the other centers.

Delores Dayton, head of PR at Thrivand, had seemed enthusiastic about the idea; she'd agreed to fly with a few of her colleagues to Dublin, Ohio, to see Growing Places' flagship facility and talk over the possibilities. Judy had asked Evan if she could invite a local reporter to tag along for the tour. The reporter had been calling her because he was working on a piece about child care in the community. "Sure," Evan had said. "Let's make it a twofer." He'd heard that Delores was incredibly warm. She could probably be counted on to coo over the little ones and ask nice questions. She'd set a pleasant tone for the coverage.

Delores did her job nicely. She fell in love with every child she met, even the rowdy preschoolers. When the group stepped into the Infant 1 room for a minute to say hello to the babies, Delores put a hand to her chest.

Evan laughed. "Sorry," he said. "We can't let you take any of them home."

"You don't know how much of a pleasure this is for me," she said. "I spend all my time talking about what's good for children, but I don't get to *spend time* with them. My own are all grown up!"

As the group headed upstairs to the corporate offices, where they had left their things, Evan heard Rob's voice in the hallway. Good, he thought. After the reporter left, they could all head to lunch together.

Evan led the way into his office, which he had kept after Rob had succeeded him as CEO four years ago and Evan had scaled back his role. He scooped up the coats that were slung on the back of his desk chair.

"What'd you think?" Rob blurted as he burst into Evan's office not 30 seconds later. As everyone turned toward the door, Evan took the opportunity to swipe some dust off his desk with his sleeve. He didn't spend a lot of time there, but it was starting to look as though he'd have to come in more often, given the additional supervision Rob had seemed to require lately.

"It was lovely," Delores said.

"What was lovely about it?" Rob wanted to know. He smiled a little, but his tone wasn't light. He wanted specifics, so he asked for them. That was his style.

Delores graciously complied. "The teachers—where did you find them? They're so seasoned. I expected to meet a bunch of kids right out of high school. There were a few, but most of your staff seem quite experienced."

"We pay them," Rob said simply. "What else?"

Evan wished Rob would tone it down a little, but he knew that probably wouldn't happen. Although Rob generated great ideas and had a gift for putting them in motion—the company had him to thank for its recent rapid growth—he didn't give two hoots about diplomacy. In fact, he took a certain amount of pride in his no-nonsense approach to business and the success it had brought him in a touchy-feely industry.

"The lactation rooms Judy told us about are a stroke of brilliance," Delores added, willing enough, at this point, to heap on the praise. She was right, too—they were one of Rob's many ideas that had paid off. Growing Places provided mostly on-site child care and preschool classes for 60 companies in the midwestern United States. At each center, the children's parents worked right next door, and Rob had spent time drumming up ways to capitalize on their proximity. Since women who breastfeed often have a hard time keeping up with it after they return from maternity leave, Rob had figured they would appreciate a convenient place to nurse their babies during breaks in the workday. The lactation rooms had been a huge draw—instrumental in winning over many parents who'd considered hiring a nanny or choosing a day care center closer to home—and the host companies were thrilled to have such an attractive perk to add to their recruitment tools.

"The moms do like them," Rob said. "What gets me, though, is how long some of these kids nurse. If they're old enough to ask for Coke, it's time to move on."

You've got to be kidding, Evan thought. Delores had tossed Rob a softball—why'd he have to go and say something like that?

Delores didn't appear to take offense, however. She patted her coat pocket for her car keys and said, "You guys want a ride to the re

Lisa Burrell (lburrell@hbsp.harvard .edu) is a manuscript editor at HBR.

aurant? I can bring you back here on my way
o the hotel."

"That'd be great," Evan said, relieved. "I
hought we'd go to LaScala. Want me to sit in
ront and help you navigate? The access roads
an be tricky." If Rob sat in the backseat, Evan
hought, maybe he'd keep his mouth shut.
Rob, giving his knuckles a quick, loud crack,
ooked oblivious. He probably had no idea
ow lucky he was that Delores hadn't reacted
o his remark.

The reporter stood by the door, quietly
cribbling.

t's Cleanup Time!

he next morning, Evan decided to brave the
ush-hour trip into headquarters for the sec-
nd day in a row. Although Rob seemed to
ave fared well with Delores—the lunch and
he good-byes went fine—Evan thought there
ould still be some fallout. He was right. When
e arrived at his office, Judy was waiting out-
de his door.

"Hey, Evan. Sorry to pester you first thing,"
he said. "I couldn't reach Rob."

"What's up? Did Delores back out?"

"Nope. But the *Sentinel* ran a raging edito-
al on Rob's nursing comment."

"Oh," Evan said. "The reporter."

"The quote's accurate, as Delores would at-
st, so there's certainly no denying it. But we
ould still be okay. I mean, bad coverage in
he *Sentinel* isn't exactly the end of the world,
s long as it doesn't spread. I've made an ap-
ointment to meet with the editor in chief to
y to contain the damage."

"In case there is some sort of uproar, PR
ould prepare a public statement of apology."

"We're already on it."

"I think you're right," Evan said. "It could be
orse. The board will be annoyed, but we can
eal with this."

After Judy left, Evan headed outside for a
uick walk around the block to clear his head.
e thought back to when the board, at his urg-
g, had brought in Rob to infuse the business
ith some fresh thinking and to shake things
a bit. During the company's first few years,
hen Evan himself was CEO, Growing Places
ad struggled just to break even. Of course, it
asn't his fault entirely: Child care was a tough
eld, and only the most innovative companies
rned even a modest profit. In the end, the
oard agreed with Evan that Growing Places

needed a leader who wasn't born and bred in
the industry—someone who had a different
perspective on the challenges the company
faced and could find creative ways to generate
profitable growth.

During the search, Rob immediately distinguished himself as an attractive, though unlikely, candidate. For nearly ten years, he had
been the president of a small insurance company. When he first had taken charge there,
the company had been stable but unimpres-
sive; by the end of his tenure, it had grown dramatically. His tack had been to focus and then
refocus the company's objectives, always tar-
geting a new goal—reducing whole-life under-
writing losses, for instance, or boosting sales of
disability policies—before he'd worked the previous one to the bone.

Rob was experimental, a little restless, and
an entrepreneur at heart, never happier than
when six or eight pots were cooking at once, all
at different temperatures. He'd seemed to be
the kind of leader Growing Places needed to
pull ahead in a field where high accreditation
standards meant that most companies worth
their salt did things more or less the same way.
To the board's delight, Rob had turned out to
be a veritable font of ideas.

For starters, he'd suggested, why not carve
out a niche and provide on-site care for client
companies? It hadn't occurred to the board before, but why not, indeed? To recruit and retain star talent, more and more companies in
major cities on the East and West coasts were
contracting with on-site child care providers. It
would take some effort to persuade large companies in the Midwest to do the same, but this
was a rare opportunity to stand out among
competitors. With that critical change in strategy, Growing Places had expanded over the
past four years from six freestanding, garden-
variety facilities in Ohio to ten times that number of on-site facilities at companies and universities in five states.

Rob also had a knack for knowing which services his clients really wanted. For example, although market research had indicated, at best,
lukewarm interest in Webcams, which allow
parents to "visit" their kids over the Internet
without leaving their desks, Rob had insisted
that Growing Places offer the service. It turned
out that more than half of Growing Places'
customers were willing to pay $50 a month for
something that cost the company next to noth-

If Rob sat in the backseat, Evan thought, maybe he'd keep his mouth shut. Rob, giving his knuckles a quick, loud crack, looked oblivious.

ing to provide.

Even before Rob was hired, though, Evan and the rest of the board had been well aware that Rob's entrepreneurial vision came with an abrasive personality and some disregard for social convention. They'd expected him to cross a line or two—and Rob had delivered. His comment at the end of the tour certainly wasn't his first verbal gaffe; in fact, it echoed earlier remarks he'd made to staff members. For example, when a few senior managers had questioned the wisdom of considering Thrivand as a sponsor because of its aggressive marketing of infant formulas—one of them had asked, "Why associate our brand with a practice that's detrimental to mother and child?"—Rob told them to get over themselves and leave the propaganda at home.

And then there was his comment about lesbian adoptions. Evan felt his shoulders tense up as he recalled the incident. At a recent staff retreat, managers had talked about ways to make sure that adopted children and the children of gay parents didn't feel different from their classmates. Rob stopped the discussion cold: "The point'll be moot if China follows through on its adoption policy and keeps lesbian couples from snapping up its girl babies." Could he be serious? Maybe it was a joke—but no one was laughing.

After that meeting, Evan had told Rob that he needed to find a coach to help him with his emotional intelligence. Rob had laughed but did begin seeing a coach recommended by Growing Places' HR chief. Evan wondered, given recent events, how much progress Rob was making and whether he'd even agree to issue a company apology if his breastfeeding comment got more press.

Choosing Rob had been a calculated risk, Evan thought as he rounded the third corner of the block—and so far, it had paid off. But had Rob crossed one line too many?

If You Don't Have Something Nice to Say...

Evan had agreed to get together with Alex Horowitz, a friend and fellow board member, at a high school gymnastics meet, where Alex's daughter would be competing. It'd been ten days since the *Sentinel* story had come out. Both men had been booked for most of the previous week, and they really wanted to talk in person. This was the only way they could

squeeze in a conversation before the board meeting.

Evan pulled into the parking lot of Dublin South High School, right behind the visiting team's bus. He hoped Alex was there already maybe they could talk before the meet began But when he made his way into the gym, h couldn't find Alex. He climbed to the top of the metal bleachers to a spot where he could get some perspective on the scene.

If Rob had managed to stay out of trouble after the nursing blooper, Evan wouldn't have needed to meet with Alex. Yet, even knowing he was on notice, Rob had done it again. At an early childhood education conference a few days after the visit from the Thrivand group he had given a spirited keynote address on the importance of student-centered preschool curricula. Afterward, he'd fielded questions. A teacher in the audience who'd identified herself as one of Growing Places' own had commented that highly customized instruction was great to strive for but not always possible to implement.

Rob's response? "If you all got off your rear ends and did a little prep work, there wouldn't be a problem. Grade school teachers do it all the time; pre-K shouldn't be any different. I'm not saying it's all on you, of course. Administrators need to pony up, too, and provide some guidelines." He'd said it with a wink and a smile, thinking, Evan supposed, that a spoonful of sugar would help the medicine go down. Of course, that's not how it had worked out.

The Growing Places employees who had attended the conference had been outraged by Rob's suggestion that they weren't pulling their weight. The ones with a lot of experience were especially irked. They didn't just teach, they nurtured. And they used lesson plans that had worked wonderfully for years. How could Rob call them unprepared? Besides, the idea of developing a curriculum based on company-wide guidelines—even if it was customizable—grated on many teachers. As child care professionals, they should be trusted to improvise and cater to the mix of children in each class.

In a matter of days, about 50 teachers, most of them highly experienced, threatened to quit. On top of that, a newswire reporter had been at the conference, so the story spread to media outlets across the United States in no time. Online columnists and bloggers had

Evan and the rest of the board had been well aware that Rob's entrepreneurial vision came with an abrasive personality and some disregard for social convention.

chimed in with headlines like "Kiddie Care Exec Demands Top Quality from His Sweatshop Team."

Evan recalled that Rob had come to the company not just to spur growth but also to whip operations into shape. Evan had to admit that, under his own leadership, an incredible amount of time was consumed by staff meetings where employees were given a chance to voice their gripes. Rob had put an end to the gripe sessions. As he was fond of saying, "I can't deal with people whose feelings bruise so easily. Are we grown-ups or babies who need coddling?" He argued that the time would be better spent improving the delivery of service. Developing a curriculum that could be used across the organization was Rob's latest initiative in this vein.

Evan's thoughts were interrupted by the sight of a sullen girl wheeling out a balance beam. Gymnasts started to filter in, with nylon bags slung over their shoulders. As Alex came through the double doors with his daughter, Evan caught his attention with a wave. Alex gave his daughter a quick kiss on the head and started his ascent. Evan smiled as he watched his friend huff his way to the top of the bleachers.

"So what's going on, besides the obvious?" Evan asked when Alex plopped down beside him.

"The board members have been informally caucusing," Alex said. "Some of them are talking ouster, and Gwen's adding an 'external relations' agenda item for the meeting Thursday."

Gwen Larson was a big shareholder. Evan had known that she, among others, would be keen to pounce; the stock price had already taken a meaningful dip since the press coverage of Rob's recent comments had kicked in.

"External relations." Evan shook his head. "I hope Rob has the good sense to leave the room and let other people defend him."

"There are several who will," Alex said. "The board's divided. Half are saying we owe every ounce of our success to Rob, we'd be stupid not to take the long view, the stock'll bounce back, there wouldn't even be a stock price if it weren't for him—that kind of thing. The others are fed up with his loose-cannon crap, and as much as I hate to say it, I can see their point. If we're getting bad press and our stock is on its way down, the last thing we need is Rob's brand of 'straight shooting.' He doesn't exactly have a history of making nice. What's to say he'll start now?"

Good point, Evan had to admit. Actually, with his hackles up, Rob could get even more outspoken. Evan thanked his friend for the heads-up and, before the gymnastics meet got ramped up, threaded himself through the assembling crowd.

On his way home, Evan remembered the company's early days, when each quarter seemed as though it might be the last. Rob had come along at just the right moment, but was his time up? Both Growing Places and its client companies felt the consequences when Rob stuck his foot in it. The clients got angry, of course, because PR gaffes compromised the employee-recruitment power Growing Places was supposed to confer in the first place. And many of the offended teachers would walk unless Rob ate his words. Evan was not going to hold his breath for that.

Everyone on the board respected Evan and trusted his strategic judgment. They'd have their say at the meeting, but, ultimately, they'd follow his lead.

Should Evan try to persuade the board to hang on to Rob, or should he back an ouster for the innovative but abrasive CEO? • Four commentators offer expert advice.

See **Case Commentary**

Rob had put an end to the gripe sessions. As he was fond of saying, "I can't deal with people whose feelings bruise so easily. Are we grown-ups or babies who need coddling?"

Case Commentary

by Ronald A. Heifetz

Should Evan try to persuade the board to hang on to Rob, or should he back an ouster for the innovative but abrasive CEO?

Rob Miranda's case isn't all that unusual. If most managers didn't bring a mixed bag of strengths and weaknesses to their jobs, the entire coaching profession would go out of business.

The first step in resolving the situation is to determine if Rob has the capacity to reflect on his weaknesses. This assessment may involve some trial and error: While one coach or colleague may conclude that Rob will never admit to a problem, another may be able to get through Rob's defenses and help him see that there's work to be done.

If it becomes clear that Rob can get past this threshold of self-reflection, there are a number of possible approaches—all of which are about more than just changing Rob's behavior. My experience is that all first-rate executives in business or politics need a constellation of trusted partners—formal and informal, members of the top team or outsiders—who can complement their strengths and compensate for their weaknesses. In Rob's case, such partners would be able not only to keep him out of trouble by bluntly telling him when to shut up but also to take on some of his more sensitive communication tasks.

We often look for a technical solution to this kind of problem—hiring a coach to "fix" the person, as if he's a piece of faulty software— when the solution involves the organization itself. Very rarely are you going to turn someone into a leader for all seasons. But you can help her maximize her strengths and minimize her weaknesses in the context of the organization she leads.

Evan Breyer needs to diagnose Rob's situation to determine if the turmoil reflects complex organizational issues that Rob has intuitively spotted but ham-handedly addressed. Yes, Rob has a communication problem. But Rob's poorly packaged comments may contain valuable insights into the organization's strategy that need to be teased out and examined.

For example, when he blunders into his half-joking admonition that teachers had better get off their "rear ends," he may in fact be identify-ing a basic weakness in the organization's culture. If the board's aim is simply to eliminate the disturbance prompted by Rob's comments, it may overlook the variety of possible causes for the turmoil, the validity of the turmoil, and the need to help Rob develop a better strategy for managing it productively.

The same goes for Rob's comment about Coke and breast milk. It obviously touches a raw nerve in some people and certainly was ill considered in this setting (although, you might ask, doesn't anyone have a sense of humor here?). But the howls of outrage also undoubtedly reveal women's conflicted feelings about their ability to nurture their children in a fast-paced working world. Embedded in his off-hand comment is the suggestion of perhaps a new type of service, revenue generating or not, that Growing Places might offer: classes or discussion groups, possibly led by veteran parents, in which new parents could share their anxieties and questions about—even laugh about—such charged topics as how long to breastfeed or when to let your children sleep in your bed.

Rob needs to work on his communication skills. But a fabulous communicator with well honed diplomatic skills may end up masking organizational issues and missing opportunities to generate something truly new. A terrific coach would help Rob not only manage his weaknesses better but also articulate the strategic insights embedded in some of his remarks, and turn them into new product and service ideas.

Ronald A. Heifetz (heifetz@cambridge-leadership .com) is the King Hussein Bin Talal Lecturer in Public Leadership at Harvard University's John F. Kennedy School of Government in Cambridge, Massachusetts, the cofounder of the school's Center for Public Leadership, and a principal at Cambridge Leadership Associates. He is the coauthor of "The Work of Leadership" (HBR January–February 1997) and "A Survival Guide for Leaders" (HBR June 2002).

Rob's poorly packaged comments may contain valuable insights into the organization's strategy that need to be teased out and examined.

Case Commentary

by John H. Biggs

Should Evan try to persuade the board to hang on to Rob, or should he back an ouster for the innovative but abrasive CEO?

It's clear that Rob, despite the coaching he's receiving, could use additional counsel on how to improve his communication style. The person who may really need a coach in this case, however, is the chairman of the board.

Evan doesn't seem like the kind of person who's naturally going to get tough with Rob. Consequently, he needs someone—it might be an acting instructor rather than a coach—to help him forcefully display his indignation and convey to Rob his concern about the effect of Rob's actions on the company. Indeed, Evan may need to display even more indignation than he actually feels if he wants to make Rob understand the seriousness of the situation.

When Evan does deliver his stern warning, it should focus not on Rob's failings—"Can't you see how boneheaded it was to say those things in front of a reporter?"—but instead on the consequences of his mistakes. Evan's message to Rob: "I'm proud of the company that I founded. I'm terribly upset about the potential damage to its reputation."

I've faced numerous situations in which an extremely talented contributor for one reason or another didn't get along with people. Almost inevitably, part of my task was to act as the high performer's protector. People will gang up against an abrasive personality, and you have to shield him or her from their animosity—at least long enough to give the person a chance to apologize or change course.

When I was at TIAA-CREF, an exceptionally valuable senior executive made a thoughtless comment about the outstanding performance of black athletes—to an African-American member of the board. The board member was outraged and, besides demanding that I fire him, succeeded in engaging the entire board in the matter. Part of my role in defusing the situation involved defending the executive and his value to the company. It also involved a heated conversation with the executive about his misstep. Because he was a good friend, I had to work myself into a completely different role— as I think Evan needs to in this case—in order to get across to him my displeasure.

But protection can go only so far. I once hired a brilliant young analyst who had the unfortunate tendency to let colleagues know, either directly or indirectly, how stupid he thought they were. I spoke with him numerous times about this, and he was always contrite. But then he would lose his temper a few weeks later and make the same mistake. I kept him on for a couple of years. But finally, I had to say, "Enough is enough," and I fired him.

The tragedy of situations like these is that a single mistake can undo a career of good works. Harry Stonecipher resigned as Boeing's CEO for what was arguably an awkward personal situation but not a cause for termination. While married, he had a romantic relationship with a Boeing employee. After a full investigation by an outside lawyer hired by the company, it was clear he had not used his position to help the woman in her work within the company. But at the time, Harry was leading a campaign to improve the ethical climate at Boeing following a scandal over the award of Air Force contracts. Although board members were pleased with the job he was doing as CEO, in the end the board and Harry himself concluded that, given the company's current focus on living by its own code of ethics, he would have difficulty continuing to be the standard-bearer of that initiative.

Evan may need to display even more indignation than he actually feels if he wants to make Rob understand the seriousness of the situation.

John H. Biggs (jbiggs@tiaa-cref.org), the former chairman and former CEO of fund manager TIAA-CREF, is a member of the boards of Boeing and JPMorgan Chase. He is based in New York.

by Torie Clarke

Should Evan try to persuade the board to hang on to Rob, or should he back an ouster for the innovative but abrasive CEO?

In today's information environment, it's hard for one person—no matter how charismatic, articulate, or media savvy—to be a company's sole public face.

Let's get this straight: Being honest and direct is generally a good thing. I've been the communications chief for both Donald Rumsfeld and John McCain, both of them very blunt people who like to engage aggressively with audiences of all kinds. The overwhelming majority of the time, their approach works.

Any time you adopt such a forward-leaning stance—whether you're an athlete or a public official or a business leader—occasionally you're going to look back and say, "Maybe I shouldn't have done or said that." In that case, you apologize quickly and unequivocally. But usually the pluses of a straightforward style outweigh the minuses. Take Rumsfeld's infamous comment about the attitudes of "Old Europe." While it created a minor furor at the time, it was widely if not publicly viewed as a pretty accurate assessment of most of the Western European democracies. Even some of my counterparts in those countries, while they had to fuss about the comment in public, agreed with it in private.

So what to do about Rob? Evan has to lead a frank discussion with the board about whether Rob's strengths outweigh his obvious weaknesses and then choose either marriage counseling or a divorce. My sense is that it's not too late to save the company's relationship with its CEO.

If the board members choose marriage counseling, they should demand that Rob apologize to the teachers. Not some carefully couched statement—"If I've offended anyone, I'm sorry"—but a formal public apology that makes clear that he understands his thoughtless comments hurt others and himself. Rob should also begin spending more time with the teachers and other employees—something senior managers need to do even in the best of times—thereby going beyond damage repair to the building of a positive environment. In fact, Evan himself should spend more time with the teachers to get a sense of their mood.

A crucial component of marriage counseling would be to examine Rob's role as well as his behavior. Growing Places took a long time finding Rob, and he's clearly doing good things for the company. The solution might be to let him play to his strengths and steer clear of his weaknesses. Because Rob has a tendency to spout off and say outrageous things, the board may want to find other people in the company who can play a public role.

Certainly, CEOs need to be out there representing the company to customers, shareholders, analysts, and the public at large. But in today's information environment, it's hard for one person—no matter how charismatic, articulate, or media savvy—to be a company's sole public face. Increasingly, a company needs a lot of senior people to share responsibility for telling its story.

This is particularly true when the person at the top has a tendency toward the loose-cannon syndrome. Consider Ted Turner. Over the years, he has been known for his sometimes outrageous comments that became public relations disasters—calling his marginalization as a leader at AOL Time Warner the equivalent of Third World female genital mutilation, for instance, and comparing the popularity of Fox News, which is a rival of his own CNN, with that of Adolf Hitler. Turner is a creative genius with enormous energy. Getting rid of him simply wasn't an option. So over the years his organization worked very hard to prepare other senior executives—members of the management team and heads of divisions—to act as spokespeople for the company.

Torie Clarke (torie@torieclarke.com), a former assistant secretary of defense for public affairs under Secretary Donald H. Rumsfeld and former press secretary for Senator John McCain, is a senior adviser to Comcast, an analyst for CNN, and the author of *Lipstick on a Pig: Winning in the No-Spin Era by Someone Who Knows the Game* (Free Press, 2006). She is based in Washington, DC.

Case Commentary

by Roger Brown

Should Evan try to persuade the board to hang on to Rob, or should he back an ouster for the innovative but abrasive CEO?

It's time for Evan and his board to tell Rob that he's the wrong person to be leading Growing Places. I say that for two reasons, both of which have to do with the managerial context of this case.

For one thing, child care, more than almost any field you can imagine, requires a humane, caring, and values-centered management style. Because the care of young children evokes strong passions in nearly everyone, you have to be unusually sensitive to the needs of the children, the parents, and the teachers, and to the nurturing relationships among them all. Hand in hand with such sensitivity must be an engaged and participatory management style— something that Rob clearly lacks—throughout the organization. You can't expect Rob's kind of autocratic leadership style to morph into a participatory, child-centered approach as you move down the organization and into the classroom.

Think about it. If you're in a business where extreme confidentiality is required—a defense contractor, say—and the senior leader can't keep a secret, you can be sure there will be breaches throughout the system. If you're in a business like medical equipment manufacturing, where manufacturing tolerances are in the micrometers, you don't want senior leaders regularly showing up late for meetings or missing deadlines. In software development, by contrast, a few big ideas are often more important than manufacturing precision, so the industry is often marked by a freewheeling culture—a culture that would be a little scary in the case of a medical equipment manufacturer.

None of these management styles is inherently better than the others. Rob might be an excellent leader—in fact, he apparently was— in another setting. But he's unlikely to be one here over the long term.

The other reason Rob has to go relates not to his weaknesses but to his strengths. Clearly, there's a role for creativity in this business. Child care is a tough industry with low margins; everyone has explored add-on services

An approach focused on customer transactions can't drive the culture or the business of Growing Places.

like dry cleaning that people might be willing to pay extra for. Rob's innovative programs have helped the business grow.

But an approach focused on customer transactions can't drive the culture or the business of Growing Places. Child care is a huge expense for most parents, and if financial success is the only aim of your business, this will come back to haunt you. Ninety-five percent of your revenue comes from the core service of providing child care. And you aren't going to keep your centers full with clever marketing or add-on services. You're going to achieve that through word-of-mouth recommendations across the ultimate social network: the parents of young children. Rob's business innovations mean little if he's offending the parents who serve as his marketers or the teachers in whom parents place enormous trust.

One other thought: Evan acts as if Rob is the only one who can bring a creative approach to the business. It feels almost as if he's working for Rob. This often happens in the case of a blustery, autocratic, alpha-male leader. Evan has to stop and ask himself, Is this the kind of organization I wanted to create and be associated with? Do I have to live with Rob's mistakes and insults? Is there no one else in the world who has Rob's business talents *and* values that are consistent with the organization? The answer to all three questions is no.

Roger Brown (rhbrown@berklee.edu), president of Berklee College of Music in Boston, is the cochairman and cofounder of Bright Horizons, the world's largest provider of employer-sponsored child care and an organization frequently cited on lists of employee-friendly workplaces. He is the author of "How We Built a Strong Company in a Weak Industry" (HBR February 2001).

Reprint R0612A
Case only R0612X
Commentary only R0612Z
To order, call 800-988-0886
or 617-783-7500 or go to www.hbr.org

TOUGH GUY

A mere half-block away from the office on a pleasing fall day—the kind that caught the attention of most New Yorkers—Jeremy Frazer, an associate at the investment bank Hudson Smith Gordon ("Hudson") thought about Chip Mazey, one of the vice presidents he was working with on a negotiation. Frazer and three other members working on the deal, Jean Fenster, Rich Patten, and Payton Edwards, had finally confided in each other about what it was like to work for the VP.

They found themselves in a difficult situation, one that most of them thought they had no power to change. After all, doing something about Mazey's behavior was tricky business. First was the fear of confronting Mazey. Another concern was the likelihood that Mazey would probably deny his behavior or wouldn't think that a problem existed. Then there was the unease about escalating the discussion to include a conversation with Mazey's boss. Going upstairs might cause a tense situation to become even worse. Not really knowing what to do irked Frazer, though he couldn't exactly say why. He thought about the stories his coworkers had shared.

Bulge, Middle, or Boutique?

The lure of high risk and high reward made investment banking an attractive career for many in the world of finance. Organizations employed investment banks to help work out financial problems. Offering a mix of business activities, investment banks issued securities, helped investors to purchase securities, managed financial assets, traded securities, and provided financial advice. Investment banks came in several sizes. The largest were called "bulge bracket" firms; the "middle market" companies tended to be regionally based; and "boutique" banks were smaller and more specialized. As a "middle market" firm, Hudson was oriented toward financial analysis and program trading.

To support their security sales and trading activities, investment banks hired and maintained large staffs of research analysts. As Frazer described:

> In investment banking, you make deals for companies to raise capital—debt or equity. Research supports that effort. By becoming expert in a particular field, you generate more business. My firm is considered the leading expert on wireless carriers. This reputation translates into wireless communication companies' wanting Hudson to do research on them.

Making the Deals with a Fast-tracker

Chip Mazey had been with Hudson 10 years and followed the "kiss up, kick down" mantra. His verbal lashings were sharp, unrelenting, and unprovoked. He had developed a nasty reputation among analysts and associates, which was passed to the firm's top management only through their 360° review system. Mazey was very careful not to show his true colors when senior management was within earshot, but as a result of the negative comments from below, his initial promotion to vice president was postponed. The decision came as a shock to him, because he believed he had always been submissive to upper management. Despite his poor people skills, Mazey was a solid banker, and he received the promotion as scheduled one year later.

As a vice president, Mazey's swagger and bravado increased exponentially. Mazey always had trouble interacting with his peers, but after his promotion, he was more ruthless to his subordinates than his peers. He often referred to subordinates as "you" or "analyst" and he reminded others of his new title by telling them, "I am superior to you." It was common for him to yell at a subordinate in a rage, only to discover that he had made an error and there was no problem. In such a situation, Mazey would abruptly hang up the phone when he realized his error without a goodbye or apology. The targets of his verbal abuse disliked working with him and tried to spend time working on projects with other bankers.

The first time Frazer worked with Mazey was on a project Mazey was heading up. "I was assigned to this "kick-ass multibillion dollar deal," Frazer said. "Even better than that was the fact that the deal team included the vice president, so I was extremely excited about the opportunity." The vice president was in charge of leading the deal and had a reputation of being "dynamic" and on the "fast track." Frazer's enthusiasm faded somewhat when he stepped into Mazey's office. During their initial meeting, Mazey ordered Frazer to stand "right here" and pointed to a spot on the floor in front of his desk. The associate felt uneasy about being spoken to in this manner, but because it was the first time he had worked with Mazey, he decided not to mention anything—it was best to let things go. After all, investment banks had a reputation for being infested with Type-A personalities. Some "I-bankers" had told Frazer that the biggest challenge in an investment banking career was to manage upward.

Over the next several weeks, Frazer witnessed Mazey's insulting and derogatory behavior toward other associates and analysts. Tension was part of being around him. "Fortunately, I worked on multiple assignments, reporting to various other managers at the same time," Frazer said. "The dynamics on other assignments were in stark contrast to this particular one. So I realized how much I liked the job and how well I fit in—despite being so heavily reprimanded on a continual basis with that VP."

On a Need-to-know Basis

That Mazey was difficult to deal with was hardly news to most at Hudson. What was worthy of a headline was that Frazer seemed more willing than most to talk about his supervisor's questionable behavior. Others who had been in the organization much longer than Frazer just learned to work around Mazey's behavior—he was a control freak who made a lot of money for the company and that translated into wielding a lot of power. "I became more comfortable with some of my peers and started confiding in a few of them," Frazer said. "I realized my situation was hardly unique since everyone who had at one time worked with that VP had the same story." Things became so ugly, Frazer learned, that some full-time associates within the group bluntly refused to work with him. Jean Fenster, an analyst who also worked with Mazey on a few deals, described her experience:

> When I first started, Chip asked me to complete an assignment which would typically take a novice at least three days to finish. I was handed the assignment at 8 p.m. and instructed to have it finished and on his desk to look at first thing the following morning. I sat through the night cranking on the assignment and finally completed what I thought was a pretty comprehensive product. To my good fortune, there were a few experienced staff members at the office during the night who offered to vet my product. They seemed pretty happy with my work. Slightly before dawn, I laid the finalized assignment on Chip's desk. I thought it would be a great idea to go home, catch up on a couple hours of sleep, and clean up. I arrived back at the office at least 15 minutes before Chip—ready to answer any questions.

As expected, Fenster was called over to Mazey's desk the next morning. What followed, however, was unexpected. He questioned every assumption she had made, countered every explanation she offered in a derogatory manner, and nitpicked her work for an entire hour. He then asked her to redo the work based on information he forwarded via e-mail. When Fenster sat down at her desk to rework the material, she was shocked to learn that the VP was privy to that additional information *before he handed her the assignment,* information that would have made it easier to complete the work. She just couldn't fathom why this information was not forwarded to her earlier. Even more discouraging was that although she was asked to complete the work within 24 hours, the e-mail indicated they had two weeks before it was even due. That assignment was a nightmare, and every effort Fenster made toward working on it contributed to the bad dream. "Each session I had with Chip included a series of derogatory and demeaning remarks directed toward me," she said. "From my communication skills, my accent, to the way I dressed, this VP was critical."

Duck!

Fenster's story sounded eerily familiar to Rich Patten, who described a couple of his experiences with the vice president. During a conference call with a client, Patten was unable to answer a question the client posed. Mazey became enraged and began screaming at both him and the other analyst in the room. Patten said he could have helped Mazey answer the client's questions but Mazey's ranting prevented him from even speaking. "The outburst resembled that of a 2-year-old, and both of us were speechless," Patten said. "Then, still in a rage, Chip grabbed a calculator from his desktop and shattered it against the wall, just above my head!"

Later that day, Mazey apologized for his outburst, and Patten believed his apology was sincere. "I had considered going to speak with the vice president who hired me about the incident," Patten said. "But after the apology I changed my mind," Mazey asked the associate to focus on the task at hand. It was 7 p.m. and there were still at least nine hours of work that had to be completed by an 8 a.m. conference call the next morning. Mazey instructed Patten to come in to work an hour early to prepare for the call.

"I spent the entire night working, arrived home at 4:30 a.m., slept for an hour and a half, and then returned to the office at 7 a.m." Patten recalled. "Gulping down my coffee, I went to Chip's office only to find it empty." The 8 a.m. showtime came and went without any word from Mazey, who eventually rolled into the office at 10 a.m. without a word. Patten asked him about the meeting, and Mazey simply said that the meeting was changed. Patten asked another associate who was staffed on the deal about the meeting, and found out that no such meeting was ever planned!

Get to Work—Everyone!

Payton Edwards had another Mazey characteristic to share. "He's very bright and certainly very capable, but he demands complete perfection and treats subordinates as if they were subservient to him and only him," Edwards said. "Occasionally, this man would compliment me for a 'job well done.'" Yet within five minutes, Mazey would come back with some reason why it wasn't "quite right" and force him to redo his work. He was also known for forcing people to do useless, menial tasks. For example, he frequently had his administrative assistant, as well as two analysts, complete the *exact* same task. Mazey said he just wanted to make absolutely sure that when all was said and done, the task was completed perfectly. Eventually, the analysts and administrative assistant found out that they were all assigned the same task and they were peeved. They felt like he didn't trust them—and he didn't. Edwards said:

Even when it was apparent that Chip had made a mistake, he never openly acknowledged it. One time, he denied that that there were multiple buyers on a particular deal and created a hostile deal environment for many of the concerned parties. He also did not like initiative-taking, much less even consider rewarding it. When I went to him with ideas on topics to research relevant ongoing deals, he shot down my ideas and told me to work on what he wanted me to get done. When it turned out later that my ideas were good, he never gave me credit and pretended that he had thought of them himself. In fact, he went out of his way to discredit me. For example, when I was still a very novice drinker, Chip would get a kick out of having me order the wine at closing dinners. He wanted to embarrass me in public because of my lack of knowledge about wine.

Chip also made fun of the secretary who came from a poorer part of the city and where everyone seemed to have the same last name. At Christmas parties, the support staff was not allowed to bring spouses while analysts and associates were invited to bring their spouses. Chip told me that he did not feel that it was necessary to "pay to feed the secretary's husband."

Any More Questions?

Life for support staff working for Mazey was a challenge as well. He had an incessant need to know what every person was working on at all times. This was even more pronounced the lower an employee was within the organizational hierarchy. His administrative assistant, Gabriela Salaberrios, found it surprising that the VP needed to know what a secretary was typing at a given moment. Yet Mazey had to know where all employees were at all times. He provided Salaberrios with a cell phone so that he could contact her in the middle of the night to work on last-minute deal items. He was never polite, and refused to take no for an answer. More than a few times, Mazey called in the middle of the night and demanded her presence at the office. Many times he had already sent a car to get Salaberrios before she had said yes. One time, she was vacationing in Tunisia, and he called to demand her immediate return—it seemed that his idea on how a deal should go from beginning to end was to be followed by all.

So What?

Proud of his accomplishments in his career so far, Frazer had sashayed into New York with a youthful certainty that attitude would carry him. He held a job he had thought about for some time in a firm he was convinced would offer even more opportunities. Not once had he expected to get sidetracked over some middle-aged, disgruntled vice president. Yet that same VP possessed many of the characteristics Frazer had expected and indeed admired on Wall Street. Gathering all this information on Mazey had been almost cathartic. Now what, if anything, should he do with it?

Harvard Business Review ⬥

www.hbr.org

Is George guilty of micromanagement?

The Micromanager

Four commentators offer expert advice.

by Bronwyn Fryer

Reprint R0409A

George Latour bends over backward to coach his marketing director, but she considers his management style oppressive. Can they find a way to cooperate?

The Micromanager

by Bronwyn Fryer

Nine-year-old Jill slammed her pencil down on the table in frustration.

"I *hate* word problems!"

She clearly was tired and hungry. It had been an exhausting day and not just for fourth graders. George Latour's wife was visiting her mother, leaving him to manage both his children and his company. George prided himself on being a good father and a good corporate paterfamilias, but his wife's rare absences always renewed his appreciation of her stamina and general serenity.

"It's like the last one, Jilly," George said, trying to hide his impatience as Jill slumped dramatically over her workbook. He spooned some meatballs and spaghetti onto the dinner plates. "First you have to come up with the fraction. So now, tell me what the numerator would be."

He turned to see three-year-old Bobby starting to tip a full milk carton toward his glass.

"Ooops!" George snatched the teetering car-

ton from his son before it could fall forward.

"I can pour it!" Bobby shouted.

"Trust me. It's too heavy." George filled a small plastic cup with milk and placed it on the table. He gently pushed Jill's work aside and put her plate in front of her. "Here, honey. Eat your dinner and then you can finish up the homework."

George asked his children how their days had gone. Jill was proud of a good grade on her spelling test. Bobby had drawn a picture of a scary spider.

"And how was *your* day, Daddy?" Jill asked brightly, chasing an escaped strand of spaghetti.

"Fine, thank you, Jilly," said George, pleased by her polite interest.

To be perfectly honest, the day had been anything but fine. The board members had been testy at the morning meeting, where George had spent an inordinate amount of time defending the company's sales strategy.

HBR's cases, which are fictional, present common managerial dilemmas and offer concrete solutions from experts.

Everyone in the room knew that Retronics needed a boost, and he had felt the heat.

As CEO, George's mandate was to grow revenues with an eye toward taking the software-engineering firm public by 2006. Retronics had been a Silicon Valley darling during the 1990s, enjoying generous venture capital funding and boasting a long list of big-name clients. When the dot-com bubble burst, Retronics had suffered. First came the layoffs and cutbacks; then the board fired the founder. In 2003, the directors hired George, who was a seasoned executive with impressive engineering credentials and significant experience in enterprise-scale systems and operations. He had brought in some important new business. But 16 months later, revenues hadn't rebounded enough to impress investors, and other firms were beginning to pick off Retronics's market share. The board was stamping its collective feet, and George was running out of ideas.

"The business is out there," Pete Dmitrijevich, the chairman, had said. "And you have talented marketing people. Your lead stream should look better than this."

Tempted to reply that the storehouses of talent weren't as helpful as he'd hoped, George had bitten his tongue.

Bobby saw the crease deepening between his father's eyebrows. "What's wrong, Daddy?" he asked.

"Oh, nothing, Bobby," George said. "Just thinking. Eat your spaghetti."

If You Want Something Done Right
At 4:30 the next afternoon, George felt the need to stretch his legs. Walking down the hall, he saw Shelley Stern, the new marketing director, coming toward him. She was deeply engrossed in a press release draft, and he swerved to avoid her.

"How's it coming, Shelley?" George called out.

She started.

"Mind if I take a peek?" he asked.

"Uh, sure," Shelley said, handing the papers over—a little reluctantly, George thought. "I'm...still just messing around with it."

George read the press release headline aloud. "'Mortimont Corporation Adopts Prex-Pro.' Isn't that kind of a soft—"

"It's just a working title," Shelley interrupted. "I write the headlines last."

He continued to read. "How about a stron-

ger quote? Maybe something like, 'According to CEO George Latour, anyone who isn't using the PrexPro Toolset is using Stone Age technology'?"

"I just don't think they'd print that," Shelley countered. "We might have a better chance with something a little more measured."

George said patiently, "I see your point, Shelley, but it's not like they ever print these things verbatim. Any self-respecting reporter is going to assume a certain amount of hyperbole and discount it. So if you come out the gate sounding humble, they're going to figure there's really nothing there. A quote with some attitude might just get them to sit up and take notice. So," he concluded, "I'd really like to see this copy do two things: one, emphasize the innovation and, two, exude confidence."

Pursing her lips, Shelley nodded slightly.

"Thanks, Shel," George said with edgy cheeriness. "You're the best."

George knew Shelley hated to have her work criticized. But he tried to keep things constructive. If she was going to rise to her potential, she needed the feedback. And, anyway, he couldn't afford underperformance. As far as the rest of the organization was concerned, Shelley Stern was his hire—one of the first he'd made, in fact. The quality of her work reflected directly on him.

In truth, Shelley hadn't been his recruit but had come into the company by way of the board's chairman. Pete loved to describe a rock-climbing event that Shelley had invented for a trade show. The booth included a replica of the Matterhorn, a climbing wall, and a 30-foot bungee-cord drop that had been the talk of the show and produced a flood of new leads. "Just you wait," Pete had told him when George announced that Shelley had taken the job. "She's a thoroughbred. Train her in the business. Then give her her head, and you'll see what a difference she can make."

To bring her up to speed, George had had her sit in on some of the developers' meetings. She'd accompanied the sales force on client calls to see and hear from customers directly. He'd even asked the CFO to explain the company's cash flow situation to her. But he still found many of her decisions a bit off target. She was a solid project manager who knew how to produce handsome marketing collateral and wade through the logistics of trade shows. But that direct mail campaign she'd

Bronwyn Fryer (bfryer@hbsp. harvard.edu) is a senior editor at HBR.

launched? Or the format of the seminar Retronics hosted? Not how he would have done it. So he kept editing her work, explaining what really mattered to customers, how they arrived at their purchasing decisions, and how Retronics's value proposition could be made clearer. If she became more effective in the long run, that was time well invested, and it could even be personally fulfilling to mentor someone with real potential. The problem now was Shelley seemed increasingly disengaged—not as hungry to learn as she'd seemed at first. Maybe she was dealing with some personal problems. Whatever the issue was, it would have to be addressed. He couldn't keep doing her job forever.

Every Move You Make

Shelley fell onto the sofa, kicked off her shoes, and turned on the evening news. Scenes of carnage halfway across the world flared into her living room. Disgusted and depressed, she turned off the set, poured herself a glass of wine, and picked up the phone. She craved advice. She left a message for Laura, her friend and former boss, who had put a successful career on hold to raise two small children.

Shelley sipped her wine thoughtfully. She'd left a comfortable position at a successful computer hardware firm, where she'd received high accolades for her marketing work. She thought ruefully of the now-retired CEO of her previous firm, who had told her that Retronics was a "perfect next step" for her. Laura, too, had said good things about George Latour, with whom she'd worked earlier in her career. And then there were all those stock options. It seemed like a no-lose proposition. Despite the fact that she didn't know a lot about software engineering, she knew she could learn quickly.

Shelley thought again of George's breezy "You're the best." The man certainly wanted to be liked. And she had liked him, at least originally. He had enthusiastically spoken about Retronics's need to "get out there and make some noise." She thought that meant he would let her try creative things. Ha.

The phone rang.

"Hey, Shel. How's it going?"

The sound of her old friend's cheerful voice lifted her mood a little. Then Shelley heard Max, Laura's five-year-old, calling in the background.

"Why is it they start the second you get on the phone?" Laura asked rhetorically. "Hang on, Shel." Shelley heard the handset click onto a surface and listened to her friend mollify the little one. "Here is some nice white paper. Can you draw some more aliens for me?"

"Okay, all settled," said Laura as she picked up the phone. "Go ahead, Shel."

"Laura, I could use your advice. It's about George. He's driving me crazy!"

Laura listened sympathetically while Shelley described the situation. George was in her face, Shelley complained. He didn't trust her judgment. He haunted the hallways and got into conversations with her staff—sometimes getting them off track by signaling what he thought was important. He insisted on issuing a minimum of two press releases each month, even when there wasn't any real news to report. He made her tag along on sales calls to "listen in," despite the fact she had mountains of other work to do. Shelley was spread too thin. When she'd asked for help—if not additional staff, at least an outside contractor—he'd said to list everything she was working on, and he'd help her prioritize.

"Honestly, Laura, I've never had to deal with someone breathing down my neck like this. What should I do?"

"I'm sure George is under a lot of pressure," Laura offered. "Maybe he's unloading some of that on you. I'm tempted to say you should just tell him to back off and let you do your job. He might respect that. But, of course, I don't know the specifics. I guess you need to be sure, for all these things he's second-guessed you on, that he wasn't right."

Shelley bristled a little but conceded the point. "OK, a few things I admit I got wrong. But on most of it, I think my instincts have been good. I don't know the business like he does, but he should give me credit for being the better marketer. He's an engineer, for Pete's sake."

Laura laughed. "Well, maybe you shouldn't put it to him in those terms, but you ought to point out that you have some basis for your opinions. Your only other option is to just ignore him, do what you think is right, and let the results speak for themselves. Let the proof be in the pudding." There was a sound of something crashing to the floor. "Oh, Max, you should have asked for help with that! Sorry, Shel, gotta go. Can you send me an e-mail? Hang in there. Bye."

Whatever the issue was, it would have to be addressed. He couldn't keep doing her job forever.

Shelley hung up the phone reluctantly. "Maybe I should just call in sick tomorrow," she thought. "Let George make the edits himself. He's bound to change it anyway."

Sweating the Details

Early the next morning, Shelley met with Rich Hannon, who had been the project manager on one of Retronics's recent success stories—a large deployment at a national bank. She was working with him to draft a trade magazine article on the project. He'd resisted at first, worrying that the client wouldn't want to reveal what was behind its new competitive advantage. But she'd persuaded him to invite the client to coauthor the article, and, to his surprise, the client had jumped at the idea.

"Tell me about the most challenging moments in the project," she prompted the manager. "Were there any setbacks you can recall that had to be dealt with creatively?"

Rich leaned back and rubbed his chin. "I guess we were most nervous around April, when we thought we were looking at a significant overrun. But I don't think we want to put that in the article."

"You had to go back to the well with the client?" Shelley sympathized. "That's never pretty."

Rich assured her that hadn't been an option. But fortunately, he explained, a big chunk of code from another project turned out to be reusable, which his team hadn't counted on. "Good thing you thought of that," Shelley said, though she doubted it could ever be turned into exciting copy.

"To tell you the truth, it was George who thought of it," Rich explained. "He called me one night. He had the project plan right in front of him. Found some other stuff, too."

Shelley sat straighter in her chair at the mention of George. So she wasn't alone. She studied Rich's face to see whether she'd found a kindred spirit. "Kind of a mixed blessing, isn't it?" she ventured. "When George takes an interest, I mean. He can be pretty hands-on."

"Hands-on isn't the beginning of it," laughed Rich. "He's elbow deep in the stuff." But something in his manner told her not to pursue the subject further.

Is It Me or Is It Him?

"Shelley, can I speak to you for a minute in my office?" George asked.

"When George takes an interest, hands-on isn't the beginning of it. He's elbow deep in the stuff."

Shelley thought instantly of her resolve the night before to call in sick. Why hadn't she? She surely felt sick now. "What's he going to have a problem with this time?" she wondered.

George's wife and children smiled happily from a frame on his shiny desk, but he didn't look nearly as welcoming, despite his casual-Friday jeans and denim shirt.

"Hi, George," Shelley said and attempted a smile.

"Come in. Have a seat." He waved her to one of two leather chairs in front of his desk. "I want to talk about this release. This draft you sent me this morning—it's not the final one, right?"

"Should be. It's scheduled to go out this afternoon, so the reporters will have it first thing Monday. Just waiting for your blessing," Shelley answered.

"Um, I can't bless this yet," George said tensely. "Shelley, I asked you to work on the tone of this yesterday, did I not? And look at this," he said, handing her the paper. She saw that he'd crossed out some sentences and inserted new ones in his hard-to-read handwriting. "I caught two typos." He paused. He could feel the blood throbbing in his temples, but he held down his temper. "Look, I count on you to get these things right. I don't have time to worry about them myself."

Shelley's heart pounded as Laura's advice came back to her. "If I'm going to object, I'd better be right," she thought.

"I can certainly change those things," she began. "But first I should explain better why I wrote it the way I did." She took a breath and plunged ahead. "And I also wonder if we can talk a little more generally. The fact is that lately I've been fairly distressed myself."

George raised an eyebrow. "I just knew she had personal problems," he thought.

"Go ahead," he said, trying to display some emotional intelligence.

Encouraged, Shelley opened up. "Well, to be honest, I've felt a lot of pressure here lately. I believe I'm a pretty smart, talented person who knows my job and who has a lot to contribute. I deliver great results if I feel my judgment is trusted." She wanted to add, "and if I'm treated like a professional," but thought better of it. "On the other hand, I really don't do very well if I feel like someone's micromanaging me."

George's jaw worked as he struggled to keep

his composure. "Please understand that the last thing I want to do is micromanage," he said. "There are a lot of things competing for my time, and I would dearly love to take my eye off one of them and feel it was being well managed. But the fact is, if I see errors in the last draft of a press release, I begin to wonder what else is going wrong."

Shelley's lips were pressed tightly together and her eyes shone. "Whatever you do, don't cry!" she chided herself. Not trusting her voice, she simply rose from her chair, nodded, and walked out of the office.

George's first thought was to call after her, to get her to come back and resolve the issue. But he checked the impulse, suddenly aware that he would be telling her what to do. In any case, he was in no frame of mind now to listen politely while she offered a rationale for her tepid press release. "Micromanaging!" He thought of the term with disgust. Wasn't it interesting how he'd never heard really capable people complain about being micromanaged?

Is George guilty of micromanagement?
· Four commentators offer expert advice.

See Case Commentary

Case Commentary

by Jim Goodnight

Is George guilty of micromanagement?

Cut through all the psychoanalytical clutter in this case, and you're left with some basic facts. First, the company isn't meeting its goals for visibility, leads, and sales. Second, the marketing manager hasn't been successful at meeting those objectives. And, third, the CEO is ultimately responsible and will lose his job if these conditions aren't reversed.

Any CEO who ignores a situation like this doesn't deserve to drift under a golden parachute. As a CEO, I believe in trusting and empowering employees to do their jobs. I don't have the time or the interest to do it for them; I step in only when there's a clear need for new direction. That may mean telling my R&D team which new products they should be developing, setting hiring goals for my sales organization, or pushing my PR team to be more aggressive in their news releases.

The difference between setting direction and micromanagement is knowing when to get involved and when to get out of the way. Sometimes the numbers speak for themselves. If the numbers are out of line, I know I need to invest more time in a particular area. Sometimes I know just by walking the halls and listening to people. When I detect a problem or believe we need to try something new, I drill down and work with my managers to find a solution. I may have ideas, but it's up to them to show me a plan for moving forward.

Shelley may be good at marketing, but she hasn't demonstrated much leadership. She hasn't produced numbers, plans, or results to show George that she can help solve the firm's visibility and lead-generating problems. Shelley needs to get over her narrow-minded view that her professional experience makes her the only person qualified to set marketing direction. She clearly doesn't respect George's opinions because his background is in engineering. It's been my experience that creative, competent people from any background can make intelligent suggestions about other areas. Good ideas can come from anywhere, including from the customer. Shelley seems to resent George's attempt to mentor her by, among other things, inviting her on sales calls. She considers her own agenda more important than learning what's important to her target audience. Her ego is getting in the way of her development.

Shelley needs an attitude adjustment, or George needs a new marketing manager. If she disagrees with George's guidance, she should present some evidence that she has a workable strategy. Ignoring George's directives is not an effective way to get her views across; neither is walking out of a meeting without explanation. Both will ensure only that her tenure at Retronics is short-lived. She needs to develop a thicker skin and learn to accept feedback. Any employee who considers calling in sick to avoid confrontation isn't prepared for the rigor of managing the marketing program for a future IPO.

This may sound like tough talk coming from a CEO at a company that prides itself on treating its employees well. But having a cushy work environment doesn't mean being soft on performance. Employees who perform well earn the right to make decisions without having the CEO look over their shoulders. When that happens, the employees get the satisfaction of being able to exercise their creativity independently, and I get the exercise that comes from playing more golf with customers. Everyone wins.

Jim Goodnight is the CEO of SAS Institute in Cary, North Carolina.

> *Shelley needs an attitude adjustment, or George needs a new marketing manager.*

Case Commentary

by Mark Goulston

Is George guilty of micromanagement?

It sounds as though Retronics has followed the path of so many Silicon Valley start-ups founded by entrepreneurial visionaries: It has thrown out the vision with the visionary. Think about what happened at Apple. At a critical juncture, the company replaced its visionary founder with the strong operational manager John Sculley. Then Sculley failed to grow Apple, too.

The Retronics board is probably undergoing similarly painful contortions. Thinking it is better to be safe and predictable than sorry, it no doubt believed that firing the founder and replacing him with a hands-on operations guy was the solution to the company's problems. Now it is relying on a nonvisionary but highly responsible (and apparently controlling) personality to develop and articulate the company's vision.

Quite possibly, Shelley could help George formulate and communicate that vision, but her self-confidence has taken a hit. Controlling personalities have a tendency to stifle rather than nurture creative people. The need to do things in a regulated way constricts the space in which creative people need to grow. If you put a plant in a tight pot, it will not flower. Shelley's creative desire is withering at Retronics. Her initiative is being worn down and transformed into the "learned helplessness" so well described by positive-psychology expert Martin Seligman. She's falling into negative patterns: debating whether to call in sick and whining to her friends.

If Retronics's board members truly care about the company, they should consider seeking advice from the CEO they fired. Remember what happened at Apple when it asked back a more circumspect and mature Steve Jobs to revitalize its vision and passions? Jobs welcomed the opportunity. Retronics's founder may also be willing to come back to the company.

This would, of course, require that George get over his habits of control and condescension. He should begin that transformation by delivering what I call a "power apology" to Shelley. He should tell her that he delegated tasks to her and then undermined her decisions by imposing his style. He needs to apologize and say he was wrong. He should recognize that he criticized her and then tried to put a lid on her reaction by saying, "You're the best," which he now knows only made her feel worse, and how that was wrong as well. He may add—as an explanation, but not an excuse—that he was projecting his own anxieties onto her.

Power apologies also require an effort at remediation. George could tell Shelley that he will correct his actions by putting her in charge of a significant project, perhaps even having her work with the former founder to articulate a more compelling and convincing mission statement for the company. If George shows Shelley that he has faith in her, Shelley might respond by rising to the occasion.

For her part, Shelley should try to empathize with George. She should try to understand his approach to growing the company, why it may or may not be working, and what she might do to assist him. She should also try the "feedforward" technique developed by executive coach Marshall Goldsmith, which involves telling a person very specifically what he can do differently to have a positive effect on you. Feedback about misdeeds nearly always triggers defensiveness, even in those who say they want to hear it. The feedforward technique gives those receiving feedback the opportunity for positive behavior in the future.

Mark Goulston (mgoulston@shrwood.com) is a psychiatrist and the senior vice president at Sherwood Partners, an executive-coaching and consulting firm in Palo Alto, California.

Controlling personalities have a tendency to stifle rather than nurture creative people.

Case Commentary

by J. Michael Lawrie

Is George guilty of micromanagement?

George needs to manage much more than Shelley's output. He needs to gain better control of Retronics as an organization. George is uncomfortable with his role as CEO, and he's not performing his job adequately. He's relying on his engineering skills, such as attention to minute detail, to get the job done.

Yet like every top executive, George has at his disposal a variety of management tools that he can use to lead the company. These include hard tools, such as the company's financial structure, leadership team, corporate strategy, and M&A strategy. They also include soft tools, like personal leadership and communication skills, which have a powerful effect on corporate climate and culture. George has failed to use the soft tools available to him. Without fully leveraging them, he cannot hope to run his company well or take it to the next level.

Because the CEO is the chief model of behavior in a company, it is likely that everyone else at Retronics is emulating his behavior by planning and executing with too much focus on minutiae. And like Shelley, they may be negatively affected. To escape this cycle, George needs to apply true leadership skills to hone the organizational capabilities within Retronics. In particular, he needs to engage in what I call "straight talk" with his direct reports. This means having honest discussions about the vital roles they play in meeting Retronics's critical objectives.

In his straight talk with Shelley, George should stop focusing on the press release and identify the larger issues facing the marketing department. He should tell Shelley that he holds her accountable for improving the department's capabilities, performance, and effectiveness. Together, they must also set specific objectives and measures for demonstrating improvement. At the same time, he should let her

George needs to engage in straight talk with his direct reports.

know that he's willing to coach her. George should also make it clear that he will evaluate Shelley within a three- to six-month period and decide whether she is a good fit for the position. If Shelley does not perform as hoped, he should replace her with someone who better meets his expectations. This type of interaction with Shelley will establish clear goals and instill a climate of trust and delegation. George must ensure he does this with all of his direct reports.

George also needs to speak frankly with the chairman of Retronics's board about Shelley. Because the chairman recommended Shelley, George seems to believe that he should treat her differently than he treats everyone else. This is a mistake. George should let the chairman know about the specific marketing problems that are impeding the company's performance. He must emphasize that he will work with Shelley to help her set objectives and measures and that he will coach her as necessary. But he must tell the chairman that if Shelley does not markedly improve the marketing department's performance within the set time frame, she will not remain in her current position.

Finally, Shelley needs to take some responsibility for the impasse. She owes it to herself, to her company, and to George to tell him directly what she wants professionally. Likewise, she needs to take an honest look at herself and her team and assess whether, as a group, they have the skills required to help the company succeed. If those skills are lacking, she should determine how best to improve them. She should play an active role in setting the objectives and measures for her department and start living up to them.

J. Michael Lawrie is the CEO of Siebel Systems in San Mateo, California.

Case Commentary

by Craig Chappelow

Is George guilty of micromanagement?

Most of us can relate to this case because, chances are, we have been micromanaged at some point in our own careers. The problem is, George doesn't see that he's a micromanager, even though Shelley thinks he has already reached the subatomic level. She wants to be left alone to produce, but George thinks that he can't count on her to maintain quality. On the surface, what we see are two well-intentioned, hardworking individuals who want the same thing—freedom to do the best they can for the organization. Obviously, George and Shelley need to stop butting heads and resolve their differences before there's an interpersonal crisis. But what if, for each of these individuals, this is not just a personality conflict? Let's assume these are longtime patterns of behavior.

The Center for Creative Leadership has been studying the phenomenon of executive derailment since 1983. We have tried to learn as much as we can about specific behaviors that can lead to an executive being fired, demoted, or passed over for promotion. Like George and Shelley, the executives we study are talented, dedicated individuals who have established solid track records of professional success. But then something happens to knock them offtrack. In one North American study, the leading reason for derailment was the inability to develop or adapt. George's behavior is a prime example of this. His hands-on, detail-oriented management style served him well as an engineer. As a senior executive, however, the rules have changed. Executives are expected to be less hands-on with the day-to-day details and more focused on the big picture while motivating team members to perform.

George consistently succumbs to his natural tendency to take action, without considering the consequences. From helping his son pour milk to editing typos in press releases, George can't resist being involved. Because he's already made up his mind that Shelley is not motivated to learn, not open to feedback, and, ultimately, just not capable, he has created a poor working relationship with her.

A better strategy for Shelley would be to recognize that bosses come and go, but careers last a long time.

Both the derailed and successful executives we studied had potential flaws. One major difference was that successful executives were aware of their tendencies and their risk of responding with detrimental behaviors when under high stress. George, by comparison, seems oblivious to those dangers. Our advice to him would be to seek some honest feedback from a wide variety of coworkers, ideally through 360-degree review and a neutral third-party facilitator. If, as the case suggests, George is heading for derailment because he tends to overmanage people, he can develop a plan for gradually changing his approach.

Shelley risks derailing her career because of her approach to conflict with her boss. Our research shows that disagreement with the boss is a common issue and not in itself a derailment risk. The risk is how Shelley manages her disagreements with George. The wrong approach would be to decide that she is right, George is wrong, and right will win out if she just fights harder. Our studies show that if she picks a win-or-lose battle, she will lose. A better strategy for Shelley would be to recognize that bosses come and go, but careers last a long time. In a low-stress moment, she should speak openly and honestly to George about how she feels he's micromanaged her, giving specific, recent examples. Shelley should then remain open to George's perspective on the problem. If that fails, she needs to adopt a survival strategy for determining how she can learn as much as possible from George until one or the other moves on. ▽

Craig Chappelow (chappelow@leaders.ccl.org) is the senior manager of assessment and development resources at the Center for Creative Leadership in Greensboro, North Carolina.

Reprint R0409A
Case only R0409X
Commentary only R0409Z
To order, call 800-988-0886
or 617-783-7500 or go to www.hbr.org

To Order

For reprints, *Harvard Business Review*
OnPoint orders, and subscriptions
to *Harvard Business Review:*
Call 800-988-0886 or 617-783-7500.
Go to www.hbr.org

For customized and quantity orders
of reprints and *Harvard Business
Review* OnPoint products:
Call Frank Tamoshunas at
617-783-7626,
or e-mail him at
ftamoshunas@hbsp.harvard.edu

Harvard Business Review ⚜

www.hbr.org

U.S. and Canada
800-988-0886
617-783-7500
617-783-7555 fax